W9-BDV-661

25¢

SETTING
NATIONAL
PRIORITIES
The 1972 Budget

Charles L. Schultze
Edward R. Fried
Alice M. Rivlin
Nancy H. Teeters

SETTING NATIONAL PRIORITIES

The 1972 Budget

THE BROOKINGS INSTITUTION
Washington, D.C.

Copyright © *1971 by*
THE BROOKINGS INSTITUTION
1775 Massachusetts Avenue, N.W., Washington, D.C. 20036

ISBN 0-8157-7756-6 (*cloth*)
ISBN 0-8157-7755-8 (*paper*)
Library of Congress Catalog Card Number 74-161599

2 3 4 5 6 7 8 9

Board of Trustees

Douglas Dillon
Chairman

Sydney Stein, Jr.
Vice Chairman

William R. Biggs
Chairman, Executive Committee

Dillon Anderson
Vincent M. Barnett, Jr.
Louis W. Cabot
Robert D. Calkins
Edward W. Carter
John Fischer
Kermit Gordon
Gordon Gray
Huntington Harris
Luther G. Holbrook
John E. Lockwood
William McC. Martin, Jr.
Robert S. McNamara
Arjay Miller
Herbert P. Patterson
J. Woodward Redmond
H. Chapman Rose
Robert Brookings Smith
J. Harvie Wilkinson, Jr.
Donald B. Woodward

Honorary Trustees

Arthur Stanton Adams
Daniel W. Bell
Eugene R. Black
Leonard Carmichael
Colgate W. Darden, Jr.
Marion B. Folsom
Raymond B. Fosdick
Huntington Gilchrist
John Lee Pratt

THE BROOKINGS INSTITUTION is an independent organization devoted to nonpartisan research, education, and publication in economics, government, foreign policy, and the social sciences generally. Its principal purposes are to aid in the development of sound public policies and to promote public understanding of issues of national importance.

The Institution was founded on December 8, 1927, to merge the activities of the Institute for Government Research, founded in 1916, the Institute of Economics, founded in 1922, and the Robert Brookings Graduate School of Economics and Government, founded in 1924.

The general administration of the Institution is the responsibility of a Board of Trustees charged with maintaining the independence of the staff and fostering the most favorable conditions for creative research and education. The immediate direction of the policies, program, and staff of the Institution is vested in the President, assisted by an advisory committee of the officers and staff.

In publishing a study, the Institution presents it as a competent treatment of a subject worthy of public consideration. The interpretations and conclusions in such publications are those of the author or authors and do not necessarily reflect the views of the other staff members, officers, or trustees of the Brookings Institution.

Foreword

THIS IS THE SECOND in a series of annual books by Brookings staff members analyzing the major issues in the President's budget. No other single document exerts as much influence as does the federal budget on how the nation allocates resources and exercises its spending priorities. Yet it receives relatively little attention in public discussion of the nation's goals and the resources for achieving them. A year ago, in *Setting National Priorities: The 1971 Budget*, three Brookings staff members—Charles L. Schultze, with Edward K. Hamilton and Allen Schick—identified the major decisions on allocating national resources that the President had made in formulating his 1971 budget proposals, outlined the alternative choices available in each principal sector, and discussed the costs and benefits of each alternative, both immediate and longer range.

This year, Mr. Schultze and three other Brookings staff members— Edward R. Fried, Alice M. Rivlin, and Nancy H. Teeters—undertook a similar but more comprehensive analysis of the President's budget for fiscal 1972. The budget is the central focus of their discussion; but other presidential messages to the Congress, including the Economic and Foreign Policy Messages and the special messages on revenue sharing, as well as the Defense Report presented to the Congress by the secretary of defense and the secretary of state's report on foreign policy, provide elaboration on the proposals outlined in the budget and form part of the background for the analysis.

The authors have not sought to provide a critique of the budget or to construct an alternative budget. Rather, they have concentrated on presenting an array of policy choices and explaining how those proposed by the President compare to the alternatives available. The choices are of various kinds—how much emphasis should be put on one national objective as against another; which of various possible means to achieve a given objective should be chosen; and when objectives conflict with each other, as they often do, which of the feasible compromises among them is most desirable.

This year's *Setting National Priorities*, like last year's, presents an analysis of several alternative defense postures and their consequences, both strategic and budgetary. But it also examines in some depth the defense programs relating to tactical air forces, tactical nuclear weapons, naval forces, and strategic nuclear forces. Moreover, it includes a chapter that explicitly seeks to relate the defense budget to basic foreign policy assumptions, and another that analyzes the foreign security and economic assistance programs.

Two chapters are devoted to revenue sharing. They analyze the state and local "fiscal crisis" and examine several alternative revenue sharing proposals. Other chapters discuss welfare reform, financing medical care, and public job creation programs; another evaluates the national housing goals laid down in the Housing and Urban Development Act of 1968, which still form the basis of national housing policy. A chapter on environmental quality projects water pollution and waste treatment costs to the year 2000. How changes in the accounting treatment of certain federal programs during the past seven years have affected the official budget totals in a major way is the subject of a separate chapter.

In preparing many of the chapters, the authors relied on background papers furnished by other members of the Brookings staff and by outside experts. Those who provided background papers or other significant contributions to the analysis are named in the table of contents with the chapters to which they contributed; where a contribution dealt with a specific part of a chapter, the contributor is identified in a footnote. In all cases, however, the four authors bear full responsibility for the contents and conclusions of the chapter, and the listing of a contributor's name does not necessarily imply his or her agreement with the way the authors have used the contributions.

The materials assembled in the preparation of this year's and last year's *Setting National Priorities* form a growing body of organized analytical and statistical information that can be used to illuminate budgetary choices. For example, statistical models have been prepared to project future federal, state, and local revenues and expenditures; to relate housing starts to both economic conditions and national goals; to extrapolate trends in water pollution and treatment costs; and to examine the distribution of funds among the states by various revenue sharing devices. Techniques for allocating overall defense costs among various forces, geographical areas, and alternative defense postures have been developed. These and other materials will continue to be assembled as part of the Brookings Foreign Policy Studies program, which is supported by a grant from the Ford Foundation, and its program of research on public expenditures and budgeting, which is supported by a grant from the Carnegie Corporation of New York under which this book was prepared.

Editorial assistance by the Brookings publication staff made it possible to publish this study three months after the President's budget was released on January 29, 1971. John Yinger carried out the computer program used in projecting revenues and expenditures, and John A. Gardecki the program underlying the estimate of housing allowances in Chapter 14. Nancy C. Wilson provided general research assistance and performed much of the computer work underlying the evaluation of national housing goals. Mary S. von Euler provided research assistance in several chapters, and Khadija Haq assisted in the preparation of Chapter 16. To produce a volume of this size, with its many tables and numerical references, in a short period of time incurs serious risk of factual errors. This risk has been substantially reduced by Evelyn P. Fisher, who organized the checking of statistics.

The views expressed in this book are those of the authors and are not presented as the views of the trustees, officers, or other staff members of the Brookings Institution, the Carnegie Corporation, or the Ford Foundation.

KERMIT GORDON
President

April 1971
Washington, D.C.

Contents

1. An Overview   1

The Budget and Economic Policy *2*
Priorities in the 1972 Budget *12*
Two Important Features *19*
Commitments for the Future *22*
Summary *24*

INTERNATIONAL AFFAIRS AND DEFENSE

2. Foreign Policy Assumptions   25
with Henry D. Owen

U.S.-Soviet Relations *26*
Europe *27*
The Middle East *28*
Asia *29*
Foreign Assistance *29*
Alternatives *30*
Conclusion *32*

3. Major Defense Options   33
with Laurence E. Lynn, Jr., Jerome H. Kahan, and Edward C. Meyer

SHAPING THE DEFENSE POSTURE *36*

STRATEGIC FORCES *39*
Six Strategic Issues *40*
Strategic Arms Limitation Talks *46*
Budget Alternatives *47*
Decisions in the 1972 Budget *49*

GENERAL PURPOSE FORCES *51*
Implications of the Nixon Doctrine *52*

Alternative Postures *63*
The Administration's Program *65*

LONG-TERM TRENDS AND ALTERNATIVES *66*

4. Special Defense Issues   71
with Jerome H. Kahan, Arnold M. Kuzmack, and Edward C. Meyer

ROLE OF THE AIRCRAFT CARRIER *71*
Vulnerability Considerations *72*
The Soviet Surface Fleet *75*
The Adequacy of ASW Forces *77*
Alternative Approaches to the Issues *77*
Specific Budgetary Decisions *81*

TACTICAL AIRCRAFT ISSUES *83*
Tactical Air Missions *84*
Land-based versus Sea-based Aircraft *90*
Budget Decisions *91*

TACTICAL NUCLEAR WEAPONS IN EUROPE *94*
The Underlying Situation *95*
How a Tactical Nuclear War Might Be Fought *96*
Size and Mix Criteria *98*
Impact on Force Decisions *100*

VIETNAM AND THE PEACE DIVIDEND *102*

STRATEGIC SYSTEMS AND COSTS *107*
Composition of the Strategic Budget *108*
Strategic Weapons Issues *108*
Budgetary Impact of SALT *116*
Strategic Doctrine and Budgets *117*

5. Foreign Assistance   118
Security Assistance *119*
Development Assistance *127*
Future Possibilities *130*

FISCAL FEDERALISM

6. General Revenue Sharing   134
with Allen D. Manvel and Robert D. Reischauer

Pros and Cons of Revenue Sharing *136*
Major Issues *146*
Alternative Proposals *148*

7. **Special Revenue Sharing** 158
   with Robert D. Reischauer

   Why Special Revenue Sharing? *159*
   The Six Programs *163*
   The Implications of Special Revenue Sharing *169*

   HUMAN RESOURCES

8. **Welfare and Family Assistance** 172
   with Josephine Allen

   The Welfare Problem *173*
   What FAP Would Do *175*
   Dilemmas in the Design of FAP *178*
   Integration with Other Welfare Programs *180*
   Alternative Futures *184*

9. **Job Creation** 191
   with Robert A. Levine

   Six Major Questions *193*
   Job Creation Programs: A Brief History *195*
   What Has Been Learned? *198*
   Current Status of Public Employment Proposals *201*

10. **Social Security** 204

    Current Status of Social Security Proposals *204*
    Major Long-term Issues *207*

11. **Financing Medical Care** 214
    with Robert W. Hartman

    What Is the Problem? *214*
    Criteria for a National Financing System *219*
    Current National Financing Proposals *227*

    PHYSICAL RESOURCES

12. **Environmental Quality** 238
    with Robert H. Haveman and Ivars Gutmanis

    Water Pollution *240*
    Air Pollution *253*
    The Total Environment *257*

13. Transportation   259
with Gordon Murray and Gerald R. Jantscher

Highways *261*
Aviation *264*
Merchant Marine Subsidies *267*
Rail Passenger Service *271*

14. Housing   276

Housing Assistance in the 1972 Budget *277*
The 25 Million Goal *280*
Housing Subsidies *289*

15. Agriculture   297
with John A. Schnittker

Consequences of Recent Legislation *299*
Price and Income Supports *300*

SPECIAL ISSUES

16. Expenditures Outside the Budget   306
with Henry J. Aaron

Changes in Budget Coverage *307*
New Forms of Federal Assistance *309*
Sales of Assets *311*
Adjusted Expenditures *313*
Measuring Long-term Subsidy Commitments *316*

17. The Fiscal Dividend Through 1976   319

The Projections *320*
The Fiscal Dividend *325*
Implications *331*

POSTSCRIPT

Continuing Problems in Some Older Programs 334

Farm Price Supports *334*
Impacted Aid *334*
Merchant Marine Subsidies *335*
Public Works Projects *335*
General Aviation *335*

Tables

Chapter 1: An Overview

1-1. The Federal Budget: Revenues, Outlays, and Surplus or Deficit on Actual GNP Basis and Full Employment GNP Basis, Fiscal Years 1970, 1971, and 1972   2

1-2. Changes in Original and Revised Estimates of Federal Budget Out-Lays, Fiscal Year 1971   5

1-3. Major Components of Federal Budget Outlays, Selected Fiscal Years, 1955–72   13

1-4. Major Changes in Federal Budget Outlays from Fiscal Year 1971 to Fiscal Year 1972   15

1-5. Summary of Changes in National Defense Outlays, by Cause, from Fiscal Year 1971 to Fiscal Year 1972   17

1-6. Federal Outlays for Human Resources Programs, Selected Fiscal Years, 1964–72   21

Chapter 3: Major Defense Options

3-1. Financial Summary of the Department of Defense Budget, Fiscal Years 1964, 1968, 1971, and 1972   34

3-2. Funds Authorized for Strategic and General Purpose Forces, by Category, Selected Fiscal Years, 1961–72   35

3-3. Structure of Department of Defense Military Forces, Various Significant Fiscal Years, 1961–72   37

3-4. Average Annual Federal Budget Costs of Alternative Strategic Force Postures   48

3-5. Possible Distribution of Proposed Fiscal Year 1972 General Purpose Forces, by Geographic Contingency   54

3-6. Allocation of Costs of Proposed Fiscal Year 1972 General Purpose Forces, by Geographic Contingency   55

3-7. Budgets for Alternative General Purpose Force Postures, Fiscal Year 1972   64

3-8. Comparison of Total Obligational Authority for Procurement and Research, Development, Testing, and Evaluation, by Service, Fiscal Years 1971 and 1972   66

3-9. Projections of Optional Department of Defense Budgets, by Military Program, Fiscal Years 1972 and 1976   67

3-10. Comparison of Manpower and Budget Costs Per Active Military Unit, by Service, Fiscal Years 1964 and 1972   69

Chapter 4: Special Defense Issues

4-1. Investment in Tactical Air Programs by Primary Mission and Type of Aircraft, Fiscal Years 1971 and 1972   91

4-2. Vietnam and Non-Vietnam Defense Outlays, and Real Change in Outlays, Fiscal Years 1968–72   103

4-3. Trends in Total Obligational Authority for Military Procurement, by Use, Fiscal Years 1964–71   105

4-4. Troop Levels and Incremental Costs of the War in Southeast Asia, Fiscal Years 1968–73   107

4-5. Estimated Direct and Indirect Cost of Strategic Forces, Fiscal Years 1971 and 1972   109

4-6. Estimated Allocation of the Strategic Budget by Major Weapons Categories, Fiscal Year 1972   110

4-7. Estimated Ten-year Program Cost of Selected Strategic Systems   111

Chapter 5: Foreign Assistance

5-1. Funds for U.S. Security Assistance Programs, Selected Fiscal Years, 1964–72   121

5-2. Estimated Allocation of Budget Authorizations for U.S. Foreign Security Assistance Programs, by Purpose and Country, Fiscal Year 1972   122

5-3. Funds for U.S. Foreign Development Assistance and Welfare and Emergency Relief, by Program, Selected Fiscal Years, 1964–72   128

5-4. Funds for U.S. Foreign Assistance, in Current and 1972 Dollars, by Major Program Category, Selected Fiscal Years, 1949–72   131

Chapter 6: General Revenue Sharing

6-1. Comparison of State and Local Expenditures, by Function, Fiscal Years 1955 and 1969   139

6-2. Comparison of State and Local Revenues, by Source, Fiscal Years 1955 and 1969   141

6-3. State and Local Expenditures, by Function, and Revenues, by Source, Fiscal Year 1969, and Estimates, Fiscal Year 1976   142

6-4. Per Capita Distribution of Fiscal Relief to States under the Administration's General Revenue Sharing Proposal Compared with Compensatory Public Service Grants and Federal Assumption of Public Assistance, by State, Fiscal Year 1972   156

Chapter 8: Welfare and Family Assistance

8-1. Comparison of Estimated Full-year Cost of the Family Assistance Plan and the Current Welfare System, by Level of Government and Program, Fiscal Year 1972   176

8-2. Distribution of Families under the Aid to Families with Dependent Children Program in 1969, and of Families Eligible for the Family Assistance Plan in 1972, by Selected Characteristics   177

Chapter 10: Social Security

10-1. Total First Full-year Cost of March 1971 Social Security Benefit Increases and of Other Liberalizations Proposed in 1971 by the Administration, the House, and the Senate 205

10-2. Combined Employer and Employee Social Security Tax Rates on Wages and Salaries, Existing Law and House and Senate Proposals, 1969–87 and After 211

Chapter 11: Financing Medical Care

11-1. Distribution of Family Personal Health Expenditures, 1963 220

Chapter 12: Environmental Quality

12-1. Distribution of Federal Water Pollution Control Act Grants and Population, by Size of Community, January 31, 1969 245

12-2. Appropriations and Expenditures of Environmental Protection Agency for Water Pollution Control Programs, Fiscal Years 1965, 1969, 1970, 1971, and 1972 246

12-3. Wasteloads Generated (before Treatment) in the United States, by Type of Waste, 1960, and Projections for 1973, 1980, and 2000, Assuming No Change in Industrial Technology in Future Years 250

12-4. Increases in Wasteloads Generated in the United States, by Type of Waste and Major Source, 1960–80 251

12-5. Wasteloads Discharged in the United States in 1973, 1980, and 2000, Assuming Continuation of 1970 Percentages of Waste Treatment by Each Industry and Sector 251

12-6. Wasteloads Discharged in the United States, Assuming Secondary Treatment of All Waste, 1973, 1980, and 2000 252

12-7. Annual Costs of Primary and Secondary Treatment of All Wastewater in the United States, by Source, 1973, 1980, and 2000 253

12-8. Estimated Nationwide Air Pollutant Emissions, by Source, 1968 254

Chapter 13: Transportation

13-1. Federal Budget Outlays for Transportation, by Major Program, Fiscal Year 1972 260

13-2. Federal Budget Outlays for Transportation, by Agency or Program, Fiscal Years 1955, 1960, 1965, 1970, and 1972 260

13-3. Federal Highway Outlays, by Program, Fiscal Year 1972 261

13-4. Estimated Revenues and Expenditures for Federal Airway System, Fiscal Years 1971–76 265

Chapter 14: Housing

14-1. Federally Assisted Housing Starts, by Program, for Fiscal Year 1968 and Estimates for Fiscal Years 1971, 1972, and 1975 279

14-2. Housing Starts, New Mobile Homes, and Net New Households, Subperiods during Calendar Years 1950–69, and National Housing Goals for Fiscal Years 1969–78   281

14-3. Number of New Housing Units and Their Use, Calendar Years 1960–69, and National Housing Goals, Fiscal Years 1969–78   282

14-4. Number of Household Formations, by Age Groupings, Subperiods during Calendar Years 1950–69, and High and Low Projections for Fiscal Years 1970–79   283

14-5. Number of New Housing Units, by Type, Subperiods during Calendar Years 1950–69   284

14-6. New Housing Units, Fiscal Years 1965–70, and Comparison of National Housing Goals with Projections Based on Economic Factors, by Type, Totals for Fiscal Years 1969–78, and Annual Averages for Three-Year Periods, Fiscal Years 1970–78   285

14-7. Comparison of National Housing Goals with Projections Based on High and Low Rates of Household Formation and Varying Economic Conditions, Ten-year Totals by Type of Housing Unit, Fiscal Years 1969–78   287

14-8. Comparison of National Housing Goals for New Units and Their Use with Projections Based on a High Rate of Household Formation and Contrasting Economic Conditions, Ten-year Totals, Fiscal Years 1969–78   288

14-9. Number of Substandard Housing Units, by Location and Income Class of Occupant Households, 1966   291

14-10. Percentage of Households Paying More Than 25 Percent of Their Income for Rent and Household Utilities, by Income Class and Location, 1967   292

14-11. Number of Eligible Households and Cost of a Housing Allowance Program for Low- and Moderate-income Families That Subsidizes Housing Expenses in Excess of 25 Percent of Personal Income, 1976   294

Chapter 15: Agriculture

15-1. Government Payments to Farmers under Feed Grain, Wheat, and Upland Cotton Programs, Crop Years 1965, 1969, 1970, and 1971   300

15-2. Feed Grain Economic Indicators, Crop Years 1965, 1969, 1970, and 1971   302

Chapter 16: Expenditures Outside the Budget

16-1. Illustration of the Value of Federal Below-market Interest Rate Loans and Annual Supplements Relative to Commercial Loans   309

16-2. Official and Adjusted Budget Outlays, by Source of Differences, Fiscal Years 1965, 1970, 1971, and 1972   312

16-3. Adjusted Budget Outlays and Excess over Official Budget Outlays, by Program Area, Fiscal Years 1965, 1970, 1971, and 1972   314

16-4. Actual and Full Employment Budgets, Adjusted to Include Long-term Subsidy Commitments, Fiscal Years 1965, 1970, 1971, and 1972   317

Chapter 17: The Fiscal Dividend Through 1976

17-1. Economic Indicators Used in Budget Projections, Calendar Years 1970, 1974, and 1976   321

17-2. Projected Federal Revenues, by Source, Fiscal Years 1972, 1974, and 1976   322

17-3. Projected Changes in Federal Outlays, Fiscal Years 1972–74 and 1974–76, and Selected Total Outlays, Fiscal Years 1972, 1974, and 1976   325

17-4. Major Changes in Outlays and Full Employment Revenues Influencing the Fiscal Dividend, Fiscal Years 1974 and 1976   326

17-5. The Fiscal Dividend in Relation to Social Security Surpluses and the Balance of Other Revenues and Outlays, Fiscal Years 1972, 1974, and 1976   327

17-6. The Fiscal Dividend for Fiscal Year 1976 under Alternative Assumptions about the Path of Inflation   330

SETTING NATIONAL PRIORITIES
The 1972 Budget

1. An Overview

THE PRESIDENT'S BUDGET for fiscal 1972, presented to the Congress in January 1971, reflects a number of major decisions in both its overall budgetary magnitudes and its choices among national priorities. With respect to its total expenditures and revenues, the budget:

• drastically revises the estimates presented a year ago for the current fiscal year, 1971, changing a forecast $1.3 billion surplus into an $18.6 billion deficit (see Table 1-1);

• calls for a deficit of $11.6 billion in fiscal 1972—the twelve months beginning July 1, 1971—and indicates a willingness to accept an even larger deficit if the economy does not expand rapidly;

• adopts the "full employment budget" concept (under which the tax revenues yielded by a fully employed economy, rather than the actual revenues collected, become the guide to federal spending) and proposes expenditures in both fiscal years 1971 and 1972 that are practically in balance with full employment revenues but substantially above estimates of actual revenue collections; and

• proposes expenditures of $229 billion for the coming 1972 fiscal year, $28 billion above those originally proposed for fiscal 1971 and $16 billion higher than the now-revised expenditures for that year.

In its choices about national priorities, the new budget:

• necessarily devotes a substantial part of the increased expenditures to meeting the costs imposed on the federal government by rising wages, prices, and workloads;

• provides a slightly increased defense budget, under which projected reductions in the budgetary costs of the Vietnam war would be more than offset by the cost of military and civilian pay increases, rising prices, and somewhat expanded weapons procurement;

1

Table 1-1. The Federal Budget: Revenues, Outlays, and Surplus or Deficit on
Actual GNP Basis and Full Employment GNP Basis, Fiscal Years 1970,
1971, and 1972

Billions of dollars

Basis	1970 actual	1971 original estimate	1971 revised estimate	1972 current estimate
Actual GNP basis				
Revenues	193.7	202.1	194.2	217.6
Outlays	196.6	200.8	212.8	229.2
Surplus (+) or deficit (−)	−2.8	+1.3	−18.6	−11.6
Full employment GNP basis				
Revenues	199.2	214.5	214.2	229.3
Outlays	196.6	200.8	212.8	229.2
Surplus (+)	+2.6	+13.7	+1.4	+0.1

Sources: *The Budget of the United States Government* for fiscal years 1970, 1971, 1972. Figures are rounded
and may not add to totals.

• proposes a program of general revenue sharing with state and
local governments and a regrouping of many existing grant programs
into new "special revenue sharing" categories that would add a major
new element to federal-state-local relationships; and

• requests the Congress to inaugurate a new Family Assistance
Plan and a new set of health financing plans—major proposals whose
costs would fall principally in subsequent fiscal years.

From this brief summary of the 1972 budget submission, five major
questions arise: What does the concept of a "full employment budget"
mean, and what will be the consequences of adopting it? What caused
the 1971 budget to differ so markedly from the original estimates of a
year ago? What will be the effect of the total revenues and expenditures in the revised 1971 budget, and of the new 1972 proposals, on
unemployment, inflation, and other important measures of the nation's economic health? What priorities in the use of national resources are set by the new budget—how does it propose to allocate
the increased federal outlays toward meeting national goals? And
what is the size and significance of the proposed shift from specific
federal grant-in-aid programs to revenue sharing grants as a means
of helping state and local governments?

The Budget and Economic Policy

The federal budget can help achieve the overall economic goals of
a high level of employment and reasonable price stability. To serve

this purpose, the amount of stimulus or restraint coming from the budget must be responsive to the needs of the economy at any particular time. When the economy needs to speed up, an expansionary budget policy is appropriate; when the economy needs to slow down, a restrictive policy is in order. The economic stabilization aspect of the budget is referred to as "fiscal policy."

The Full Employment Budget

No one measure of the federal budget adequately states its complex impact on the national economy, but perhaps the most useful summary indicator of fiscal policy is the full employment surplus or deficit. This measure differs from the budget surplus as usually presented because the revenues and expenditures are calculated as they would appear if the economy were at full employment. The surplus or deficit that would prevail at full employment—the level of activity associated with 4 percent unemployment—is a better indicator of fiscal policy than is the actual surplus or deficit because it separates the effect of the budget on the economy from the effect of the economy on the budget. The federal budget, through expenditures and taxes, exerts an influence on the economy, and this is the effect to be isolated as a measure of fiscal policy. But actual federal revenue collections, and even to some extent the behavior of expenditures, are themselves strongly affected by how the economy is behaving.

In a recession, incomes, sales, and profits decline. Less income and excise taxes are paid to the government. Even though no positive fiscal action may have been taken to stimulate the economy, the federal budget may show a declining surplus or may shift from surplus to deficit. Similarly, expenditures of the federal government for unemployment compensation will automatically rise and fall as unemployment rises and falls. As a result, changes in the actual surplus or deficit from year to year will reflect both positive government fiscal policy decisions and the impact of economic conditions on the budget. Only the former should be considered as a measure of fiscal action.

By calculating revenues and expenditures each year as they would be at full employment, it is possible to exclude the effects of changing economic conditions on the budget and to isolate those changes in the surplus or deficit that result from fiscal policy decisions. A decline in the full employment surplus is an indication that the government is taking additional budgetary action to stimulate the economy; an increase in the surplus indicates greater efforts by the government to restrain the economy. Since the degree of fiscal stimulus appropriate to any given time depends on the strength of private demands and on how much economic expansion is desired, there is no uniquely correct full employment surplus or deficit for all times. When private demands are excessively strong and policy calls for a slowdown in the rate of economic expansion, a larger full employment surplus is appropriate. When private demands are weak and policy calls for a speedup in the economy, a full employment deficit may be called for.

The Revised 1971 Budget

The revisions of the estimates for fiscal 1971 illustrate these interrelations. More than a year ago, the President's budget proposed a small surplus of $1.3 billion for fiscal 1971. The full employment surplus implicit in last year's original budget submission was much larger—$13.7 billion. The difference between the two estimates of the surplus reflected the expected revenue loss associated with a less-than-full employment level of economic activity. This large full employment surplus reflected the administration's view at the time that substantial fiscal restraint was needed to bring inflation under control.

A year later, in January 1971, the revised estimates for fiscal 1971 showed a swing of almost $20 billion in the budget forecast—from a projected surplus of $1.3 billion to a projected deficit of $18.6 billion. Part of this shift was caused by an even slower pace of economic activity than was anticipated a year ago, which means that revenues are now expected to be $8 billion below the amount originally forecast. This is the direct result of the impact on the budget of changing economic conditions. Gross national product in calendar year 1970 was $977 billion, $8 billion below the forecast of a year ago and nearly $50 billion below the estimated gross national product that would hold the unemployment rate to approximately 4 percent. Of most significance for federal tax collections is the fact that corporate profits were more than $20 billion below the level that could be expected at relatively full employment, a shortfall much greater than was forecast a year ago. The fact that federal revenues decline under the impact of falling output and profits, however, is not to be deplored, but rather to be welcomed. The federal government, by absorbing some of the fall in national income, softens the impact of declining income on consumer and business purchases and thereby automatically helps limit the extent of the decline.

The remainder of the $20 billion shift from surplus to deficit in fiscal 1971 came from a $12 billion increase in expenditures above those proposed a year ago. It was this $12 billion rise in expenditures that caused the planned full employment surplus to drop from $13.7 billion to $1.4 billion. As the figures in Table 1-2 indicate, the expenditure increases stemmed from a number of sources. About $6 billion came from legislative action, over half of which was the result of a larger pay increase for federal employees than had originally been proposed by the administration, although the final action had the administration's approval. A 10 percent increase in social security benefits has been enacted and made retroactive to January 1971. Since the increase was limited to this across-the-board figure at this time, the expenditures in fiscal 1971 have been kept close to the $1.1 billion estimated under the administration's proposal for that year. (The Congress has indicated that legislation later in the year will further liberalize benefits.) The $1.7 billion by which the Congress increased the President's appropriations is the net result of an $800 million cut in military spending (which the administration did not welcome) and

Table 1-2. Changes in Original and Revised Estimates of Federal Budget Outlays, Fiscal Year 1971

Billions of dollars

Original estimate of 1971 outlays		200.8
Changes in estimate, by cause		
Legislative action, net		6.3
Social security benefit increase	1.1	
Veterans' benefit increases	1.1	
Additional pay increases	3.2	
Congressional appropriation action	1.7	
Failure to enact welfare reform and revenue sharing	−0.8	
Failure to achieve proposed reductions, total		2.6
Sale of assets	1.0	
Failure to enact postal rate increase	1.2	
Failure to enact other reductions	0.4	
Major overruns, total		4.0
Public assistance and Medicaid	0.9	
Unemployment insurance	1.6	
Interest	1.5	
Other changes, net	−0.9	
Total increase above original projection		12.0
Revised estimate of 1971 outlays		212.8

Sources: *The Budget of the United States Government* for fiscal years 1971, 1972.

a $2.5 billion rise in civilian outlays (parts of which the administration opposed vigorously, in several cases through veto action).

Another $2.5 billion of additional net budget expenditures in 1971 stemmed from the failure of the Congress to enact several expenditure-reduction measures that the administration had suggested, and from a shortfall in planned sales of financial assets. Major overruns in expenditures, due to increases in prices, workloads, or interest rates above the earlier budget estimates, accounted for a further $4 billion of the rise in expenditures. The fact that unemployment rose by substantially more than was forecast a year ago accounted for $1.5 billion of this figure.

As noted earlier, it was primarily the $12 billion rise in expenditures above the earlier estimate that caused the full employment surplus in 1971 to fall from the originally planned $13.7 billion to only $1.4 billion. But in view of the relatively large rise in the number of jobless persons and the administration's stated goal of reversing that trend sharply and providing the budgetary stimulus for a return to lower unemployment rates, this major reduction in the full employment surplus should be welcomed. If the current $1.4 billion full employment surplus is now considered appropriate to the present state of the economy, the originally projected $13.7 billion surplus would have proved far too large if it had materialized; unemployment would have risen and profits fallen even further had this surplus not virtually disappeared. The administration has, in fact, accepted the currently projected small full employment surplus as appropriate to its fiscal policy.

The Economic Setting and the Forecast

The fiscal 1972 budget was planned in an economic setting of recession—high levels of unemployment along with continuing inflation. During 1970 the unemployment rate rose from 3.6 percent to 6.2 percent, with 5 million people unemployed at the year's end. In the final quarter of 1970 the consumer price index was increasing at an annual rate of 5.6 percent, and industrial wholesale prices by 4.5 percent. With high unemployment and continued inflation existing side by side, the policy decisions this year were particularly difficult.

The administration chose to pursue a goal of rapid economic expansion that would reduce unemployment; and it argued that such a policy would be consistent with a gradual reduction in the rate of inflation. The budget is based on a forecast of a 9 percent rise in GNP in calendar 1971 to a level of $1,065 billion. This is $15 billion to $20 billion higher than the majority of private forecasts, but is consistent with the goal of a very rapid expansion. The administration argues that its policies, in conjunction with a policy of aggressive monetary ease by the Federal Reserve, could achieve the forecast.

An unusual amount of attention has been given to the government forecast this year, in large part because it anticipates a much stronger economic advance than most private economists and business forecasters expect. The official forecast appears to be based on assumptions about the rate of increase in prices (4 to 4.5 percent) that are similar to those of private forecasters, but on somewhat larger estimates of the rate of real growth. Three kinds of issues are raised by the forecast. First, what does the rise in the dollar value of GNP forecast by the administration imply for real growth, unemployment, and inflation over the next year? Second, is the policy outlined by the administration strong enough to produce the projected expansion in GNP, and, if not, what policies would be needed? And third, from a longer-term standpoint, would the projected expansion in GNP be desirable at this time if it could be accomplished?

How rapid the expansion of GNP would have to be to meet this forecast is best appreciated when it is translated into a rate of expansion during the year 1971—that is, from the fourth quarter of 1970 to the fourth quarter of 1971. Over this interval, GNP would have to expand by nearly 12 percent. The fourth quarter of 1970 was particularly depressed by the automobile strike; adjusting for this still implies about a 10.5 percent advance in GNP, apart from the effects of the strike.

The 12 percent gain forecast between the fourth quarter of 1970 and the fourth quarter of 1971 appears to be composed of an estimated 4 percent rise in prices and an 8 percent increase in real output. With such a strong advance in real output, by year's end the unemployment rate could be expected to fall by roughly one percentage point from the 5.9 percent average in the fourth quarter of 1970. There is some reason to question whether so rapid an advance, accompanied by a substantial new tightening of labor markets over a short period of time, could be achieved without renewing inflationary pressures and causing a noticeably larger increase in prices than the projected 4 percent. Many private forecasters expect a comparable rate of inflation with a much slower rise in total GNP. Past experience suggests that a more rapid advance would lead to greater inflationary pressures than would a more modest rate of advance in the economy. However, this is not an economic environment with which we have had much past experience, and it would be inappropriate to imply that there is a great deal of agreement on how much inflation would accompany a GNP expansion at the projected rate. The official forecast about the inflation that would accompany the projected GNP growth seems optimistic, but it cannot be considered unrealistic.

The administration has indicated specifically that it has forecast such a high rate of GNP expansion because it has formulated policies designed to bring it about. These include both the fiscal policy implied in the budget and a monetary policy which, though not spelled out in the budget, was thought to be consistent with recent experience and within the range of what the Federal Reserve Board can be expected to do during 1971.

Fiscal Policy in the 1972 Budget

As was shown in Table 1-1, unified budget expenditures are projected to rise by $16.4 billion to $229.2 billion. About one-fourth of the increase in expenditures is associated with the proposed revenue sharing program. Looking at the absolute magnitude of the proposed expansion in government outlays, it seems at first glance to be a very large growth, but it is a rise of 7.7 percent, somewhat less than the normal year-to-year increase in a fully employed economy in which prices are rising at the rate expected this year. The revenues estimated at full employment are expected to rise by $15.1 billion, leading to a small decline in the estimated full employment surplus from $1.4 billion in fiscal 1971 to $0.1 billion in fiscal 1972. This small decline in the full employment surplus is not enough by itself to provide a significant stimulus to the economy.

A number of changes in the budget have already occurred, and there may be others that could significantly change the full employment surplus planned in the 1972 budget. The social security bill enacted in March 1971 provided larger across-the-board benefits than the administration requested, and postponed until January 1972 an increase in payroll tax revenues originally scheduled for January 1971. In combination, these actions reduced the surplus by $3 billion. Public assistance caseloads are currently increasing at a much faster rate than was foreseen in the budget, and may raise budget expenditures by more than $1 billion. On the other hand, some $4 billion of the total expenditures contemplated in the budget depend on enactment of the President's revenue sharing proposals. If these fail of enactment and if expenditures on other programs are not increased by an equal amount, the full employment surplus would increase.

While it is too early to predict how these divergent forces will balance out, it is most unlikely that the rapid economic advance forecast by the administration will derive its primary thrust from the federal budget. That expansion will have to come from the private sector—a resurgence of consumer demand (both for goods and for housing), a resumption of the investment boom of the late 1960s, or a sharp rise in inventories. With fiscal policy offering no major new thrust, the administration is counting primarily on monetary policy to induce the projected expansion in private demand.

Monetary Policy

There are different ways to assess monetary policy—for instance, by prevailing interest rates, by the growth in the money supply, or by the growth in a more inclusive measure of private liquidity, such as the money supply plus time deposits. During 1969 and 1970, all of these measures have varied considerably.

The money supply (currency plus demand deposits) grew at a 5 percent rate in the first half of 1969, then at a rate of 1 percent during the second half of that year, and at a 5.5 percent rate during 1970. The more comprehensive measure of the money supply that includes commercial bank time deposits declined by 1 percent during 1969 and then rose by 12 percent during 1970. Interest rates moved sharply and erratically during this two-year period; the rates on long-term government bonds rose by a full percentage point between the beginning and end of 1969, fell for a brief period, and then rose to new highs by the middle of 1970. In the following nine months they declined by a full point. Over this period, as at all times, the behavior of these different measures has reflected the interplay of the various demands for cash and the monetary policy of the Federal Reserve System.

Discussions of monetary policy for 1971 have centered around the needed rate of growth in the money supply. As Arthur F. Burns, Chairman of the Board of Governors of the Federal Reserve System, pointed out in testimony earlier this year before the Joint Economic

Committee of the Congress, too much attention to the money supply can divert attention from other important monetary variables, such as interest rates. Nevertheless, it may be useful to examine what the administration's forecast may imply about needed monetary growth.

To judge from past experience, the 9 percent rise in GNP from calendar 1970 to 1971 forecast by the administration (roughly half of which would come from increased prices) would require a growth in the money supply of between 6 percent and 9 percent. However, as private demands are not projected to be particularly strong, interest rates will have to be kept low. To accomplish this, the growth in the money supply may have to be closer to 9 percent than to 6 percent. It seems doubtful, on the basis of recent history and from the February 1971 testimony of Chairman Burns, that these rates of monetary expansion are being contemplated.

Policy Choices for 1972

Restrictive monetary and fiscal policy, if carried far enough, can eliminate inflation—but at the cost of high and too long sustained levels of unemployment. Expansionary monetary and fiscal policy can produce full employment but, if done too rapidly, at the cost of an unacceptably high rate of inflation. Faced with this dilemma, many economists and politicians have stressed the need for a direct attack on inflation so that monetary and fiscal policy would be freer to work for a faster reduction of unemployment with less fear of inflationary consequences.

Most advocates of a direct attack on inflation favor a two-pronged approach. The first step would include administrative and legislative measures to reduce inflationary pressures through a freer trade policy, a less inflationary policy toward subsidized or regulated industries (such as reduced price supports in agriculture and the removal of minimum rate regulations in the transportation industry), attacks on structural unemployment, less inflationary procurement and pay policies on the part of the government, and other actions to increase competition in particular sectors of the economy. The administration has taken some steps in this direction and has increasingly indicated a willingness to take others.

The second element of this approach would be an "incomes policy," through which the government would try directly to moderate wage and price increases by setting standards of anti-inflationary behavior for industry and labor. Opinions differ on the extent to which these standards should be voluntary or mandatory. Some advocates of an incomes policy believe that legal wage and price controls, at least in key industries, may be necessary. However, the majority believes that these standards, once established and promoted with the full prestige of the federal government and the presidency itself, could operate on a voluntary basis. They contend that, while individual wage and price decisions would conform only roughly to the standards, on balance, voluntary standards would moderate wage and price increases in periods when the economy was not overheated.

The evidence about the effectiveness of incomes policies when they were used in this country during the early and mid-1960s is mixed. There is some evidence that such policies had an effect in moderating wage and price advances that were not being fed by an overheated economy. But even the advocates of an incomes policy do not believe that they would themselves completely remove the dilemma currently posed by the simultaneous existence of inflation and high unemployment. The administration has moved to establish a form of wage and price standards in the construction industry. And in January 1971 it pressed for and got a partial rollback in the originally announced increase in steel prices. But it has not announced a formal incomes policy for labor and industry generally that would include voluntary wage-price standards, on grounds that such standards would have little effect on inflation while at the same time encouraging false hopes of a relatively quick solution to the unemployment-inflation dilemma.

If, as the year proceeds, it becomes evident that the economy is expanding at a slower rate than is now foreseen by most private forecasters, and should the administration retain its objective of a more rapid growth, fiscal policy must become more expansionary. In adopting the full employment budget concept, however, the President not only proposed to use it as a measuring rod for fiscal policy, but advanced the proposition that federal expenditures "must never be allowed to outrun the revenues that the tax system would produce at reasonably full employment."[1] Since expenditures in the unified budget, about which the President was speaking, are already projected to equal full employment revenues, this would seem to rule out the possibility of further expansionary fiscal action, either by raising expenditures or by lowering taxes. But this is a needless constraint.

For assessing the fiscal impact of the budget, it is useful to calculate

1. *The Budget of the United States Government, Fiscal Year 1972*, p. 9.

its full employment surplus or deficit. But a balance in this full employment budget is not necessarily an appropriate target for policy at all times. When the economy needs stimulation from the budget, expenditures can appropriately exceed full employment revenues. Conversely, a full employment budget surplus is appropriate when the economy needs restraining. Thus only by the happiest coincidence would a fixed budget rule of full employment balance correspond with the fiscal needs of the economy at any particular time, and in no event would it meet those needs at all times. Adhering to the rule of full employment balance in the budget would deprive the administration of any further possibilities for stimulative fiscal action should the economy fall significantly short of the forecast.

The final question to ask of this year's fiscal policy is whether the $1,065 billion forecast is a desirable goal, quite apart from whether it is obtainable with the present strategy. The rate of economic expansion implied by the standard economic forecast of a $1,045 billion GNP in 1971 would not produce a significant drop in unemployment. As a target, most would find it insufficiently ambitious. Reaching the administration's target of a $1,065 billion GNP, on the other hand, would significantly reduce unemployment, but at some risk of adding to the rate of inflation. In general the administration's target might be characterized as being at the upper end of a reasonable set of policy choices. The greater weight one gives to the desirability of reducing unemployment and the less one fears inflation, the more appropriate this target seems. A vigorous and effective incomes policy might make it possible to achieve the employment target with less inflationary impact. The question is whether this possibility is worth the risks, difficulties, and commitment of presidential prestige necessary to secure union and management cooperation.

Priorities in the 1972 Budget

In determining priorities and formulating the federal budget, the President and his advisers do not start with a clean slate, deciding de novo how the $229 billion of expenditures for fiscal 1972 should be allocated in meeting national goals. Recent history, prior commitments, current political realities, relations with the Congress, economic and social events beyond the control of budget makers—all play a major role in limiting their ability to change radically the current shape of the budget. What they consider desirable must be tempered by what they consider feasible. Even in a budget of $229 billion, the margin of truly free choice is surprisingly small.

Understanding what the current budget says about the administration's priorities therefore calls for a brief look at past trends. Table 1-3 summarizes the development of the federal budget in the past fifteen years. Several facts stand out. The combined outlays for national defense, space, and foreign affairs rose sharply during most of the 1960s under the impact of successive decisions on the "missile gap," the moon landing, and most significantly the Vietnam war. The peak in expenditures for the moon landing was passed several years ago, and troop withdrawals in Vietnam have led to some reduction in defense spending.

Outlays for the federal government's various income maintenance programs have become by far the most rapidly growing component of the budget. Payments under the social security system continue to rise sharply year after year, in part because the number of retired persons is increasing, but mostly because benefit levels are periodically raised by legislation. In the mid-1960s, Medicare became a new and rapidly growing element in the budget. Public assistance payments have also escalated sharply because eligibility provisions

Table 1-3. Major Components of Federal Budget Outlays, Selected Fiscal Years, 1955–72
Billions of dollars

Component	1955	1960	1965	1970	1972
National defense, space, foreign affairs	42.3	49.5	59.3	87.8	85.6
Income maintenance	15.1	24.7	34.6	64.2	84.6
Investment in human resources (education, training, health)	1.5	2.3	3.8	11.5	14.4
Investment in physical resources and industry	1.6	5.9	9.3	11.3	15.0
Housing and community development	0.5	0.7	1.2	5.3	8.1
Interest on the debt (net)	4.7	6.9	8.7	14.4	14.4
Other outlays[a]	2.8	2.3	2.5	3.5	7.6[b]
Revenue sharing	—	—	—	—	4.0
Less: Sale of assets	—	−0.2	−1.1	−1.4	−4.5
Total budget expenditures	**68.5**	**92.2**	**118.4**	**196.6**	**229.2**

Sources: *The Budget of the United States Government* for fiscal years 1957, 1962, 1967, 1972. Figures are rounded and may not add to totals.
a. Other outlays are net of the federal government's contribution to employee retirement funds. These contributions are included in each functional category above but are netted out of the government total since they are intragovernmental transactions.
b. Includes pay increases for agencies other than defense and contingency allowance.

have been liberalized, a growing proportion of those eligible have taken advantage of their entitlement, and benefit levels have been raised. Each year when the budget is made up, a significant part of the available increase in budgetary resources must be set aside for growth in these programs, which accounted for more than 60 percent of the increase in expenditures between 1970 and 1972.

In the mid-1960s, a number of new programs providing federal investment in human resources—health, education, and manpower training—were inaugurated, and expenditures for these purposes grew rapidly. In the last few years the rate of growth has slowed, but part of each year's budget increment continues to be devoted to these programs. Previously, federal investment in physical resources was concentrated primarily on traditional public works affecting water resources, to which a major highway grant-in-aid program was added in the mid-1950s. These traditional investments continue to grow slowly, joined in recent years by sharply increasing federal grants for airports, urban mass transit, water pollution control facilities, and recreational development.

The growth in expenditures for housing and community development is largely the result of accelerated outlays in a longstanding federal program (urban renewal) and one major new thrust (housing subsidies for low- and moderate-income families). For both of these last two categories (housing and community development and investments in physical resources), most of the expenditure increases in any given year are the result of commitments for grants and subsidies made one or more years earlier.

Finally, the President has proposed the addition of an important new category, "general revenue sharing" with state and local governments, as well as a consolidation of many existing programs into a few special revenue sharing categories. Table 1-4 indicates how revenue sharing and the other factors mentioned above are reflected in changes in budget outlays between fiscal 1971 and fiscal 1972.

The budget planners started with three sets of facts. First, given a fiscal policy that aimed at a full employment budget balance, expenditures could not significantly exceed $229 billion. Projected expenditures for 1971 had been reestimated at about $211.5 billion before allowing for the recent increase in social security benefits, about $1.1 billion of which will fall in fiscal 1971. This made room for a total increase in expenditures of some $17.5 billion. Second,

Table 1-4. Major Changes in Federal Budget Outlays from Fiscal Year 1971 to Fiscal Year 1972

Billions of dollars

Vietnam withdrawal		−4.0
"Built-in" changes, net		12.2
Unemployment compensation	−0.8	
Other income maintenance	6.4	
Military and civilian pay	2.0	
Remaining built-in	4.6	
Reductions, total		−4.7
Financial transactions	−2.3	
Medicare and Medicaid proposals	−0.8	
Postal rate increase	−1.5	
Other	−0.1	
Major discretionary increases, total		14.0
Defense	3.7	
Volunteer army	1.2	
Other defense	2.5	
Social security	3.0	
Revenue sharing	4.0	
General revenue sharing	3.8	
New outlays for special revenue sharing	0.3	
Other civilian outlays	3.2	
Welfare reform	0.5	
Education and manpower training	0.5	
Rural housing	0.6	
Contingencies	0.7	
Other	0.9	
Unadjusted total		17.5
Less: Adjustment for cost of social security increase		
falling in 1971		−1.1
Total change in budget outlays		**16.4**

Sources: *The Budget of the United States Government, Fiscal Year 1972; The Budget of the United States Government—Appendix, Fiscal Year 1972; Special Analyses, Budget of the United States Government, Fiscal Year 1972.* Figures are rounded and may not add to totals.

continued withdrawals from Vietnam were expected to reduce budgetary costs by some $4 billion, although this amount could not be predicted with certainty. Third, even after some vigorous pruning, more than $12 billion was needed to pay for "built-in" changes required by law or for prior commitments. The list of built-in changes is formidable:

• Rising numbers of retired workers swell the costs of social security and Medicare; rapidly advancing medical prices drive up expenditures for Medicare and Medicaid; sharply growing numbers of welfare recipients under state programs increase the cost of the public assistance grant-in-aid program.

• In a number of rapidly growing programs—water pollution control, urban renewal, housing subsidies for low- and moderate-income families, urban mass transit, and the like—commitments in 1971 and earlier years to states, local governments, and private groups require added expenditures in 1972.

• Both law and policy provide for raising the pay of federal military and civilian employees in line with increases in the private sector.

• A relatively optimistic economic forecast, implying an estimated sharp reduction in unemployment during the 1972 fiscal year, provided some offset to these increases through a projected $800 million decrease in federal payments for unemployment compensation.

Starting with the $17.5 billion in expenditure increases allowed by fiscal policy, adding the $4 billion of budgetary savings made possible by planned withdrawals from Vietnam, and subtracting the $12.2 billion required to meet "built-in" increases, budget makers were initially left with $9.3 billion in discretionary funds for program expansion or for new programs.

To broaden this leeway, the budget sets forth several proposals designed to reduce expenditures by some $4.7 billion and make the savings available for the administration's high priority programs. Sales by the government of mortgages, other financial paper, and strategic stockpile materials that it holds are scheduled to expand by $2.3 billion. The proceeds from these sales are treated as deductions from expenditures and hence would serve to reduce the expenditure total. (In the past, projections of such asset sales have tended to be over optimistic, and the results have usually fallen below expectation.) A postal rate increase was announced, designed to reduce the Post Office deficit—which is a government expenditure—by $1.6 billion in 1972 (and by $0.2 billion in 1971). Since the reorganization of the postal service, this increase is no longer legislated by the Congress, but is handled through a complex administrative procedure. Savings of $800 million in the Medicare and Medicaid programs are proposed, primarily through requiring beneficiaries of the program to pay a larger share of the costs. Other proposed reductions will have their main impact in the years after 1972.

The $9.3 billion in net budgetary leeway, plus the use of some $4.7

billion in budget reductions, made possible a $14 billion discretionary expansion in outlays. The term "discretionary" is used to distinguish expenditure increases over which the administration can exercise some control from those built-in changes that are required by law or prior commitments. The $14 billion of discretionary increases in the 1972 budget consist of five major elements:

1. *Defense outlays.* Apart from expenditures attributable to Vietnam and those required to meet built-in changes in pay and retirement benefits, defense outlays are increased by some $3.7 billion. Slightly more than $1 billion of this total would finance the first step in special pay increases designed to attract more volunteers and thus move toward an all volunteer army. Increases of about $2.5 billion are proposed for other defense programs, about half of which may be necessary to cover rising prices. A summary of changes in defense outlays is shown in Table 1-5. The defense budget is discussed in Chapters 3 and 4.

2. *Social security.* A 6 percent increase in social security benefits, along with the liberalization of certain other benefits, was proposed by the administration at a cost of $3 billion in fiscal 1972. From the administration's standpoint, however, this increase was discretionary only in a technical sense. In 1970 both the House and the Senate approved increases in social security benefits that were larger than the administration's proposal. They failed to be enacted only because they became entangled with more controversial legislation in the closing days of the session. In a sense, the proposed liberalization does

Table 1-5. Summary of Changes in National Defense Outlays, by Cause, from Fiscal Year 1971 to Fiscal Year 1972

Billions of dollars

Cause of change	1971	1972	Change
Department of Defense and military assistance, total	**74.5**	**76.0**	**1.5**
"Built-in" factors	4.3	6.1	1.8
Military and civilian pay raises	(0.9)	(2.4)	(1.5)
Military retirement	(3.4)	(3.7)	(0.3)
Vietnam war costs	12.6	8.6	−4.0
Non-Vietnam defense costs	57.6	61.3	3.7
Volunteer army	(—)	(1.2)	(1.2)
Other defense programs	(57.6)	(60.1)	(2.5)

Source: *The Budget of the United States Government, Fiscal Year 1972*, p. 86. Vietnam war costs are authors' estimates.

represent a "discretionary" decision to liberalize social security benefits, but politically the administration had little choice but to propose the increase. Indeed, the Congress in March 1971 enacted a 10 percent across-the-board benefit increase, and is likely to enact other benefit liberalizations later in the year. The social security program is discussed in Chapter 10.

3. *Revenue sharing.* The administration proposed to use $4 billion of discretionary funds for its new revenue sharing proposals. The general revenue sharing proposals would cost $3.8 billion in fiscal 1972. The proposed plan is to take effect in October 1971, three months after the fiscal year begins. As a consequence, only three-fourths of the $5 billion first-full-year cost would fall in 1972. An additional $250 million would be used in fiscal 1972 to supplement $9.6 billion of expenditures under 130 existing grant-in-aid programs, which the administration proposes to group together into six special revenue sharing plans. Detailed examinations of general and special revenue sharing, and of various alternatives for aiding state and local governments, are the subjects of Chapters 6 and 7.

4. *Welfare reform.* The administration plans to resubmit its welfare reform proposal to the Congress. The fiscal 1972 cost would be $502 million, primarily for advance planning and organization. The major budgetary impact of this program would begin in fiscal 1973, when it is expected to cost about $4 billion. These costs are the *net* addition to existing federal costs for public assistance that would be incurred with the new plan. Welfare reform is discussed in Chapter 8.

5. *Education and Manpower.* Education and manpower programs account for only $0.5 billion of the increase in outlays. An extensive revision of aid to college and university students is proposed, to ensure that "no qualified student who wants to go to college should be barred by lack of money." The revision would consolidate grant and work study programs and provide subsidized loans for needy students and unsubsidized loans for all students. A National Student Loan Association (NSLA) would be set up to help in financing the volume of subsidized and unsubsidized loans by raising capital in the private market and lending to the originators of student loans. Because of the emphasis on guaranteeing loans by private lenders and the fact that NSLA activities would not appear in the budget, the magnitude of the administration's proposals for student aid financing are not fully reflected in budget expenditures. Except for student aid, outlays for higher education are projected to decline in fiscal 1972, reflecting cut-

backs in facilities construction and other institutional aid programs that would be only partially offset by the proposed new National Foundation for Higher Education. No increase in the federal support for elementary and secondary education is apparent in the budget. Funds are requested for assistance to school districts that are desegregating their schools, but this program would be a short-term effort, not a continuing support program for education.

6. *Other programs.* The five programs listed above would absorb $12 billion of the $14 billion discretionary expenditure increases. The remaining $2 billion is allocated among several other programs. An allowance for contingencies of $1 billion is provided, up $700 million from 1971. This allowance is made in the budget totals to provide room for unexpected developments and to cover proposals not firmly decided on when the budget is submitted to the Congress. Outlays for subsidized rural housing will rise by $600 million and for higher education by $200 million. Since $1.1 billion of the social security increase was scheduled to occur in fiscal 1971 and be added to that year's total, only $16.4 billion of the $17.5 billion overall increase will affect budget totals for fiscal 1972.

To summarize, the 1972 budget starts with a fiscal policy decision to operate within a balanced full employment budget, providing for total outlays of $229 billion, an increase of $17.5 billion over 1971 (before allowing for the cost of the social security increase in 1971). Some $12.2 billion of unavoidable expenditure increases must be provided for, offset partly by perhaps $4 billion of savings from continued Vietnam withdrawals, assuming that withdrawals continue at roughly the same pace as in fiscal 1971.

To the remaining $9.3 billion may be added some $4.7 billion of various proposed expenditure reductions, making $14 billion available for discretionary increases. Of this amount, $3.7 billion has been allocated to defense, $4 billion to revenue sharing, $3 billion to new liberalizations of social security benefits, and $500 million to the 1972 costs of welfare reform. The other $2.7 billion has been allocated among a wide range of programs, the largest specific items being for education and rural housing loans.

Two Important Features

On the domestic side of the budget, two overriding priorities stand out. One is the continuation of rapid growth in income support programs, explicitly called an "income strategy" in the President's Budget Message. The other is the introduction of revenue sharing.

The "Income Strategy"

The portion of the budget devoted to human resource programs—those designed to improve individual well-being and to help people function better in the future—has been growing for nearly a decade. This broad category encompasses two types of programs: (1) income support for individuals and families, and (2) programs to improve the provision of services such as education, manpower training, and health care.

In the mid-1960s, the primary federal emphasis was on improving services. Federal support for education and manpower training grew rapidly from a very small base. Major new legislation—the Elementary and Secondary Education Act, the Higher Education Act, the Equal Opportunity Act—provided federal funds for services to the poor and for strengthening health and education institutions generally. With the enactment of Medicare and Medicaid, the federal government took on a major new responsibility for helping individuals finance medical care, but cash transfer programs grew relatively slowly.

Beginning in 1967, the emphasis changed. The defense buildup associated with the Vietnam war produced pressure to curtail increases in federal contributions to health, education, and manpower services, while a number of other developments led to a rapid rise in income support payments. As may be seen in Table 1-6, the 1972 budget continues the emphasis on income programs rather than service programs. The growth of income programs is partly due to uncontrollable factors such as continued increases in the number of public assistance beneficiaries, and partly to a deliberate "income strategy" designed to ensure more adequate incomes for all families with children and better access to such important services as health and higher education.

Revenue Sharing

Chapters 6 and 7 discuss revenue sharing in detail, but a preliminary explanation of the size of the program is in order here. In his budget the President proposes to spend $13.6 billion on various reve-

nue sharing programs. These programs are to start part way through
the 1972 fiscal year; measured on a full twelve-month basis, they
would provide $16 billion a year for revenue sharing.

Of the $13.6 billion in proposed spending for revenue sharing, $3.8
billion would be for *general* revenue sharing—money made available

Table 1-6. Federal Outlays for Human Resources Programs,
Selected Fiscal Years, 1964–72[a]

Billions of dollars

Program	1964	1968	1971	1972
Income strategy, total	**30.4**	**46.1**	**73.3**	**79.7**
Cash transfers (including food assistance)	**30.0**	**38.1**	**59.4**	**64.6**
Social security[b]	19.1	27.2	39.9	43.6
Public assistance[c]	3.3	4.3	7.9	9.8
Unemployment insurance benefits	3.7	2.1	5.9	5.1
Veterans' pensions and compensation	3.9	4.5	5.8	6.2
Access to health care	**0.2**	**7.1**	**11.5**	**12.4**
Medicare	...	5.3	8.3	9.0
Medicaid	0.2	1.8	3.2	3.4
Access to education	**0.2**	**0.9**	**2.4**	**2.7**
Student assistance	0.1	0.4	0.7	0.8
G.I. Bill	0.1	0.4	1.7	1.9
Human resource development, total	**4.7**	**10.9**	**14.7**	**15.7**
Health resources	**3.0**	**3.8**	**5.4**	**5.8**
Research	0.9	1.1	1.3	1.4
Health manpower training	0.2	0.4	0.5	0.6
Construction of medical care facilities[d]	0.3	0.3	0.4	0.4
Health services, planning, and grants to states[d]	1.7	1.9	3.2	3.4
Education, manpower, and work incentives	**1.7**	**7.1**	**9.3**	**10.0**
Preschool, elementary, and secondary education[e]	0.3	2.4	3.2	3.6
Manpower training, vocational education, and vocational rehabilitation	0.3	1.9	2.4	2.5
Higher education, except student assistance	0.3	1.0	0.8	0.5
Other	0.8	1.8	2.9	3.4
Grand total	**35.1**	**57.0**	**88.0**	**95.4**

Sources: *The Budget of the United States Government* for fiscal years 1966, 1970, and 1972, and *The Budget of the United States Government—Appendix, Fiscal Year 1966.*

Note: The income strategy category in this table differs from the income maintenance category in Table 1-3 principally because the latter includes and the former excludes farm price supports.

a. Includes relevant programs of the Department of Health, Education, and Welfare; the Department of Agriculture; the Manpower Administration of the Department of Labor; the National Science Foundation; the Office of Economic Opportunity; the Veterans Administration; and the Environmental Protection Agency.

b. Includes old-age, survivors, and disability insurance, railroad and civil service retirement, and related benefits; excludes Medicare.

c. Includes the proposed Family Assistance Plan, food stamps, and other food and nutrition programs.

d. Includes outlays for this purpose by the Veterans Administration.

e. Excludes vocational education.

to state and local governments to use as they saw fit. In addition, the President proposes to group 130 existing federal grants into six major "special revenue sharing" categories through which funds would be distributed under six different formulas to state and local governments. Some $9.9 billion would be spent in 1972 for the latter grants. As Chapter 7 points out, state and local governments would in most instances have wide discretion in how they used the special revenue sharing funds. Indeed, except that funds would be distributed under the six different formulas rather than one, the latter program would in many respects be much like general revenue sharing.

Should the President's revenue sharing proposals be enacted, the federal government's grant-in-aid program to state and local governments for fiscal 1972 would be composed of four major categories, with funds allotted to each as shown below (in billions of dollars):

Income maintenance grants	14.6
Revenue sharing, general and special	13.6
Interstate highways	3.1
All others	7.0
Total	38.3

Of the total $38.3 billion in grants, $14.6 billion would be the federal government's share of the cost of various income maintenance programs—public assistance, Medicaid, food stamps, and the like. An almost equal amount would be general and special revenue sharing grants. The 90 percent federal grant for the interstate highway program would account for slightly more than $3 billion. Finally, the remaining categorical grants, in which the federal government stipulates in some detail the purposes and conditions under which state and local governments could spend the funds, would amount to only $7 billion, about 3 percent of the total federal budget.

Commitments for the Future

Analyzing the 1972 budget solely in terms of expenditures does not bring out the full flavor of the decisions it reflects. In many cases, expenditures respond to budgetary decisions only after a long time lag. New commitments to states and localities for pollution waste treatment plants will result in expenditures only as the plants are built, which may not occur for one or more years. New orders for Navy ships may represent large new commitments in 1972 but lead to little in the way of expenditure increases until 1973 and later years. Similarly, expenditures under the proposed Family Assistance Plan, scheduled at only $500 million in 1972, would rise to about $4.0 billion in 1973. A new health financing plan for poor families is proposed in the 1972 budget, but expenditures would not begin until 1973, when they would amount to more than $1 billion. The President's general revenue sharing program is scheduled to start in October 1971 and would cost $3.8 billion in fiscal 1972, but $5.4 billion in fiscal 1973.

There are several measures of the extent to which the 1972 budget incorporates decisions that will lead to increased spending in future years. For example, it gives figures based on the amount of *obligations* the federal government plans to make. "Obligations" is the term used in the budget to denote contracts signed, grant-in-aid commitments made to state and local governments, and similar actions by which the federal government binds itself to pay out funds. In fiscal 1972, total federal obligations are scheduled to be $9 billion higher than expenditures in the same period, suggesting future increases in federal spending to meet that higher level of contracts and commitments. Between 1971 and 1972, while expenditures are scheduled to rise by $16.4 billion, obligations would increase by $18.9 billion. Thus the excess of obligations over expenditures would rise between the two years.

Of the $9 billion excess of obligations over expenditures in fiscal 1972, defense would account for $2.1 billion, suggesting future rises in defense spending. Provision is also made in the defense budget for substantial research and development expenditures for a series of new weapons systems—including a long-range underwater strategic missile system, the new B-1 bomber, a new Air Force fighter plane (the F-15), and a new attack aircraft (the A-X). Final decisions have not been made to procure any of these weapons, but some of them are highly likely to be included as procurement items in future budgets. Other major areas in which obligations exceed expenditures include water pollution control grants, public works construction, transportation programs, and various activities of the Department of Health, Education, and Welfare.

How the 1972 budget decisions affect future expenditures, the relationship of these expenditures to future revenues, and the budget-

ary resources available for new or expanded programs in later years
are the subjects of Chapter 17.

Summary

This year's budget documents reflect a number of the administration's priorities. With respect to overall economic objectives, the administration seeks a very ambitious rate of expansion in economic activity. Its budgets for both the current and the coming fiscal year entail large deficits. But those deficits stem from the depressed revenues yielded by low profits and income in the private economy; the budget itself is not expansionary. An expansion of money and credit by the Federal Reserve is sought as the chief policy instrument for rapid economic recovery.

In terms of priorities, the new budget necessarily envisions expanded outlays to allow for rising prices and workloads. It allocates a slightly higher amount to defense than last year. On the domestic side, provision is made for a major new system of revenue sharing with state and local governments, for an increase in social security benefits, and for small expansions in a number of existing social programs. Two new programs directed toward the poor are proposed—the Family Assistance Plan and a health insurance scheme. The major spending consequences of these new programs, together with new commitments made in existing programs, will show up primarily in budgets of future years.

2. Foreign Policy Assumptions

WHILE THIS BOOK IS NOT INTENDED to offer an in-depth analysis of foreign policy issues, a brief review of the President's publicly stated view of those issues is needed as background for the discussion of defense questions that follows.

Roughly one-third of the nation's budgetary outlays are for national defense and foreign assistance. Whether one considers that these expenditures are excessive, approximately right, or inadequate depends in the first instance on how one looks at the risks the United States faces in the world, on how one assesses the U.S. interests that could be exposed to risk, and on the importance one attaches to the U.S. role in trying to influence world events. The assumptions underlying these judgments are discussed in this chapter.

At least equally important, however, are judgments on such matters as allied and enemy capabilities, the military responses that would be most effective in dealing with specific contingencies, the relative military roles of different types of forces, and the degree of confidence the United States needs (and is prepared to pay for) in its ability to deal with risks. These judgments combine political, military, and technical considerations, which are discussed in Chapters 3–5.

Both political and technical judgments are necessary in deciding whether to spend money on international programs rather than on competing domestic demands.

The President's 1971 message on the state of the world outlines his view of the foreign policy assumptions that underlie expenditures on international programs. The keynote of that message, as of the secretary of state's later report on U.S. foreign policy, is continuity. The President foresees no major change in U.S. interests or commitments overseas, as compared with those that existed in the 1960s. Thus, he expects no large shift in U.S.–Soviet relations or in the U.S. commitment to Europe; he projects a continuing willingness on the part of the United States to match Soviet power in the Middle East; he calls for increased effort by Asian countries, particularly in combating insurgency, but suggests no change in the existing definition of U.S. interests in Asia or in U.S. willingness to fulfill its commitments in the area. He does, however, project some important changes in the means by which the United States pursues these interests and fulfills these commitments.

In general, the President's message is intended to convey to foreign powers an impression of firmness and of continuing involvement; it is, in itself, a means of bargaining with potential adversaries and of maintaining allied confidence and cohesion. In this sense, the defense budget is also an instrument of policy. It should reinforce the President's Foreign Policy Message by showing expenditure and force requirements that are consistent with the President's statement of the U.S. role in the world.

Different assumptions regarding the world scene and the U.S. world role presumably would have called for a different budget for international programs—either larger or smaller. The purpose of this section is, first, to outline the administration's foreign policy assumptions in the main areas of U.S. concern—U.S.–Soviet relations, Europe, the Middle East, Asia, and the developing countries as a group; and, second, to describe in general terms some possible alternative views in some of these areas.

U.S.–Soviet Relations

At the heart of the President's message is his view of U.S.–Soviet relations. Nothing in the message foreshadows any drastic near-term change in the uneasy mixture of competition and cooperation that now marks those relations.

In the strategic field the President assumes that the Soviet Union's minimum goal is to maintain nuclear parity with the United States. To do so gives the Soviet leaders greater confidence in their ability to neutralize U.S. strategic nuclear power. It is also a matter of pride and prestige for a country that lags several decades behind the United States in industrial power and technology. The President points out some ambiguity in the USSR's strategic arms policy, suggesting at least the possibility that it may envisage a goal more ambitious than parity. This emphasis on the ambiguities of the Soviet position, both in the President's message and in other administration statements, probably has the dual objective of seeking clarification of the Soviet position and of generating domestic support for major U.S. defense programs, such as the Safeguard program to protect missile sites with antiballistic missiles (ABMs).

The President's response to Soviet strategic programs is to continue present U.S. efforts to assure strategic "sufficiency." He eschews any attempts to regain strategic "superiority" over the USSR, because "small numerical advantages in strategic forces have little military relevance" and because "the attempt to obtain large advantages would spark an arms race which would, in the end, prove pointless." For this reason as well, he expresses serious interest in reaching some form of strategic arms limitation agreement with the USSR. He is not prepared to accept any diminution in the effectiveness of our strategic deterrent and seems determined to prevent any significant adverse change in the overall U.S.–Soviet strategic balance. Current U.S. programs keep virtually all options open as to future U.S. decisions in developing and deploying new strategic weapons systems—offensive and defensive—on the premise that this course is most likely both to preserve sufficiency and to enhance prospects of a realistic arms limitation agreement.

In general, the President's Foreign Policy and Budget Messages and Secretary Laird's Defense Report show evidence of cautious concern, rather than great expectations, regarding Soviet intentions and policies. They show interest in making this an "era of negotiations," but they also view Soviet moves on the seas, in the Middle East, and in the strategic weapons field as new challenges that must be offset.

Europe

The President takes a cautious position toward détente in Europe. He favors East-West negotiation through all available channels, but he is anxious that it not be conducted in ways that might compromise Western unity and strength, and implies that there is considerable risk that this will occur. Clearly, he does not expect Chancellor Brandt's *Ostpolitik* and other approaches to the Soviet Union on European issues to produce early and important changes in Soviet policy. He sees Soviet policy as being designed to maintain, and to secure Western acquiescence in, the status quo in Central Europe, but he does not exclude the possibility of new Soviet pressures on the West, should weakness in NATO upset the military balance in Europe.

These judgments play a part in the President's decision that the U.S. forces in, and committed to, Europe should not be reduced, except in balanced withdrawals of both U.S. and Soviet forces, and that an effort should be made to upgrade the quality of NATO forces.

This decision regarding U.S. forces also reflects the President's view of allied attitudes. While he believes that the NATO allies are ready to join the United States in a continuing effort to sustain NATO, and that likely progress toward Western European unity will strengthen this resolve, he also judges that they are not prepared to mount a greatly increased defense effort and that a cut in U.S. forces now would only lead to corresponding cuts in allied forces.

More than military factors, however, underlie the decision to maintain U.S. forces in Europe. It reflects not only the President's view of Soviet intentions, but also his assessment of the primary importance of Europe, of the U.S. connection with Europe, and of the U.S. role in Atlantic affairs, as elements in the world balance of power.

The Middle East

The other crucial area where U.S. and Soviet policy and power interact is the Middle East. Here, too, the President implicitly projects continuity in Soviet policy. The USSR wants to extend its power, he believes, but not at the cost of a major confrontation with the United States. He concludes that the United States needs to emphasize the risks of such a confrontation; he hopes that, if this is done, the Soviet Union will be deterred from adventurous policies and may eventually join us in trying to bring greater stability to the area.

Similarly, in regard to the Arab-Israeli conflict, the President hopes for progress in negotiations, but does not assume that it will occur. The continued possibility of new hostilities presumably reinforces his disposition to avoid what he fears might be unsettling changes in U.S. force planning for the Middle East.

Asia

The President discusses the Nixon doctrine in terms that make clear that it is an attitude, rather than a specific program. He expects increased allied effort, particularly in meeting internal threats; but he projects no great change in past definitions of U.S. interests and commitments in East Asia. He envisages a continued U.S. willingness to fulfill those commitments when local forces are not sufficient to deter or repel external attack.

Thus, if the reduction in U.S. general purpose forces (discussed in Chapter 3) has its roots in a reduction in forces earmarked for Asia, the explanation does not lie in a basic reappraisal of U.S. interests in the region. Rather, it rests on the force planning assumption (which the President makes explicit) that the United States will not have to meet serious threats in Asia and Europe simultaneously, principally because of growing hostility between Russia and China, but possibly also because the likelihood of large-scale Chinese aggression in Asia has been downgraded in view of China's domestic problems and a reassessment of Chinese strategy.

Changes in the way the United States will respond to threats in Asia are also involved. The President's message and the Defense Report both indicate that major reliance will be placed on allied rather than on U.S. ground forces in meeting what the secretary of defense describes as "subtheater" Asian threats, though ground forces continue to be maintained in the U.S. force structure for these contingencies. Whether or not ground forces are involved, U.S. air and naval support will be available to meet those threats. These changes also raise a question whether greater reliance will be placed on U.S. nuclear forces to deter Chinese aggression or attempted nuclear blackmail.

Foreign Assistance

The President's message distinguishes between two kinds of foreign assistance:

• security assistance, to enable allied countries to play a larger role in their own defense, which will be provided by bilateral U.S. economic and military programs; and

• economic development assistance, for humanitarian reasons and to increase long-term prospects for a viable world order, which will be provided increasingly through multilateral means.

The Nixon doctrine shapes the President's view of both. It calls on allied countries to assume a larger responsibility for their own defense; this is consistent with the view that the United States should help them to attain self-reliance through security assistance and that such assistance is a good bargain because it enables the United States to reduce its ground forces. In development aid, the President proposes that U.S. bilateral programs be gradually replaced by multilateral programs in which other donor countries, as well as the United States, play a growing part.

Indeed, the general tenor of the President's Foreign Policy Message—that the United States should avoid the extremes of direct military involvement and of withdrawal from its responsibilities—suggests his belief that the need for both kinds of aid may well increase in the coming decade. But the relationship between the two types of foreign assistance, and the extent to which one type might or should substitute for the other, are questions that are not addressed in the message. These questions could affect future expenditure requirements.

Thus, in its treatment of security needs—whether in Asia, Europe, the Middle East, or the strategic area—the President's message foresees no basic shift in U.S. interests. Proposed changes in the force structure relate to conventional forces and derive from a different set of factors. In Asia, at least, the President has chosen to gear defense policy to what he considers to be the more likely threat rather than to the worst case. Changes in either set of factors—interests or threats—would provide justifiable grounds for revising the force structure; indeed, both must be subject to constant reassessment.

Alternatives

This is not the place for a detailed discussion of alternative foreign policy assumptions, but it may be useful to mention four key issues on which differing views could lead to different defense budgets.

1. *Strategic.* One view would be that the numerical balance between U.S. and Soviet strategic power is of no particular importance, so long as the United States retains an effective survivable retaliatory capacity, even though it may be a single system. This view would be based on a belief that a possible Soviet strategic quantitative advan-

tage could no more be put to political use in the 1970s than U.S. superiority was put to use in earlier years. Its proponents would favor both more far-reaching arms control agreements than have yet been proposed by the administration and less ambitious unilateral strategic arms goals than the administration appears intent on pursuing.

On the other hand, it could be argued that Soviet strategic moves create a strong presumption of intent to seek nuclear "superiority" and to try to exploit that "superiority" in ways that could threaten peace. Proponents of this view would feel that, in this circumstance, a clearer demonstration of a U.S. desire to negate Soviet strategic moves would have a healthy effect on Soviet intentions. They might, therefore, favor more vigorous moves to bolster U.S. strategic strength.

2. *Europe.* Some would see in Europe a steadily diminishing threat of Soviet military pressure, a decline in the importance of a continuing close connection between the United States and Western Europe, and an abundant economic capacity among European nations to take care of their own defense. These assessments, which differ from the President's assessment of the European defense equation, could lead to the view that the U.S. troop commitment in Europe should be substantially reduced.

Alternatively, it might be argued that the indication of U.S.-Soviet nuclear parity warrants a more determined effort to improve NATO's capability for meeting an attack without early use of nuclear weapons. This might mean expensive moves (1) to improve the quality of NATO forces in Europe, (2) to enhance U.S. air and sea lift, and (3) to increase the readiness of U.S. reserves earmarked for Europe.

3. *Middle East.* Here an alternative view to that held by the President would downgrade both the Soviet threat and the importance of the U.S. military presence in this area. Those holding this view would tend to discount the possibility of either Soviet offensive action or effective Arab action against Israel; and they would argue that U.S. intervention in lesser contingencies (such as the crisis that occurred when Syrian armor menaced Jordan) would worsen, rather than help, the situation. In this case, different planning assumptions would have little effect on the defense budget since U.S. forces in this area—principally the carrier task forces in the Mediterranean—have as their major mission the defense of NATO. Nevertheless, a downgrading of our role in the Middle East could remove a constraint against reducing the present level of U.S. forces in the Mediterranean.

A more pessimistic view of prospects in this area would emphasize the Soviet/Arab threat to Israel and the consequent need for stronger measures to meet it. In the first instance at least, this would probably mean more security assistance to Israel, rather than strengthened U.S. forces.

4. *Asia.* An alternative view here would redefine U.S. Asian commitments to reflect the judgment that Japan is the single vital U.S. interest in the region, and that only commitments that directly relate to this interest should be sustained. For force planning purposes, this could mean U.S. involvement in the defense of Korea and Taiwan, in view of their close connection with Japan, but not necessarily future U.S. involvement in the defense of Southeast Asia. Since the requirement for U.S. ground forces in the defense of Korea or Taiwan should be substantially less than for defense of Southeast Asia, this view might permit significant reductions in the U.S. force structure.

Conversely, it might be argued that (1) the possibility of simultaneous Soviet and Chinese threats in Europe and Asia cannot be ignored, and that (2) on the basis of past experience, it seems highly unlikely that the United States would be able to fulfill its commitments, at least in Southeast Asia, without the use of large-scale U.S. ground forces. If either or both of these arguments were accepted, the requirement for U.S. general purpose forces would be greater than is projected in the President's budget.

Conclusion

The President's Foreign Policy Message and his 1972 budget need to be considered in relation to each other. Taken together, they highlight the fundamental foreign policy questions that underlie the consideration of every defense budget. First, are the forces proposed in the budget consistent with the President's view of the U.S. role in the world and the threats it faces? Second, what changes in forces would be implied by different views of this role and these threats? Since a host of other factors also enter into defense budget decisions, these questions have neither simple nor unique answers. The following three chapters deal with both general and technical considerations that need to be taken into account in judging the place of national security in the nation's spending priorities.

3. Major Defense Options

THE PRESIDENT PROPOSES that the United States spend $76.0 billion in fiscal 1972 for defense and an additional $1.1 billion for the defense-related outlays of the Atomic Energy Commission. The total would be $1.5 billion more than last year and would represent the first increase in defense spending since 1969. On the other hand, not since the period immediately preceding the Korean war has defense made so low a *proportionate* claim on the nation's resources; $76.0 billion in defense outlays would be 33 percent of total federal outlays and less than 7 percent of projected gross national product.

Future expenditure levels arising from this budget are likely to be higher than these figures suggest. The budget requests authority for the Defense Department to commit $79 billion in 1972, or $3 billion more than the estimated level of outlays. These defense budget data, with comparisons for selected past years, are shown in Table 3-1.

At the risk of oversimplification, the 1972 defense budget can be characterized as follows:

For strategic forces, it requests funds about one-fifth below the pre-Vietnam level in dollars of constant purchasing power. These funds provide for maintaining a three-fold diversified nuclear deterrent composed of sea-based missiles, ABM-protected land-based missiles, and bombers, and for the continued installation of new weapon systems to increase the capability of the deterrent. The funds also provide for the further development of other advanced systems, but the decision to procure them is left open.

For baseline conventional forces—that is, for general purpose

Table 3-1. **Financial Summary of the Department of Defense Budget,**
Fiscal Years 1964, 1968, 1971, and 1972

Billions of dollars

Description	1964	1968	1971	1972
Outlays				
Current dollars	50.8	78.0	74.5	76.0
Constant 1972 dollars[a]	74.4	98.5	78.2	76.0
Percentage of gross national product	8.3	9.5	7.4	6.8
Total obligational authority				
Current dollars	50.8	75.9	75.3	79.2
Constant 1972 dollars[a]	74.3	96.1	79.0	79.2

Source: U.S. Department of Defense, News Release 72-71, Jan. 29, 1971.

a. The cost of the volunteer service budgeted for fiscal year 1972 is not treated as an element of inflation and therefore is not used in calculating the effect of pay and price increases on the figures for prior years. Except for this, the effect of inflation was estimated on the same basis as that used by the Department of Defense.

forces other than additions for Vietnam—it requests funds somewhat above the pre-Vietnam level in dollars of constant purchasing power. These funds, however, support fewer divisions, air wings, and ships than were in the pre-Vietnam force and place somewhat heavier emphasis on sophisticated weapons. Despite the sizable reduction in combat units, manpower has been reduced very little; the ratio of support forces to combat forces has clearly gone up.

For Vietnam, it implies a continued decline in the cost of the war. Savings from further withdrawals of troops will be offset only in part by increased assistance for Southeast Asian allied forces. The war will absorb about 11 percent of defense outlays in 1972 compared to 30 percent in 1968.

Defense budget trends, with an estimated distribution of costs among these three major categories, are shown in Table 3-2.

Another way of looking at the defense budget is to see the broad relationship in current dollars among the savings on the Vietnam war, the effect of pay and price increases, and the proposed expenditures on other defense programs. Vietnam war costs will decline by another $4.0 billion in 1972 if U.S. troop withdrawals continue at the current rate. On the other hand, price increases and the general pay raise for military and civilian employees will add $3 billion to the cost of non-Vietnam programs. After allowing for these effects of inflation, the cost of non-Vietnam programs is to go up by $2.5 billion in fiscal 1972, of which $1.2 billion is for the first installment of the incentive pay increases for an all volunteer service. To put these data in other

Table 3-2. Funds Authorized for Strategic and General Purpose Forces, by Category, Selected Fiscal Years, 1961–72

Billions of dollars

Category	1961	1964	1968	1970	1971	1972
In current dollars						
Strategic nuclear forces	15.7	17.0	16.9	17.7	18.6	19.7
General purpose forces (other than additions for Vietnam)	29.2	33.8	36.0	41.5	44.1	50.9
Vietnam additions	...	...	23.0	17.6	12.6	8.6
Total	44.9	50.8	75.9	76.8	75.3	79.2
In 1972 dollars						
Strategic nuclear forces	23.8	24.8	21.4	19.7	19.3	19.7
General purpose forces (other than additions for Vietnam)	44.3	49.5	45.6	46.2	45.7	50.9
Vietnam additions	...	...	29.1	19.6	13.0	8.6
Total	68.1	74.3	96.1	85.5	78.0	79.2

Sources: 1961 in current dollars is from *Setting National Priorities: The 1971 Budget*, Table 2-1; totals for other years in current dollars are for total obligational authority (TOA) from Department of Defense, News Release 72-71, Jan. 29, 1971. All figures represent budget authorizations except those for Vietnam additions, which represent outlays. The basic data for strategic and general purpose forces are from *ibid.* The costs of the strategic nuclear forces are the sum of the strategic forces program, half of the intelligence and communications program, 40 percent of the research and development program, and a varying percentage of three support programs: central supply and maintenance, training, medical and other general personnel activities, and administration. The costs of the general purpose forces are the sum of the general purpose forces program, half of the intelligence and communications program, the airlift and sealift program, the National Guard and Reserve forces program, 60 percent of the research and development program, the support of other nations program, and a varying percentage of other support programs. Vietnam additions are based on Table 4-2. Differences between the figures in this table and those in Table 2-1 in *Setting National Priorities: The 1971 Budget* result from refinements by the Department of Defense of TOA figures for past years and adjustment of the breakout by authorization category to reflect these refinements. The amount of $1.5 billion proposed by the administration for an all volunteer force is not included for years before fiscal year 1972 in the calculations in 1972 dollars. The conversions to 1972 dollars are based on data supplied by the Department of Defense.

terms, increased spending on the baseline defense force—that is, the force the United States would maintain if it were not in Vietnam— will exceed reductions in the cost of the war by $1.5 billion.

General purpose forces continue to account for the major part of the defense budget and for almost all of this year's increase in costs associated with the baseline defense posture. Because their costs weigh so heavily in the defense budget, these forces will be the major arena for considering how military spending should weigh in the nation's priorities.

Outlays for strategic forces, on the other hand, remain relatively stable. Nevertheless, the spending issues here are potentially significant, though they are not likely to have a major influence on the size of the budget in the next year or two. Achievement of an agreement in the strategic arms limitation talks (SALT)—at least an agreement of the kind now in prospect—would not appreciably reduce strategic outlays, but it would greatly reduce the risk that such outlays could get out of hand.

A comparison of the military force structure contemplated by the 1972 budget with force structures in selected years of the past decade is shown in Table 3-3.

Shaping the Defense Posture

As is pointed out in Chapter 2, the administration's proposed defense program and budget reflect its view of U.S. interests and commitments, the major threats to our security, and the appropriate strategies for meeting them. But other factors are also involved.

The defense program, force structure, and budget are affected by a complex internal bargaining process in which important decisions are made one by one at various policy levels, using facts and analyses of widely varying quality. In the present administration, moreover, greater reliance than in the recent past is placed on presidentially determined fiscal guidance to scale the total size of the defense establishment, while within that total, more reliance is placed on the military services to make internal allocations of resources. Taken together, these management practices tend to mute debate within the Defense Department over the proper size of the defense budget and to discourage interest elsewhere in the administration in the proper allocation of defense resources.

Moreover, force planning analysis cannot resolve a number of basic uncertainties in defense requirements, capabilities, and alternatives. The range of uncertainty within which reasonable men can and do disagree about what is needed to satisfy given defense objectives is probably 25 to 30 percent, or about $20 billion a year. The same budget and force structure could be interpreted as a risky way to achieve an ambitious worldwide strategy or as a safe means to carry out a restricted and more selective strategy. Given such wide uncertainties, decision makers are pressed to accommodate conflicting viewpoints on specific programs even in the absence of agreement on objectives. Furthermore, the long lead time between the conception and the deployment of a weapon system magnifies both the pressure to come to a decision and the budgetary cost of being wrong.

Table 3-3. Structure of Department of Defense Military Forces, Various Significant Fiscal Years, 1961–72ª

Description	Last Eisenhower year, 1961	Pre-Vietnam, 1964	Peak Vietnam, 1968	1970	Estimated 1971	Estimated 1972
Military personnel (thousands)	**2,484**	**2,685**	**3,547**	**3,066**	**2,699**	**2,505**
Civilian personnel (thousands)	**1,042**	**1,035**	**1,287**	**1,161**	**1,104**	**1,082**
Strategic offensive forces						
Land based missiles	28	654	1,054	1,054	1,054	1,054
Sea based missiles	80	336	656	656	656	656
Strategic bombersᵇ	1,654	1,277	648	517	569	521
General purpose forces						
Divisions (Army and Marine Corps)	14	19⅓	23⅔	20⅓	16⅔	16⅓
Tactical air wings						
Air Force	21	22	28	23	21	21
Navy	16	15	15	13	12	11
Marine Corps	3	3	3	3	3	3
Attack carriers	15	15	15	15	14	13
Antisubmarine carriers	9	9	8	4	4	3
Nuclear attack submarines	13	19	33	46	53	56
Total number of ships	819	932	932	743	710	658
Airlift and sealift forces						
C-5A squadrons	...	...	...	1	2	4
All other squadrons	31	33	30	17	15	13
Total obligational authority (billions of constant 1972 dollars)	**68.1**	**74.3**	**96.1**	**85.5**	**78.0**	**79.2**

Sources: *The Budget of the United States Government*, various years; *The Budget of the United States Government—Appendix*, various years; Department of Defense, News Release 72-71, Jan. 29, 1971; *Defense Report: Statement of Secretary of Defense Melvin R. Laird before the House Armed Services Committee on the Fiscal Year 1972–1976 Defense Program and the 1972 Defense Budget* (March 9, 1971); unpublished data from the Department of Defense.

a. All figures, except those for total obligational authority, are for the end of the fiscal year.

b. Includes, before 1968, some medium range bombers, forward based, that were used in the strategic role. The FB-111 is included in the 1971 figure.

Events beyond the administration's control can greatly complicate matters, more so in defense than in many other areas of government activity. For example, the attempt to keep defense expenditures in check could be frustrated by a buildup in international tension, quite aside from any outbreak of hostilities. Defense requirements would be sensitive to a variety of external developments, such as new communist pressures in Southeast Asia, or a steady expansion in Soviet strategic capabilities, or the provocative deployment of Soviet conventional forces, or a dramatic breakdown of SALT.

The defense budget—and particularly the one for 1972—is also vulnerable to internal cost pressures. Notable examples would be unplanned cost increases in the procurement of new weapons, which could weigh very heavily in view of the number of sophisticated weapons systems now under development, and difficulties in recruiting skilled manpower and maintaining strength levels through the pay incentives now projected for a volunteer force.

Finally, the size of the defense budget in relation to the limited discretionary funds available each year to any administration for policy initiatives gives it a central position in the examination of national priorities. Potential gains from additional defense spending, or potential losses from cuts, must be weighed against alternative uses of these funds. Since rising prices and wages in the defense budget are absorbing the reductions in Vietnam costs, savings from defense can come only from modifications of the baseline program, and the feasibility of such modifications depends on careful analysis. Thus, there are compelling reasons to subject the defense posture to public examination—to test the underlying political, military, and technical assumptions, despite the limitations of publicly available information; to focus attention on the most important issues; and to explore alternative possibilities.

The budget covers two broad military categories: strategic nuclear forces and general purpose forces. Each is concerned with a different kind of threat to U.S. security.

The United States maintains strategic forces to deter nuclear attacks against ourselves and our allies. In designing them, we have in mind the Soviet nuclear capability and the complex of factors that enter into our assessment of Soviet intentions. More recently, the small but growing Chinese Communist nuclear arsenal has had to be taken into account.

We maintain general purpose forces to deter conventional and tactical nuclear attacks, such as could occur in a range of contingencies, principally in Europe and Asia. In examining the size and composition of these forces, it is useful to separate those added for Vietnam from what might be called the baseline or peacetime defense structure.

Somewhat distinct policy issues enter into planning the two types of forces, and within fairly wide limits the requirements for each are determined independently of the other. These issues, together with their budgetary consequences, are therefore examined separately for the two types of forces. On the basis of this analysis, implications are drawn regarding the current defense budget and trends over the longer term.

Strategic Forces

Strategic nuclear forces absorb about 25 percent of the 1972 defense budget. According to the President's 1971 Foreign Policy Message, the primary purpose of these forces continues to be "political and defensive"—that is, deterrence of nuclear attacks, of nuclear blackmail, and of acts that could lead to nuclear war.

During the 1960s, the most widely used measure of deterrence was the ability of the United States to absorb an all-out Soviet attack and still have enough forces left to destroy a significant part of the USSR's population and industry—often put at 20 to 25 percent of its population and 50 percent of its industry—in retaliation. This form of deterrence is commonly known as an assured destruction capability. Force planning policy in the 1960s defined adequate confidence in our ability to inflict urban–industrial damage as requiring that each of our three survivable force components—bombers, land-based missiles, and sea-based missiles—have an independent capability to inflict retaliatory damage. This redundant deterrent is called a "triad."

The strategic environment of the 1970s will be different. Most significantly, the Soviet Union has largely overcome its former position of strategic inferiority. The USSR currently has more land-based intercontinental ballistic missiles (ICBMs) than we do, and reports suggest that it could develop an advanced multiple warhead system for its large SS-9 ICBMs, or for an advanced version reported to be under construction. Within three to four years, the Soviet Union could match the United States in numbers of Polaris-type missile-firing submarines. On the other hand, our present strategic position is strong, and new programs are being pursued. Our multiple independently-targetable reentry vehicle (MIRV) program gives us an advantage in the number of independent warheads, and we lead in intercontinental bomber capabilities. The USSR has a small and relatively ineffective antiballistic missile (ABM) defense around Moscow, while we are deploying a new ABM system (Safeguard) and may have an edge in ABM technology.

On an overall basis, therefore, the Soviet Union has reached a position of strategic comparability with the United States. In addition, before the end of the decade the Chinese will probably acquire a small ICBM force; apparently they have already developed medium-range missiles that could reach targets in Asia. These changes in the underlying situation require a reassessment of the kind of strategic force we need. Many issues that were central to strategic debates in past years —for example, whether we should build a large anti-Soviet ABM or seek strategic superiority—are no longer considered to be serious policy options. On the other hand, arms control and mutual stability are now generally accepted as important criteria for force planning.

Six Strategic Issues

Looking to the future, six issues are likely to shape our strategic posture.

The Multiple Deterrent

A central issue for the 1970s is how much assurance or confidence we need in our ability to retaliate. Specifically, should we continue to maintain a strategic posture comprising three independent and survivable force components? Since the Soviet Union could acquire the ability to endanger the survivability of our land-based forces within a few years, it will be not only expensive but also technologically difficult for the United States to maintain a triad in the future.

The administration has begun taking action to ensure that we will have an invulnerable and diversified deterrent in the future—for example, by continued deployment of Safeguard ABM sites to defend our ICBMs and by strengthening our missile silos. In his Foreign

Policy Message, the President emphasized the importance of the triad, indicating that "it provides insurance against surprise enemy technological breakthroughs or unforeseen operational failures and complicates the task of planning attacks on us." But it may prove very difficult to find reliable and cost-effective ways of protecting our ICBMs. Thus far, none of the options—ABM defense, silo hardening, or mobility—looks promising as a long-term solution.

The basic question therefore persists: Is the confidence gained from pursuing full redundancy worth the cost? Even if we invest substantial resources, we cannot be certain of success; for the Soviet Union may be able to increase its forces and offset our protective measures.

As an alternative, the United States could decide to maintain a "diad"—a diversified deterrent with only one survivable land-based system, either missiles or bombers, to supplement the sea-based force. This would still provide some insurance through redundancy. It may be easier to protect bombers than missiles, principally through such techniques as improved alert procedures, better radar warning, and base dispersal. This would suggest a diad composed of Polaris submarines and bombers. Since missiles and aircraft have different characteristics and capabilities, this combination might be a more effective deterrent than a combination of sea-based and land-based missile forces.

Another alternative would be to rely entirely on the sea-based deterrent. Those favoring this solution point to the fact that a MIRVed Poseidon force alone would have 5,000 warheads—enough to satisfy the assured destruction objective and to penetrate moderate levels of Soviet ABM defenses. They contend that such a force would not be a single deterrent, but that each of the forty-one submarines would be an independent deterrent; that no antisubmarine warfare (ASW) breakthroughs are likely to occur; and that we could take effective countermeasures against improvements in Soviet ASW or, if these failed, accelerate the development of an advanced sea-based system. They conclude, therefore, that a sea-based deterrent alone would give sufficient assurance that we could retaliate against a Soviet first strike.

Other experts argue that we cannot count on our submarines' remaining invulnerable and, indeed, that sole reliance on submarines would stimulate the USSR to find ways to make them vulnerable. They also argue that the President's ability to maintain communications with, and control over, a dispersed submarine fleet during a crisis would be uncertain. For both reasons, these experts contend that the United States would assume unjustified risks in relying solely on a sea-based deterrent.

Vulnerability of Land-based Systems

An associated question is whether the United States should phase out its land-based systems, if and when they become vulnerable. One widely held view, shared by the administration, is that the presence of vulnerable land-based forces would be risky in a crisis and could detract from security. In a severe crisis, the Soviet Union might be tempted to attack our land-based forces as a preemptive move to limit damage to its society—even if our submarine force could inflict assured destruction. Why, then, the argument goes, leave such an option open to Soviet leaders? Furthermore, the existence of vulnerable ICBMs might lead us to adopt a firing doctrine under which we would plan to launch our missiles in response to a radar warning of attack; this could increase the risk that error would result in an inadvertent launch. These are strong reasons to phase out vulnerable systems if we cannot, or choose not to, protect them.

A contrary view is that it would be preferable to retain vulnerable land-based forces because a mixed force of any kind would complicate a Soviet attack—and therefore add to our deterrent strength. Specifically, it would be easier to ensure the survivability of either bombers or land-based missiles if both exist.

Mutual Stability

Whether the United States can have confidence in its ability to satisfy its strategic objectives depends on Soviet forces and policies. We must therefore look at U.S. force and policy decisions in light of their real or apparent threat to the Soviet retaliatory capacity. If the USSR felt threatened by what we do, the almost certain result would be some form of Soviet force buildup that would provoke additional costly and possibly dangerous rounds of weapon deployments.

The President noted the importance of mutual stability in his 1971 Foreign Policy Message. "In light of the negotiations on strategic arms limitations," he said, "we are acting with great restraint in introducing changes in our strategic posture." He also indicated that the U.S. doctrine of sufficiency means "numbers, characteristics, and deployments of our forces which the Soviet Union cannot reasonably interpret as being intended to threaten a disarming attack. . . . We seek to obviate the need for costly, wasteful, and dangerous cycles of strategic arms deployment."

Nevertheless, two practical problems remain. The first is that we do not fully understand the basis for Soviet strategic decisions. Whether a U.S. program is provocative of new rounds of strategic arms spending depends on Soviet objectives and perceptions of the purposes and consequences of our actions. And the fact is that some systems lend themselves to ambiguous interpretations and some do not. The second is the question of priority. How much importance should be attributed to bilateral stability as opposed to other objectives when an inconsistency is involved?

MIRVs illustrate these points. The President emphasized that the installation of multiple warheads on the large Soviet SS-9 ICBMs would represent a potential threat to the survivability of our Minuteman ICBMs. On the other hand, he described our MIRVs as necessary to strengthen our retaliatory deterrent, but not having "the combination of numbers, accuracy, and warhead yield to pose a threat to the Soviet land-based ICBM force." The obvious question is whether the USSR will see the issue in quite the same way.

Modest Damage Limitation

All U.S. administrations, including the present one, have ruled out attempts to seek a major damage-limiting capability, either through heavy ABM deployments or through offensive forces specifically designed to attack and destroy Soviet offensive weapons before they could be launched. The principal argument against such systems is that they would cause the Soviets to take countermeasures, thus making our investment nonproductive and destabilizing.

But what about modest damage limitation achieved through building "thin" area ABM defenses to guard the U.S. population against limited missile attacks? The administration favors such an ABM because we cannot be certain that deterrence will work against China once it acquires ICBMs, and because the system would guard against an accidental launch from any source. A further argument is that an ABM could make our guarantees against Chinese nuclear threats more credible to our Asian allies.

Opponents contend that an anti-Chinese ABM is unnecessary and even undesirable. They argue that our strategic offensive forces will be sufficient to deter the Chinese; that the system would be costly and might not work; and that Soviet leaders would be likely to view it as the first step toward a large ABM and as a threat to their deterrent, with adverse consequences for mutual stability and SALT. Most opponents of an area ABM also oppose the Safeguard defense of missile sites because they fear that even this limited use of ABMs will set off another round of Soviet countermeasures.

Decisions on bomber defense, which are also a damage limitation issue, are strongly influenced by two facts: (1) the Soviet strategic bomber force—the only one that could threaten us—is small and has not changed for a decade; and (2) our air defense system needs a great deal of costly rehabilitation if it is to provide a serious defense against advanced bombers. Advocates of air defense argue that the system is necessary both to guard against the present Soviet bomber force as well as the possibility that the USSR will build new bombers in the future, and that air defense would complicate Soviet attack plans and thereby strengthen our strategic deterrent. Opponents argue that the large Soviet missile force makes a defense against bombers meaningless and wasteful. Some go further and oppose air defense, as they do missile defense, on the grounds that both run counter to mutual stability and SALT.

Limited Response

An issue the administration has brought to the surface is whether the United States should equip its strategic forces to carry out limited strategic exchanges. In his 1971 Foreign Policy Message, President Nixon reiterated his view of the importance of having this option. "I must not be—and my successors must not be—limited to the indiscriminate mass destruction of enemy civilians as the sole possible response to challenges. This is especially so when that response involves the likelihood of triggering nuclear attacks on our own population." To this end, the President concluded that "we must insure that we have the forces and procedures that provide us with alternatives appropriate to the nature and level of the provocation."

Improving communications, control, and targeting capabilities would be one way to give the President the option of limited response against a limited attack. Most experts believe that such measures would be prudent.

Disagreement centers on a different kind of limited response capability—one designed to deal with the following situation. Suppose the Soviet Union attacked with only part of its missile force and destroyed some of our strategic forces, holding in reserve a substantial follow-on nuclear attack capability to threaten our cities. Some experts believe that to deter such attacks we need the capacity to respond in kind. By maintaining a conservatively designed multiple deterrent, we automatically would have such a numerical reserve. But if we wanted to destroy hardened Soviet missile sites, improvements in missile accuracy would also be necessary.

Critics argue that the United States need not develop this kind of capability because such a Soviet nuclear attack is inconceivable. The reasoning is that the USSR would recognize from the outset that an attack limited to U.S. missile sites, for example, would cause so much damage that it would be difficult to distinguish from an attack on population and thus would inevitably lead to catastrophic nuclear war. As an additional argument, critics contend that measures to improve missile accuracy could be interpreted by the Soviet Union as a move toward a first-strike capability; such measures would thus run counter to the objective of mutual stability and, in the end, prove self defeating.

Some argue against developing any form of limited response capacity, simply because it would suggest that strategic war could be fought without large-scale destruction and thereby increase the danger that it could happen.

Force Comparisons

The present likelihood is that the United States will hold its lead in the number of warheads. But what if the USSR attempted to gain superiority in numbers of strategic delivery systems or in the types of systems deployed? Such moves might have little direct effect on our strategic capability. But could they have a political impact on our security? For example, would such a force imbalance tempt the USSR to take risks; or cause U.S. leaders to lose confidence in a crisis; or create concern among our allies? Or should we assume that with effective military deterrence, political leaders will not be influenced by mere numerical comparisons of strategic power?

Since 1970, administration spokesmen have repeatedly expressed concern over the possible adverse political consequences of the changed U.S.–Soviet strategic relationship. President Nixon seemed sensitive to this issue in his Foreign Policy Message. "In its broader political sense," he stated, "sufficiency means the maintenance of forces adequate to prevent us and our allies from being coerced. Thus the relationship between our strategic forces and those of the Soviet Union must be such that our ability and resolve to protect our vital security interests will not be underestimated." Secretary Laird also referred to the problem in his Defense Report.

Nevertheless, for some, the weight to be given U.S.–Soviet force comparisons remains an open question. The range of positions is wide: (1) maintaining one invulnerable deterrent force is all that matters; or (2) we should retain a multiple deterrent comparable to that of the USSR; or (3) we should rapidly modernize our forces and attempt to stay ahead in all important forms of striking power.

Strategic Arms Limitation Talks

Many U.S. strategic objectives—military as well as political—could be satisfied at less risk and cost under a SALT agreement than in the absence of agreement. In his 1971 Foreign Policy Message, the President committed himself to seek "a stable strategic relationship with the Soviet Union through negotiations" and concluded that there is no inconsistency between doing so and keeping our strategic forces strong. He also indicated willingness to forego certain unilateral options in order to negotiate an effective agreement—for example, by placing limits on ABM systems, or modifying or even abandoning plans for a nationwide area ABM. (No funds are requested in the 1972 budget to install a nationwide ABM.)

Although substantial progress has been made in the SALT discussions to date, several important differences between the U.S. and Soviet positions need to be resolved. If an agreement is reached, it would probably take the form of ceilings on numbers of strategic systems on both sides, but an agreement could cover defensive weapons alone or both offensive and defensive weapons.

In general, an agreement on numerical limitation would be consistent with our unilateral strategic objectives. We could maintain our assured destruction requirements with the currently programmed force. A limit on Soviet ABMs would, in fact, increase our confidence in the ability of the sea-based Poseidon force to perform its retaliatory mission. For this reason, even an agreement confined to ABMs would be beneficial. But limits on offensive weapons are also important: a ceiling on the number of Soviet offensive missiles would mitigate the threat to our land-based ICBMs and bombers. This, however, would only gain time. It would not solve the problem, for if the Soviet Union were still allowed to deploy MIRVs, our land-based ICBMs could still become vulnerable.

Thus, even with a numerical limitation agreement—whether covering ABMs only, or covering offensive systems as well—our ICBMs could eventually be endangered. If the agreement precluded defending those missiles with ABMs, we would either have to find other ways of protecting them (as allowed by the agreement) or abandon the goal of a triad. One possible solution would be for SALT to lead eventually to a mutual reduction of ICBMs.

If the talks fail to achieve an agreement within a year or so, political pressure for the procurement of strategic systems may rise in the United States. If the talks break down and the Soviet Union continues its strategic buildup over the next few years, the United States may feel compelled on security grounds to go beyond its current programs into the procurement and deployment of new strategic weapons systems.

Budget Alternatives

Decisions on the foregoing policy issues—and the outcome of SALT—will determine the general shape of our strategic posture, affect our strategic weapons decisions, and thus influence the size of the strategic budget. But many different combinations of policy and weapons systems are possible, with varying effect on the budget. (The costs associated with different weapons systems are discussed in Chapter 4.)

For present purposes, it is useful to outline four important decisions on weapons that shape our strategic posture and show how they would affect the level of strategic spending. These variables are (1) the number of survivable force components we decide to maintain—that is, a single deterrent, a diad, or a triad; (2) the rate at which we modernize our offensive forces, replacing Polaris and Poseidon with the undersea long-range missile system (ULMS), the B-52 bomber with the B-1, and providing hard-point ABM defense and MIRVs for land-based missiles; (3) the decision whether to preserve active air defenses by investing in surface-to-air missiles (SAMs), interceptors, and associated radars; and (4) whether we decide to install a thin nationwide area ABM.

Table 3-4 shows the annual budgetary costs associated with these choices. Depending on the decisions made in each area of choice, it is possible to derive average annual strategic budgets for the 1970s ranging from a minimum of $13 billion to a maximum of $27 billion. The following three illustrations are based on the cost components shown in the table:

Low Budget. For $13 billion, the United States could rely solely on its sea-based Poseidon/Polaris force for deterrence and deploy no defenses. Land-based missiles and bombers would be phased out. This posture would rest on the premise that such a system is sufficient for assured destruction; that defense against either bomb-

Table 3-4. Average Annual Federal Budget Costs of Alternative Strategic Force Postures[a]
Billions of dollars

		Possible cost additions[b]		
Basic posture[c]	*Basic cost*	*For rapid offensive modernization*[d]	*For retaining bomber defenses*[e]	*For a nationwide antiballistic missile system*[f]
Single deterrent: Sea-based force	13	+2	+2	+2
Diad: Sea-based plus one survivable land-based force	15	+2 to 4	+2	+2
Triad: Sea-based plus two survivable land-based forces	17	+2 to 6	+2	+2

Source: Authors' estimates.

a. Costs are taken over fiscal years 1973–80.

b. Includes both direct and indirect costs. Indirect costs are taken as 50 percent of direct costs.

c. The three force alternatives assume the following: vulnerable land-based forces are not retained; existing air-defense systems (surface-to-air missiles, interceptor aircraft, and associated radars) are eliminated; warning and surveillance systems are retained; intercontinental ballistic missiles are protected through the mid-1970s by completion of a four-site Safeguard defense, additional SPRINT interceptors, site radars, and silo hardening. Bomber protection includes improved alert procedures, base dispersal, and installation of additional warning systems. Offensive forces are modernized gradually—that is, procurement decisions on new systems are made in the late 1970s and a phased replacement program extending into the 1980s is adopted.

d. Assumes introduction of new-generation offensive systems as soon as they are ready for procurement— that is, in the early 1970s—and their production and deployment as rapidly as practicable, replacing existing systems. The spread in figures corresponds to the number of forces being modernized in each posture.

e. Assumes retention of only a small portion of the existing air-defense system and modernization as soon as practicable with an airborne warning and control system, improved manned interceptors, and an advanced surface-to-air missile system.

f. Assumes deployment of a nationwide antiballistic missile system starting in fiscal year 1973, with completion in the early 1980s. A defense limited to the National Command Authorities would be substantially less expensive. Large-scale "anti-Soviet" city defenses would be far more costly.

ers or missiles is unnecessary, costly, and destabilizing; and that the prospects for SALT would be furthered by such a move. The preferred outcome of SALT would be a joint U.S.–Soviet movement toward a single sea-based system; but even if SALT failed, we would rely solely on a sea-based deterrent. This policy would stimulate pressure for rapid modernization—ULMS for Poseidon—thus increasing the annual costs to $15 billion.

Intermediate Budget. For $15 billion, we could support a diad in which either land-based missiles or bombers would supplement the sea-based force. But rapid modernization of one of these forces would increase the budget to $17 billion. Retaining air defenses would raise it to $19 billion.

We could also maintain a triad for $19 billion or $20 billion, with either some modernization or some air defense—but not both.

In general, this middle range of $15 billion to $20 billion could provide funds for a multiple or redundant deterrent that would still be consistent with the negotiation of a worthwhile arms limitation agreement. The lower end of the range might be based on the assumption that redundancy provides the margin of safety for slow or very gradual modernization of the systems making up the force. The high end of the range would give little weight to this relationship, but would place more emphasis on extra confidence.

High Budget. Modernizing all three offensive forces at the same time, retaining air defenses, and building a thin nationwide ABM would drive up the strategic budget to $27 billion a year. This posture would aim at gaining strategic advantage through a highly reliable multiple deterrent, a "strategic reserve," programs designed to provide force superiority, and modest damage limitation. Some kind of SALT agreement might be consistent with this posture, but in general, mutual stability and SALT would receive low priority. Removing the requirement for a nationwide ABM, in the event of a SALT agreement, could lower the budget to $25 billion.

Decisions in the 1972 Budget

The President's Budget Message makes clear that the United States intends to maintain a triad, at least for the time being. Deterrence is to be assured "through three major strategic systems . . . each capable of surviving a first strike and inflicting unacceptable damage upon any aggressor. . . . These forces are supported by an early warning system and extensive command and control systems to direct defensive and retaliatory forces."

The budget calls for continuation of the MIRV program, through Poseidon and Minuteman III; strengthening silos and installing four Safeguard ABMs to defend land-based missiles; development of advanced concepts for area as well as hard-point defense of ICBM sites; and stepped-up development of the B-1, ULMS, and the new airborne warning and control system (AWACS). Air defense force levels would be virtually unchanged. Three squadrons of older-model B-52s would be deactivated.

The policy underlying these force and budget decisions seems to include the following elements:

- maintenance of multiple survivable forces;
- increased interest in modernizing offensive forces, but not to the point of procurement decisions;
- development of some form of limited response capabilities;
- retention and improvement of air defenses;
- concern for the political consequences of any sizable disadvantage in force balance comparisons with the USSR; and
- continuing interest in mutual stability and SALT.

In sum, the 1972 strategic budget of almost $20 billion could prove to be transitional. Its future direction will depend on SALT and procurement decisions on new systems. Both the budget and the decisions on weapons systems reflect uncertainties and ambiguities in the administration's policy. Costs might be held to about the present level if Poseidon and the B-52s are not modernized simultaneously, or if a nationwide ABM is not deployed. If the administration maintains its interest in air and missile defense and moves rapidly toward modernization, the annual costs of strategic forces would rise substantially. On the other hand, under current policy, the possibility of a decline in the strategic budget looks dim. A SALT agreement of the type that now seems most likely would not have much effect in reducing U.S. strategic spending over the next three or four years, since a wide range of qualitative improvements could and probably would be pursued, and older systems would continue to be replaced. But an agreement could keep the budget from rising much above $20 billion.

General Purpose Forces

General purpose forces comprise the U.S. land forces—Army and Marine Corps combat and support forces, land-based and sea-based tactical air forces, antisubmarine warfare (ASW) forces, airlift and sealift forces, tactical nuclear warfare forces, and all other force elements, both active and reserve—making up our conventional and tactical nuclear war capabilities. Excluding incremental costs for Vietnam, these forces together absorb about 65 percent of the 1972 defense budget.

The primary mission of general purpose forces is to protect the United States and its interests and commitments overseas and to deter conflicts. The extent of these commitments is open to varied interpretation. One version, for example, might be that the United States is committed to preserving the independence and stability of its Asian allies, to defending NATO against all plausible threats, to avoiding war, and to the continued existence of an independent Israel in the Middle East. Other versions might be less explicit. But even if there were no differences in interpretation of what we are committed to do, we would still be far from having adequate criteria to decide how many and what kinds of land, naval, tactical air, and mobile forces we should maintain to fulfill them.

Over the years, analysts have tried to identify the principal factors governing the size and character of U.S. general purpose forces. They include the specific contingencies we use in designing our posture, for example, an attack by the Warsaw Pact countries on NATO in Central Europe, a Chinese-assisted North Korean attack on South Korea, a Chinese/North Vietnamese invasion in Southeast Asia; the strategies we plan to employ in each contingency—rapid deployment and forward defense or slower deployment and the willingness to yield ground initially; the strategic warning time of an attack that is assumed to be available; the actual and projected capabilities of the potential enemy; the length and intensity of the war; the capabilities of our allies; the extent to which we maintain peacetime forces in a fully active rather than a reserve status; and the concepts used in designing new weapons and modernizing the force structure.

Implications of the Nixon Doctrine

The present administration has made judgments of its own on a number of these issues. Many of these judgments flow from the Nixon doctrine, which forms the general framework within which U.S. general purpose forces are being designed. As the plans are outlined in the budget, the baseline general purpose force resulting from the application of the Nixon doctrine will cost in 1972 slightly more than did general purpose forces prior to Vietnam, after adjusting for the effects of inflation during the intervening period. As compared with 1964 force level objectives, the present force is smaller by three Army divisions, two aircraft carriers (and four carrier air wings),[1] and one Air Force air wing. While there are a number of changes in details, both up and down from the pre-Vietnam posture, on balance most of the budgetary saving from this reduced number of combat units is offset by a substantial increase in the ratio of support to combat forces and by the cost of introducing new sophisticated weapon systems.

Contingencies Used for Planning

According to the Nixon doctrine, the United States will maintain in peacetime general purpose forces adequate for meeting a major communist attack in either Europe or Asia, but not simultaneously in both. We will also assist our allies against limited threats in Asia and be able to contend with a minor contingency elsewhere without the necessity of drawing on forces committed to NATO.

This is the "one and one-half war" strategy. It supersedes the previous administration's policy, known as the "two and one-half war" strategy, of maintaining forces against the contingency of fighting simultaneously the Warsaw Pact countries in Europe, as well as Communist China and its allies in Asia, and also being able to contend with a small contingency elsewhere.

The basic rationale for this strategy shift stems from the following reasoning:

   • A full Soviet or Chinese attack taken by itself has always seemed

1. In 1964, each of the fifteen attack carriers had its own air wing. In the late 1960s two air wings were dropped, on the ground that at any one time two carriers are normally in port for repairs; therefore it is unnecessary to maintain active air wings for all fifteen carriers.

improbable for a variety of reasons, including the great risk that either could trigger the use of nuclear weapons.

• The occurrence of these two contingencies simultaneously is even less likely. The likelihood is now further reduced because China and the Soviet Union are at odds with each other, which not only rules out the kind of Sino-Soviet cooperation that seemed feasible in the late 1950s, but also requires these two powers to maintain large forces for defense against each other.

But the Nixon doctrine is at least partly hedged. In his Foreign Policy Message the President endorsed "the desirability of insuring against greater than expected threats by maintaining more than the forces required to meet conventional threats in one theater—such as NATO Europe." As a consequence, ground forces previously committed to meeting a major Chinese attack in Asia, while reduced, will still be sizable. How much and in what form we will assist allies is another hedge. The indicated range is wide: military and economic grants only, or such assistance plus sea and air combat support, or in certain cases ground support as well.

Alternative assumptions that would call for increased force requirements are

• a return to the view that we must be prepared to fight a conventional war with China and the Soviet Union simultaneously, rationalized on the grounds that (1) nuclear weapons have no deterrent effect on conventional attacks in an era of Soviet-U.S. strategic parity, and (2) a two-front war is possible without Soviet-Chinese cooperation, though the forces each side could commit might be smaller;

• adding a Middle East contingency to the worst case, assuming in effect that we might want to assist Israel or Iran under circumstances in which we did not want to draw down our forces committed to NATO or our Asia-oriented strategic reserve.

On the other hand, reduced force requirements could stem from a policy of restricting the requirement for land forces in Asia to Northeast Asian contingencies or dropping it altogether. The latter could mean, for example, that if South Korean, Thai, Cambodian, and South Vietnamese forces, reinforced by U.S. air and naval support, could not cope with internal and external threats, the cost of further U.S. support would be much greater than our interests could possibly justify. A still narrower definition of U.S. interests could reduce this force even further by eliminating the air and naval capability of inter-

Table 3-5. Possible Distribution of Proposed Fiscal Year 1972 General Purpose Forces, by Geographic Contingency[a]

Type of force	Europe	Asia	Other areas	Strategic reserve	All areas plus strategic reserve	Net change from fiscal year 1964
Active divisions (Army and Marine Corps)	9	4 (7)	1	2⅓	16⅓	−3
National Guard and Reserve divisions	6	...	...	3	9	...
Navy attack carrier task forces[b]	4	6	1	2 (4)	13	−2
Marine air wings	1	2	...	...	3	...
Air Force tactical air wings	16	5 (6)	...	...	21	−1

Sources: Based on Table 3-3 and *Setting National Priorities: The 1971 Budget*, Table 2-9 and pp. 37–45. In view of the primacy accorded to the defense of Europe in the President's foreign policy message, 1971, and in other administration statements, the rationale supporting the allocation of U.S. forces for European contingencies remains valid. But one active division has been added to, and one reserve division subtracted from, forces for Europe to accord with the listing of armored and mechanized divisions (all of which would be for Europe) shown in *The Military Balance, 1970–71*, Institute for Strategic Studies. The reduction in forces proposed in the fiscal year 1972 budget is assumed to come entirely out of forces maintained for Asian contingencies. Three points should be stressed: (a) this distribution of forces represents an estimate of current planning to relate forces to specific geographic contingencies; (b) the actual use of forces in a crisis or a war could be very different; and (c) it is based on the force structure at the end of fiscal year 1972, after proposed reductions have been made.

a. Estimated force allocations for the 1964 force that differ from the 1972 distributions are shown in parentheses.

b. Two carriers would normally be in overhaul but could be expected to be prepared for deployment quickly and thus are considered in strategic reserve. However, only 11 carrier air groups are in the budget.

vening in Asian conflicts on the ground that, once out of Vietnam, we should not again become involved in any war in the area.

To help in assessing the relation of forces to contingencies, a projected distribution of the 1972 force by geographic contingencies is shown in Table 3-5. Estimated costs applicable to these forces are shown in Table 3-6. The discussion that follows examines different ways of looking at these forces and at the contingencies they are designed to meet.

Force Requirements for NATO

The administration continues to support the NATO strategy of "flexible response." This means maintaining the capability to respond to an attack on NATO with conventional, tactical nuclear, or strategic nuclear forces, depending on what action is appropriate to the circumstances. The administration has also decided to keep U.S. forces in Western Europe at the present level; the United States will reduce its forces only if the Warsaw Pact countries take reciprocal actions.

Table 3-6. Allocation of Costs of Proposed Fiscal Year 1972 General Purpose Forces, by Geographic Contingency[a]
Billions of dollars

Type of force and research and development category	*Europe*	*Asia*	*Other areas*	*Strategic reserve*	*Total obligational authority*
Active divisions (Army and Marine Corps)[b]	9.3	4.6	1.0	2.3	17.2
National Guard and Reserve divisions	2.1	...	...	1.0	3.1
Navy attack carrier task forces	2.6	4.0	0.7	1.3	8.6
Air Force tactical air wings	6.4	2.0	...	...	8.4
Antisubmarine and antiair warfare forces[c]	3.3	3.3	...	...	6.6
Amphibious and other forces	1.1	1.1	...	...	2.2
Airlift and sealift forces	0.6	0.6	...	...	1.1
Research and development					3.7
Total	25.4	15.6	1.7	4.6	50.9

Sources: General purpose force total obligational authority is based on fiscal year 1972 aggregation contained in Table 3-2. Breakout by type of force is based on the possible distribution of proposed fiscal year 1972 general purpose forces contained in Table 3-5. Allocation of costs to forces is based on Table 2-10 in *Setting National Priorities: The 1971 Budget*, updated to take into account the fiscal year 1972 defense budget and the impact of inflation and pay increases on general purpose forces. Figures are rounded and may not add to totals.
  a. The incremental costs of the war in Vietnam are excluded.
  b. Includes Marine air wings, estimated as $0.9 billion.
  c. Excludes escorts for attack carriers.

These decisions were based on the view that the current state of strategic nuclear parity with the Soviet Union strengthens the rationale for strong conventional forces to deter conventional aggression in Europe. Conventional forces committed primarily to NATO are a major determinant of the size of the defense budget and represent at least half of the total cost of our general purpose forces. They include one active Marine and eight active Army divisions, of which four and one-third are based in Western Europe; sixteen land-based tactical air wings, eight of which are based in Western Europe; four carrier task forces, two of which are continuously on station with the Sixth Fleet in the Mediterranean, together with other ships in the Mediterranean and Atlantic fleets; and varying percentages of other general purpose forces. Six National Guard and reserve divisions and about six Guard and reserve tactical air wings could also be earmarked for NATO. As shown in Table 3-6, the annual cost in 1972 dollars of the total NATO-oriented force is estimated at about $25 billion. Forces actually deployed in Europe account for about one-third of this total. These figures include estimated allowances for overhead and other across-the-board costs applicable to all general purpose forces.

Strong pressures have developed in the Congress to cut our NATO deployments as a means of reducing defense and foreign exchange costs. Some favor this course because they believe that the threat has greatly diminished; others contend that it would be the most effective way of getting our allies to increase their contribution to Europe's defense.

Bringing forces back from Europe merely to keep them in the United States rather than in Europe cannot in itself save money. In fact if they were kept at home, additional airlift would be needed to bring them back quickly to Europe in case of an emergency, which would mean an increase in costs. Budgetary savings could result only if the withdrawn forces were deactivated, that is, if the total size of the active force we maintained for NATO were reduced—both the forces stationed in Europe and those stationed in the United States and maintained for European contingencies. We could, for example, save money by shifting units from active to reserve status and accept the reduction in the readiness of our NATO posture. But another calculation must be made before it can be assumed that cutting forces for NATO would result in savings. So long as we assign primary importance to the defense of Europe, we would not deactivate forces returned from there until we had cut the forces we maintain for Asian contingencies to the minimum—or even eliminated them entirely. In the context of force allocations projected in Table 3-5, this reasoning would suggest that we would not start cutting forces for Europe until we had eliminated the four divisions maintained for Asia—or in other words, until after our total force structure had been reduced from the presently projected sixteen and one-third divisions to twelve and one-third divisions.

How would a net reduction in the capabilities of our NATO posture affect the military balance between NATO and the Warsaw Pact? Proposals to withdraw forces from NATO frequently reflect the view that NATO is heavily outmatched by the Warsaw Pact anyway, and that the most feasible course is to rely on nuclear weapons to overcome NATO's disadvantages on the battlefield. For this reason, the argument goes, U.S. forces can be reduced to a "trip wire" role; if Europeans want a strong conventional option, they should build it and bear the cost themselves.

But is NATO presently outmatched? In terms of manpower and tactical air forces deployed in Eastern and Western Europe, the two sides are comparable: about 1,100,000 NATO troops face 1,270,000 Pact troops, and about 3,000 sophisticated NATO aircraft face about 5,000 Pact aircraft of widely varying quality. NATO certainly has important deficiencies: its forces are poorly placed to counter a Pact thrust across northern Germany; they are overly concentrated, inadequately protected, and therefore vulnerable; and they have insufficient logistic support, especially the forces of our allies. Furthermore, it is argued, but by no means proved, that the USSR could reinforce the Pact more rapidly than we could reinforce NATO. Thus, at most, some question exists whether NATO forces are in reasonable balance with Pact forces, and hence whether a defense with conventional forces against Pact moves is in fact feasible.

On the other hand, the feasibility of using tactical nuclear weapons as a substitute for conventional forces is open to very serious question. The arguments are discussed at greater length in Chapter 4. Briefly, they are (1) that no one can predict whether or how either side could control or operate on a nuclear battlefield; (2) that the advantage would go to the side that could recover most rapidly and bring to bear sufficient troops to take and defend terrain, in which case the accessibility of Soviet reinforcements and the relative vulnerability of NATO ports and airfields through which U.S. reinforcements would have to pass suggest that tactical nuclear warfare might be more advantageous to the Pact; (3) that massive casualties are likely; and (4) that escalation to strategic war is both likely and as much a threat to us as to them in an era of mutual deterrence.

What of the possibility that European members of NATO might do more for the defense of Europe while the United States reduces its total force structure? It is self-evident that these countries could make room to spend more on defense if they had a sharpened perception of the need. In economic size and size of population, Western European countries combined are more than a match for the Warsaw Pact nations. But Western Europe is neither a bloc nor a community; it is an assortment of countries with different priorities and a general tendency to see the security threat as diminishing, not growing. The presence of U.S. forces certainly enables Western Europe to take a more relaxed view of its defense needs, but in present circumstances it does not follow that the withdrawal of U.S. forces would shock

Western Europe into a larger defense effort. That could happen. An at least equal possibility is that the reverse—reduced defense spending —would follow, accompanied by greater reliance on détente politics, even though the underlying justification was imagined rather than real.

The central question for the United States, therefore, is whether the effective defense of Europe is a primary U.S. security interest. So long as we believe that it is, continued assurance of this defense is essential. The second question is whether that assurance can be sought through reduced U.S. and increased Western European effort. The only way to find out is by negotiating with the Europeans. But until that negotiation yields useful results, the continued commitment of U.S. forces to European defense is dictated by our own security interest in that defense.

The realistic alternatives for NATO forces then appear to be as follows:

1. Withdraw from one to three of the U.S. divisions now in Europe, two or three tactical air wings, and one of the carrier task forces in the Mediterranean on the grounds that (a) a Soviet conventional attack is a remote possibility, or that (b) defects in the NATO conventional posture are serious and it is unlikely that the United States would find it economically or politically possible to correct them. The position then would be that the real deterrent to war is our nuclear capability and, if that is the case, we might as well save money on conventional forces. At the same time we should improve the survivability and war-fighting qualities of our tactical nuclear weapons in Europe. Savings could amount to perhaps $3 billion to $5 billion—but only if bringing those units back from Europe resulted in an equivalent reduction in the total force structure. As is noted above, this would be unlikely to occur until after the total force structure dropped below twelve divisions.

2. Maintain the current NATO posture and costs on the grounds that they provide a credible deterrent to a conventional attack; that, with modest increases in cost, it could be significantly improved; and that it costs no more to maintain forces in Europe than it does to keep them in the United States.

3. Significantly increase our outlays for NATO to leave no question about the adequacy of conventional forces for the defense of Europe. This could mean heavier investments in readiness, in pre-

positioning equipment, in antitank capabilities, in aircraft protection, and in NATO-wide training exercises. Extra costs could amount to $2 billion to $4 billion annually in 1972 dollars.

The administration's decision, as it emerged from a review of NATO strategy, was to maintain the current NATO posture. This is not a fixed choice. It will have to be reviewed over time in terms of changes in the political climate in Europe and a reassessment of the consequences in Europe of a reduction in U.S. forces. In addition, U.S. force levels will be affected by the possibility of achieving an agreement with the USSR on a mutually balanced reduction of forces, and by changes in our assessment of the Soviet threat. In turn, the forces the United States maintains for Europe will affect the possibility of achieving mutual force reductions and will be a factor in shaping ultimate security arrangements in Europe.

Force Requirements for Asia

In his Budget Message the President stated, "Our general purpose forces, together with those of our allies, must be adequate to counter . . . a Chinese attack in Asia [and] to assist our allies against lesser threats in Asia. . . ."

As is suggested in Table 3-5, the pre-Vietnam forces maintained for Asian contingencies consisted of an estimated seven active divisions, about fifteen active tactical air wings, including six operating from carriers, plus varying percentages of other general purpose forces. The Nixon doctrine suggests that we will reduce the ground forces maintained for Asia. The question is by how much? The two most commonly assumed contingencies that would call for ground forces are a communist attack in Southeast Asia and one against South Korea. The latter presumably would give rise to the smaller requirement in view of the strength and size of South Korean forces.

To take the Korean contingency first: a 570,000-man Republic of Korea (ROK) force, which the United States is committed to modernizing, plus about 35,000 U.S. troops, including one U.S. division, face a North Korean force of 370,000. ROK forces seem more than adequate to cope with North Korea alone. It is at least questionable that China would be able to deploy enough forces to Korea—diverting them from positions opposite Taiwan and the Soviet Union—to overrun the ROK defenses, even if the latter were supported only by U.S. tactical air capability. But if it is judged that this could occur and that

U.S. divisions would be needed, the number required probably would be considerably fewer than the seven divisions we deployed to Korea during the Korean war, though fairly high levels of air and naval support might be needed.

Post-Vietnam war requirements to deal with various contingencies in Southeast Asia are much more difficult to estimate. We do not have a reliable assessment of the balance of forces now in the area. South Vietnamese and Cambodian forces are growing stronger, but their capabilities to counter by themselves a concerted North Vietnamese drive is yet to be tested. Nor is it clear how much North Vietnam would commit to such a drive so long as it believed that the threat of a counterinvasion existed. Our experience in the Vietnam war does not help much in calculating requirements. At the peak of U.S. involvement in the war we deployed ten divisions there. But the political and military constraints that operated in Vietnam may have made a difference. If so, the seven divisions in the pre-Vietnam force planned as the initial deployment for Asian contingencies might not be out of line with potential requirements for dealing with a wide range of contingencies in Southeast Asia.

This neglects the problem of China, however. As few as 100,000 Chinese troops, plus a contingent of civilian workers, operating solely in North Vietnam could free an equal number of North Vietnamese to fight in South Vietnam, Cambodia, and Laos. This change in the balance of forces would leave us with the options of (1) bombing China or using nuclear weapons, either of which would raise profound political and moral issues quite apart from questions about their military utility; or (b) using available forces to hold the major cities or other limited areas, inflict maximum casualties and disruption on the enemy force, and seek a political settlement. The main point is that it would take a very large increase in U.S. forces to improve the outcome.

A choice among alternative force requirements involves a definition of U.S. interests in the outcome of various potential conflicts in Asia as well as a determination of force levels appropriate to those interests. Given these considerations, the alternatives may be outlined as follows:

1. Limit the number of active divisions available for Asia to perhaps one Marine division/wing team as a threat to North Vietnam and North Korea plus one or two carrier task forces and up to seven

Air Force fighter/attack wings for allied support. This posture would assume "no more land wars in Asia." As a hedge we could, if necessary, use our strategic reserve and possibly restructure and divert some of the divisions stationed in the United States and committed to NATO, until reserves were mobilized.

2. Maintain three or four active divisions for Asia, three deployable carrier task forces, and seven Air Force fighter/attack wings. These forces for Asia, plus the possibility of drawing on the three and one-third active divisions in the strategic reserve (including one allocated to Western Hemisphere contingencies), would be geared to dealing with an attack against South Korea as the primary planning contingency for Asia. The forces would be large enough to give the President options for responding quickly to a variety of crisis situations in Southeast Asia. Responding to a full-scale Chinese attack would require drawing on some forces oriented toward Europe.

3. Maintain the pre-Vietnam Asian force levels at least until the current war in Southeast Asia is ended and we can assess the consequences.

The posture outlined in the 1972 budget suggests that we will maintain perhaps four divisions for Asia, along with continued high levels of air and naval capabilities. It seems closest to the second of the above alternatives but on the high side. As compared with the pre-Vietnam posture, forces for Asia have been reduced by three divisions. But by drawing fully on the active strategic reserve it would still be possible to commit close to seven divisions to an Asian crisis, as in the two and one-half war strategy. Further, as noted in the Defense Report, forces stationed in the United States but earmarked for NATO could also be used to deal with a major communist attack in Asia. This is oversimplified arithmetic, but it serves to illustrate the wide range of Asian contingencies that this force could seek to meet.

The Contribution of Allies

The Nixon doctrine emphasizes that the United States will expect its allies to play an increasingly larger role in their own defense, especially in maintaining the ground forces needed to counter external threats. Our primary role will be one of assistance—in peacetime through providing equipment and funds, and in wartime through providing the kinds of combat support, primarily air and naval forces, that are too costly for our allies to provide for themselves.

The presumption is that we will be prepared to increase military assistance to the degree that it can be used effectively to enhance the defense capabilities of our allies. Unfortunately, it is almost impossible to relate our various military assistance efforts to any specific yardsticks of adequacy. Data on the total flow of U.S. arms and equipment to other countries are one thing; circumstances in individual countries are quite another. Prospects are distinctly different in Thailand, South Korea, Turkey, and Cambodia—the major recipients of assistance. Some of the issues involved in foreign assistance are examined in Chapter 5.

Other Implications

In reducing active forces, the Nixon doctrine would rely more on reserves in the event of a major contingency. A force buildup such as that in the Vietnam war would not be attempted without calling up the reserves. There is to be no increase in the number of reserve units, but with a smaller active land force structure, both active and reserve forces are to be in a relatively high state of readiness.

The budget calls for ". . . increased readiness for our Guard and Reserve forces. New concepts in Reserve organization and training will be tried. High priority will be placed on better equipping and supporting these forces." But two major questions immediately arise: (1) What will be the effect on the reserve components of eliminating the draft? At a time when the United States increases its dependence on trained reserve manpower to counter major risks to its security, it may be concurrently removing the major incentive for men to join the reserves. (2) Will it be possible to make significant improvements in reserve readiness? This has always been a problem because the reserves must compete for attention and funds with the active forces. At a time when the services will be wrestling with the problems of meeting their manpower requirements for active forces through an all volunteer structure, the reserves may continue to suffer from relative neglect.

There are no ready answers to these questions, but they bring into focus a larger issue. By cutting active forces, is the administration in reality shifting to greater reliance on nuclear weapons both for deterrence and for fighting wars? The fact that the President said (in his Foreign Policy Message) that our strategic forces "face an aggressor contemplating less than all-out attacks with an unacceptable risk of escalation" might seem to support such a view. But the administration has also said that the passing of the era of U.S. nuclear superiority has increased the importance of conventional forces in coping with conventional threats.

Deciding on the appropriate roles for tactical nuclear weapons remains a difficult problem, and the administration has not given a clear statement of its views on this issue. Most experts would agree that such weapons are needed to keep an enemy from using them first. In this connection, we should be certain that our weapons are survivable against first use by an enemy and controllable in retaliation. Most would also agree that their value in fighting a war is highly questionable and that, if anything, the need for non-nuclear forces increases if a tactical nuclear strategy is contemplated. The most difficult problem, then, is not to know the extent to which we should rely on nuclear weapons as a substitute for conventional forces, but to know how, for what purposes, and with what results, we would use them if deterrence failed and we were in fact struck first.

Alternative Postures

Based on the discussion above, Table 3-7 describes alternative general purpose force structures. They range in cost from $37 billion to $58 billion, measured in 1972 dollars and excluding any Vietnam war-related costs. The least expensive posture would be to reduce land forces to eight to ten active divisions, though the reserve force could be increased over the present nine divisions. Active forces of this size probably would require some reduction in U.S. forces for NATO. Only a token land force would exist for Asian contingencies. Tactical air forces would be reduced by about one-fourth and would be oriented toward close air support and air superiority, not deep interdiction bombing. Modernization (the replacement of older weapons systems with new and more sophisticated versions) would be highly selective. By implication, much greater emphasis would be placed on nuclear weapons for deterrence of conventional Chinese and Soviet attacks.

Starting from this posture, one might add a further range of forces that would give us greater confidence that we could deal with a variety of contingencies with less reliance on nuclear deterrence, and that also would cost more money. These alternative postures would in-

Table 3-7. Budgets for Alternative General Purpose Force Postures, Fiscal Year 1972[a]
Billions of 1972 dollars

Posture	*Annual cost*
Heavier reliance on nuclear deterrence	**37–40**

Strategy implications: Some reduction in U.S. forces for Europe but at least enough remaining to assure a "pause" in any crisis; no land war in Asia but air and naval support capabilities; strategic reserve for reinforcements and other contingencies.

Size of force: 8–10 active Army and Marine divisions; 15–17 U.S.A.F. tactical air wings; 9 carriers; modernization if economical or essential; all volunteer force; all military assistance that allies can effectively use.

Austere Nixon doctrine	**43–45**

Strategy implications: Capability for initial stage of conventional defense of Europe and modest ground forces for minor contingencies in Asia or elsewhere; air and naval support for Asia; capability for major contingency in Asia dependent on use of troops oriented toward Europe as well as on strategic reserve.

Size of force: 12–13 active Army and Marine divisions; 15–17 U.S.A.F. tactical air wings; 11–12 carriers; modernization if economical or essential; all volunteer force; moderate military assistance to allies.

Nixon doctrine (current posture)	**51**

Strategy implications: Capability for initial stage of conventional defense of Europe plus sizable ground forces for Asian contingency; air and naval support for Asia; modernization concentrated on Navy.

Size of force: 16⅓ active Army and Marine divisions; 21 U.S.A.F. tactical air wings; 13 carriers; heavy modernization of naval tactical air forces; all volunteer force; all military assistance that allies can effectively use.

Nixon doctrine with heavy modernization	**55**

Strategy implications: Capability for initial stage of conventional defense of Europe plus sizable ground forces for Asian contingencies; air and naval support for Asia; rapid modernization of all services and reserves.

Size of force: 16 active Army and Marine divisions; 21 U.S.A.F. tactical air wings; 13 carriers; heavy modernization of all active and reserve forces; improved airlift and sealift capability; all volunteer force; all military assistance that allies can effectively use.

Pre-Vietnam 2½ war strategy	**58**

Strategy implications: Forces to fight initial stages of conventional war with Soviet Union and the Peoples Republic of China simultaneously.

Size of force: 19 active Army and Marine divisions; 22 U.S.A.F. tactical air wings; 15 carriers; heavy modernization; manpower draft utilized as necessary; moderate military assistance to allies.

Source: Authors' estimates.
a. Excludes Vietnam war costs.

volve adding active land force divisions and tactical air capability for the conventional defense of Europe and for Asian contingencies. The larger the number of Army and Marine divisions, the closer the posture approximates a two and one-half war strategy. The total cost of each posture varies not only with the number of forces, but also—and importantly so—with the degree of modernization assumed to be required.

The Administration's Program

The forces proposed in the President's budget (shown in Table 3-7 under the heading of the Nixon doctrine) include the following:

• Sixteen and one-third active divisions (thirteen and one-third Army, three Marine), which are consistent with nine divisions for the conventional defense of Europe, four divisions for Asian contingencies, and three and one-third divisions for a strategic reserve.

• Nine National Guard and reserve divisions, mostly for Europe.

• Thirteen attack carriers, which would make it possible to maintain two carriers on station in the Pacific and two in the Mediterranean.

• Twenty-one active Air Force and three Marine Corps fighter/ attack wings, which would provide seventeen for Europe and seven for Asia.

• Modernization is concentrated on the Navy—for ship construction (including five more high speed nuclear attack submarines, a nuclear guided missile frigate, seven antisubmarine destroyers, and high speed patrol boats with surface-to-surface missiles) and for increased procurement of the F-14 fighter. In all, Navy procurement is to go up by $1.8 billion.

• Continued development of the Air Force F-15 fighter and the A-X close air support system—together with procurement of the F-14 and the Marine Corps Harrier aircraft—strongly indicates higher future levels of investments in the modernization of tactical air capabilities.

Research and development is programmed at $6.1 billion in 1972, an increase of $900 million over 1971, which could be an indication of higher future levels of investment in weapon system modernization. The comptroller general's annual reports on new weapons systems that are being developed or procured provide another indication. The 1971 report shows 129 new systems involving an estimated procure-

Table 3-8. Comparison of Total Obligational Authority for Procurement and Research, Development, Testing, and Evaluation, by Service, Fiscal Years 1971 and 1972
Millions of dollars

	Total obligational authority		
Service	1971	1972	Change, 1971 to 1972
Army	5,174	5,751	+577
Navy	9,924	11,749	+1,825
Air Force	9,444	9,495	+51
Other	541	614	+73
Total	25,083	27,609	+2,526

Source: Department of Defense, News Release 72-71, Jan. 29, 1971, Table 12.

ment cost of $150 billion. The comparable figures in the 1970 report were 131 new systems and $141 billion.

The same strategic emphasis as in the administration's posture could be obtained at lower cost if a more selective approach to modernization were taken. Alternatively, a different emphasis would be possible within the same budget: a smaller investment in weapons, but larger land forces. The funds for new weapons provided in the 1972 budget, allocated among the services, are shown in Table 3-8.

Long-term Trends and Alternatives

This is the first defense budget that reflects force structure decisions arising out of the Nixon doctrine and the influence of the strategic arms limitation talks with the Soviet Union. The most immediate consequence has been a reduction in ground combat forces, but the full implications are by no means clear and probably have not yet been worked out. In any event, the ultimate effects on force planning, on the force structure, and on the budget probably must await the end of U.S. participation in the Vietnam war and could depend to an important degree on the final outcome of that conflict.

In summary, current force planning, as indicated by the 1972 budget, means:

• The reduction of three divisions from the prewar level leaves enough divisions in the baseline structure to deal with a wide range of contingencies in Asia and still keep intact the strong conventional force the United States maintains for deterring a war in Europe.

• A moderate reduction in the number of attack carriers from fifteen to thirteen, along with an accelerated pace of naval modernization.

• A moderate reduction in the number of air wings, from forty in 1964 to thirty-five now, along with a projected modernization of tactical air capabilities both to deal with a Soviet challenge and to support allies in Asia.

• Maintenance of a redundant diversified strategic deterrent at fairly stable cost, but with the possibility that the United States might move toward rapid modernization in both offensive and defensive forces—and higher budgets.

The cost implications of this posture over the next five years are compared in Table 3-9 with those under a lower-budget option and under a higher-budget option. In five years the current posture, taking

Table 3-9. **Projections of Optional Department of Defense Budgets, by Military Program, Fiscal Years 1972 and 1976**

Billions of dollars

Option and program	1972	1976[a]
Option 1		
Austere Nixon doctrine	44	52½
Diversified strategic deterrent with only essential modernization	17	20½
All volunteer army	[b]	1½
Vietnam	8½	1
Total	69½	75½
Option 2		
General purpose forces as in 1972 budget	51	61
Strategic forces as in 1972 budget	20	24
All volunteer army	[b]	2
Vietnam	8½	1
Total	79½	88
Option 3		
Nixon doctrine with heavy modernization	55	65½
Diversified strategic deterrent with rapid modernization	23	27½
All volunteer army	[b]	2
Vietnam	8½	1
Total	86½	96

Source: Authors' estimates.

a. Outlays other than for the cost of the all volunteer army and Vietnam have been adjusted for projected increases in pay and prices.

b. The $1.5 billion provided in the fiscal year 1972 budget for the volunteer force is included in the 1972 cost of the general purpose and strategic forces in each option. The figure shown for this purpose in 1976 is the estimated additional cost that will be required to put the proposal into effect: $1.5 billion for Option 1 (with a smaller number of troops) and $2 billion for Options 2 and 3.

into account pay and price increases, could cost $88 billion, as compared with the lower option costing $75.5 billion and the higher option costing $96 billion. The three budgets are based on the alternatives shown separately for strategic forces and for general purpose forces in Table 3-4 and Table 3-7. They by no means represent an extreme range; each in fact would be consistent with different interpretations of the Nixon doctrine. The lowest-cost option combines the general purpose forces needed for a literal interpretation of the one and one-half war strategy, with a lower rate of modernization than is now contemplated and with a diversified strategic deterrent costing somewhat less than the current posture. The highest-cost option provides for general purpose and strategic forces as proposed in the 1972 budget, but with more rapid modernization of weapons systems. In each case, additions for Vietnam and the cost of a volunteer service, where applicable, are shown separately.

This way of looking at the budget suggests some additional implications that can be drawn from the current defense posture. At the end of five years, defense costs would be down only slightly in real terms, even after completion of the withdrawal from Vietnam, but they would represent about 6 percent of national output, as compared with slightly under 7 percent today. Part of the remaining savings from closing out the Vietnam war would be used to finance a volunteer service and, by implication, a somewhat stepped-up pace of force modernization.

Choosing among force structure alternatives and translating the choices into specific defense budgets involves more than military strategy, national security and foreign policy. There is also a range of technical issues that underlie force planning and influence defense costs. These include (1) the degree to which the United States should rely on attack carriers, which involves an assessment of their vulnerability and their effectiveness compared to land-based aircraft; (2) the appropriate ratio of tactical air wings to divisions, which involves an assessment of how much importance we should attach to the different ways of employing tactical air power; (3) whether we would plan to fight a long conventional war in Europe or, given the risk of nuclear confrontation, assume that any war there would be of relatively short duration; (4) the degree to which nuclear forces, either strategic or tactical, can substitute for conventional forces; (5) the tradeoff between modernization and force levels; and (6) the tradeoff between active and reserve forces. Some of these issues are explored in Chapter 4.

Analysis of the fiscal 1972 budget strongly suggests, moreover, that the range of issues underlying the relationship between support forces and combat strength deserves more attention. The fact, noted throughout this chapter, that the cutback in strategy and combat units did not result in a commensurate reduction in the defense budget is enough to flag the problem. Pay and price increases, together with higher modernization costs, are only a partial explanation of this phenomenon. An apparent decline seems to have taken place in the efficiency of general purpose forces as compared with the pre-Vietnam period.

Publicly available data are not sufficient for a careful exploration of the issues, but a few highly simplified comparisons may serve to illustrate their potential importance. For example, as is shown in Table 3-10, between 1964 and 1972, military manpower will have declined less than in proportion to the reduction in major force components (for example, divisions, air wings, and so on), and civilian manpower will actually have increased.

The analysis can be taken a step further by showing for each of the services the relationships between total manpower and total budget costs, on the one hand, and the number of major force components on the other. The difference between these statistically crude relationships in 1964 and 1972 is shown in Table 3-10. In each case, the im-

Table 3-10. Comparison of Manpower and Budget Costs Per Active Military Unit, by Service, Fiscal Years 1964 and 1972

Service and manpower or budget item	1964	1972	Change
Army			
Total manpower per active division	59,632	70,827	+19%
Total budget per active division			
(billions of constant 1972 dollars)	$1.13	$1.61	+42%
Navy			
Total manpower per active ship	716	918	+28%
Total budget per active ship			
(millions of constant 1972 dollars)	$23.3	$35.5	+52%
Air Force			
Total manpower per active aircraft	67	78	+16%
Total budget per active aircraft			
(millions of constant 1972 dollars)	$2.2	$2.4	+9%

Sources: Derived from Table 3-3, supplemented with information in the sources listed for that table.

plied budget cost of an Army division, or a carrier task force, or an air wing, in dollars of constant purchasing power, is considerably higher in 1972 than in 1964. Also in each case the total manpower associated with each of these major force components is higher, and this, of course, is a fundamental reason why budget costs are up.

By implication, these figures suggest that today's forces, manned and supported at the 1964 level, would cost $10 billion to $15 billion less than the current budget provides. But this conclusion perhaps pushes the available data too far and does not allow for the oversimplifications inherent in this kind of analysis. For example, the data do not take into account the effect on Air Force costs of the change from manned bombers to missiles; on Navy costs of the increase in the number of submarines in relation to carriers; and on Army costs of the inordinately large support base required for Vietnam.

Nevertheless, these figures clearly raise an issue that will be increasingly important as U.S. participation in Vietnam continues to decrease. Support requirements will go down automatically as the Vietnam pipeline dries up and as related adjustments are made in military manpower needs. However, unless a conscious effort is made to reduce the support base—in the naval shore establishment and in Army and Air Force training bases and logistic systems—the cost of combat forces will remain much higher than they were in 1964, and the United States will be getting less defense for its budget dollars.

4. Special Defense Issues

THIS CHAPTER EXAMINES five defense issues: the role of the aircraft carrier, tactical air needs, uses of tactical nuclear weapons, Vietnam war costs, and the costs of strategic systems. All of these issues affect the budget and all affect national security. The discussion of strategic systems illustrates an additional characteristic: different approaches to selecting the systems we should have raise policy issues that can be critical to the nation's security, but it is quite possible that different approaches could be fitted into the same budget total.

Role of the Aircraft Carrier

One of the primary military functions performed by the U.S. Navy is the operation of floating air bases—that is, aircraft carriers. In turn, the decision on the number of carriers to be maintained is by far the major single determinant of the Navy budget. The purpose of this section is to explore some of the factors underlying this decision and to examine their implications for alternative Navy budgets.

Aircraft carriers and their aircraft can perform a variety of missions:

- providing tactical air support to deployed land forces;
- protecting the merchant shipping that provides logistic and economic support to allied armies and populations;
- protecting other naval forces, such as amphibious assault forces; and
- attacking enemy navies engaged in their own operations.

Carriers also have unique political-military capabilities. They can

71

be sent to a crisis area and be held offshore in international waters, thus signaling a capability and readiness to intervene in advance of a final decision to do so. They can show strength without actually committing force. Therefore, the use of carriers could provide greater political flexibility and a wider range of policy options in crisis situations than could sole reliance on land bases in the area. Similarly, the continuous presence of carriers in one place—such as the two carrier task forces the United States maintains on station in the Mediterranean and the three it deploys in the Far East—is in itself a first order political factor in areas of potential crisis.

In fiscal 1972 the Navy plans to operate thirteen attack carriers (CVAs) and three antisubmarine aircraft carriers (CVSs). This force, including aircraft and logistic support ships, will cost about $8 billion. A part of this cost is for protection of the carriers themselves. In addition, a significant part of what is spent on antiair (AAW) and antisubmarine (ASW) warfare forces can be allocated to the protection of the aircraft carriers and their support ships. By an extremely rough estimate, for each dollar spent on the carrier's mission, an additional 25 to 50 cents is spent on carrier protection.

The proper size and character of the carrier forces depend in important measure on how much capability is wanted to perform the missions described above. Virtually all of the missions can be performed at least to some extent by forces other than carriers—land-based fighter/attack and ASW aircraft and submarines, for example. Carriers, however, because of their mobility, have some unique advantages over land-based weapons systems. They also have an important disadvantage: vulnerability to attack both in absolute terms and relative to land-based systems. The vulnerability issue involves more than the cost of protection. Low confidence in the survivability of the carriers may put important constraints on when and where we can or will use them.

Thus the proper carrier force level depends on assessments of their vulnerability to various threats, the feasibility and costs of protecting them against these threats, and the utility of the force in comparison with alternatives.

Vulnerability Considerations

Technology and other developments in recent years have made the aircraft carriers more rather than less vulnerable.

- Large air-to-surface missiles with conventional warheads and terminal guidance have made it possible to launch the equivalent of the Second World War Kamikaze attacks, without sacrificing pilots and aircraft.
- Satellite and long-range aircraft reconnaissance has greatly reduced the ability of naval task forces to hide in the broad expanses of the oceans.
- More sensitive submarine sonars and higher speed submarines make it much easier for submarines to find and attack the carriers.
- Developments in carrier defense have lagged behind. The effectiveness of ASW devices in any particular engagement is limited by the inherent variability of the underwater acoustic environment. AAW measures are likely to be overwhelmed by improvements in offense, such as higher-speed and lower-altitude missiles. Both types of defense can cause large enemy losses over a long period of time but cannot provide strong assurances that a carrier could survive a determined attack.

As a result of these developments, a strong case can be made that the carriers would not be able to remain on station in areas where the Soviet Union could concentrate land-based aircraft or submarines against them.

The Navy argues correctly that it is very difficult to sink an aircraft carrier and that no modern carrier (Essex class or later) was sunk in the Second World War. However, it is comparatively easy to damage a carrier enough to make flight operations impossible and force the ship to return to port for a long period of time for repairs. In anything but a protracted conventional war with the USSR, to force the carrier out of action for three months or more would be almost as good, from the enemy's point of view, as sinking it.

In the Second World War, 60 percent of the carriers that took one hit by a Kamikaze and all the carriers that were hit more than once were forced to return to port for repairs. (New carriers with improved damage control features that came into action toward the latter part of the war—Essex class and later—did not fare any better.) Based on this evidence and making ample allowance for improvements in damage control since the Second World War, it is estimated that four or five hits by Soviet air-to-surface missiles (ASMs) would force a carrier to retire. Similarly, four or five hits on the carrier's four screws by submarine-launched acoustic homing torpedoes should cause enough loss of propulsion power to make normal flight operations impossible and to greatly reduce the carrier's ability to avoid further damage.

Only about ten carriers would be deployed at any one time, the remainder being in overhaul. Against this relatively small number of targets, the enemy could mount a concentrated and sophisticated attack by land-based aircraft or submarines. Since only a few hits on a carrier would force it to retire, it seems unlikely that the carriers could be successfully defended, within foreseeable limits of technological advance and funds likely to be available for carrier defense.

This fundamental point is worth elaborating by a purely illustrative and highly simplified model. Suppose the USSR is willing to expend twenty-five bombers, each capable of carrying one ASM, and their fighter escorts, in order to disable one carrier. (The Soviets have in their naval aviation force some three hundred ASM-capable bombers, whose primary mission would be to attack U.S. carriers.) Suppose also that the ASMs have 80 percent reliability and, very optimistically, that our fighter defense would have a 40 percent chance of shooting down a bomber in a single engagement and our surface-to-air missile systems (SAMs) an 80 percent probability of shooting down an incoming ASM. With these assumptions, the bombers would get six hits on the carrier, more than enough to force it to retire. Less optimistic assumptions on defense would sharply reduce the number of bombers needed to put a carrier out of action.

Given these considerations, prudence would argue strongly against planning to use our aircraft carriers for strikes against land targets in situations where the USSR could concentrate land-based aircraft or submarines against them. The USSR could use land-based aircraft in the eastern Mediterranean (from bases in Bulgaria or the United Arab Republic), the northern Norwegian Sea, the Sea of Japan, and the Yellow Sea (from bases in North Korea). It could concentrate submarines virtually anywhere. Thus, the use of aircraft carriers for strikes against land targets, where they would be constrained by the mission radius of their aircraft (about 600 miles) to operate in a restricted area, seems unsustainable in any war in which the Soviet Union were fully involved.

On the other hand, the USSR is the only potential enemy with the large and sophisticated air and submarine forces needed to mount an intensive attack on the aircraft carriers. China does not have such forces, nor do the smaller powers against which we might intervene.

Against these adversaries, it should be possible to defend the carriers, although the possibility of substantial damage remains. And, of course, there may be many contingencies in which the carriers would be able to operate from sanctuaries, as they did in Korea and are now doing in Vietnam.

The Soviet Surface Fleet

Do developments in the Soviet surface fleet affect the decision on how many carriers should be in the U.S. fleet and on how to protect them? Until recently, the Soviet fleet of surface warships did not play a large role in U.S. defense planning. It was much smaller than ours and did not include aircraft carriers; thus the assumption was that it could easily be destroyed by carrier-based aircraft. However, after the sinking of an Israeli destroyer in 1967 by an Egyptian Soviet-built patrol boat with surface-to-surface cruise missiles (SSMs), the realization has spread that these ships with their SSMs could pose a substantial offensive threat to the U.S. fleet. The effect of the SSMs on a carrier would be similar to the effect of the air-to-surface missiles discussed earlier. As of the summer of 1970, the Soviet fleet contained 18 cruisers and destroyers, 150 patrol boats, and 47 submarines that could fire these missiles. In addition, the Soviet Union has given substantial numbers of SSM patrol boats to its allies.

In considering ways in which the Soviet surface fleet might be used against our aircraft carriers, one of the first that comes to mind is a situation in which the U.S. and Soviet fleets are in continuous contact during a crisis leading to war. A crisis in the Mediterranean would be an example. If the USSR decided to strike first, it could suddenly launch a coordinated volley of SSMs without warning and do substantial damage to the U.S. fleet. The Navy is working on several programs and tactics to improve its ability to deal with this situation, including: the development of its own SSM (Harpoon) with a 35-nautical-mile range to counter the Soviet SSM patrol boats, without having to wait until aircraft can be launched; the development of patrol boats to carry it; the use of helicopters to improve warning; and an increased emphasis on jamming and other electronic countermeasures to deflect the approaching missiles. But none of these measures could prevent the initial volley of missiles from being launched.

Therefore, the threat of a Soviet first strike against the U.S. fleet is not likely to be eliminated in the foreseeable future.

If the U.S. carrier task forces survived the initial attack, or if the war developed in a way that such an attack did not occur, then the outcome would depend largely on whether the Soviet surface ships had land-based air cover. If they did not, U.S. aircraft carriers could remain outside missile range of the Soviet surface fleet and still attack it with carrier-based aircraft. Some U.S. aircraft would be lost, but most of the Soviet surface ships would be sunk. On the other hand, if the battle occurred in an area where Soviet land-based aircraft could be used (for example, in the eastern Mediterranean), the Soviet surface fleet could be defended, and our carriers would probably be forced to retire from the battle area.

Thus the main contribution of the Soviet surface fleet is to increase the USSR's confidence in its ability to damage our aircraft carriers enough to force them to withdraw—a result it probably could achieve with land-based aircraft and submarines alone.

What about the use of the Soviet surface fleet against U.S. merchant ship convoys carrying logistic support for our armies overseas and civilian goods required by our allies' economies? Soviet tactics presumably would concentrate on sinking the convoy's escorts with SSMs while remaining outside the range of their guns; if this were successful, Soviet surface ships and submarines could then easily move in to sink the merchant ships.

In such maneuvers, Soviet surface ships would be operating outside land-based air cover and would therefore be vulnerable to strikes by carrier-based aircraft while the carriers themselves remained outside missile range. On the other hand, the carriers would face the opposition of Soviet submarines. They would not be as vulnerable as when launching strikes against land targets since they would not be constrained to operate in a restricted area. Consequently they could more effectively use speed and mobility to keep enemy submarines from getting close enough to attack and would remain in any given area only long enough to sink the enemy surface ships. Therefore, the carriers would have a reasonable chance of being able to carry out this mission. If the enemy submarine threat proved too great, two further options would remain: to suspend convoys while ASW aircraft wore down the deployed enemy submarine force or to use attack submarines against the Soviet surface ships.

In summary, the Soviet surface fleet reinforces the USSR's ability to deny the United States the use of its aircraft carriers for strikes against land targets in any war in which the Soviet Union was heavily involved. But the USSR could do so even without using its surface fleet. It could also use its surface fleet against merchant ship convoys, but this use could be countered.

The Adequacy of ASW Forces

The arguments concerning the vulnerability of the carrier also affect requirements for ASW forces. An evaluation of the ability of planned ASW forces to defeat the Soviet submarine force is subject to considerable uncertainty. Nevertheless, some useful qualitative observations can be made.

First, if we accept the thesis that aircraft carriers used against land targets cannot be adequately protected, at reasonable cost, against concentrations of Soviet submarines, the needs for ASW forces are greatly reduced. It is inherently harder to protect a small number of high-value targets, such as carriers, than a large number of low-value targets, such as merchant ships. If one or two submarines penetrated a carrier's defenses and made, say, five hits on the carrier's screws, they would disable the task force. The same submarines penetrating a convoy would sink perhaps five to ten merchant ships. In order to have an effect on the land war by sinking merchant ships, Soviet submarines would have to sink a large number of them, which would be easier to prevent than the small number of successful attacks necessary to force aircraft carriers to withdraw.

Second, the United States has a substantial investment in ASW platforms—ships, aircraft, and submarines—which are expensive to procure and to operate. Measures to improve the performance of these forces would seem to have a much greater payoff than would expenditures on new forces. Such measures include the development of new and more effective sensors (sonars, sonobuoys, and the like) and weapons such as torpedoes and mines, as well as improvements in operational proficiency and maintenance. When budget constraints force a choice, a strong case can be made for continuing these programs even if it requires reducing the number of ships or aircraft.

Alternative Approaches to the Issues

A set of attitudes toward the future development of the Navy can be derived from an evaluation of these issues—carrier vulnerability, the threat of the Soviet surface fleet, and the adequacy of ASW forces. Such attitudes can be related only loosely to force level recommendations; hence, while the discussion here describes three alternative sets of attitudes, and three force levels associated with them, this caveat should be kept in mind.

All three alternatives assume that aircraft carriers are useful for providing a presence during peacetime or during a crisis. The requirements for this function therefore set the minimum carrier force level. For present purposes, this minimum is taken to be nine carriers, in the belief that this is a reasonable number to support the U.S. political posture and to deal with all war contingencies except those involving the USSR. As a rule of thumb in peacetime, three carriers are needed in the force to maintain one carrier continuously deployed in a forward area. The backup carriers make it possible to rotate men and provide for maintenance. On this basis, the force level of nine would allow one carrier to be continuously on station in the Mediterranean and two in the Western Pacific, or vice versa. Each of the deployed carriers could be reinforced during a crisis by one or two of the backup carriers. In a wartime situation, an even larger number could be continuously deployed on station.

How many additional carriers, over and above these nine, should the United States have?

The first alternative accepts the argument that the carriers would be vulnerable in any war with the USSR if they were used for strikes against land targets. In this case, no additional carriers would be required, and reliance would be placed solely on land-based aircraft for tactical air needs against the USSR. In a major war in Asia with the Chinese, carriers would be used in addition to land-based aircraft, but a force of nine carriers should be adequate for this purpose. If the Soviet surface fleet should become involved and be used against merchant ship convoys in the open ocean, the nine carriers would probably be enough to handle it, although several might be severely damaged by Soviet submarines. Very substantial ASW forces would have to be maintained, under this alternative, to protect merchant shipping, but less than the United States already maintains, since we would not attempt to use aircraft carriers under conditions where they would be most vulnerable. Efforts to improve the performance of the ASW forces would have high priority.

Other important consequences would follow from this approach.

First, the new F-14 fighter, which is designed to protect the carriers from an advanced Soviet air threat, would lose its main justification. A replacement for the existing F-4 fighter might still be needed, but one of a much less expensive design than the F-14 would be adequate. (See the section on tactical air issues below.) Second, the air defenses we provide for the carriers, including the surface-to-air missile systems on escort ships, would be designed for high reliability against less sophisticated weapons, rather than lower reliability against the most advanced weapons. Third, we would still have to worry about the SSM threat to the carriers, since a number of countries have Soviet-built SSM patrol boats. But in this case, the missiles to protect against would be shorter in range and fewer in number than if the Soviet fleet had to be considered.

Such an approach would mean a large reduction in the number of ships. It would require detailed planning as to how the reduction could best be made and would take several years to carry out. When completed, it could result in a Navy budget of about $16 billion, compared with the budget request of $22 billion in fiscal 1972.

A variation of this approach—which might also fit into a low-cost budget—might have some long-term attractions. Assuming that aircraft carriers would not be used against land targets in a major war with the USSR, how would we design a carrier task force for more limited wars? Such a force would probably have a much lighter screen of escort ships. The carrier itself might be smaller and less expensive, and its aircraft might be designed more with a close air support mission in mind. If these changes were made, the cost advantage of land-based aircraft would be greatly reduced, or even disappear. In these circumstances, additional carriers might be more attractive than land-based aircraft to meet our needs for tactical air capability in situations where Soviet forces were not involved—for example, in the event of a Chinese and North Korean attack on South Korea.

The second alternative might be characterized as being based on only a partial acceptance of the arguments on carrier vulnerability. Carriers would neither be counted on for air strikes in a major war with the USSR nor written off. Although the difficulties would be recognized, it would be argued that, under this approach, a combination of improved defenses, successful electronic countermeasures, enemy mistakes, and luck might make the survival of carriers sufficiently likely to make a modest gamble worthwhile. We would therefore be willing to operate more than the minimum nine aircraft carriers.

At the same time, some reduction from the force level of fifteen attack carriers maintained in recent years would be in order—say, to a level of eleven or twelve. Because of the need to defend the aircraft carriers against enemy submarines, any reduction in ASW forces would at most be small. Emphasis would be placed on measures for defense against cruise missiles, both surface-to-surface and air-to-surface, including electronic countermeasures, the new Harpoon anti-ship missile, helicopter-borne early warning sensors, and the like. Most of this work would be in the research and development stage, and the full cost would be several years off.

Actions to counter the Soviet surface fleet as a threat to our carriers would also have high priority. The reasoning would be that the Soviet surface fleet might make a crucial difference in our ability to maintain carriers on station, in contrast to the first approach, which viewed the Soviet surface fleet as being essentially redundant in this respect, since Soviet land-based aircraft and submarines already gives them the ability to deny us this use of our carriers.

Procurement of the F-14 fighter would continue, since that aircraft would be relied upon to defend the carriers against advanced Soviet planes. This could also mean that it would be necessary to buy the F-14 only for carriers planned for NATO contingencies rather than for the entire carrier fleet.

This approach could result in a Navy budget of about $20 billion to $21 billion.

The third alternative would reject entirely the arguments concerning carrier vulnerability and cost. This position was expressed by Admiral Thomas H. Moorer, then chief of naval operations and now chairman of the Joint Chiefs of Staff, as follows:

I certainly don't accept the allegations that the carrier is vulnerable to the degree that often has been mentioned. . . . I don't believe surface ships are vulnerable. I believe in the next war we will perhaps suffer greater losses than we have in the past, but I am confident that we can stay out there and operate.[1]

1. *Authorization for Military Procurement, Research and Development, Fiscal Year 1971, and Reserve Strength,* Hearings before the Senate Armed Services Committee, 91 Cong. 2 sess. (1970), Part 2, p. 1308.

Essentially, this approach would continue the force levels maintained in fiscal 1971 or increase them if additional mission capability were thought to be needed. The current relative priorities in and among tactical air, ASW, and other forces would also be maintained. The real cost of this approach, after allowing for inflation and pay increases, would be greater than current funding levels would allow, for two reasons. First, maintenance of these force levels into the 1980s would require a large and sustained increase in new ship construction to replace Second World War ships still operating today. Second, increases would be required to fund a large F-14 program—enough for the entire carrier force. The resulting Navy budget might be about $24 billion to $25 billion.

Specific Budgetary Decisions

The 1972 budget provisions for the Navy suggest that the administration is moving in the direction of the second alternative discussed above, but at the high end of the budget range that would be consistent with that alternative.

• It provides for operating thirteen attack aircraft carriers and three antisubmarine aircraft carriers. As an experiment, one of the attack carriers is to have a mixed air wing with both attack and ASW aircraft. The objective is to maintain the capability to operate more sea-based ASW aircraft with a smaller number of carriers.

• The Navy is emphasizing cruise missile defense, including for the first time the building of patrol boats with surface-to-surface missiles as a counter to Soviet surface ships trailing U.S. carriers.

• In spite of the reduction in carrier force levels, funding for ASW is expanding rapidly. Of the $1.6 billion increase in total obligational authority for Navy procurement, about half is taken up by increased spending on four major ASW systems: the SSN-688 nuclear attack submarine, the DD-963 destroyer, the S-3A sea-based ASW aircraft, and the P-3C land-based ASW aircraft. A substantial portion of the remainder may well be intended for less visible ASW systems. This emphasis is consistent with a belief that the vulnerability of aircraft carriers is a serious, but probably soluble, problem that needs increased emphasis.

The evidence as to where the current posture will lead, however, is somewhat ambiguous. Heavy concentration on new ASW forces and procurement of the F-14 represent a strong effort to defend the carrier against Soviet opposition. This would also be consistent with the third alternative discussed above, though based on a smaller number of carriers.

A somewhat lower force level than the one provided in the 1972 budget may, in fact, be envisaged for the future. In addition to military considerations, the age distribution of the present carriers will determine the final outcome.

By Navy standards, thirty years is the "maximum useful life" of a ship, and carriers are no exception. In practice the length of service can be extended, but at about this age carriers become more expensive to operate and less effective in performing their mission.

When the two nuclear powered carriers now being built are completed in the mid-1970s, the total carrier force, if maintained at the present level, would consist of three new nuclear powered carriers, eight conventionally powered carriers of post-Second World War design, and five Second World War carriers. Those in the last group would have reached or be nearing obsolescence: by 1975, three would already be thirty years old or older, and the other two would be twenty-five and twenty-eight years old. The probability is that the three ASW carriers, which are the oldest, would be phased out as they become over-age.

The lead time for building carriers and putting them into service is long—roughly six years from the time the initial funds are authorized. Thus, if the attack carriers were to be replaced soon after thirty years of service, a rough schedule can be outlined relating the construction of new carriers for the rest of the decade to the intended size of the carrier force. This schedule is as follows:

• To maintain the present force of thirteen attack carriers, it would be necessary to start construction of three new carriers over the period 1973–79. This would mean starting one new carrier every two to three years.

• For a force of twelve carriers, one could be started by 1974 and a second by 1979.

• To maintain a force of eleven carriers, it would not be necessary to start a new carrier until fiscal 1979.

No funds are provided in the 1972 budget for a new carrier. In the Defense Report, Secretary Laird said that U.S. responsibilities abroad "will require construction of an additional nuclear powered carrier for the Navy to ensure adequate attack carrier capabilities for the 1980's and beyond." He indicated that authorization of this new carrier might be requested in fiscal 1973 or 1974.

This timetable would be consistent with an eventual force of twelve attack carriers. If construction of a new carrier is postponed until much later in the decade, the Navy would be moving toward a force of eleven carriers.

Phasing out the ASW carriers as they become over-age would mean relying more heavily on carriers with mixed air wings combining attack and ASW aircraft, should the current experiment with such an air wing prove successful. The alternative would be to replace the existing ASW carriers with new ones, which would involve large budgetary costs and severely strain existing shipbuilding capacity.

Tactical Aircraft Issues*

The 1972 defense budget provides for thirty-five active wings of tactical aircraft (Air Force, Navy, and Marine) and eleven and one-third reserve wings. These forces are a major cost element in the defense budget. This section examines some of the principal issues involved in determining tactical aircraft requirements and the cost implications of administration decisions in this area.

The total cost of tactical air programs in the 1972 budget would be approximately $15 billion. While useful for present purposes, this estimate is very rough because the data needed to allocate overhead and other costs to tactical aircraft are inadequate and there is disagreement over what costs to include. Of the $15 billion total, procurement of aircraft accounts for only $2.4 billion. The bulk consists of the cost of operating all tactical aircraft, some airlift, Navy attack carriers, and some logistic support ships, as well as an allowance for indirect costs, such as research and development. Perhaps $2 billion to $3 billion represents incremental costs of the Vietnam war—that is, the attrition and the higher operating, maintenance, and ordnance costs arising from the war.

An estimated allocation of these forces among geographic contingencies was shown in Table 3-5. Twenty-one of the thirty-five air

* Based on a background paper by Donald G. Ogilvie and Bruce F. Caputo.

wings are allocated to the European theater, where, in conjunction with other NATO aircraft, they would face sophisticated Soviet aircraft that will probably continue to be replaced by technologically more advanced aircraft. Warsaw Pact forces are equipped primarily with light maneuverable aircraft (MIG-17s, 19s, and 21s), designed to perform air interception and defense missions rather than long-range bombing or close air support. In recent years the Soviet Union is reported to have developed the MIG-23 Foxbat, which is believed to be superior to the MIG-21, though the missions of the two aircraft may not be identical.

Most of the remaining air wings are for Asian contingencies, the most demanding of which would involve combined North Korean and Chinese Communist opposition. Most enemy aircraft in Asia are older and short range, though the Chinese have a limited number of MIG-21s. Neither the Koreans nor the Chinese have a significant long-range bomber capability, and the bulk of their tactical aircraft are designed for air defense. However, in the air war over North Vietnam, U.S. air wings faced modern Soviet-built aircraft.

Tactical Air Missions

The United States buys tactical air forces for four major missions; the relative weight assigned to each is another determinant of requirements. These missions are

- interdiction and destruction of targets deep inside enemy territory;
- close air support for U.S. and allied ground combat forces;
- air defense of U.S. and allied military and civilian installations;
- air superiority against enemy fighter aircraft.

It is difficult to allocate the cost of tactical air programs among these missions since most U.S. tactical aircraft are multipurpose weapon systems. Some planes, though not all, have one principal mission; but even so, subsidiary capabilities to perform other missions are important. Nevertheless, it is useful to outline the principal issues involved in each mission since they enter heavily into the ultimate force level and procurement decisions.

Deep Interdiction

The primary purpose of deep interdiction bombing is to halt or reduce the flow of enemy troops and supplies in one of the following ways: by destroying transportation facilities such as roads, bridges, railroads, trucks, ships, and aircraft; destroying industrial capacity; or weakening the enemy's will to fight. In addition, deep interdiction is used to reduce enemy air capability by attacking enemy aircraft on the ground or by bombing airbase facilities.

The ability of tactical aircraft to achieve any or all of these objectives depends on the war situation. (In certain cases, such as Vietnam, B-52 strategic bombers are used for deep interdiction, but the Air Force does not normally plan on using strategic planes for this purpose.) The results would obviously vary in a country with a relatively limited, as opposed to a highly developed or redundant transportation system, or with an industrial as opposed to an agricultural economy. Political factors are also crucial, as is the ability to be supplied from outside sources.

Similarly, the costs of deep interdiction can vary greatly. U.S. bombing in Cambodia was relatively inexpensive because of the short flying distance from South Vietnam and the lack of effective anti-aircraft defenses. On the other hand, the bombing of North Vietnam was expensive, with estimates of the total cost ranging as high as $20 billion to $25 billion. Against targets in the USSR, Eastern Europe, or Communist China, where air defense is highly effective, the costs of conventional bombing would run much higher.

The characteristics of the opposing air defense system also affect the procurement cost of tactical aircraft. To counter sophisticated air defense systems, the United States has attempted to develop sophisticated, high-performance, less vulnerable aircraft, but costs have risen with performance goals. For example, the F-111A, designed to fly beneath enemy radar to the target area and automatically release its bombs, costs several times more than the F-105 it was to replace, which in turn cost a few times more than the various aircraft it replaced.

These possible wide variations highlight the principal issue in deep interdiction bombing. Are the results worth the costs? How much should we invest to purchase and operate planes that are designed principally for this mission? The issue has been hotly debated since the first U.S. deep interdiction raids against Germany in the Second World War.

Opponents argue that bombing raids have never reduced an enemy's will to resist or significantly impaired his capability to continue fighting. They read the historical record of the bombing of Britain in the 1940s and the bombing of North Vietnam—one an industrial and the other an agricultural economy—as supporting their position. In both cases the will to resist did not seem to be impaired. Production losses were offset by outside support and increased internal effort, and the victims continued to fight with seemingly undiminished capabilities.

Opponents of deep interdiction bombing would argue that a campaign against Eastern Europe would have similarly disappointing results. For example, assuming that such bombings could permanently destroy 50 percent of the lines of communication in Eastern Europe (which would be the most a massive conventional bombing campaign could achieve), Warsaw Pact forces in all likelihood would continue to be able to move the necessary men and supplies—given the redundancy of the Eastern European transportation system. Moreover, in a sixty or ninety day war, the outcome could be determined before enemy forces had to rely on supplies brought up from the rear. Critics also argue that deep interdiction bombing is costly and ineffective against enemy air bases that are protected, camouflaged, and dispersed.

Supporters of deep interdiction, on the other hand, contend that such bombing could be a decisive factor in a war, if it were properly used. They argue that the results of the bombing campaign in North Vietnam do not provide valid evidence because it was limited by political constraints; unrestricted air strikes would have greatly impaired North Vietnam's military capacity. They also believe that deep interdiction would be highly effective against industrial economies in Eastern Europe and the Soviet Union, both in disrupting the reinforcement of men and supplies and destroying critical production facilities.

Close Air Support

Another principal mission of tactical aircraft is to provide close support to U.S. and allied troops engaged with enemy land forces. Such support consists of air strikes to prevent enemy troops from massing and to destroy them when they have massed, to attack enemy armor and artillery, and to bomb heavily fortified positions. At least half of our tactical air capability is earmarked for this mission, though the aircraft are multipurpose.

By the nature of the mission, requirements for close air support are linked to the number of ground combat divisions the United States maintained. And given the importance of this mission in determining total tactical air requirements, a reduction in army divisions generally should result in a reduction in air wings. The 1972 budget reflects this relationship, but it provides for a reduction in air wings that is less than proportionate to the reduction in divisions.[2] For example, both immediately before the war in Vietnam and at the peak period of U.S. involvement there, the force structure contained roughly 1.4 Air Force air wings per Army division. Recent changes in force levels, however, have not been based on this ratio. Between fiscal 1970 and 1972 the number of active Army divisions has been reduced by four, while the number of active Air Force air wings has been reduced by only two, leaving a somewhat higher tactical air capability per division. This change may be the temporary result of the withdrawal of divisions from Vietnam, but it could reflect a force planning concept stemming from the Nixon doctrine: increased air support for allies in Asian contingencies.

There is no convincing way to determine with precision how much close air support is required per division. The answer depends on the kind of war we anticipate and where it is to be fought. In South Vietnam, greater reliance on tactical air forces at the expense of ground forces would probably have been unwise, since men were needed on the ground to locate the enemy. On the other hand, in a more contained conflict such as the Korean war, greater reliance on tactical aircraft may be feasible. Still again, in Europe, determining requirements for close support aircraft is complicated by the existence of a sophisticated air defense system.

There is also debate about which weapon system can most effectively provide close fire support for U.S. and allied ground forces. The Army believes this mission can best be performed by an integrated fire support capability ranging from light and heavy ground artillery to advanced helicopter gunships, and operating as an organic part of an Army unit. Tactical air support is viewed as being complementary to close fire support. If a choice had to be made, the Army probably would want more close fire support, such as advanced helicopter gunships, at the expense of close tactical air support. The Air

---

2. This calculation is based solely on the relation between active Air Force wings and active Army divisions. Naval air wings are excluded because they would not be employed for close support missions in Central Europe, where the major requirement exists.

Force, on the other hand, argues that tactical aircraft can do most of the jobs that a helicopter gunship can do and perform other missions as well. In its view, tactical aircraft are a better buy, and the Air Force is designing a new plane for this mission. The Marine Corps has been buying the AV-8A Harrier, which is primarily a close support plane.

Finally, there is considerable controversy about the design characteristics that can most effectively carry out the mission. Here the issue is whether we should concentrate on specialized aircraft or rely more on multipurpose aircraft. In the past we have purchased primarily multipurpose aircraft on the assumption that they could perform several missions and serve as a hedge against the uncertainties of enemy air defenses. The F-4 is an example; it can perform the four principal tactical air missions. Alternatively, we could invest more in aircraft specially designed for close air support. Such aircraft would be simple, reliable, and cheap, and would be able to deliver large tonnages of ordnance at relatively low speeds and altitudes. In Vietnam the older, slower Air Force planes (the A-1 and the T-28) provided more effective close air support than did the supersonic jets. On the other hand, such specialized planes would be more vulnerable to enemy air defenses and would probably not be able to operate in heavily defended areas.

Air Defense

Tactical aircraft (along with land-based systems) are used to defend military and civilian installations. In addition, Navy fighter aircraft defend aircraft carrier fleets from enemy air attacks. The air defense mission requires tactical aircraft that can locate and destroy enemy aircraft and cruise missiles at long range. They must be able to take off quickly, cruise at high speeds to intercept attacking forces, and destroy the enemy aircraft with long-range missiles or cannon fire.

The Navy has given high priority to the F-14, a sophisticated aircraft to defend the carrier. This plane was developed primarily as a replacement for the unsuccessful F-111B (the Navy version of the F-111). The F-14 is expensive to build and will be costly to operate. It is designed to carry the Phoenix missile, which will cost anywhere from $200,000 to $800,000 each, depending on the number procured. Use of this missile requires a large, complex air frame that reduces the F-14's air-to-air combat capability. It could turn out that the F-14

will not be as effective for one aspect of air defense and air superiority
—close air-to-air combat—as the F-4, which it is to replace.

Air Superiority

We need air superiority in a war situation in order to be able to
move U.S. and allied troops freely, resupply them, and give them
close air support; to conduct air reconnaissance operations in forward
areas; and to defend installations.

This mission requires an aircraft with the ability to accelerate
rapidly and with high top speeds, excellent maneuverability, and good
visibility. Many of the performance characteristics of an effective
deep interdiction aircraft (long range, heavy payload capacity, and
sophisticated avionics equipment) or an effective close air support
aircraft (long loiter times, slow delivery speeds, and survivability)
reduce the effectiveness of the aircraft as an air superiority fighter.

The ability of present U.S. forces to maintain air superiority over
the most advanced Soviet and Chinese aircraft is unclear. Some of
these aircraft, such as the latest version of the MIG-21 and the new
MIG-23 Foxbat, could put U.S. control of the air in doubt. But these
planes have a limited range and for the most part could not fight more
than 300 to 400 miles beyond their bases. This means that U.S. and
allied planes have air superiority over most of Western Europe today.
But that would not necessarily be the case in a conventional war
situation if ground were lost and enemy planes could fly from forward
bases.

Given these uncertainties about the present balance, what kind of
planes, and how many, could maintain air superiority or improve
the present position?

One way to deal with these questions would be to build tactical
aircraft armed with sophisticated air-to-air missiles designed to attack and destroy enemy aircraft at long range. This characteristic is
called a "stand-off" capability. As a result of development difficulties
with stand-off missile systems, this approach thus far has not been
fully successful. Development of the Phoenix stand-off missile system,
which as noted earlier is a central component of the F-14, represents
a new attempt to deal with this problem. Should it fail, the F-14 could
not effectively perform any part of the air superiority mission. Aircraft
designed to use these missiles sacrifice the maneuverability and speed
needed for close-in air-to-air combat.

The major alternative to this type of stand-off air superiority fighter is the more conventional interceptor aircraft, which has little sophisticated electronic equipment but is fast, highly maneuverable, and relatively inexpensive. The "international fighter," which we provide to allies in some military assistance programs and which is now under further development as the F-5-21, is an example.

Both the Navy and the Air Force are building sophisticated aircraft to replace the F-4, currently our principal air superiority fighter. The Navy F-14 is a stand-off aircraft, as noted earlier. If its missile performs well, it will gain air superiority at long range; at short range, on the other hand, its design characteristics could put it at a disadvantage against advanced Soviet planes. The Air Force F-15 is designed primarily for close-in air-to-air combat, but it too will carry a missile and have very sophisticated electronic systems. Given its complexity and weight, the question arises whether it will have the speed and maneuverability needed to match the most advanced Soviet combat aircraft. The F-14 and the F-15 will be expensive planes, costing several times more than the planes they will replace. Both design and cost factors therefore enter into the question whether these planes are the most appropriate ones to provide air superiority in the 1970s.

Land-based versus Sea-based Aircraft

Another issue is whether the missions described above can be performed better by land-based or by sea-based aircraft, and the appropriate mixture of the two in our force structure. Two factors are involved: relative vulnerability and relative cost.

As the foregoing discussion indicates, the vulnerability of the attack carrier—and hence of sea-based tactical air forces—is most open to question for contingencies in which the Soviet Union is heavily engaged, and particularly in the event of a war in Europe. Land-based planes are also vulnerable because they must rely on fixed bases. But they can be dispersed more readily, and their support installations can be protected against attack and more easily repaired.

On the question of costs, a valid comparison is difficult to make since disagreement is possible about which costs to charge against the two alternatives. Taking all factors into consideration, it is probable that a sea-based air wing, while having greater mobility, is more expensive because of the cost of its sea-based logistic support and the needed protection against submarines (a threat the land-based wing does not face). Recent congressional hearings suggest that the cost of the sea-based wing might be as much as 40 percent more than the cost of a comparable land-based wing. The premium may be worth paying for particular contingencies, but this difference in costs should not be overlooked.

Budget Decisions

In making the 1972 budget, the administration faced four major procurement decisions that are directly related to the foregoing discussion of tactical air missions. These decisions concern four planes— the Air Force F-111, F-15, and A-X, and the Navy F-14. How they fit into total tactical aircraft procurement can be seen in Table 4-1.

Table 4-1. Investment in Tactical Air Programs by Primary Mission and Type of Aircraft, Fiscal Years 1971 and 1972

Millions of dollars

Primary mission and type of aircraft	Investment	
	1971	1972 proposed
Close air support		
A-6A	23	0
A-6E, A-7E	108	192
A-X[a]	28	47
AV-8A (Harrier)	86	110
A-7D	241	208
Cheyenne[a]	18	13
Subtotal	504	570
Air superiority and air defense		
F-4E	78	143
F-15[a]	348	415
F-14[b]	995	1,034
Subtotal	1,421	1,592
Deep interdiction		
F-111A	666	190
Total	2,591	2,352

Sources: *Defense Report: Statement of Secretary of Defense Melvin R. Laird Before the House Armed Services Committee on the Fiscal Year 1972–1976 Defense Program and the 1972 Defense Budget* (March 9, 1971), pp. 87–88; *Armed Forces Journal*, Feb. 15, 1971, p. 35; supplemental information from the Department of Defense.

a. In various stages of research and development.

b. Includes some costs for research and development in both years, but more in 1971 than in 1972.

The grouping of planes by primary mission is somewhat arbitrary, since many are multipurpose, but it is useful for comparisons.

These were the major budgetary decisions:

Sharply reduced procurement of the F-111. This suggests lower priority for the deep interdiction mission, though the poor performance of the plane may have been the more decisive factor.

A heavy commitment to the Navy F-14. This plane is now in the stage of continuing procurement. Since its primary mission is to defend the carrier and to gain air superiority over advanced aircraft, this decision underlines a force planning conclusion that the carrier can operate successfully in contingencies involving Soviet forces.

A heavy commitment to develop a sophisticated air superiority fighter for the Air Force—the F-15. There are no indications in the budget that we intend to develop a less expensive, more maneuverable aircraft for close air-to-air combat.

Continuing investment in a new close air support plane—the A-X. The funds are still small. It is not yet possible to determine whether the plane will in the end be more like a slow, specialized close support plane or like a high performance, sophisticated multipurpose plane. As a hedge, the administration is continuing to purchase the A-7 and the F-4 for close support. In general, procurement decisions in this area—including additional procurement of the Marine Corps Harrier —support the Air Force view that tactical aircraft are necessary for close support, rather than the Army position emphasizing advanced helicopter gunships (though the budget requests funds for continued development of the Cheyenne helicopter).

These decisions in turn provide a base for assessing the current level of expenditures on tactical aircraft; they have implications for the level of future expenditures as well.

As was indicated at the outset, total expenditures for tactical aircraft are approximately $15 billion a year. This amount is not very different from the estimated level of annual expenditures in the early 1960s, calculated in dollars with the same purchasing power. Then, however, the United States was building up tactical air capability and introducing new planes into the system. This would suggest that the current level of expenditures is comparatively high, an implication supported by the fact, noted above, that Air Force tactical air capabilities have not been reduced in proportion to the reduction in Army land forces. On the other hand, allowance should be made for the substantial incremental cost of tactical aircraft attributable to Vietnam.

The fact that we are moving in the direction of introducing two very expensive planes into the force structure could create budgetary pressures in the future. Expenditures on the F-14 for procurement and development, and on the F-15 for development only, make up more than half of the 1972 investment budget for tactical aircraft. The experimental A-X close support plane is still an unknown quantity, but it too could turn out to be a high cost plane for the mission it is to serve.

With respect to the F-14, the main question is how many are needed, since most of the research and development has been completed and the 1972 budget requests funds to buy 48 planes. In congressional hearings during 1970, the Navy indicated that procurement could total 722 aircraft, but the final decision has not been made. If purchased only for contingencies involving Soviet aircraft, the F-14 would be needed on only about half of the Navy's attack carriers, which might mean about 300 aircraft at a cost of about $5 billion. If it is to replace the aircraft in all carrier tactical air wings, the number of aircraft and the total cost could be double.

In the case of the F-15, the procurement decision is still in the future but not far distant. The March 1971 Defense Report notes that procurement is expected to begin in fiscal 1973 and that the plane will join the active forces by 1976. The budgetary implications hinge on two questions: How sophisticated will the plane become, and how many will we decide we need? If the F-15 turns out to be a highly sophisticated aircraft, as now seems likely, we could keep tactical air expenditures at current levels only by substituting one F-15 for something like four or five F-4s. Substituting them on a one-to-one basis would rapidly drive up budgetary costs.

The size of this problem is dramatized by an example based on the unrealistic assumption of a one-to-one substitution. The Air Force now has 1,400 F-4s costing about $4 million each at current prices. The cost of the F-15 has not yet been estimated. A reasonable assumption is that it might end up costing somewhat less than the F-14, say, $12 million to $14 million. On this basis, replacing all the Air Force F-4s over a ten-year period would cost about $17 billion to $19 billion. This would mean annual procurement costs of almost $2 billion for this one plane, or almost as much as the total cost of procurement for all tactical aircraft in fiscal 1972. Also, operating costs probably would be much higher in view of the plane's greater complexity.

Fewer than 1,400 F-15s probably will be purchased. Some F-4s, for example, will be replaced by new aircraft designed for missions other than air superiority, and which will be much less expensive than the F-15. Nevertheless, the impact of the F-15 on the budget, given its high cost, will be considerable.

Tactical Nuclear Weapons in Europe[*]

Tactical nuclear weapons have a controversial history. To some, they are the essential ingredient that holds NATO together. To others, they are a liability because they increase the risk of nuclear war and because they give Western European NATO countries an excuse for not doing as much as they should to strengthen the conventional force posture of the alliance.

Two roles for these weapons can be distinguished: (1) to deter the use of similar weapons by Soviet forces, and (2) to deter a Soviet attack with conventional weapons and to counter such an attack should it occur. Most strategists would agree on the first role—that the ability of the United States to respond in kind helps to deter a Soviet tactical nuclear attack against our forces in Europe. The major disagreements concern the right size and combination of forces to give us a high degree of confidence in our ability to do the job, and whether tactical nuclear weapons add enough to the deterrence created by strategic forces to justify their cost.

The second role—to deter a Soviet attack in Europe with conventional forces—is more controversial. As a *supplement* to conventional forces, tactical nuclear weapons can contribute to deterrence by adding an element of uncertainty to Soviet plans for non-nuclear aggression. Looked at in this way, they present no serious issues. The crucial and controversial question is this: To what extent should we rely on tactical nuclear weapons as an *alternative* to conventional forces for deterrence and defense in Europe?

The budgetary consequences of reliance on tactical nuclear weapons depend on the role assigned to them. For example, our tactical nuclear arsenal costs about $500 million a year to operate, mostly for weapons

---

[*] Based on a background paper prepared by Han Swyter.

in Europe.[3] If these weapons are thought of solely as a deterrent to tactical nuclear war, the only issue is whether we have the right size and mixture. Possible changes in size and mix could alter costs—either up or down—but not by enough to make this a major budgetary issue. On the other hand, if the United States were to rely heavily on tactical nuclear weapons to deter and defend against a Soviet conventional attack, it could substantially reduce the conventional forces maintained for European contingencies, and this would greatly reduce the total defense budget.

The discussion that follows examines these issues by: (1) indicating the present balance of forces, (2) projecting how a tactical nuclear war could be fought, and (3) from this projection, drawing implications regarding the possible role of these weapons and questions as to their size and composition.

The Underlying Situation

We now arm the general purpose forces in Europe—both U.S. and allied—with nuclear weapons. We have some 7,000 such weapons in Europe, ranging from several kilotons to hundreds of kilotons. Additional weapons are stored in the United States. Army delivery systems consist of tube artillery, surface-to-surface missiles, surface-to-air missiles, and atomic demolition munitions. Air Force and Navy tactical aircraft have nuclear bombs. These weapons are designed for defense against an invasion of Germany, mostly by ground forces, but also for the defense of Norway, Greece, and Turkey. In most cases the nuclear weapons would be delivered by weapon systems that would also be used to deliver conventional warheads. Soviet forces are armed with similar nuclear weapons systems, probably with about the same number of nuclear warheads but with longer range and higher yields.

Both sides in Europe intend these weapons for use on each other's ground and air forces, not on strategic forces or cities. A "tactical nuclear war" would involve combat between conventionally armed forces—infantry, tanks, and their artillery and aircraft fire support—that could also use their weapons to fire nuclear warheads. The military purpose of such a war would be to occupy or defend territory.

3. If indirect costs are added, such as the cost of the artillery and planes to deliver the weapons, this amount would be several times larger. But this approach involves some double counting, since the planes and artillery are also in the force structure for delivering conventional firepower.

The distinction between these "tactical" or "theater" nuclear weapons and strategic nuclear weapons could turn out to be academic. A war in Europe between armies firing nuclear weapons at each other's forces could devastate cities and gravely increase the possibility of a U.S.–Soviet strategic exchange. But the possibility of a tactical nuclear exchange does exist, and it is therefore worth examining the role of these weapons in Western Europe.

How a Tactical Nuclear War Might Be Fought

The destructive force of nuclear weapons makes the battlefield different in kind, not merely in degree, from the battlefield in a conventional war. This difference is basic to the problems associated with the use of these weapons.[4] Nuclear war would be chaotic. Nuclear detonations could so disrupt the atmosphere, especially the ionosphere, that most radio and radar would be inoperable for hours or days. Logistics could fall apart. As a result, the control and the effectiveness of forces on both sides in Europe would deteriorate rapidly, even if individual units survived.

Once the nuclear threshold were crossed, both sides would be under pressure to use their nuclear weapons quickly before they were destroyed, and to use them on targets far beyond the front lines in order to attack the enemy's nuclear launchers, as well as its reserve troops, supplies, airfields, communications, and supply routes. These circumstances would compound the problems of using these weapons in a controlled or measured way—and in particular of limiting exchanges once they had begun.

A serious problem could arise about targets. In conventional war, locating the enemy's forces and reporting in time to direct firepower at them is vital to the United States in defending against an invasion of Europe by the highly mobile Warsaw Pact forces. Forward ground units and aircraft perform this mission. However, in tactical nuclear warfare, the breakdown in communication that in all probability would occur would seriously hamper rapid and accurate target acquisition. As a result, discrete use of tactical nuclear weapons on specific military targets could quickly turn into uncontrolled use of these weapons against likely areas of enemy concentration. The problem

---

4. The description presented here is based on an analysis of war games and extrapolation from data about Hiroshima, Nagasaki, and numerous U.S. tests.

would be aggravated further if airfields and forward deployed ground forces were both struck in the first nuclear exchange.

Finally, a tactical nuclear exchange would be devastating to the civilian economy of NATO and Warsaw Pact nations on whose territory the war was fought. If, for example, nuclear weapons were used initially after the Warsaw Pact forces had penetrated well into West Germany, the bulk of our detonations, as well as those of the Pact, would occur in West Germany. Conceivably, some 20 percent or more of the built-up areas could be destroyed and some 12 million Germans killed. A moderately extensive attack along the German front by both sides, with an attack on some targets in depth, including air bases and supply depots, could quickly kill 25 million West and East Europeans from the blast and thermal effects alone. Extensive additional non-fatal casualties would result.

In these circumstances, what can be said about the role of tactical nuclear weapons? The main point that emerges is that reliance on these weapons for defense against a Pact invasion would not reduce NATO conventional force requirements. Why is this so?

If NATO relied on tactical nuclear weapons to counter a large-scale Pact invasion of Germany, it might expect to inflict casualties of up to 50 percent. The Pact in turn could be expected to employ tactical nuclear weapons in a similar manner with comparable results. In theory, tactical nuclear weapons alone could stop the invading Warsaw Pact force. In practice, this would not be the case.

Manpower, firepower, and natural and man-made obstacles are needed to cause attacking troops to mass. Thus, Pact forces would become vulnerable nuclear targets only if NATO defensive forces were strong enough in the first place, in both numbers and firepower, to require the invading forces to mass. Further, NATO would need strong conventional force reserves to counter reinforcing Pact troops and to defend against threats to the rear area. Pact doctrine calls for rapid reinforcement to exploit successes, a tactic particularly suited to nuclear conflict and consistent with the Pact's mobilization capability. In the absence of NATO replacement forces, Pact forces could infiltrate through the battlefield. Hence, adequate conventional forces are necessary if tactical nuclear weapons are to be used effectively. If one side has substantially more conventional forces available for reinforcement than the other, that side has a major advantage, just as in conventional war.

Nor can the side with fewer conventional forces hope to offset its disadvantage through the use of tactical nuclear weapons. Its opponent not only can respond in kind but, with larger forces, can bring in reinforcements and disperse them more widely, thus retaining its conventional advantage—even after an exchange of nuclear salvos. For the side that stands to lose territory using conventional forces, initiating a tactical nuclear exchange would only worsen its position and cause the same result to be reached more quickly.

In short, it would be dangerous as well as impractical to rely on tactical nuclear weapons as a substitute for conventional forces to deter a Soviet conventional invasion of Europe. Of course, such weapons inhibit aggression, as does the array of strategic nuclear forces. But to rely more on them for this purpose by relying less on conventional forces could increase the risk that, in a crisis situation, the USSR might be tempted to move because it had an advantage in conventional forces and miscalculated both NATO intentions and the nuclear consequences of its action. The present situation of nuclear parity between the United States and the USSR makes this danger the more serious. The essence of the NATO doctrine of flexible response is to prevent such miscalculations, as well as to give the President military options other than early use of nuclear weapons of any kind in a crisis. Maintaining a balance of conventional forces in Europe helps to meet both objectives.

On the other hand, it is also important to recognize that NATO tactical nuclear weapons can be an effective deterrent against the use of tactical nuclear weapons by Pact forces. So long as both sides have these weapons, each would be dissuaded from initiating their use by the destructive consequences, by a realization that no net advantage would be gained, and by the risk of causing strategic nuclear war.

Size and Mix Criteria

Assuming that for planning purposes the United States relies on tactical nuclear weapons solely as a deterrent to Soviet first use of similar weapons, questions still arise as to whether our current tactical nuclear arsenal is too large or too small, or whether the weapons have the right characteristics. A large number of technical issues are involved, but they can be grouped in two categories: (1) whether our weapons could survive a Soviet first use, and (2) whether the President could effectively control the initiation of the use of these weapons, the number used, and termination of their use.

Survivability

Enough weapons and launchers must survive a Pact theater nuclear attack to enable us to destroy a major fraction of Pact theater forces in response. This criterion calls into question the characteristics of our present weapons systems and tactics for their employment. Our 155-millimeter and 8-inch tube artillery have a maximum range of less than twenty miles. Hence, a major fraction of our launchers would be in a belt within one hundred miles of the front. Both systems would be well within range of the Pact weapons and thus would be destroyed in an initial attack. Aircraft-delivered nuclear bombs are extremely vulnerable since the aircraft and the bombs are located on fixed, known airbases.

U.S. procedures call for leaving many nuclear weapons in fixed, known nuclear supply depots when troops deploy to the field in emergencies, with the intention that the weapons would be brought forward when needed. Because of their fixed nature, supply depots would be priority targets for tactical nuclear weapons. Weapons left behind when troops deploy to their wartime positions cannot be depended upon to be available when needed.

Our tactical nuclear force structure is based on the "discrete fire" concept; namely, that tactical nuclear weapons will be fired against specific or known enemy targets, as in conventional warfare, and that they will be controlled and fired from forward positions. This structure is another factor contributing to vulnerability.

The Pact's tactical nuclear arsenal, on the other hand, contains longer-range and higher-yield weapons that could destroy our forward deployed weapons and have greater prospects for survival themselves. This difference in weapons also suggests a difference in tactics. Pact weapons are suitable for saturating and destroying a specific geographic area. They are much less dependent on specific target acquisitions and can therefore rely on fewer higher yield weapons.

The vulnerability of weapons on both sides adds to the danger of a preemptive strike. Should war break out, military commanders on both sides would be concerned about the survivability of their weapons and therefore could make a case for early release against the other side's nuclear arsenal. This is precisely the kind of dangerous situation that has been avoided in the area of strategic nuclear weapons, where neither side's delivery system could be destroyed in a first strike. It highlights the need to make these systems survivable or to eliminate them entirely.

Presidential Control of the Weapons

The characteristics of a weapon system and tactics for its use also affect the degree of presidential control over this form of warfare. Some disturbing questions arise in this connection:

• Deployment of weapons to a large number of units near the front means that once the President authorizes their use, control over firings would be diffused in the very areas where communications are likely to be disrupted early in a war and where confusion could most readily occur. Thus, local commanders might well have to make decisions about what weapons to use and when, and the President would have difficulty in controlling, moderating, or terminating their use once the tactical nuclear battle had begun.

• The problem arising from this diffusion of weapons is compounded because we provide these weapons, under U.S. guard, to allied units. In the confusion of a war situation, allied units might want to use tactical nuclear weapons in defense of their territory earlier than we would, and might try to take control of them for this purpose.

• The diffusion of control once tactical nuclear war has begun would also reduce the range of options open to the President. In practice, diffusion means that the President might have little choice but to authorize using all the weapons or to decide not to use them at all. Thus, he might be inclined in a crisis to postpone the decision, even if that meant risking the destruction of most of the weapons. Of course, the other side of this situation is that, if he decided on use, events could rapidly get out of control.

Impact on Force Decisions

In his 1971 review of foreign policy, the President, in referring to NATO, indicated that we would develop concrete programs to ensure the provision of "modern and sufficient" theater nuclear weapons. The considerations mentioned above would argue that modernization should move in the direction of more centralized control over the use of tactical nuclear weapons and delivery systems with longer range and higher yields. What would be the cost?

A theater nuclear force for Germany alone, designed along these lines, might consist of 2,000 to 2,500 nuclear weapons. This would mean virtually the complete replacement of existing tactical nuclear weapons in Europe. The annual cost could be somewhere between $1 billion and $1.5 billion a year for procurement and operations over a ten-year period, or two to three times more than the United States spends now for tactical nuclear weapons in all of Europe from Norway to Turkey. For this we might hope to get a weapon system that would (1) be able to survive an enemy first strike and could effectively destroy a major fraction of Pact forces, (2) make it possible for the President to make an informed and deliberate decision in any contingency that might involve the use of tactical nuclear weapons, and (3) enable the President to halt immediately the use of these weapons if any had been fired.

The issue here involves a tradeoff between cost and the degree of safety to be sought in dealing with a highly improbable set of contingencies. Given the improbability that a tactical nuclear exchange will occur, the cost of developing a survivable long-range system seems high. On the other hand, the present forces have grave deficiencies that cast doubt on their deterrent value and that could generate critical problems in the event of war. To do nothing, therefore, carries serious risks.

Alternatively, the United States could stay close to current spending levels by phasing out existing short-range systems and making the remainder more survivable and more responsive to centralized control. This approach could include such actions as removing the nuclear capability of artillery and tactical aircraft; moving toward longer-range missile systems rather than introducing the comparatively short-range Lance; making missile systems more mobile; and developing better information systems to strengthen control procedures. The limitations of current U.S. forces would still exist, but we would be moving gradually to eliminate them.

Or the United States could phase out these weapons altogether, on grounds that our strategic forces are sufficient to deter Soviet first use of tactical nuclear weapons and that NATO's conventional forces provide an adequate buffer against Soviet conventional attacks. The reasoning would be that any use of nuclear weapons in Europe, however small their yield and however restrained their use, would rapidly result in escalation to strategic nuclear war between the United States and the USSR. Since there can be no practical distinction among different kinds of nuclear weapons, it is argued that spending on our part for tactical nuclear forces in Europe is wasteful.

Eliminating all the weapons could create political problems in Europe by generating allied fears that the U.S. nuclear shield was being withdrawn and by undermining our allies' sense of participation in this important area of European defense. Leaving these important problems aside, however, the difficulty in this approach is that it puts the President in the position of either doing nothing or launching strategic nuclear war in response to a limited Soviet tactical nuclear attack. The burden of escalation would then be on the United States; even with adequate conventional forces, there would be a large gap in the strategy of flexible response.

Improbable as this form of warfare is, the fact that both sides in a potential conflict in Europe have tactical nuclear weapons makes it necessary to address these issues. The wrong kind of weapons could reduce their deterrent capabilities. And weapons that would be both vulnerable and inadequately controlled in a crisis increase the risk of a preemptive attack and create pressures for their early, if not premature, use.

Vietnam and the Peace Dividend

Decreasing U.S. participation in the Vietnam war has focused attention on three questions: (1) What has happened to the savings in war costs achieved thus far? (2) Have the pressures of financing the war deferred requirements for modernization that should now be made up? (3) What are the prospects for future savings from Vietnam? This section briefly discusses each of these questions.

What has happened to past savings from Vietnam? An estimate of how much has been saved by reducing U.S. participation in the Vietnam war depends, in the first instance, on how one estimates the costs of the war. The approach taken here is that the most useful way to measure them is to view them as incremental: How much spending did the war require over and above what would have been spent on the baseline force? Cost estimates derived through this approach, and the underlying reasoning, were shown in *Setting National Priorities: The 1971 Budget.*

In testimony before the House Appropriations Committee, the comptroller of the Defense Department has submitted estimates of Vietnam war costs for 1969 and 1970 based on the incremental cost concept. These data have been used as the basis for making comparable estimates for 1968, the peak year, and for 1971 and 1972; they are compared in Table 4-2 with changes in the rest of the defense budget.

Two seemingly contradictory conclusions emerge. Total defense outlays between fiscal 1968 and 1972 declined by only $2 billion, which would suggest that most of the $14 billion reduction in Vietnam war costs has been offset by increased expenditures on other parts of the defense budget.

A different picture emerges when account is taken of the effect of pay and price increases between 1968 and 1972 on the cost of non-Vietnam forces. Pay increases alone totaled $9.5 billion, both to compensate for inflation and to fulfill the legislative requirement to make military and civil service pay comparable with private pay scales. (Between 1964 and 1972, military pay increased by about 10 percent more

Table 4-2. Vietnam and Non-Vietnam Defense Outlays, and Real Change in Outlays, Fiscal Years 1968–72

Billions of dollars

Description	1968	1969	1970	1971	1972	Net change, 1968–72
Outlays						
Vietnam	23.0	21.5	17.6	12.6	8.6ᵃ	−14.4
Non-Vietnam	55.0	57.2	60.3	61.9	67.4ᵃ	+12.4
Total	78.0	78.7	77.9	74.5	76.0ᵃ	−2.0
Real change in non-Vietnam outlays from preceding year						
Total outlays	...	+0.7	−0.8	−3.4	+1.5	−2.0
Less: Pay increasesᵇ	...	−1.9	−3.6	−2.1	−1.9	−9.5
Price increases	...	−1.1	−1.4	−1.2	−1.1	−4.8
Plus Vietnam savings	...	+1.5	+3.9	+5.0	+4.0	+14.4
Net real change in non-Vietnam outlays	...	−0.8	−1.9	−1.7	+2.5	−1.9

Sources: Total outlays are from p. 163 of *Defense Report* for 1972–1976, cited in Table 4-1, and from *Department of Defense Appropriations for 1971*, Hearings before a Subcommittee of the House Committee on Appropriations, 91 Cong. 2 sess. (1970), Pt. 1, p. 486; Vietnam data for 1969 and 1970 are in *ibid.*, p. 488 (1970 has been updated to include pay raises); these data and accompanying testimony were the basis for estimates made by authors for 1968, 1971, 1972.

Real change in outlays is based on U.S. Department of Defense, News Release 72-71, Jan. 29, 1971, and other information from the Department of Defense.

a. Includes cost of all volunteer armed force.

b. Excludes cost of all volunteer armed force in 1972 and includes active and retired pay.

than the average increase in private sector pay over the same period.) At the same time, price increases for military procurement and other military activities caused an increase of almost $5 billion in spending on non-Vietnam forces.

Thus, for purposes of comparison, if one reduces 1972 expenditures on the non-Vietnam portion of the military budget to adjust for pay increases, the total comes to $57.9 billion, or almost $3 billion more than the 1968 level. If, in addition, a further adjustment of $5 billion is made for price increases, current non-Vietnam spending is about $2 billion less than the 1968 level.

How one looks at this question therefore depends on the approach taken. In current dollars, the defense budget has not been reduced nearly as much as the Vietnam war costs. Had the defense program been required to absorb all or most of the pay and price increases (as a few other government programs have been), much greater reductions in the defense forces would have had to be made. Or if account is taken of the reduction in the number of baseline divisions, air wings, and carriers, the reductions in the defense budget should have been greater.

On the other hand, if one considers the amount of real resources (men and production capacity) being devoted to defense, one can conclude that resources devoted to the war in Vietnam are being returned to nondefense programs and to the private sector as the war effort is reduced. They are not being devoted to non-Vietnam military programs. However, one important qualification should be noted. Although outlays on non-Vietnam military programs in dollars of constant purchasing power are about $2 billion less in fiscal 1972 than at the peak of the war, funds requested for the development and procurement of new weapons will result in increased outlays of several billion dollars in future years, barring a change in policy.

Has modernization been deferred? If financing the Vietnam war had caused funds to be diverted from the replacement of obsolete equipment, an additional requirement for defense expenditures would exist. Stated differently, the existence of a modernization backlog might require that part of any future savings from Vietnam be used for catchup expenditures. In presenting the 1972 budget, the Department of Defense in fact stated that one reason for the increased emphasis on weapon modernization was "to offset prior year deferrals because of Southeast Asia requirements."

When this subject was examined in *Setting National Priorities: The 1971 Budget*, it was concluded that no clear case could be made that the war had delayed modernization of the armed forces. Three points were made in support of this conclusion: (1) Funds obligated for non-Vietnam general purpose forces have continued at about the 1964 level, after allowing for price and pay increases; (2) the end of U.S. participation in the war will leave more modern equipment in the U.S. inventory than there was in 1964; (3) present weapons are more effective than their prewar equivalents.

The trend in procurement figures for general purpose forces lends additional weight to this conclusion. (Spending on strategic forces is not considered here because it was influenced by factors independent of the Vietnam war; procurement declined after the buildup of Minuteman and Polaris was completed in the early 1960s.) On the average, budget obligations for procurement over the period 1965–71 were higher than the 1964 level, as is shown in Table 4-3. This is true whether the figures are presented in current dollars or in dollars of constant purchasing power. Some of these funds have not yet been spent, both because of normal lead times and because of the priority given to war-related production. Hence, much of the equipment that has been authorized, and for which funds have been obligated, has not yet entered the military inventory.

One may question whether the 1964 base is proper, but it can be pointed out that the early 1960s were a period of military buildup and

Table 4-3. Trends in Total Obligational Authority for Military Procurement, by Use, Fiscal Years 1964–71

Billions of dollars

	Current dollars		Constant 1972 dollars	
Procurement use	*1964*	*1965–71 average*	*1964*	*1965–71 average*
Total	**15.1**	**20.5**	**19.3**	**23.7**
Strategic nuclear forces	4.8	2.9	6.1	3.3
Vietnam[a]	...	5.0	...	5.6
Non-Vietnam general purpose forces	10.3	12.6	13.2	14.8

Sources: Compiled from *The Budget of the United States Government*, various years; Secretary of Defense Posture Statements, various years; House Appropriations Committee Reports on Defense Department Appropriations, various years; *Department of Defense Appropriations for 1970*, Hearings before a Subcommittee of the House Committee on Appropriations, 91 Cong. 1 sess. (1969), Pt. 6, p. 297; *Department of Defense Appropriations for 1971*, Hearings, Pt. 1, p. 487; Department of Defense, News Release 72-71, Jan. 29, 1971; authors' estimates.

a. Outlays; not available in terms of total obligational authority. The error introduced is small, since it is unlikely that there would be large unexpended balances of Vietnam-related procurement.

generally high procurement. There is also the question whether the greater sophistication of today's weapons makes for higher or for lower spending requirements. In addition, serious modernization problems may exist in a particular area, as in the block obsolescence of naval vessels dating from the Second World War.[5] The main point, however, is that a case for deferred requirements is not apparent from the data and that judgments regarding modernization needs should be made independently of the effects of the Vietnam war.

Are future Vietnam savings possible? Up to now, reduced U.S. participation in the Vietnam war has brought budgetary savings from two sources—the deactivation of units withdrawn from Vietnam, which is the principal source, and the smaller operating and support costs associated with a lower level of U.S. combat activity. The increase in military assistance to South Vietnam and Cambodia, which accompanied the withdrawal of U.S. troops, is an offset to these savings.

The future situation will be somewhat different. The force structure recommended in the 1972 budget would leave room to deactivate about 200,000 more troops, who could be drawn from those returning from Vietnam or from military personnel stationed outside Vietnam and engaged in support activities for Vietnam. This could mean that of the troops now in Vietnam, the last 50,000 to 100,000 would be retained in the military force structure—whether they stayed in Vietnam as a residual force or were returned to the United States. Bringing them back would save operating costs because of the absence of combat activity. But the major part of their cost—normal investment, operating, and maintenance expenses—would not be saved, since it probably would be about the same whether these troops remained in Vietnam or were stationed in the United States. On the other hand, it would seem reasonable to assume that the cost of military assistance will level off and then decline moderately as the task of equipping and training Vietnamese troops is completed.

To clarify these issues, Vietnam war costs over the future are estimated on the basis of alternative assumptions as to the number of forces remaining in Vietnam both on and after June 30, 1972, as shown in Table 4-4. These estimates lead to the following conclusions:

With no future change in the total force structure and level of military manpower, maintaining a residual force of 100,000 men in Vietnam would incur continuing costs of $4.7 billion a year, of which $2

5. See Arnold M. Kuzmack, *Naval Force Levels and Modernization: An Analysis of Shipbuilding Requirements* (Brookings Institution Staff Paper, 1971).

**Table 4-4. Troop Levels and Incremental Costs of the War in Southeast Asia,
Fiscal Years 1968–73**

Costs in billions of dollars

	Vietnam troop level		
Fiscal year[a]	Number of troops	Basis for number of troops	Incremental cost[b]
1968	534,700	Actual	23.0
1969	538,700	Actual	21.5
1970	414,900	Actual	17.6
1971	250,000[c]	Estimate	12.6
1972	100,000	Assumption	8.6
1972	50,000	Assumption	7.8
1972	0	Assumption	7.0
1973	100,000	Assumption	4.7[d]
1973	50,000	Assumption	3.5[e]
1973	0	Assumption	2.0[f]

Sources: Troop levels, 1968–70: Department of Defense, Public Affairs for Vietnam office; costs, 1968–71: Table 4-2; costs, 1972–73: extrapolation of 1968–71 data.

a. Troop level data are as of June 30.

b. Federal budget outlays. Includes security assistance of about $1 billion in 1968, $2.5 billion per year in 1969–72, and $2 billion in 1973. Does not include about $0.5 billion per year in economic supporting assistance in 1971–72.

c. Reflects the President's announcement of troop withdrawals of April 7, 1971.

d. Assumes that the troop level as of June 30, 1972 was 100,000.

e. Assumes that the troop level as of June 30, 1972 was 50,000.

f. Assumes that the troop level as of June 30, 1972 was 0.

billion would be for military assistance. On these assumptions, only about $4 billion would still be available as savings from the level of Vietnam war costs estimated for fiscal 1972.

To save more over the future would require a reduction in the rate of U.S. combat activity, or reductions in manpower associated with support operations for Vietnam, or a reduction in the level of military assistance, or any combination of the three.

Strategic Systems and Costs

The United States faces a number of important strategic weapon decisions that could significantly affect the size of the strategic force budget through the 1970s. The major policy issues underlying these decisions were discussed in Chapter 3. This section describes the composition of the strategic force budget and outlines the choices that must be faced in the light of these policy issues.

Composition of the Strategic Budget

The figure shown in the budget for strategic force programs accounts only for the direct costs of strategic systems that are already deployed or are being procured. Direct costs include investment costs (procurement, construction, and development and testing of approved systems), as well as operating costs (material and personnel). To obtain the total cost of strategic forces, allowance must be made for indirect costs, including associated intelligence warning, and communications programs, basic research and development on possible future strategic systems, and a variety of support costs. For the most part, these indirect costs appear in the budget as across-the-board costs for all forces and services; hence, the proportion that can reasonably be allocated to strategic forces and systems must be estimated. In addition, about $1 billion in costs of the Atomic Energy Commission (AEC) support U.S. strategic programs.

The estimated total costs of strategic forces in fiscal 1971 and 1972 are given in Table 4-5. The figures show that direct costs remained roughly the same in the two years, but total costs increased by about $1 billion in 1972, primarily because of pay raises and increased research and development costs.

Strategic Weapons Issues

The strategic posture of the United States is built around five major categories of weapons: (1) land-based missile forces, consisting of the Minuteman and Titan ICBMs; (2) submarine-launched ballistic missile forces, notably the Polaris/Poseidon system; (3) strategic bombers, primarily the B-52s and related air-to-surface missile systems; (4) the antiballistic missile system (ABM), including radars and missile interceptors; and (5) the air defense system, including surface-to-air missiles (SAMs), fighter interceptors, and radars. Part of the antisubmarine warfare forces—which are funded under general purpose forces—serve strategic missions, but the cost attributable to strategic purposes cannot be realistically estimated. (The problem is further complicated because ASW forces would be purchased for general purpose forces even if they had no mission in connection with strategic forces.) A rough estimate of the relative importance of each of

**Table 4-5. Estimated Direct and Indirect Cost of Strategic Forces,
Fiscal Years 1971 and 1972**
Billions of dollars

	Cost	
Type of cost	*1971*	*1972*
Direct		
Investment (procurement, construction, development and testing)	4.8	4.7
Operating (material and personnel)	2.9	2.9
Subtotal	7.7	7.6
Indirect		
Intelligence and communications	2.7	2.8
Research and development	2.1	2.7
Support	5.9	5.6
Pay raises and all volunteer armed force[a]	0.2	1.0
Subtotal	10.9	12.1
Total	18.6	19.7

Sources: Total direct costs are the costs officially given as strategic forces costs in the defense budget in *The Budget of the United States Government, Fiscal Year 1972*, p. 89. The allocation between investment and operating costs is estimated from *Department of Defense Appropriations for 1970*, Hearings, and *Department of Defense Appropriations for 1971*, Hearings.

Intelligence and communications costs are estimated at 50 percent of total defense intelligence and communications costs from p. 89 of *The Budget . . .*, cited above. Support costs are estimated at varying percentages of (a) central supply and maintenance, (b) training, medical, and general personnel activities, and (c) administration and associated activities, from *ibid*. Pay raises and volunteer force costs are estimated at 25 percent of those categories in *ibid*.

Research and development estimates are based on testimony in the Appropriations Hearings cited above, and on data in *Armed Forces Journal*, March 15, 1971, p. 16.

a. Volunteer force costs apply to 1972 only. A distribution of the portion of these costs that would be allocated to direct costs was not made.

these weapon categories in the total strategic budget is shown in Table 4-6.

As the table indicates, the indirect costs for all of the strategic forces are greater than the direct costs. This relationship holds for each category of weapons. Many indirect costs, such as intelligence, communications, and basic R&D, would change very little in response to changes in either the number of strategic systems or their composition. On the other hand, certain indirect costs, such as support and training, could vary with weapons programs. Therefore, changes in direct costs resulting from the introduction of new systems or the elimination of existing systems would not necessarily be accompanied by proportionate changes in indirect costs.

The administration faces decisions in each of the five weapons categories that will have significant budgetary consequences and policy

Table 4-6. Estimated Allocation of the Strategic Budget by Major Weapons Categories, Fiscal Year 1972

Costs in billions of dollars

Weapons category	*Direct costs*	*Indirect costs*	*Total cost*	*Percentage of total*
Intercontinental ballistic missiles	1.1	1.8	2.9	15
Submarine-launched ballistic missiles	1.4	2.2	3.6	18
Bombers	1.9	3.0	4.9	25
Antiballistic missiles	1.5	2.4	3.9	20
Air defense	1.7	2.7	4.4	22
Total	7.6	12.1	19.7	100

Sources: All strategic weapons programs have been divided among the above categories. Each category consists of cost estimates for the major delivery systems and related weapons. Direct costs are based on: proposed programs shown in *The Budget of the United States Government, Fiscal Year 1972,* and the *Defense Report;* other programs which fall in each category; and estimates of operating costs for each weapons category. Indirect costs are allocated among each of the systems in proportion to direct costs. Atomic Energy Commission costs for strategic systems and antisubmarine warfare costs are excluded.

implications. Technical and timing considerations are also involved. Some of the major issues are examined below; the estimated investment and operating costs for each weapon system are shown in Table 4-7.

Land-based Missiles

The United States is currently replacing 550 of its 1,000 single-warhead Minuteman ICBMs with advanced versions that carry up to three multiple independently-targetable reentry vehicles (MIRVs). The investment in these advanced missiles will run to about $6 billion (the cost in fiscal 1972 will be about $840 million); the program is scheduled for completion by 1973. What about the rest of this force? Will 550 advanced versions of the Minuteman be enough, or will it be necessary to modernize the rest of the force? Alternatively, could we work toward an agreement with the USSR that would make it possible for us to freeze the Minuteman/MIRV program at the present level?

A less important question concerns the increasing obsolescence of the fifty-four Titan ICBMs, the only U.S. missile capable of carrying a heavy warhead. Should we phase them out and save operating costs or keep them for purposes of bargaining with the USSR?

The most crucial issue concerning land-based missiles is their potential vulnerability to Soviet attack. If the USSR develops accurate

Table 4-7. Estimated Ten-year Program Costs of Selected Strategic Systems[a]
Billions of dollars

	Cost[b]	
Program and system	*Investment*	*Operating*
Approved programs[c]		
Minuteman III[d]	6.0	1.2
Safeguard missile-site defense[e]	9.0	1.3
Poseidon[f]	7.0	3.5
Short range attack missile	1.7	...
Possible new programs[g]		
Undersea long range missile[h]	15.0	2.5
B-1 intercontinental bomber[i]	9.0	6.0
AWACS/IMI/SAM[j]	10.0	7.0
Safeguard nationwide area defense[k]	13.0	2.0

Source: Authors' estimates.
a. The period covered by the ten-year program costs depends upon the year in which any system is introduced into the active forces.
b. Investment cost includes research and development, procurement, and military construction costs. Operating cost includes direct personnel and operation and maintenance costs over a ten-year period. No allowance is made in the cost figures for indirect costs associated with these systems. In the approved programs, substantial parts of the investment costs have already been spent.
c. Assumes completion of programs in progress in fiscal year 1972.
d. Includes 550 new missiles, silo hardening, and retention of older missiles.
e. Estimate of cost independent of area defense; includes completion of Safeguard for four sites, augmented with additional antiballistic missiles and radars.
f. Missiles and conversion of submarine-launched missiles.
g. Programs in research and development stage in fiscal year 1972; assumes that a decision is made to procure weapons for the system.
h. Cost figures provide for 20 boats and 400 missiles.
i. Cost figures provide for 200 bombers.
j. Involves procurement of 42 airborne warning and control systems (AWACSs), 350 new improved manned interceptors (IMIs), over-the-horizon radars and surface-to-air missile batteries (SAMs).
k. Estimate of incremental cost of eight-site area defense system plus some augmentation.

MIRVs for its large SS-9 ICBMs, it could endanger the Minuteman force. The administration is now deploying the Safeguard ABM at four Minuteman complexes and strengthening existing missile silos to improve the survivability of this system. The investment cost of these programs could run to $9 billion. Other options are also being investigated. For example, R&D programs are exploring the possibility of making the ICBM force mobile and of developing a more effective ABM defense system specifically to protect the ICBMs. These systems, if adopted, could cost anywhere from $10 billion to $20 billion.

It is entirely possible that no feasible solution to the problem of making ICBMs survivable will be found. This consideration alone might suggest that the United States should go slow in the Minuteman/MIRV and the Safeguard ABM programs—until we know that adequate protection of the missiles is technically possible.

Sea-based Missile Systems

The conversion of U.S. nuclear-powered Polaris submarines to accommodate the Poseidon/MIRV missile as a replacement for the Polaris missile is currently under way; the first Poseidon boat became operational in early 1971. Each Poseidon missile can carry as many as ten to fourteen small-yield warheads. As in the Minuteman/MIRV program, the purpose of increasing the number of warheads is not to add to total destructive power but to add to deterrence. More warheads would increase the chance of having enough left after a Soviet first strike to penetrate Soviet ABM defenses, should those defenses become more extensive in the future than they are now.

Present plans call for the conversion of thirty-one of the forty-one Polaris submarines; it is not technically feasible to convert the ten earlier-model Polaris submarines. The conversion program will be completed in 1976 at a cost of almost $7 billion, of which $800 million is provided in the 1972 budget. But once a boat is converted, it cannot again accommodate the older Polaris missile. Hence, if we should decide not to complete the MIRV program because fewer warheads are needed than are now planned—possibly because the USSR did not install additional ABM defenses by agreement with the United States —the decision would have to be made before all the boats were converted. (If they had already been converted, it would be technically possible to develop a single warhead for the Poseidon missile to replace the MIRV warhead.)

A far more important decision, in terms of both policy and cost, centers on a program currently in R&D—the undersea long-range missile system (ULMS), an advanced missile-firing submarine capable of carrying some twenty ICBMs. The administration attaches high priority to this system, principally as a means of keeping the sea-based deterrent secure in the event of significant progress in Soviet ASW capabilities. The R&D funding for ULMS has increased from $45 million in fiscal 1971 to $110 million requested in fiscal 1972. Secretary of Defense Laird has indicated that our present submarines probably will remain secure, but that, as a prudent planner, he could not be certain whether this will be true five to seven years hence. For this reason, the administration is moving ahead with the development of ULMS.

Most experts agree in principle with the need for prudence, but they argue that our currently programmed sea-based force will be safe at least through the 1970s; hence they believe that we could move more slowly on a new sea-based weapon system. Others favor moving ahead rapidly with ULMS, relying on this system as our sole deterrent if it proves successful, and then phasing out the other systems.

ULMS may be ready for a procurement decision within two or three years; if it is then decided to go ahead, the system could become operational no sooner than the late 1970s. Building a force of twenty boats with their associated missiles might cost $15 billion.

Strategic Bombers

U.S. long-range B-52 bombers have been in the force for more than a decade and have been continuously modified to keep them operational. They are the most expensive component of the strategic offensive force to operate, costing about $1 billion a year.

The Defense Report shows that 36 B-52s will be phased out in fiscal 1972. At the end of the year, the strategic bomber force will be reduced to 450 B-52s and 71 medium-range FB-111s. Another 200 B-52s probably will be phased out over the next few years. The remaining 250 B-52s are late-model planes that have been extensively modified; they are scheduled to carry a new air-to-ground nuclear missile and probably could be retained at least until 1980.

The survivability of the bomber force could be endangered by Soviet submarine-launched missiles fired from close range, which might destroy our aircraft before they could leave their bases. To counter this threat, new radars and warning systems are being installed. Toward the same end, alert procedures could be improved and air bases be established in the interior of the country. Taken together, these measures could significantly increase the cost of the present bomber fleet.

At some point, the United States will have to decide whether it wants to retain a bomber force at all. If it does, the B-52s will eventually have to be replaced, simply because of age.

The Air Force is now developing a new bomber, the B-1. The 1972 budget requests a large increase in funding for this program: $370 million, compared with $75 million in fiscal 1971. Included in the 1972 program are funds to build a prototype. If a procurement decision were made within the next few years, this system could enter the force by the early 1980s. To build 200 planes would require an investment of at least $10 billion, and the system would be costly to operate.

Apart from costs is the question whether the B-1 is the appropriate follow-on bomber to the B-52. The B-1 is being developed to perform a number of sophisticated nuclear missions as well as conventional bombing missions. The design characteristics needed to satisfy these multiple requirements raise the cost of the system. An alternative design that some experts believe should be investigated because it would optimize survivability and penetration—which are essential to the plane's primary strategic mission—amounts to an airborne missile-firing platform capable of firing air-to-surface nuclear missiles and remaining aloft for long periods of time.

In any event, the Defense Department plans to spend almost $2 billion to develop and procure advanced air-to-surface missiles (SRAM and SCAD) in order to increase the penetration capabilities of the B-52s, and for eventual use on a new bomber if we should decide to retain bombers in the strategic force structure.

Nationwide ABM

As was noted above, the Safeguard ABM system, currently being installed at four sites, is for the protection of our ICBMs, not our cities. In fiscal 1971 the administration proposed the initiation of a thin nationwide area ABM to guard against possible Chinese ICBM attacks and accidental missile launches, but the Congress did not approve the request. This year, the administration asked for R&D funds to investigate new and improved area ABM concepts, but not for area ABM deployment. In effect, it is seeking authority to keep open the option of moving in the direction of such a system, depending on how the technology develops and on the outcome of the strategic arms limitation talks with the USSR. One variation that could result from SALT would be to install an area ABM only around Washington.

Much of the debate over the ABM centers on policy considerations set forth in Chapter 3. For example, would the system be destabilizing and thus be a factor in setting off an arms race? But technical and cost factors also enter. While the administration is confident that such a system is feasible, some private experts argue that it is not. If a decision to move forward with deployment were made within the next year or two, a thin nationwide ABM could become partly operational by the end of the decade. The cost of constructing a full nationwide ABM composed of eight sites and radars, in addition to the four Minuteman sites, could run as high as $13 billion.

Air Defense and Warning

The U.S. air defense system consists of about 900 surface-to-air missiles (SAMs), 600 manned interceptors, and associated radars and command centers. The costs of operating this system are high—about $1 billion a year. To reduce these costs, air defense components that are not effective against advanced bomber tactics have been eliminated, and this process continues. The system could well become virtually obsolete within the next few years. Thus, if we want to retain an air defense system through the 1970s, we would have to decide soon whether to replace radars, interceptors, and SAMs with new equipment.

There are no signs that the Soviet strategic bomber threat is increasing and, as was noted in Chapter 3, there is controversy over how much (if anything) air defense contributes to our strategic deterrent. These reasons suggest that the United States should not move toward procurement of new air defense systems at the present time.

As a hedge, the administration is requesting $145 million in 1972 to develop an advanced airborne warning and control system (AWACS) against bombers. The possibilities of building a new manned interceptor aircraft (IMI) and new versions of surface-to-air missiles are under consideration; relatively small research programs continue for each. If these weapons eventually were introduced into the system, the investment cost could amount to $9 billion, and annual operating costs would be high.

Programs to warn against missile attack are also being pursued, specifically the development of a new over-the-horizon radar to improve detection and a satellite surveillance system to provide longer warning time. They would replace components of the present system that are not only less effective but also more costly to operate. Strategic experts generally agree on the usefulness of pursuing these programs.

Cost Summary

Estimated costs of these strategic programs, both those that are now in procurement and those that might be proposed in the future, are summarized in Table 4-7. The indicated investment costs would represent new procurement. However, the operating costs for each system shown in the table would not necessarily represent an increase in budget costs. That would depend on whether they were greater, or less, than the operating costs of the systems they would replace. The B-1 or a new air defense system, for example, probably would result in a saving in operating costs over the B-52 or the current air defense system. The Safeguard ABM, on the other hand, is a new type of system, and therefore the cost of operating it would be additional. Similarly, if ULMS supplemented rather than replaced existing sea-based systems, the cost of operating it would also be additional.

These estimates also highlight the potential budgetary significance of research and development costs. Total R&D costs for new strategic weapons in the 1972 budget can be estimated roughly at less than $1 billion. The total ten-year investment cost of the systems that might result could come to almost $50 billion. Should decisions be made within the next few years to procure two or more of these new systems (for example, ULMS and the B-1), the annual strategic budget could show a rising trend.

Budgetary Impact of SALT

As is indicated in Chapter 3, the most likely type of strategic arms agreement would call for a limitation on numbers of weapons. If such an agreement limited ABMs to zero or to a defense of the national capital only, current outlays for Safeguard would be reduced, and follow-on programs would no longer need to be considered for future funding. But a numerical limitation agreement would not necessarily rule out other programs, such as a new bomber system (B-1) or a new sea-based system (ULMS), nor would it in any way restrict MIRV programs for the Minuteman or Poseidon missile.

Further, under any agreement the United States probably would increase spending on intelligence collection and research and development as a hedge against Soviet cheating or a possible breakdown of the agreement. We would still have to be concerned about the potential vulnerability of the ICBMs and would have to decide either to phase them out or find new ways to protect them. Thus, an agreement could be as much an argument for spending on permitted activities as an argument against such spending, depending on the kind of technical problems that arose as well as on the overall state of East-West relations. To be sure, with numerical constraints placed on future Soviet threats, major *increases* in U.S. strategic forces would probably not be necessary over the next five years and this in itself could be of considerable budgetary significance.

Administration officials have often implied that U.S. spending for strategic arms might have to increase significantly if we could not reach an agreement with the Soviet Union on limiting strategic arms, and they point to ULMS and the B-1 as projects waiting in the wings. But failure to reach an agreement of even a limited kind need not add materially to the case for either the B-1 or ULMS. Decisions on these systems should depend on a continuing assessment of the Soviet threat.

Strategic Doctrine and Budgets

It might seem logical to assume that decisions on the strategic policy issues discussed in Chapter 3 will determine weapons decisions and that these decisions will determine the level of future annual strategic budgets. But this will not necessarily be the case. Three points should be kept in mind:

First, there is no automatic way of translating strategic doctrine into weapons decisions. Cost-benefit analysis would help but would not necessarily provide a unique solution to the problem. A variety of force structures could be developed to support a given doctrine. For example, a force planning goal, such as inflicting a specified level of retaliatory damage against an assumed attack, tends to determine the total number of survivable weapons needed, not the quality or mixture of weapons systems.

Second, decisions on particular weapons systems need not have a near-term effect on the strategic budget as a whole. Slowing the schedule under which a new system is introduced and phasing out obsolete systems at the same time could make it possible to go forward with new programs while staying within a fixed expenditure limit. For example, in fiscal 1970 the administration *reduced* spending on strategic programs by $2 billion, while continuing both the MIRV and ABM programs.

Finally, many crucial strategic policy decisions do not entail large expenditures. Qualitative modifications, such as improving missile accuracy, increasing silo hardness, or enhancing command and control, are relatively inexpensive—at least in comparison to the cost of new systems. Yet these and other low-cost decisions can have important consequences for the strategic balance and for SALT. Therefore, the level of spending may not always be the most significant measure of our strategic policy.

5. Foreign Assistance

FOR FISCAL 1972 the President requests authority to spend $7.5 billion on foreign assistance programs, compared with $6.9 billion in 1971 and $5.7 billion in 1970. The total in each of the three years includes roughly $2.2 billion in military assistance for Vietnam, Laos, and Thailand, funded in the Defense Department budget. The 1972 foreign assistance budget consists of three elements: security assistance, accounting for 58 percent; economic development assistance, for 36 percent; and welfare and emergency relief, 6 percent. Security assistance programs have expanded steadily in recent years, mostly in connection with the Vietnam war, but also because of increased assistance to Korea and Israel. An increase is also projected in 1972 for international development assistance that would restore the appropriation to the level of the mid-1960s—but without compensating for the effects of inflation. This increase in development aid—about $0.5 billion—is for funds that would enable the United States to meet its share of contributions to international lending institutions, as previously negotiated with other nations.

The budget also foreshadows changes in the organization and emphasis of U.S. foreign assistance programs that the President had previously indicated he would seek. Furthermore, in presenting its program, the administration seeks to clarify the various uses of foreign assistance and the amount of resources devoted to each.

Security assistance is a new budget category. In addition to military grants and credits, it includes military-related economic programs for Vietnam, Laos, Thailand, and Cambodia, designed to help those countries bear the cost of fighting the war. These programs, called supporting assistance, were formerly part of the economic aid appro-

118

priation. Military and supporting assistance are to be coordinated in a new security assistance program.

In the case of development assistance, the President proposes to establish two new organizations to replace the Agency for International Development (AID): a U.S. International Development Corporation for bilateral lending and a U.S. International Development Institute to promote technical cooperation with poor countries. (A third organization, the Overseas Private Investment Corporation, was established in 1970 and is already in operation.) Similarly, emergency relief and other forms of humanitarian assistance are to be differentiated from other programs and coordinated by the Department of State, though they will continue to be carried out for the most part by U.S. voluntary agencies and international organizations.

The buildup in foreign assistance reflects two major aspects of the administration's foreign strategy: (1) the use of increased military and economic aid as a counterpart to reduced dependence on U.S. ground forces in Vietnam, Korea, and elsewhere in Asia, and hence to fewer army divisions in the U.S. force structure; and (2) increased financial support for international financial institutions in keeping with the object of placing primary reliance on a multilateral rather than a bilateral framework for promoting international development.

This chapter outlines the main elements of these programs and the trends in appropriations for them. It concentrates on three issues: (1) the tradeoff between security assistance and the U.S. force structure; (2) the feasibility of moving toward greater multilateralism in development assistance; and (3) the relationship between security assistance and development assistance and its implications for future U.S. foreign aid programs.

Security Assistance

Security assistance in essentially its present form has been a feature of U.S. policy for more than two decades. The program has had a variety of purposes, but its central goal is to help countries in which the United States has a security interest to do more in their own defense. This definition leaves wide latitude for selecting the countries, deciding how much defense is enough, and determining the most effective way to help.

President Nixon described the goal in terms of helping friends and allies do more for themselves. What seems to be envisaged is a division of labor in which the United States provides military equipment and training that will enable these countries to provide effective manpower for their own defense. In his 1971 Foreign Policy Message, the President pointed out that security assistance is also an integral part of his effort to reduce the involvement of U.S. military forces abroad:

Particularly in the areas of the world where we are reducing our manpower, we must make resources available to help them complete the transition with us. In some cases this will require substantial assistance during the period of adjustment. This is central to our new approach to American foreign policy in the 1970's.

Recent appropriations for security assistance bear out this projected trend. The total 1972 budget request for all forms of security assistance (military and economic) is more than double the pre-Vietnam level, as is shown in Table 5-1.

Between 1970 and 1972, assistance to Vietnam and Cambodia is projected to increase by almost $1 billion, mostly for the new security assistance program to Cambodia and for increased supporting assistance to Vietnam. During the same period, reduced U.S. participation in the war will result in budgetary savings of many times that amount.

But what about the future? Does the Nixon doctrine imply that security assistance will continue to be needed at anywhere near the current levels? If so, will there be further savings in U.S. forces? In examining these questions, it is useful to assess the program and the expenditures in terms of the purposes they are designed to achieve. These purposes are

• To assist "security countries"—that is, countries to whose defense against external aggression the United States is committed by treaty, or countries where the United States has some other direct security interest. Groups of countries in this category include Vietnam, Laos, Cambodia, and Thailand; Korea and Taiwan; Greece and Turkey; and probably Israel and Jordan.

• To maintain base rights or other privileges useful to U.S. military policy and strategy. Examples are found in Spain, the Philippines, and Ethiopia.

• To promote a variety of general interests, such as gaining influence among military leaders, helping to maintain a balance of military

Table 5-1. Funds for U.S. Security Assistance Programs, Selected Fiscal Years, 1964–72[a]
Millions of dollars

Program	1964	1966–67 average	1970	1971	1972
Military security assistance					
Military assistance program grants	1,415	938	350	750	705
Foreign military credit sales	83	144	70	700	510
Department of Defense funded grants for Thailand, Laos, Vietnam	—	1,167	2,174	2,177	2,200[b]
Surplus stocks[c]	(41)	(111)	(424)	(300)	(600)[d]
Subtotal	1,498	2,249	2,594	3,627	3,415
Economic security assistance					
Supporting assistance	334	690	388	523	778
Public Law 480 common defense grants	132	121	108	110[e]	100[e]
President's foreign assistance contingency fund	100	124	33	26	100
Subtotal	566	935	529	659	978
Total	2,064	3,184	3,123	4,286	4,393

Sources: *The Budget of the United States Government, Fiscal Year 1972;* Agency for International Development (AID), Office of Program and Policy Coordination (OPPC), *Operations Report, Data as of June 30, 1969* (AID, 1970); AID, OPPC, "U.S. Overseas Loans and Grants, Preliminary FY 1970 and Trend Data: Obligations and Loan Authorizations, July 1, 1945–June 30, 1970" (AID, 1970; processed); *U.S. Overseas Loans and Grants and Assistance from International Organizations: Obligations and Loan Authorizations, July 1, 1945–June 30, 1969,* Special Report Prepared for the House Foreign Affairs Committee (AID, 1970); various statements submitted for Hearings on Military Assistance before the Subcommittee on Economy in Government of the Joint Economic Committee, 92 Cong. 1 sess. (January and February 1971; processed); unpublished information from AID.

a. Data for 1964 and 1966–67 average are net obligations and loan authorizations, except for the supporting assistance program, which are commitments. Data for 1970–72 are for budgetary authority, except for the President's contingency fund, 1970 and 1971, which are budget outlays.

b. Estimate.

c. Parentheses indicate that no budgetary expenditure is involved. Stocks are valued at acquisition cost. (The utility value is usually taken as one-third of the acquisition cost.)

d. Assumed to be double the 1971 level because of the additional stocks made available as a result of the withdrawal of troops from Vietnam.

e. Estimate based on 1969–70 average.

forces in an area, restraining arms races, or furthering other diplomatic and political objectives.

An estimate of how the security assistance budget request for 1972 might be allocated among countries in these three categories is shown in Table 5-2. Because no analysis of this kind is publicly available for fiscal 1972, the figures in the table are estimated on the basis of published data for past years or, where those are not available, on fairly arbitrary judgments. The totals for the major countries or groups of countries probably are not so far from the mark as to distort the analysis for which they are used.

Table 5-2. Estimated Allocation of Budget Authorizations for U.S. Foreign Security Assistance Programs by Purpose and Country, Fiscal Year 1972
Millions of dollars

Purpose category and country	Department of Defense funded grants	Military assistance program grants	Foreign military credit sales	Public Law 480 common defense grants	Supporting assistance	President's foreign assistance contingency fund	Total
Security countries							
Vietnam	2,000	...	...	65	500	...	2,565
Laos	100	...	...	...	50	...	150
Cambodia	...	175	...	...	125	...	300
Thailand	100	...	...	...	50	...	150
Korea	...	250	...	...	...	...	250
Taiwan	...	20	50	35	...	...	105
Greece	...	20	...	...	...	...	20
Turkey	...	100	...	...	...	...	100
Israel	...	...	300	...	...	...	300
Jordan	...	30	...	...	...	...	30
Base rights countries							
Spain	...	20	...	...	...	...	20
Ethiopia	...	10	...	...	...	...	10
Philippines	...	15	...	...	...	...	15
Other	...	10	...	...	...	...	10
General interest countries							
Other Near East and South Asia	...	20	50	...	...	...	70
Other East Asia	...	15	20	...	...	...	35
Other Africa	...	10	10	...	...	...	20
Latin America	...	10	40	...	...	...	50
Unallocated	...	...	40	...	53	100	193
Total	2,200	705	510	100	778	100	4,393

Sources: Total authorizations are from Table 5-1. Allocations are authors' estimates. In most cases, estimates are based on data for previous years, for which the sources are: U.S. Department of Defense, *Military Assistance and Foreign Military Sales Facts* (March 1970), and Joint Economic Committee hearings cited in Table 5-1. See text for discussion of the purpose categories.

The possibilities for a tradeoff between these assistance programs and the budget costs of U.S. forces are limited to the security countries, and even there the possibilities vary widely. They occur in countries where U.S. forces are stationed, as in Vietnam and Korea, and countries for whose defense the United States maintains specific forces in its peacetime defense structure, such as Taiwan, Thailand, Greece, and Turkey. In both categories of countries it is at least conceivable that increased security assistance might make it possible to reduce the size of U.S. forces maintained for contingencies relating to them. These possibilities and some of the issues they raise are examined below.

Security Countries Related to Vietnam

We now spend more than $3 billion a year on military and supporting assistance to Vietnam, Laos, Cambodia, and Thailand. This estimate does not allow for the share of the security assistance program to Korea that might be viewed as support of Koreans serving in Vietnam. Since the total security assistance program comes to something more than $4 billion, this means that about three-fourths of the program is related directly to the Vietnam war. Assuming that this large sum is an essential element in the withdrawal of most or all U.S. forces from Vietnam, a number of important issues arise that have implications for future programs.

First are military issues that involve important policy choices. We are equipping and training Vietnamese forces with weapons designed for U.S. forces—for example, helicopters, tanks, personnel carriers, and other kinds of relatively sophisticated equipment. This course has several advantages. It promises to give the Vietnamese forces greater mobility, greater control over roads, and the capacity to influence a wider area of the country. It will permit fewer troops to do more jobs. On the other hand, it gives lower priority to helping Vietnamese troops to develop greater effectiveness in areas off the main roads and in the countryside generally, where communist forces have had the most consistent success. Moreover, it will leave the Vietnamese forces with a relatively complicated and costly supply system; it will tend to perpetuate Vietnamese dependence on U.S. advisers, training, spare parts, and replacements; and it could result in slowing the pace of U.S. withdrawal.

The relative emphasis to be placed on rural pacification and development raises a second set of issues that have stirred a recurrent controversy. In fiscal 1971 the Congress appropriated funds to help finance a land reform program in Vietnam. Would it be more effective to use a greater proportion of U.S. assistance to underwrite more ambitious programs of this type in the countryside, and somewhat less on supporting the Vietnamese armed forces? Again, the decision could have important implications for the future level of Vietnam's dependence on the United States.

There are economic issues as well. The present level of commodity support and other kinds of economic assistance to Vietnam is probably about $600 million a year. This program will cushion the impact on the economy of losses in foreign exchange resulting from reduced expenditures by U.S. forces as they are withdrawn. In fixing the amount of this aid, a judgment is required as to whether the Vietnamese are doing enough themselves. Would it be possible to mobilize more resources domestically through higher taxes, and impose more effective cost controls to ensure that fewer resources would be needed to control inflation—or will continued warfare make the political fabric too weak to support this burden?

Finally, what level of assistance might be appropriate if the war grew less intense and something closer to a stable military situation developed, uneasy though it might be? The current level of U.S. military and economic assistance to Vietnam is probably about equal to its total GNP, but this amount reflects the buildup phase of the Vietnamization program and could be expected to decline under almost any circumstances. Korea in the 1950s provides a useful reference point. The cease-fire there was followed by U.S. economic and military assistance through the 1950s that averaged about $500 million a year in dollars of today's purchasing power. The situation in Vietnam could, of course, be different in fundamental respects, but the Korean experience suggests that a sharp reduction below present levels should be expected over the future in security assistance for Indo-China.

Other Security Countries

Outside Vietnam, the possibility of a tradeoff between increased security assistance and budget savings in U.S. forces is clearest for *Korea*. We have been providing Korea with about $200 million a year in security assistance on the grounds that it is unable to support by itself the very large force required for its defense. More important, two U.S. divisions have remained in Korea as an integral part of the defending force.

We are now withdrawing one combat division (20,000 troops) from Korea; during the transition, we will provide an additional $150 million in military assistance in fiscal 1972, as part of a five-year program to modernize the Korean forces. The costs of this *special* program will probably continue at this level and come to about $750 million for the five years; the total security assistance program for Korea over this period will probably cost twice this amount.

The tradeoff calculation would then run as follows. Savings from the withdrawal and subsequent deactivation of the U.S. combat division would come to about $250 million a year. (Contrary to the situation for troops in Europe, deactivation of the troops to be withdrawn from Korea can be assumed, since it would be consistent with the reduced number of divisions forecast in the budget for the end of fiscal 1972.) Given the projected cost of $150 million a year for the special five-year assistance program, net annual savings would thus amount to $100 million over the period. The budgetary savings would be even more impressive if, over the period, the total security assistance program of perhaps $300 million a year helped to make possible the withdrawal of the second U.S. division from Korea, leaving behind only a relatively small number of specialized units.

This calculation would seem to indicate a clear budgetary benefit to the United States. Nevertheless, three questions can be raised: (1) Does Korea have more divisions than it needs and is its equipment more costly than necessary? If so, Korea's defense burden could detract from its economic potentialities and perpetuate its dependence on the United States. (2) Could the Koreans, with a rapidly growing economy, be asked to bear a larger share of their defense costs? (3) Would it be more effective, as measured by the long-term strength of the Korean society, to provide some or all of this help in the form of economic, rather than military, assistance?

Elsewhere in the security countries there are no clearly identifiable U.S. forces that could be disbanded if the military capabilities of those countries were strengthened. In *Taiwan*, military assistance is used principally to strengthen that country's defense against Chinese Communist air attacks. It can be argued that by strengthening Taiwan's air defense, U.S. military assistance could postpone the need for direct U.S. intervention in a crisis, and this would be an important benefit from the program. On the other hand, Taiwan's defense against Chinese Communist air attacks rests ultimately on U.S. naval and air power in the area. Military assistance programs cannot lessen that dependence.

In *Greece* and *Turkey*, U.S. security assistance is part of a NATO-wide program. Should war break out, Greek and Turkish forces, though poorly equipped in comparative terms, probably would help defend NATO's southern flank, since the opposing Warsaw Pact forces are not front line troops and are not as well equipped as those on the central front.

Critics argue that these assistance programs no longer make much sense, since (1) Greece and Turkey are more concerned with defense against each other than with defense against Soviet attack; (2) Turkish forces would be more effective if they were fewer in number and better equipped, but our programs are not influencing Turkey in that direction; and (3) assistance to Greece has adverse political implications.

The Middle East is a special case because our security assistance programs, which are designed to achieve military stability in the area, hinge more than usually on actions beyond our control—namely, those of the Soviet Union, Israel, and the United Arab Republic. Military credits to Israel and military grants to Jordan are the principal U.S. programs; their purpose is to offset, in varying degree, Soviet military assistance to the area. But in an arms race of this kind, the distinction between action and response often becomes blurred and comes to depend heavily on the viewpoint from which it is seen. The main purpose of these programs may well be to provide a means for exercising influence toward a political settlement.

Base Rights Countries

Programs that in one sense or another might be viewed as "rent" for U.S. bases probably total little more than $50 million a year. In theory, one might argue that the U.S. interest in these bases could be weighed by comparing the cost of these programs with the cost of making alternative arrangements for, or adjustments in, U.S. forces if we did not have access to the bases. In practice, these computations prove difficult to make; nevertheless, the concept can provide a useful perspective for base rights negotiations. One of the problems in this area is a tendency to delay reassessment of whether changes in technology or politics make it necessary or desirable to maintain an existing base arrangement.

General Interest Countries

The remainder of the security assistance program costs about $200 million and is spread over more than forty countries. Assistance to these countries is designed to further a wide range of largely political interests. Proponents of this assistance argue that it is an inexpensive and efficient means of promoting U.S. objectives. Critics contend that these military grant programs should be discontinued because the means are inappropriate to achieve such objectives, and that the programs run the risk of unintentionally generating U.S. military commitments.

Development Assistance

In his 1971 Foreign Policy Message, the President pointed to his proposed approach to providing development assistance as a "major application of the Nixon doctrine." This approach is based on the following three elements in the world situation he projects for the 1970s:

• Many developing countries are now able to determine their own development priorities, intend to do so, and are mobilizing domestically the major part of the resources to carry them out.

• The United States, though still the largest single supplier of development assistance, now provides less than other industrial countries combined.

• The international lending institutions have the capacity for "fusing the efforts of all countries into a true multilateral partnership for development."

For these reasons, the President proposes that a growing proportion of U.S. development aid be provided in the form of contributions to the international lending institutions, and that U.S. bilateral programs be reorganized into three specialized government corporations designed to support this international effort.

To help in assessing these proposals, Table 5-3 shows changes in the size and composition of U.S. programs since the pre-Vietnam period. For fiscal 1972, the budget request for all forms of development assistance amounts to $2.7 billion. This level is appreciably higher than that of the past few years but about equal to the programs of the mid-1960s, when considerable emphasis was given to building up development assistance. If account is taken of price changes, the

Table 5-3. Funds for U.S. Foreign Development Assistance and Welfare and Emergency Relief, by Program, Selected Fiscal Years, 1964–72[a]

Millions of dollars

Assistance program	1964	1966–67 average	1970	1971	1972
Bilateral[b]	**2,463**	**2,281**	**1,470**	**1,666**	**1,648**
Financial	1,258	1,087	539	627	655
Technical cooperation	259	288	331	354	315
Peace Corps	76	109	90	88	73
Food loans[c]	802	733	478	553	517
Other	68	64	32	44	88
Multilateral	**215**	**446**	**609**[d]	**544**[d]	**1,063**
Total development assistance	**2,678**	**2,727**	**2,079**	**2,210**	**2,711**
Welfare and emergency relief	569	442	473	450[e]	450[e]

Sources: Same as Table 5-1.

a. Data for 1964 and 1966–67 average are net obligations and loan authorizations, except for the financial and technical cooperation programs, which are commitments. Data for 1970–72 are for budgetary authority, except for the Peace Corps and food loans programs, which are budget outlays.

b. Bilateral programs exclude economic supporting assistance and the President's foreign assistance contingency fund, which are shown in Table 5-1 under economic security assistance.

c. Title I of Public Law 480 (83 Cong.), less common defense grants, which are shown in Table 5-1 as part of economic security assistance. Title II is included in welfare and emergency relief (last line of this table).

d. Excludes budgetary authority for callable capital to the International Bank for Reconstruction and Development and the Inter-American Development Bank, on the assumption that such authority will not result in outlays.

e. Estimate.

1972 budget request is about one-fifth less than the mid-1960s level. The figures in these comparisons have been adjusted to accord with the approach and changes proposed by the administration. Supporting assistance, though economic in form, is omitted and instead shown in Table 5-1 as a security program; welfare and emergency relief—mostly agricultural food grants under the Food for Peace program of Title II of the Agricultural Trade Development and Assistance Act (Public Law 480)—is shown separately.

Changes in the composition of the programs are also significant. Bilateral lending has been greatly reduced; the $650 million requested for financial programs for 1972 is about the same level as in fiscal 1971 and only half the amount provided in 1964. (Repayments of interest and principal on past loans will increase this amount, but no appropriation is required.) On the other hand, multilateral aid—principally for the U.S. share of contributions to international lending institutions—is to increase from about $200 million in 1964 to more than $1 billion in 1972. This form of assistance is likely to increase over the years. The two major components of the 1972 budget request—the U.S. share for the Inter-American Development Bank (IDB) and for the International Development Association (IDA), the "soft loan window" of the World Bank—are both parts of internationally negotiated multi-year agreements. Furthermore, the lending operations of the Asian Development Bank should grow rapidly in the near future, and it is possible that the United States and other industrial countries will reach agreement with African nations to help finance the African Development Bank.

How would this move toward greater multilateralism affect the U.S. share of total world development assistance? The shares for contributing countries are fixed for each international lending institution, but the distribution varies among them. For example, the United States provides 40 percent of the contributions to IDA, roughly two-thirds for the IDB, and 20 percent for the Asian Development Bank. The total U.S. contribution of about $1 billion for all multilateral organizations would be accompanied by contributions of $1.25 billion from other countries. From the U.S. point of view, this relationship is about the same as, or somewhat better than, that between U.S. bilateral assistance and the bilateral assistance of other industrial countries combined. This represents good burden-sharing in a financial sense, apart from its political advantages. It also means that with U.S. bilateral programs remaining constant at the present low level, and those of other industrial countries rising, the U.S. share in the world development effort will continue to decline.

Another issue is the capacity of these institutions to carry the greatly increased responsibilities envisaged by the administration's program. Critics argue that the international organizations are not well prepared to assume leadership in the world development effort. Changes in the policies, procedures, and staffing of these organizations will certainly be required, but for the most part this argument has not caught up with the facts. The expansion of the international financial institutions over the past five years has already made them a major factor in development lending. They account for one-third of total world development lending on concessional terms, and for a considerably higher proportion of world development lending if the large volume of World Bank loans at near market rates of interest is taken into account. In building up to this level, they have greatly increased their capabilities —and the new capital they are scheduled to receive as a result of recently negotiated international agreements will permit this process to continue.

The third issue is the extent to which explicit or implicit U.S. obligations exist that would argue against cutting these expenditures or call for them to be increased. Obligations and interests do exist, but they take a variety of forms.

As was indicated earlier, the budget request for multilateral assistance represents U.S. compliance with international agreements—and these funds account for about 40 percent of the $2.7 billion program. Another $500 million consists of food loans under the Food for Peace program. The food will come from U.S. stocks and would not be produced were it not for our domestic agricultural legislation; perhaps half the cost would be paid in any event to support farm prices. A specific domestic interest is served in the remainder of the bilateral program. Development lending is now tied to procurement in the United States, which makes it a form of export promotion, particularly for some of our high-cost industries. The tying requirement, however, greatly reduces the value of these appropriations to the recipients, since they must pay prices higher than those on a competitive world market. The administration is seeking to eliminate it if all other industrial countries agree to do the same in their programs. More generally, to the extent that the United States is prepared to view the promotion of economic development in poor countries as a shared responsibility, it can be argued that an obligation exists to strengthen the U.S. development assistance program.

Future Possibilities

A brief examination of the history of these programs provides some useful insights into the two central issues for the future: the size of the foreign assistance program and the mixture between security and development assistance. The data are shown in Table 5-4.

For more than two decades the total size of this program in dollars of constant purchasing power has stayed within a range of $6 billion to $8 billion. The proposed 1972 program is about 10 percent less in constant dollars than the average level during both the Marshall Plan period and during the first years of the Mutual Security Act period. Twenty years ago, foreign aid amounted to roughly 1.75 percent of GNP, while now the proportion is about 0.70 percent.

In size, then, the current program is not out of line with the past and represents a declining proportion of GNP. The 1972 budget request

Table 5-4. Funds for U.S. Foreign Assistance, in Current and 1972 Dollars, by Major Program Category, Selected Fiscal Years, 1949–72[a]

Millions of dollars

Program category	Marshall Plan period 1949–52 average	Mutual Security Act period 1953–57 average	Mutual Security Act period 1958–61 average	1964	1966–67 average	1970	1971	1972
In current dollars								
Security assistance	1,155	4,680	3,050	2,064	3,184	3,123	4,286	4,393
Welfare and emergency relief	20	233	346	569	442	473	450[b]	450[b]
Development assistance	4,133	615	1,425	2,678	2,727	2,079	2,210	2,711
Total	5,308	5,528	4,821	5,311	6,353	5,675	6,946	7,554
In 1972 dollars								
Security assistance	1,842	6,954	3,983	2,636	3,853	3,360	4,436	4,393
Welfare and emergency relief	32	346	452	727	535	509	466	450
Development assistance	6,592	914	1,861	3,420	3,300	2,237	2,287	2,711
Total	8,466	8,215	6,296	6,782	7,687	6,106	7,189	7,554
Percentage of total								
Security assistance	21.8	84.7	63.3	38.9	50.1	55.0	61.7	58.2
Welfare and emergency relief	0.4	4.2	7.2	10.7	7.0	8.3	6.5	6.0
Development assistance	77.9	11.1	29.6	50.4	42.9	36.6	31.8	35.9
Total	100.0	100.0	100.0	100.0	100.0	100.0	100.0	100.0
Foreign assistance as percentage of gross national product	1.75	1.40	1.00	0.85	0.80	0.60	0.70	0.70

Sources: Tables 5-1 and 5-3, and sources for Table 5-1. Figures are rounded and may not add to totals.
a. In general, the funds for each program are classified as noted in Tables 5-1 and 5-3, footnote a.
b. Estimate.

for all forms of foreign assistance is not far from the target set by the Pearson Commission in 1969 for development assistance alone. But the major part of the total consists of security assistance; development assistance is now very low in comparison to past U.S. levels or to the contrasting trend in other industrial countries. Which brings us to the second issue: What is the proper mixture?

Wide swings have occurred in the relative emphasis placed on security as against development assistance. During the Marshall Plan period, of course, the bulk went for economic recovery and development in the industrial countries of Western Europe. The proportion was reversed during the 1950s. The need for security assistance at the beginning of that decade seemed obvious in the wake of the Berlin blockade and the Korean war. At first the bulk of security assistance went to Western European countries through NATO to help them rebuild their defense, as we had helped to rebuild their economies through the Marshall Plan. A large amount also went to Korea, Taiwan, and elsewhere in Asia, and the amount rose during the later part of the period.

Another swing took place during the early 1960s, when development assistance again received higher priority and the program was directed almost entirely toward assisting poor countries. This trend was reversed again in the middle of the decade, following U.S. entry into the Vietnam war.

What are the prospects that a shift will take place once again, this time in favor of development assistance? An end to the war in Vietnam, or at least a reduced level of fighting, is probably a prior condition; but then the decision will have to be faced.

The mixture of military and development assistance can affect choices *within* the developing countries as between the two goals— military security and economic growth. This need not be the case if the form of assistance is neutral in its effects on internal decisions— for then the external resources would be interchangeable, and changes in the proportions of development aid and military assistance would be offset by changes in the internal resources allocated to the two purposes. Either form of assistance would contribute resources that the country could then use in accord with its own priorities. But the form of assistance is in fact not neutral. Military assistance is often designed to maximize domestic expenditures for defense, and economic assistance to maximize domestic expenditures for development. This means that our military and economic development programs can have competitive effects—which underlines the importance of reaching the right decision about the mixture of these kinds of aid.

The Nixon doctrine focuses on security, while recognizing the need for development and the relation between these two goals. Experience confirms that this relation exists and says something about where the emphasis should be placed. The countries that have been most successful in enhancing their defense and security are those that have also made the greatest progress in development. If experience is any guide to the future, a preoccupation with security in its narrowest sense could jeopardize security in the broadest sense. If so, we would be wise to give priority to development assistance, and to make that priority clear in the decisions to be made in the years just ahead.

6. General Revenue Sharing

THE 1972 BUDGET puts major emphasis on revenue sharing with state and local governments. The proposals are of two distinct kinds: special revenue sharing, which is discussed in Chapter 7, and general revenue sharing.

General revenue sharing means earmarking a portion of federal revenues for distribution to the states in accordance with a formula. The administration's proposal would allocate an amount equal to 1.3 percent of taxable personal income (about $5 billion in 1973) for this purpose. The program would start in October 1971 and make $3.8 billion available in fiscal 1972. These funds would be transferred automatically to the states—not subject to annual appropriation by the Congress—to be used for any legitimate public purpose. The states would be required to share them with their local governments in accordance with a procedure specified in the law.

The prominence given to revenue sharing in the President's messages on the budget, the state of the union, and other subjects has brought a new kind of question into the budget debate. Past budgets have precipitated controversy about their overall size or fiscal impact and about the allocation of federal funds among different purposes or priorities. The 1972 budget, however, precipitates debate about the federal system itself—how revenues and decision-making power should be shared among different levels of government.

From a fiscal point of view, the federal system is largely an accident. Nobody thought it out in advance. The Constitution specified certain

134

powers for the federal government and left the rest to the states and their constituent localities. State and local responsibilities were more costly than federal ones, but no level of government absorbed much of the national output. As recently as 1929, expenditures at all levels of government accounted for only about 10 percent of the gross national product—2.4 percent by the federal government and 7.5 percent by state and local governments combined. Then came a decade of depression, in which the federal government took on a whole new range of functions, and a decade of hot and cold war, in which the federal defense responsibility became increasingly expensive. By 1950, federal expenditures alone were 13.5 percent of GNP, while state and local expenditures were 7.8 percent. Growth continued in the next two decades, with state and local expenditures (financed partly by federal grants-in-aid) growing at a more rapid rate than federal expenditures. By 1970, total government expenditures were 32.1 percent of GNP, 18.6 percent being federal and 13.4 percent state and local.

The composition of federal revenues also changed dramatically as federal responsibilities grew. In the early days, federal revenues from customs and from sales of public land were more than adequate to cover federal expenditures, but in the twentieth century, taxes on income became the mainstay of federal finance. Taxes on personal and corporate income and payrolls now provide about 85 percent of federal revenues. State and local governments, however, rely primarily on property and sales taxes. Although an increasing number of states and even a few localities now tax income, corporate and personal income taxes still account for only 16 percent of state and local tax revenue.

General revenue sharing would change the federal system in two directions. It would increase reliance on the federal income tax as a source of funds for state and local governments, and it would give those governments greater control over the ways in which federally raised funds are spent.

Revenue sharing is but one of several possible ways of strengthening the fiscal position of state and local governments. One alternative would be to increase federal funding for existing categorical aid programs; another would be for the federal government to assume one or more major functions now financed by state and local governments. Enactment of the fully federal social security system in the 1930s, for example, undoubtedly relieved state and local governments of a major burden for support of the aged. Federalization of the welfare system would similarly relieve state and local governments of a major burden for support of the poor. The federal government could also make it easier for state and local governments to increase their taxes. It could reduce its own taxes on particular items, leaving those potential tax sources to state and local governments, or it could allow individuals to credit taxes paid to states and local governments against their federal tax bill, rather than allowing them only to deduct these payments from their taxable income as they do now. The federal government could also engage in "tax sharing"—returning a portion of federal tax revenues to the jurisdictions in which they were collected.

Pros and Cons of Revenue Sharing

There are three basic arguments for general revenue sharing. First, it is needed to alleviate an impending state and local fiscal crisis; second, it is desirable because it would shift power to state and local governments, which are more responsive to the needs of people than is the federal government; third, it would redistribute resources from the affluent to the less affluent by shifting part of the burden of government expenses from the generally regressive state and local taxes to the more progressive federal income tax and by redistributing resources from richer states to those less well off. These three arguments will be examined in turn.

Is There a Fiscal Crisis?

A fiscal crisis at the state and local level could reflect either a short-run problem related to cyclical swings in the economy or a more serious long-run imbalance between growth in desired expenditures and growth in revenues. At least part of the "crisis" reported so fully in the media in 1970 and 1971 is a result of the recession and rapid rate of inflation during the past two years.

RECESSION AND INFLATION. The recession has had a double effect. It has slowed the expansion of tax revenues and increased the demand for certain state and local services. States and localities as a whole would have obtained about $3.5 billion more revenue in calendar 1970 from taxes alone if the economy had been at the full employment level. The shortfall in tax revenues has been particularly great in a few states like New York, where income taxes provide a substantial portion of revenue.

The economic slowdown also increases the demand for certain

state and local services. Welfare rolls expand when unemployment is high. In the past year the number of welfare recipients rose by 2.4 million, or 23 percent. State and municipal hospitals, public universities, and other social services are also in greater demand in periods of recession.

The inflation of the past several years has hit states and localities especially hard. Since the beginning of 1966, prices paid by their governments for goods and services have risen 32 percent, one-third faster than consumer prices. Unionism and a new militancy among teachers and other public employees have pushed their wages up faster than wages generally. In the past four years, their salaries have risen at twice the rate in the total labor force. Since more than 42 percent of all state and local outlays are for wages, total expenditures are highly sensitive to contract settlements. Inflation has also increased state and local revenues, but by less than the rise in expenditures, at least in the last few years.

The last four years have also seen an unprecedented rise in the cost of borrowing. While the interest rate on municipal bonds hovered around 3.2 percent in the early 1960s, it had more than doubled by 1970. Although the rate paid by states and localities has declined during the past six months, it still remains far above the level of the early 1960s.

Clearly, inflation and recession have combined to intensify fiscal difficulties at the state and local level, but if these short-run developments were the crux of the problem, general revenue sharing would not be an appropriate solution. While it would provide those governments with additional funds, the size of the grant would not increase during downturns in the business cycle, nor would it respond rapidly to an increase in the rate of inflation. Had general revenue sharing been initiated several years ago, it would probably not have alleviated the fiscal problems being encountered by state and local governments in the face of recession and inflation.

LONG-RUN PROBLEMS. Advocates of revenue sharing see it as a response to a more fundamental long-run crisis. They anticipate a gap between future demands for state and local expenditures and the revenues that state and local governments could raise without increasing tax rates or tapping new sources of revenue. They argue that state and local expenditures have been rising rapidly in recent years—considerably faster than the gross national product—and may be expected to continue to rise. On the other hand, state and local revenues raised from their own sources have tended to grow more slowly. The yields from sales and property taxes, which constitute three-fourths of the tax receipts of these governments, at best rise only as fast as GNP. In the past, the gap between the growth in expenditures and the normal increase in revenues has been filled both by raising tax rates and through greatly expanded contributions from the federal government. Advocates of revenue sharing argue that continued increases in tax rates at the pace of recent years are neither desirable nor politically feasible. They contend that it would be better to shift part of the increasing burden of state and local expenditures to the federal income tax—a tax that not only is more equitable than state and local taxes, but also grows more rapidly than the gross national product. It would thus be possible to raise needed revenue at the federal level and distribute it to the hard-pressed state and local governments.

State and local expenditures have been rising over the past two decades in response to such long-run factors as population growth, rising incomes, and urbanization. Population growth creates pressure for more schools, new hospitals, and other basic services, while rising income and urbanization create more traffic, trash, effluents, crime, and other problems with which state and local governments must deal. Moreover, the long-run increase in wages pushes state and local costs up faster than costs in other sectors, because wages are an especially large component of state and local budgets and because there is little room for substituting machines for people in many state and local activities, such as school teaching and health care. Added to these general problems has been the sharp rise in welfare expenditures in the 1960s. A rapidly growing proportion of the poor has begun receiving assistance. Nearly one-half of the persons classified as poor are now on the welfare rolls, compared with about 18 percent in 1960.

The rapid rise of state and local expenditures, by major governmental functions, may be seen in Table 6-1. A rough attempt has been made to allocate the increases to workload (number of people, number of automobiles, number of school-age children, and so on), to price increases, and to increases in the scope or quality of services provided. Rising prices emerge as the most important cause of the increase, while workload appears considerably less significant. The scope and quality of state and local government services appear to have risen substantially, indicating that the level of public services we

Table 6-1. Comparison of State and Local Expenditures, by Function, Fiscal Years 1955 and 1969

Amounts in billions of dollars

Function	Amount		1955–69		Percentage of 1955–69 increase in expenditure attributable to increase in		
	1955	1969	Percentage increase	Percentage of total increase	Workload	Price	Scope and quality
All functions	**39.0**	**134.1**	**244.1**	**100.0**	...	...	...
General expenditure	33.7	116.7	246.1	87.2	26.2	43.8	30.0
Local schools	10.1	33.8	233.2	24.8	31.7	52.4	15.9
Higher education and other education, except local schools	1.8	13.5	657.6	12.3	25.1	35.5	39.4
Public welfare	3.2	12.1	282.2	9.4	...	29.7	70.3
Highways	6.5	15.4	138.9	9.4	50.8	42.3	6.9
Hospitals and health	2.5	8.5	237.5	6.3	18.8	43.8	37.4
Basic urban services[a]	4.3	14.9	243.7	11.1	22.8	50.6	26.6
Administration and other[b]	5.3	18.5	247.4	13.9	18.5	38.0	43.6
Utility deficit	0.4	1.4	234.5	1.0	...	...	...
Debt retirement and additions to liquid assets[c,d]	3.9	12.0	206.1	8.5	...	...	...
Contributions to retirement systems	0.9	4.0	339.8	3.2	...	...	...

Sources: U.S. Bureau of the Census, *Governmental Finances in 1968–69*, Series GF69—No. 5 (1970); Bureau of the Census, *U.S. Census of Governments: 1962*, Vol. 6, No. 4, *Historical Statistics on Governmental Finances and Employment* (1964). Percentages attributable to workload, price, scope, and quality are authors' estimates. All calculations are based on unrounded data.

a. Includes fire protection, police protection, correction, sewerage, other sanitation, parks and recreation, housing and urban renewal, and transportation and terminals.

b. Includes administration and general control, general public buildings, interest on general debt, employment services, and miscellaneous functions.

c. Excludes assets of social insurance funds.

d. Estimated.

are now enjoying is considerably higher than in the past. It is not surprising that taxes have had to be increased to pay for these qualitative improvements.

State and local receipts have also risen dramatically in the last decade and a half (see Table 6-2). Tax revenues alone have more than tripled. Much of the increase in tax yields has been attributable to economic growth; higher incomes, sales, and property values yield more revenue even at the same tax rates. Economic growth has also raised state and local receipts from fees and charges; more cars mean more revenue from motor vehicle licenses. About one-third of the increase in tax revenue, however, is attributable to increases in tax rates or the imposition of new taxes; about one-fourth of the rise in revenues from fees and charges was due to higher rates.

Over the same period, federal grants-in-aid increased more than twice as fast as state and local tax revenues. New debt issues of state and local governments also rose.

PROJECTIONS. How does the state and local fiscal situation look for the years just ahead? A four-step procedure can be followed in answering this question.

• Project state and local expenditures several years ahead on reasonable assumptions about the changes in workload, prices, and scope and quality of services.

• Project state and local revenues at existing tax rates and with current federal grant programs.

• Measure the resulting gap between receipts and expenditures.

• Calculate what it would take, with several alternative policies, to close the gap: further increases in state and local tax rates; an expansion of federal grants-in-aid; general revenue sharing; federal assumption of part or all of the state and local welfare burden.

Table 6-3 lays the groundwork for this analysis, projecting state and local expenditures and revenues to 1976. If state and local tax rates remain unchanged and federal grants-in-aid continue to operate as they do today (with no new programs but with an expansion in existing programs to take account of price and workload increases), total revenues of state and local governments may be expected to rise to about $251.7 billion by 1976. If the quality and scope of state and local services increase at roughly the rate observed between 1965 and 1969, then total expenditures may be expected to rise to about $261.1 billion by 1976. As was the case in the 1960s, the most rapid increases will be in higher education and welfare (assuming that the federal

Table 6-2. Comparison of State and Local Revenues, by Source, Fiscal Years 1955 and 1969

Amounts in billions of dollars

| | Amount | | 1955–1969 | |
Source	1955	1969	Percentage increase	Percentage of total increase
All sources	**38.8**	**134.1**	**245.6**	**100.0**
Taxes	23.5	76.7	226.6	55.8
Property	10.7	30.7	185.5	20.9
Individual income	1.2	8.9	620.2	8.0
Corporation income	0.7	3.2	327.4	2.6
Sales	7.6	26.5	247.0	19.8
Other	3.1	7.4	137.8	4.5
Federal grants-in-aid	3.1	19.4	520.9	17.1
Fees and charges	3.1[a]	13.3	333.7	10.7
New debt issued	7.6[a]	18.9	149.0	11.9
Miscellaneous[b]	1.6	5.8	272.1	4.4

Sources: Bureau of the Census, *Governmental Finances in 1968–69;* Bureau of the Census, *Census of Governments: 1962, Historical Statistics.* All calculations are based on unrounded data.

a. Estimated.

b. Includes special assessments, sales of property, interest earnings, profits from liquor stores, and other miscellaneous earnings.

government does not substantially increase its contribution) and general administration. The gap between state and local revenues and expenditures for 1976 would thus be about $9.4 billion. In other words, even with no new responsibilities, state and local governments would need $9 billion to $10 billion more in revenues than they would be expected to have in order to meet their obligations.

This gap is not of huge proportions. It represents less than 4 percent of anticipated state and local expenditures in 1976. The gap could be filled by any one of the following alternatives or by some combination of them:

• An average annual increase of 1.2 percent in state and local tax rates.

• An increase of 21 percent in the size of established federal grants, over and above the level they would reach in 1976 as a result only of price and workload increases. This would imply a considerably smaller rate of growth in federal grants over this period than in the past five years.

• A general revenue sharing program of $9.4 billion, which would equal 1.7 percent of the federal personal income tax base (compared to the 1.3 percent proposed by President Nixon).

• Assumption by the federal government of 40 percent of the cur-

Table 6-3. State and Local Expenditures, by Function, and Revenues, by Source, Fiscal Year 1969, and Estimates, Fiscal Year 1976
Billions of dollars

	Expenditure	
Function	*1969 actual*	*1976 estimate*
Total	**134.1**	**261.1**
General expenditure	116.7	229.0
Local schools	33.8	59.5
Higher education and other education, except local schools	13.5	36.7
Public welfare	12.1	34.5
Highways	15.4	19.6
Hospitals and health	8.5	18.5
Basic urban services[a]	14.9	24.7
Administration and other[b]	18.5	35.5
Utility deficit	1.4	1.4
Debt retirement and additions to liquid assets[c]	12.0	23.1
Contributions to retirement systems	4.0	7.6

	Revenue	
Source	*1969 actual*	*1976 estimate*
Total	**134.1**	**251.7**
Taxes	76.7	133.0
Property	30.7	50.2
Individual income	8.9	22.0
Corporation income	3.2	6.2
Sales	26.5	43.5
Other	7.4	11.2
Federal grants-in-aid	19.4	45.4
Fees and charges	13.3	28.5
New debt issued	18.9	34.7
Miscellaneous[d]	5.8	9.9

Source: Authors' estimates. Figures are rounded and may not add to totals.
a. Includes fire protection, police protection, correction, sewerage, other sanitation, parks and recreation, housing and urban renewal, and transportation and terminals.
b. Includes administration and general control, general public buildings, interest on general debt, employment services, and miscellaneous functions.
c. Excludes assets of social insurance funds.
d. Includes special assessments, sales of property, interest earnings, profits from liquor stores, and other miscellaneous earnings.

rent state and local welfare burden, coupled with a federal program that financed all future increases in welfare costs.

If the aggregate gap is of such manageable proportions, why such concern about the state and local fiscal crisis? There are at least three reasons. Probably the most important is that the fiscal outlook of state and local governments is much more bleak in particular states and cities than it is in the aggregate. For the prosperous suburbs and the states without large urban centers, the outlook may be fairly promising. On the other hand, in areas with large low-income populations and in congested and deteriorating central cities, the situation is desperate and likely to get worse. While the overall growth in revenues should almost balance the expected rise in expenditures, much of the revenue increase will occur in jurisdictions where the built-in growth in expenditures is least. A second reason for the attention being paid to the fiscal crisis lies in the rising resistance to tax rate increases that states and localities are encountering. Some of this can undoubtedly be explained by the desire of citizens to protect themselves from inflation and recession. It is also probably true that resistance increases as the fraction of income devoted to taxes rises.

Finally, as was mentioned above, states and localities are currently suffering from the effects of recession and inflation. They find it hard to shield themselves from rapidly rising prices or declining revenues, or to see beyond the critical problem of meeting the next budget. Competition among jurisdictions for industry and high-income residents has also made states and localities reluctant to raise their taxes.

"Returning Power to People"

The second major argument for revenue sharing is political rather than fiscal. It is an argument for using revenue sharing to shift more decision-making power from the federal level to lower levels of government, thus turning power "back to the people," as the President put it in his Budget Message. The argument is that state and local governments, because they are responsible for smaller areas than is the federal government, are more attuned to local needs, more responsive to local demands, and better able to determine priorities and to administer certain kinds of programs effectively.

In recent years, the growing number and variety of federal grants-in-aid to state and local governments have greatly complicated the planning and budgeting tasks of those governments. Each federal grant has its own formulas, conditions, and cost-sharing arrangements. As a result, the services and operations of state and local governments have become increasingly contingent on decisions made in Washington. Especially in recent years, the problem has been compounded by uncertainties and delays in the federal budget process. Appropriations for grants-in-aid have frequently been passed by the Congress long after the beginning of the fiscal year to which they pertained.

The object of revenue sharing would be to increase the budgetary control and decision-making power of state and local governments. It would reduce the role of the federal bureaucracy and allow state and local officials more freedom to design programs to suit local conditions.

Counterarguments are also advanced. Many believe that state and local governments are *less* rather than more responsive to people. A smaller proportion of the eligible population votes in state and local than in national elections. In many cases, states and localities have long ignored pressing local problems even when they have had the financial capacity to deal with them. Furthermore, many groups—especially the poor, urban dwellers, blacks, and labor unions—have found the national government far more responsive to their needs over the years than are state and local governments. It is also alleged that legislatures, city councils, and state and local bureaucracies often display a low level of competence and are susceptible to corruption. Moreover, state and local governments may give relatively low priority to those programs that are considered to be in the national interest but that have relatively little payoff in the local area. For example, a state may do little to clean up the effluents its industries pour into a river if the downstream areas lie in another state; or it may make minimal efforts to educate groups that are likely to migrate from the state. Hence, whether one favors general revenue sharing over increases in grants-in-aid or the assumption by the federal government of certain state and local functions depends at least in part on one's view of (1) the potential for improvement in state and local governing capacity and (2) the extent to which national and state and local interests converge.

The objective of giving more resources to state and local governments without the federal interference or the uncertainty involved in the grant-in-aid process might be accomplished by turning over tax sources to state and local governments, or returning some of the proceeds of federal taxes to the jurisdictions in which they were collected. This procedure would have many of the advantages of revenue sharing and one important disadvantage: rich states would get back a lot and poor states only a little.

Redistribution of Resources

Revenue sharing would have two kinds of redistributive effects. To the extent that it substituted for more revenues raised by state and local governments, revenue sharing would shift the burden of paying for government services from lower- to higher-income groups, and from lower- to higher-income states.

The federal income tax is a progressive tax. Persons with very low incomes pay nothing, while the taxes paid on additional income rise quite steeply as income increases. Despite all its loopholes and inequities, the personal income tax probably reflects ability to pay better than does any other tax on the books. State and local taxes, by contrast, are often regressive. Sales taxes fall heavily on low-income persons, who must spend a high proportion of their incomes for taxable goods. The impact of property taxes is less certain, but some part of the burden is undoubtedly reflected in the rents low-income people pay. Even state and local personal income taxes are generally less progressive than the federal income tax; in a number of cases they are simply a flat percentage of personal income above a minimum level.

If revenue sharing were substituted for state and local taxes that would otherwise be collected to support the same expenditures, the effect would generally be favorable to lower-income groups. The same effect could be achieved, of course, by encouraging state and local governments to shift to more progressive forms of taxation. For example, a tax credit that allowed individuals to deduct a portion of state and local income taxes from their federal income tax liability would encourage state and local governments to use the income tax, since part of the resulting revenue would mean a reduction in the federal tax take rather than an additional burden on their own taxpayers.

A tax credit is an indirect way for the federal government to share its income tax revenues with state and local governments. But it would not be likely to have the same effect on a particular state as would a general revenue sharing system, since the impact of the credit would depend to an important degree on the state's present taxing arrangements and the changes that would result from adoption of the credit system. Moreover, the tax credit would not serve to redistribute resources among the states.

Unlike tax credits, revenue sharing would reduce existing disparities in the ability of states to respond to social needs by offsetting part of the difference in their fiscal capacities. Revenue collected through the federal income tax would be distributed under revenue sharing in accordance with some indicator of the state's need for public services. Need might be measured by population (as in the administration's proposal) or by some other measure giving additional weight to the special needs of low-income or highly urbanized states. Even a simple per capita distribution would help the low-income states considerably. Any dollar amount per person would have a greater value for a poor state, which would have to impose higher tax rates than would a richer state to obtain an equivalent amount through its own revenue system. Also, any given amount of shared revenue would typically yield more purchasing power in the poorer states than elsewhere, because the wages and salaries of their public employees are generally below the national average. Furthermore, while all state and local governments, rich and poor, would receive funds under revenue sharing, the federal *taxpayers* in rich states would be paying more than their governments were receiving back. This is, of course, the inevitable consequence of any redistributive plan. It is impossible to redistribute so that everyone gains.

In weighing the various arguments for and against revenue sharing, one should bear in mind that the proposals under discussion envision relatively small amounts. Five billion dollars represents only 3.8 percent of total state and local expenditures in 1970. This amount could hardly transform the behavior or fiscal health of these governments, either for better or for worse. Of course the size of the general revenue sharing plan could expand markedly, once the idea had been accepted.

Major Issues

At least four sets of questions must be answered in designing a revenue sharing plan, in addition to the overriding question whether revenue sharing is a good idea.

1. *How much revenue should be shared?* The desirable size of a revenue sharing plan bears no necessary relation to the anticipated gap between state and local expenditures and revenues at present tax rates. As was pointed out above, one might decide to fill all or part of this gap by other means. Alternatively, one might decide that it was desirable to overfill the gap, allowing state and local governments to reduce their dependence on property and sales taxes and shift a larger

part of the burden to the federal income tax. The decision depends partly on the priority given to state and local expenditures and partly on the degree to which it is considered desirable to finance those expenditures from federal rather than from state or local funds.

2. *What restrictions should be placed on the use of these funds?* Should there be no strings at all, except for routine audits and enforcement of the civil rights laws? Should some uses of the funds—for example, highway building—be excluded on the ground that they are already well financed by the federal government? Or should an attempt be made to use revenue sharing to compel states and localities to modernize their governments, or at least to show evidence that they are engaging in serious planning for the use of the funds? In considering such restrictions, it should be remembered that the mere statement in the law of a limitation on uses of funds would have little actual effect. To tell a state that it could not use the revenue grant for highway construction might simply mean that it would use the grant for some other program that it was formerly supporting and transfer to highways the funds thereby released.

3. *How should the revenues shared be distributed among the states?* The simplest method would be to distribute the revenues on the basis of population, on the ground that population is a reasonable index of the need for government services in a state. One can argue, however, that population does not adequately reflect true needs—that states with high concentrations of urban populations or states with many poor persons have special needs that are not reflected in the population figure. In addition to need, it can be argued that the distribution formula should also reflect the effort being made by the state itself. Effort might be measured by expressing taxes (or total revenue from own sources) as a percentage of personal income in the state. At present, the states vary tremendously in their effort. New York's self-raised revenues are equivalent to 15.3 percent of total personal income in the state; Connecticut's are only 10.1 percent. The effort factor in a formula would serve to encourage states to maintain or increase their tax levels, rather than merely substitute federal funds for their own. Moreover, particular kinds of taxes (like income taxes) could be weighted more heavily in the effort formula if it were thought desirable to encourage the states and localities to rely more heavily on them.

4. *How should the shared revenues be distributed within states?*

Giving revenues to state governments would not necessarily aid localities. Hence, it is argued, a revenue sharing plan should require states to "pass through" part of the shared revenues to local governments to relieve their fiscal burdens. Since different states share functions with their local governments in different ways, finding an appropriate pass-through formula would be difficult. Which local governments should share the funds? Should they be *all* local governments or only general purpose governments (excluding special purpose governments, such as school or drainage districts)? Or should the pass-through be limited to large municipalities, which are assumed to have particularly difficult problems? If so, how large is "large"? Once it is decided who should share, how should the share be determined? Should the funds be divided in proportion to the revenues that the localities have raised themselves? Should indexes of need (such as density or size of low-income population) be introduced? Or should these matters be left for the individual states and localities themselves to decide?

Alternative Proposals

President Nixon is the first chief executive to propose revenue sharing to the Congress. The revenue sharing idea is not new, however. It was widely discussed in the 1950s and 1960s, and dozens of revenue sharing bills have been introduced in the Congress by members of both parties. Senators Edmund S. Muskie and Jacob Javits, for example, have sponsored such bills, as have Representative Henry Reuss and Representative (now Secretary of Defense) Melvin Laird.

The presidential candidates of both major parties endorsed the concept of revenue sharing in their campaigns in 1968. In 1964, at the urging of Walter W. Heller, then chairman of the Council of Economic Advisers, President Johnson appointed a task force on revenue sharing, headed by Joseph A. Pechman. The Heller-Pechman plan proposed that 2 percent of the federal income tax base be distributed to the states on the basis of population, revenue effort, and income. Although this plan never received administration endorsement, it did arouse considerable discussion in the press and on Capitol Hill. In 1968 the "Douglas Commission" (the National Commission on Urban Problems, headed by former Senator Paul H. Douglas) recommended revenue sharing as one of a series of measures to relieve the plight of major cities. In 1969 the Advisory Commission on Intergovernmental Relations (ACIR), composed of representatives from the local, state, and federal levels, recommended a revenue sharing bill.

President Nixon's first revenue sharing proposal was sent to the Congress in September 1969. It called for sharing a fraction of the federal income tax base with the states and localities, on the basis of both population and revenue effort. The bill was referred to the House Ways and Means Committee, headed by Representative Wilbur D. Mills, a skeptic of the revenue sharing concept. The committee held no hearings on the subject during the Ninety-first Congress.

In his State of the Union and Budget Messages in January 1971, the President gave top priority to revenue sharing. A new and more ambitious general revenue sharing bill was submitted by the administration and was again referred to the Ways and Means Committee. Chairman Mills, though repeating his opposition to revenue sharing, has promised to hold hearings on the measure.

These various revenue sharing proposals differ in the answers they give to the four questions listed above. Some of the differences are discussed briefly below.

The Administration Proposals

The latest administration proposal would earmark an amount equal to 1.3 percent of taxable personal income for allocation to the states. The 1972 budget assumes that the program would begin in October 1971 and would cost about $3.75 billion. It is estimated that the first full-year cost would be $5.0 billion, rising to about $6.5 billion by fiscal 1976.

Funds would be allocated to states on the basis of population and revenue effort (taxes, fees and charges, and so on). Within states, the shared revenue would be divided into two parts, one to be kept by the state (or distributed to localities as it saw fit), the other to go to local governments. The local share would bear the same ratio to the total that locally raised revenue bears to total state and local revenue from sources within the state. (In determining the total local share, all local revenue would be taken into account, including that raised by special purpose governments, such as school districts, although the latter would not actually receive any of the funds passed through.) Once the local share was determined, it would be divided among all *general purpose* local governments in proportion to their revenue from their own sources.

The states would be encouraged, however, to develop a different pass-through formula better suited to local conditions. The statutory formula just described would be used to allocate only 90 percent of the funds due each state. The balance would be held back until an individual state could work out an alternative formula agreeable to a majority of the governments (representing a majority of the population).

In contrast to some other proposals, the current administration bill would give no special consideration to states with particularly low income or to cities with particularly large populations. It would not directly help school districts or other special purpose governments. Indeed, it might encourage the amalgamation of these units with general purpose governments. It would pass through a relatively large portion of the funds (about 48 percent) to local governments, but this local share would have to be divided among all general purpose governments with a population of 2,500 or more. It is estimated that 38,000 local units might be entitled to some funds.

Douglas Commission Proposal

The Douglas Commission also proposed earmarking a portion of the federal income tax base for revenue sharing, but it left the exact percentage open. No restrictions would be placed on the use of the funds by recipient governments. The funds would be distributed to the states on the basis of population and tax effort. In measuring effort, double weight would be given to state income tax revenue in order to encourage this form of taxation.

The commission, whose concern was urban problems, was not content to let the states decide what funds to pass through to local governments. It recommended direct allocation by the federal government to "major municipalities and urban county governments" (cities with at least 50,000 inhabitants and counties with 50,000 or more, at least half of whom lived in "urban areas" as defined by the Census Bureau). The formula suggested by the commission for determining these allocations emphasized the special needs of large cities. Each city and urban county with a population of at least 100,000 would be entitled to a share of the entire statewide amount equal to twice its proportion of all state–local tax collections, and cities and urban counties of between 50,000 and 100,000 persons would be aided on a scaled-down basis. Fewer than 900 cities and counties would be aided in this way. Each state government would be entitled to the balance of the statewide allocation remaining after provision for the direct payments to major local governments. Under this formula it was estimated that nearly two-thirds of all the shared revenues would go to state governments, about 22 percent to major cities, and about 13 percent to major urban counties.

The ACIR Proposal

The Advisory Commission on Intergovernmental Relations tied together in a single bill both revenue sharing and tax credits for state and local income taxes. To encourage state and local taxation of personal income, individuals would be allowed a credit on their federal income tax for 40 percent of state and local income taxes paid. The revenue sharing part of the proposal also encouraged state income taxation. The amount of shared federal revenue would be equal to 1 percent of taxable personal income plus one-fourth of the preceding year's personal income tax collections by all states.

Funds would be distributed to states on the basis of population and effort. The ACIR adopted the Douglas Commission approach to the distribution of funds to local governments, with certain changes. Funds for local governments would not be paid directly by the federal government, but would "pass through" the states. All counties of more than 50,000 population would share—not just those that were more than half urban (as in the Douglas Commission proposal). There would be a bonus for cities and urban counties with more than 100,000 inhabitants similar to that suggested by the Douglas Commission. In addition, states would be required to share some of their funds with school districts. A provision was made for states, if they wished, to devise an alternative pass-through formula better suited to their individual needs. To be acceptable, however, such a formula would have to provide more money for local governments than would the statutory formula, or have the explicit support of a majority of the affected cities and counties (including those that would be due at least half of the funds under the statutory formula).

The Reuss-Humphrey Plan

In 1969, Representative Henry Reuss submitted a bill to use revenue sharing as a means of bringing about reform in state and local government. A somewhat altered version, co-sponsored by Senator Hubert Humphrey, was introduced in January 1971.

The Reuss-Humphrey bill would not tie the amount of shared revenue to the federal income tax. It would simply authorize the appropriation of $3 billion for fiscal 1972, which would rise in $2 billion increments to $9 billion for 1975. These sums would be divided among the states on the basis of population and revenue effort, but within states the division would be left to state law. However, states that were able to secure agreement to the division from counties and municipalities having a majority of the state's population would get a 10 percent bonus for so doing.

The unique feature of the Reuss-Humphrey bill is that in order to receive funds in the second and subsequent years, each state would have to file a "master plan and timetable for modernizing State–local government." This plan would include a description of the state's intentions with respect to (1) interstate cooperation on regional problems, (2) reform of state government (including such details as shortening the ballot, paying legislators "adequately," and revising state aid formulas), and (3) strengthening local government (consolidating small units, improving property tax administration, raising limits on borrowing, and so on). The bill does not specify how the state should solve these problems. The idea is to focus public attention on them and to use revenue sharing, in Reuss's words, as a "catalyst to bring about State–local governmental reform, not a crutch to allow the states to hobble along as they have."

Poverty-related Revenue Sharing

This brief survey of several of the major revenue sharing proposals in no way exhausts the supply of plausible general revenue-sharing plans. For example, one object of revenue sharing might be to help states and localities that are burdened with large concentrations of low-income persons. The rationale is that the poor, while needing special public services, are unable to contribute appreciably to the support of government services. Middle-income residents of jurisdictions with large poor populations must either accept a low level of public services or bear the costs of providing adequate services for those who are unable to pay. Faced with such a choice, the middle-income families too often have abandoned the poor by moving to a community where incomes are more like their own.

One way that has been proposed to alleviate this situation is to provide states and localities with grants equal to a fixed fraction of the particular government's per capita expenditures (financed from its own sources) on public services, multiplied by the number of low-income residents in the jurisdiction. Such a compensatory public service grant would concentrate shared revenues in the central cities, rural areas, and the southern states, bypassing many of the more affluent suburbs. It would also give relatively more aid to states that had high costs or spent comparatively large amounts on public services.

"Federalization" of Welfare

The federal assumption of state and local welfare costs is frequently suggested as an alternative to general revenue sharing. The reasoning behind it is that since rising welfare costs are a major element in the state and local fiscal burden, federal assumption of these costs would release state and local funds for other purposes and thus have much the same effect as revenue sharing.

There are several ways in which welfare might be "federalized." A simplistic approach would be for the federal government to take over the administration and full funding of those public assistance programs for which it now provides partial funding—that is, aid to the blind and the disabled, old age assistance, and aid to families with dependent children (AFDC). Since the state and local share of these programs in fiscal 1972 will be about $4.5 billion, federal assumption of this burden would *in the aggregate* provide more relief to state and local treasuries than would the administration's revenue sharing proposal. This fiscal relief, however, would be highly concentrated in a few states with large welfare caseloads and relatively high benefits. New York and California would get 39 percent of the total, while these two states together with Florida, Illinois, Massachusetts, Michigan, New Jersey, and Pennsylvania would account for more than 69 percent. Moreover, the division of the welfare burden between state and local governments varies widely. In some states, such as California, New York, New Jersey, and Wisconsin, local taxpayers pay a significant part of welfare cost. In many others, however, welfare is primarily or entirely state financed. In twenty-two states, the localities contribute less than 1 percent of the cost of welfare. Federal assumption of welfare burdens in these states, therefore, would not automatically benefit localities unless some "pass through" were specified in the law.

Moreover, a federal takeover of existing welfare programs is infeasible because of the tremendous differences that now exist in welfare benefit levels among states. It would not be considered equitable (perhaps not even constitutional) to run a federal welfare system in which AFDC recipients in Mississippi received $12 per person per month while those in New York received $78, as was the case in 1970. If the system were to be completely federal, benefit levels would have to be uniform or at least related to some objective factor, like the cost of living or prevailing wages in the community. If the federal government set a relatively high national welfare benefit (comparable to levels prevailing in New York), the cost would far exceed the fiscal relief that would be provided to the states and localities.

A more feasible approach would be to put a federal floor under welfare payments at a relatively low level and either allow or require the states whose present welfare benefits are higher to supplement the federal payments. This is essentially the approach adopted by the administration in its Family Assistance Plan (FAP), which is discussed in Chapter 8. FAP would go part of the way toward reducing the geographic disparities in benefit levels, but it would provide only limited relief to state and local governments (about $600 million in the first year) through a provision that would hold state and local welfare contributions to 90 percent of their present level.

The enactment of FAP, however, could be viewed as a first step toward federalizing welfare. If the basic benefit were raised from $1,600 to a more adequate level, geographic disparities in welfare benefits would be reduced. The state contribution to welfare programs could also be eliminated over a period of years. For example, states could be required to spend 90 percent of present levels this year, 80 percent next year, and so on. If this general approach is followed, two important questions will have to be resolved: (1) Should states with benefits above the federal floor be required to maintain their present benefit levels? And (2) should the federal government share the cost of supplementary programs in states whose benefits are already above the federal floor? The administration's proposal for FAP answers both questions in the affirmative. Maintenance of current levels would be required, and 30 percent of the cost of state supplemental programs would be paid by the federal government. An alternative version of FAP, leading more quickly to a uniform national system, would raise the federal floor to a higher level (say, $2,400 for a family of four), but would leave the states free to set any level of benefits above the federal floor, at their own expense. This version would provide more fiscal relief for the states, but might result in reduced benefits for welfare recipients in states already above the federal floor.

As an agenda for welfare reform, some version of FAP has considerable appeal (see Chapter 8), but it would not accomplish the same objectives as would revenue sharing. Since the per capita amounts spent for welfare in the poorer states—especially in the South—are relatively small, no scheme for federalizing welfare would bring much relief to the treasuries of those states. Some other form of revenue sharing, such as the administration proposal or a compensatory public service grant, would be necessary to accomplish this purpose.

State Distributions

These various approaches to revenue sharing would affect individual states in radically different ways. This point is illustrated in Table 6-4, in which per capita distributions by state are compared for three proposals: (1) the administration's general revenue sharing proposal, which would distribute the funds on the basis of population and revenue effort; (2) a compensatory public service grant, which would distribute funds according to the size of the low-income population and state and local expenditures per capita; and (3) "federalization" of welfare, that is, payment by the federal government of what states and localities spent on federally aided public assistance programs in fiscal 1972.

Federalization of welfare would save state and local governments $4.5 billion in the aggregate. But California and the District of Columbia would receive over nine times as much per capita as the two lowest states, South Carolina and Indiana. In contrast, a plan that distributed $5 billion according to the number of poor in the state, weighted by the per capita expenditures on public services, would generally aid southern states such as Louisiana and Mississippi. While the rich industrial states, like New York and California, would not receive a large amount over all, the bulk of the aid they received would be concentrated in the poor rural counties and central cities of the states. Under the administration's proposal a number of states with low population densities, such as Wyoming, New Mexico, and North

Table 6-4. Per Capita Distribution of Fiscal Relief to States under the Administration's General Revenue Sharing Proposal Compared with Compensatory Public Service Grants and Federal Assumption of Public Assistance, by State, Fiscal Year 1972

	Fiscal relief per capita, in dollars		
State	*Administration's revenue sharing proposal*	*Compensatory public service grants*	*Federalized public assistance*[a]
Alabama	23.77	36.26	10.08
Alaska	28.05	30.83	36.29
Arizona	33.88	27.73	14.40
Arkansas	22.73	33.23	8.53
California	29.69	28.00	53.35
Colorado	26.84	23.60	20.25
Connecticut	19.54	14.47	19.43
Delaware	24.44	40.17	13.87
District of Columbia	24.34	36.79	54.06
Florida	23.62	27.68	24.27
Georgia	22.83	31.45	10.46
Hawaii	29.44	25.82	25.76
Idaho	27.24	24.79	9.68
Illinois	19.98	18.82	23.19
Indiana	22.30	18.81	5.85
Iowa	26.45	24.13	17.14
Kansas	24.66	24.12	14.82
Kentucky	24.57	27.58	9.07
Louisiana	28.69	44.00	15.35
Maine	23.24	28.21	17.46
Maryland	23.66	19.30	15.04
Massachusetts	24.15	18.28	37.48
Michigan	25.89	22.40	21.90
Minnesota	28.06	23.39	18.08
Mississippi	28.17	45.22	7.35
Missouri	21.11	25.74	11.44
Montana	27.73	26.65	7.63
Nebraska	25.60	25.96	8.70
Nevada	27.06	25.15	6.75
New Hampshire	20.38	13.62	17.76
New Jersey	21.70	16.50	28.95
New Mexico	31.71	40.69	14.09
New York	29.60	28.53	38.49
North Carolina	22.12	27.73	7.16
North Dakota	33.55	36.24	7.45
Ohio	20.18	18.07	11.43
Oklahoma	25.23	30.62	18.33
Oregon	27.26	19.10	17.07
Pennsylvania	21.19	18.83	24.40
Rhode Island	22.13	17.10	24.29
South Carolina	21.62	26.60	3.44
South Dakota	29.22	30.82	9.77
Tennessee	21.38	28.76	9.81
Texas	21.64	22.40	8.49
Utah	27.29	18.37	9.82
Vermont	26.87	25.65	15.30
Virginia	22.46	27.40	8.58
Washington	27.21	19.55	22.35
West Virginia	24.55	34.83	10.66
Wisconsin	28.42	19.26	9.80
Wyoming	35.22	25.38	8.72

Source: Authors' estimates. See text for discussion of the proposals.

a. Estimate of state and local spending on categorical public assistance programs in fiscal year 1972.

Dakota, would receive the most money per capita, while a number of highly urban states, such as Connecticut, Illinois, and Ohio, would gain the least.

Finally, it should be obvious that revenue sharing, like any other government program, is not free. Taxes would have to be increased or other federal expenditures reduced to provide the necessary funds. Hence, on balance, residents of some states would gain, and residents of other states would lose, depending on how the funds necessary to finance revenue sharing were made available, as well as on how they were spent.

7. Special Revenue Sharing

IN CONTRAST to general revenue sharing, which would provide substantial new funds for state and local governments, the special revenue sharing proposals involve primarily a restructuring of current programs. Under the administration's plan, 130 existing aid programs would be consolidated into six major grants covering urban community development, rural community development, education, manpower training, transportation, and law enforcement.

Several features are common to all six of the special revenue sharing programs:

1. Recipient governments would not be required to provide matching funds or to maintain their current level of expenditures on these programs in order to obtain their grant.

2. Each of the six grants would be distributed among the states and localities by a formula (or formulas) established in law, and recipients would be free to spend the money on virtually any type of activity falling within a broad definition of the purpose of the grant, so long as civil rights laws were adhered to.

3. For the first year at least, all governmental units would be "held harmless"—that is, no state or locality would obtain less from each of the new formula grant programs than it previously received from the categorical grants that were consolidated to form each special revenue sharing category.

Why Special Revenue Sharing?

At present the federal government provides aid to state and local governments through more than 500 specific (or, as they are commonly called, "categorical") grant programs. These programs distribute funds either according to set formulas, as in the case of educational aid for disadvantaged children (under Title I of the Elementary and Secondary Education Act), or upon approval of a specific application for assistance, as for urban renewal or model cities. In some cases the grants require that the states and localities provide matching funds; in other cases they do not. Advocates of special revenue sharing argue that this system is overcentralized, strangling in its own red tape, and needlessly restrictive.

The confusion that engulfs today's grant system stems largely from the rapid proliferation of these programs over the past decade. Some grants partially duplicate others. Grants for similar purposes are often handled by several different agencies with little coordination among them. Potential recipients are often unaware even of the existence of certain grants for which they are eligible. A number of states and cities have gone so far as to set up special offices devoted solely to finding out what grants are available and applying for some of them. Others have turned to private consulting firms that specialize in selecting grants from the cluttered federal menu. Despite these efforts, an element of inequity remains for those less adept at grantsmanship.

From the viewpoint of state and local officials, another aspect of the present system is exceedingly troublesome. Most grant programs prescribe detailed procedures for applicants and have voluminous requirements and regulations to which grant recipients must adhere. Applications involve hundreds of steps. The forms designed to ensure compliance with federal laws are long, complicated documents that require experts to decipher. This maze of red tape causes inordinately long delays before projects are approved and introduces major uncertainties into the system.

In addition, many grants require that state and local governments share some of the costs of the federally assisted program, further injecting federal influence into the budgeting of state and local funds. All too often, federal officials in an agency with large grants to distribute deal directly with their bureaucratic counterparts in state or local governments, undercutting the authority of mayors and governors and weakening their control over their own budgets.

Proponents argue that the conversion of 130 of these specific programs into six broad categories would substantially reduce the problems associated with the present system. Confusion and duplication among numerous grant programs would be lessened; many regulations and much red tape would disappear; and within each of the six major areas, governors and mayors could spend the federal funds on the problems *they* regarded as most pressing.

But there is another side to the story. The current system of highly specific grants reflects an effort on the part of the federal government to direct the expenditure of funds toward purposes serving an explicit national goal. Legal services for the poor are supported by specific grants because the Congress believed that the poor needed legal assistance they were unlikely to get from state or local governments. Similarly, special grants for family planning services reflect congressional intent to give family planning higher priority than it was likely to be accorded at the state and local level. Moreover, through project-type grants, the federal government has been able to concentrate funds on large, specific projects, such as mass transit systems in metropolitan areas, which would not have received similarly concentrated funds through grants thinly spread throughout the nation by a statutory formula. The division of federal grants into numerous watertight compartments has undoubtedly been carried too far. But removing most of the compartments would reduce the federal government's ability to employ state and local governments as agents for the achievement of national objectives.

Similarly, many of the restrictions and regulations governing the use of federal grants sprang from a deliberate attempt to achieve a particular national purpose. There are scores of examples: desegregation provisions in education grants; requirements that urban highway decisions take into account the neighborhood impact; provisions to ensure that decent housing is found for low-income residents displaced by urban renewal; and regulations seeking to channel educational grant funds for disadvantaged children to the benefit of those children, rather than to the relief of local school budgets. While the red tape, regulations, and manipulation of state and local budgets that characterize current federal grant-in-aid programs reflect excessive proliferation and the zeal of bureaucracy, they also reflect deliberate policy choices by past administrations and congresses.

The matching requirements, which would be eliminated under the special revenue sharing programs, also have a purpose. The benefits of public programs often extend beyond the boundaries of a single political jurisdiction. A waste treatment plant constructed by one locality benefits the citizens of downstream communities. The provision of high quality elementary and secondary education to young people who move out of the community after high school yields public benefits primarily to the communities into which those people move rather than to the communities that paid the costs of schooling. More generally, if states and localities were to make expenditure decisions solely on the basis of the benefits accruing to their own citizens, they would often spend less on certain programs than the national interest warrants. By effectively reducing the price of a particular service to the state or community, federal grants with matching requirements induce the recipient governments to spend more on activities of the "national interest" type than they would if they considered only the costs and benefits accruing to their own residents.

Alternative Approaches to Reform

Proposals for improving the complex federal system of grants-in-aid may be placed along a spectrum. At one end lie technical suggestions for simplifying, consolidating, and streamlining the system, while retaining many of the instruments by which the federal government seeks to influence the behavior of state and local governments. At the opposite end lie those more fundamental proposals for change that would transfer a great deal of decision-making power from the federal to state and local governments.

The technical approach to grant simplification could encompass a variety of changes in current procedures. Existing grant programs could be reviewed to determine which are overlapping and duplicative, which regulations and red tape are unnecessary to achieve federal purposes, and which programs could be combined into broader categories, with the federal government still able to influence how grant funds are spent by state and local governments. Some individual programs in education, for example, might be consolidated (while retaining many of the present controls) simply on grounds that the current excessive categorization serves no valid federal purpose. Or existing categorical grant programs could be retained, but with governors and mayors allowed some discretion in shifting funds from one category to another, so long as they met the requirements of each program they selected. Application procedures could be streamlined and regulations pared down to those that served important federal purposes. All of these changes would bring technical improvements while retaining some substantive federal control.

The alternative approach would involve political and philosophical issues. To what extent can and should the federal government seek to influence state and local spending decisions? Should the federal role be primarily to provide financial assistance without any effort to determine how the funds are spent? Are there national objectives to be sought through grants-in-aid in specific fields, such as elementary education and urban development, or is the national objective primarily to help local governments to achieve their own objectives?

In answering these questions, few would choose the extreme of either complete federal dominance or the removal of all controls in federal aid programs. However, various proposals for improving the current state of federal grant-in-aid programs can be distinguished by the emphasis they give to one side of the choice or the other. The administration's special revenue sharing programs clearly belong to the class of proposals that would transfer substantial decision-making authority to state and local governments.

Although the two approaches are separated by major differences, the complexities of the real world would ultimately bring about results that are somewhat closer to the middle than to either end of the spectrum. Those who would maintain the federal government's influence over state and local spending should recognize that despite all the federal rules, regulations, and formulas, state and local governments are able by one device or another to divert federal grants partially to their own purposes. Indeed, as time passes and recipients increase their understanding of new programs, their ability to divert grant funds increases, leading to more complex and detailed regulation as federal officials seek to keep ahead of them. That is why regulations tend to burgeon. On the other side, even if most federal controls were removed from grant programs and decision-making powers were transferred to state and local governments, new national problems would continue to emerge and particular groups would go on seeking explicit federal aid. Along with general and special revenue sharing grants would grow a new series of categorical grants with specific federal regulations, competing with revenue sharing for budgetary funds. Moreover, while special revenue sharing may initially have seemed quite simple in concept, the problems encountered in developing the six specific programs resulted in a set of proposals that already are highly complex in their distributional formulas, "hold harmless" provisions, pass-through allowances, regulatory requirements, and reporting procedures. This is clear from the summary of the main features of the six programs presented below.

The Six Programs

The full details of the six proposed special revenue sharing programs have yet to be worked out. However, it is possible to sketch a rough picture of them from information contained in the 1972 budget and the several presidential messages on the subject.

Urban Community Development

The urban community development fund would consolidate the four categorical grant programs administered by the Department of Housing and Urban Development (urban renewal, model cities, water and sewer facility grants, and rehabilitation loans). In 1973 the Community Action Program administered by the Office of Economic Opportunity would be merged with them. Eighty percent of the $2 billion that would be authorized for the first full year of the program would be divided among the nation's 243 standard metropolitan statistical areas (SMSAs), on the basis of a formula that would take account of population, housing conditions, the degree of overcrowding in the housing, and the number of families living below the poverty level. Within each SMSA, the same formula would be used to allocate a share of the funds to every city of more than 50,000 persons. In the first year of the program, any remaining funds would be used to ensure that no jurisdiction within the SMSA received less than it had been receiving in recent years (the "hold harmless" provision). If additional funds remained, they would be divided by HUD among the smaller governmental units within the SMSA or used to encourage areawide development activities. The 20 percent of revenue sharing funds not distributed to the SMSAs would be available to HUD to provide any additional financing needed for the "hold harmless" provision, and for funding "innovative" programs in urban areas.

Cities would be free to spend the money for any community development purpose allowed under the four original programs that were consolidated into the urban community development program. These include such activities as manpower training, sewer and water construction, rehabilitation of blighted areas, health centers, and adult education. While no formal application would be necessary, the federal government would require a general statement of how the recipient planned to spend the money.

Many federal grants are now distributed to state and local recipients under a formula specified by law. But this is not the case with any of the programs being consolidated into urban community development. Grants under these programs are currently distributed by HUD on the basis of applications from each community, often involving extensive negotiations with HUD. Through these negotiations HUD has sought, with mixed results, to influence the shape of urban development in recent years—for example, by emphasizing that low- and moderate-income housing should be part of urban renewal programs. Under the new special revenue sharing program, this kind of relationship would disappear. Perhaps more than in any other case, the urban special revenue sharing program would represent a significant transfer of federal decision-making power to local officials.

If the Community Action Program of OEO is merged with the urban community development program in 1973, as proposed by the administration, another element of decision-making power would be transferred to local officials. Perhaps the chief characteristic of the Community Action Program, particularly in its early days, was that it provided federal funds in poverty areas to community organizations that were often quite separate from the official local bureaucracy or political organization. As a consequence, the community action organizations injected a new element into publicly funded poverty programs—sometimes creative, sometimes disruptive, but almost always different from the traditional approach. These organizations have, in many cities, come increasingly under the influence of city officials, but they still retain some independence. If the funds for their programs are turned over to those officials, it is fairly predictable that in most cases these organizations will become a part of the local government.

Rural Community Development

The special revenue sharing proposal for rural community development would replace eleven programs now administered by the Departments of Commerce and Agriculture with a single program controlled by the secretary of agriculture. The main components of this group are the Appalachian regional program, the economic development assistance program, the agricultural extension service, the agricultural conservation program, and the rural water and waste disposal grant programs now administered by the Department of Agriculture. The $1 billion in funds now devoted to these separate programs would be divided among the states by a formula based on the number of rural inhabitants, the per capita income of these residents, and the rate of net out-migration from the rural areas of each state. There would be no mandatory pass-through of this money to local governments in rural areas. States would be required to spend the funds on programs of direct benefit to rural persons. Such activities might include subsidizing business firms for locating in rural areas, building sewer and water systems, financing agricultural extension services, or any of the general purposes now covered by the rural-oriented grant-in-aid programs. For the purposes of the programs, all counties that lie outside the nation's 243 SMSAs, plus those metropolitan counties that have fewer than 100 inhabitants per square mile, would be considered "rural."

Several programs now included in the new fund (the agricultural conservation and Great Plains conservation programs) do not provide grants-in-aid to state or local governments. The funds currently go directly to individual farmers. They would now be provided to state governments. The Appalachian regional program has channeled special development funds into Appalachia. One difficulty in securing acceptance of the new special revenue sharing program may be that after the first year, when the "hold harmless" provisions apply, the Appalachian states are likely to receive significantly less than they would under the existing grant system.

Education

The special revenue sharing program for education would consolidate the present grant programs for compensatory education for disadvantaged children, vocational training, programs for the handicapped, children of federal employees in impacted areas, school lunches, libraries, and a few other purposes. The total amount involved is $3 billion. It is doubtful, however, that the existing patterns of federal aid for elementary and secondary education would be significantly changed, since the proposed method of distributing the funds is in many respects the same as the present one.

One portion of this special revenue sharing grant would be distributed directly to school districts on the basis of the number of school children whose parents live on federal property located in each district. This subgrant would be similar to one part of the existing impacted aid program. Another portion, representing over half of the $3 billion total, would be earmarked for school districts with large concentrations of children from low-income families. As a condition for receiving this grant, districts would be required to demonstrate to the state administering agency that, out of their own funds, they provide educational services to low-income children comparable to those provided other children.

The balance of the $3 billion remaining after the allocations described above would be shared among states according to a formula that is based upon the size of their school age population and the number of children whose parents work but do not live on federal property. The amount each state received on the basis of its school age population would be earmarked in fixed proportions for programs benefiting handicapped children, vocational education, and support services (such as school lunch programs, libraries, purchases of textbooks, or support of the state planning agencies). The fraction of the grant deriving from children of federal employees would be devoted to educating these school children. A state could, however, transfer up to 30 percent of the funds designated for any one of the four program areas to any other one. States would also have a good deal of latitude in determining whether and how these funds were distributed to the school districts.

Most of the current federal grants for elementary and secondary education are distributed by formula, unlike the bulk of HUD's urban grants, which are based on the approval of specific applications. The proposed revenue sharing program would not significantly change this arrangement. The main departures would be (1) consolidation of many small grant programs (for equipment, school lunch programs, and so forth) into a larger category designated for support services, and (2) as yet unspecified provisions that would allow children in non-public schools to benefit from federal aid for support services, vocational education, and aid to the handicapped. Furthermore, states and school districts would be allowed greater flexibility in shifting funds among programs. But the part of the new program that distributed funds to school districts that provide comparable educational services to both upper- and lower-income groups would undoubtedly generate substantial regulations and reporting requirements, probably at the state level.

Manpower Training

The manpower revenue sharing plan would replace the numerous categorical grants established under the Manpower Development and Training Act and the manpower provisions of the Economic Opportunity Act. In the first full year, the plan would have $2 billion in budgetary authority; however, when the unemployment rate exceeded 4.5 percent for three consecutive months, additional funds would automatically become available. The secretary of labor would distribute these extra funds to areas of high unemployment. Eighty-five percent of the regular grant would be divided among states, cities, and counties with populations of more than 100,000, using a formula based on the size of the labor force, the level of unemployment, and the number of low-income adults. Certain bonuses would be given to labor markets in which area-wide manpower programs were undertaken by a consortium of local governments.

The money could be used at the discretion of the recipients for a wide range of manpower-related activities, including education, on-the-job training, child care, aid in relocation, job counseling, recruitment and placement services, and *temporary* public service employment. Payments to any individual in this last category would be limited to two years, and the state or local government would have to satisfy the federal government that the public service jobs would be a transitional step toward better employment for the job holder.

Because its manpower training assistance funds are now divided among several kinds of training programs, the federal government through its budgetary allocations exercises some influence over who is trained (unemployed, skilled workers, the hard-core disadvantaged, the young) and over the kind of program (job creation, skill training, work experience). Basic decisions about these matters would be transferred to state and local governments under the special revenue sharing program.

Transportation

Twenty-three categorical aid programs would be combined to form the transportation special revenue sharing package. Although the interstate highway system is left out, the plan does encompass federal aid for other roads, the highway safety and beautification programs, and urban mass transit and airport grants.

On a full-year basis, $2.57 billion would be allocated. One-fifth of this ($525 million) would be designated as the mass transit capital investment element. Four-fifths of the mass transit money would be distributed to the states according to their share of the total U.S. population living in SMSAs with more than 1 million inhabitants. In turn, 50 percent of this money would have to be "passed through" from the states to local governments in these large SMSAs; the other 50 percent would also have to be spent in these SMSAs, but at the state's discretion. The remaining one-fifth of the mass transit funds would be allocated among the states according to each state's share of the nation's population living in SMSAs of less than 1 million population, with the states deciding how the funds should be used. Since there are thirty-three SMSAs with populations exceeding 1 million, the formula would allocate an average annual direct grant of $6.3 million to each, with another $6.3 million available for use in the area at the state's discretion.

The share of this program's funds for general transportation would be $2.04 billion. Ten percent of this would be spent at the discretion of the secretary of transportation. The remaining $1.8 billion would be divided into four parts, each to be distributed to the states under different criteria. Twenty-five percent would be allocated on the basis of population, 35 percent according to urban population, 20 percent by geographic area, and the remainder on the basis of star and rural postal route mileage. That part of each state's grant that is based on the distribution of urban population would have to be passed on to local governments within the state.

A major issue concerns the future of highway building under this plan. Currently, most roads (except the interstate highway system) are constructed under federal grant programs that require either 30 or 50 percent matching with state or local funds. The total federal contribution is determined largely by gasoline tax revenues deposited in the highway trust fund. But states may reduce their spending on highways when the matching requirements are eliminated under special revenue sharing. Road building would no longer appear cheap to those governments. On the other hand, state highway departments wield strong influence in most states and might be able to keep highway expenditures at a high level.

Some part of the funds for the general transportation program would be derived from the highway trust fund. Although the President's proposals spell out broadly how this portion would be determined, it is most unlikely that spending from the highway trust fund for interstate highways and for its share of the general transportation program would equal the large and growing trust fund revenues from gasoline taxes and the like (see Chapter 13). Would the remaining funds be spent on some new form of federal assistance to highway construction? No answer has yet been provided, though the President's special message on transportation revenue sharing did indicate that the money in the trust funds "would still go to achieve the general purposes for which the funds were established." More than $1 billion a year might depend on how this question is answered.

Law Enforcement

The special revenue sharing package dealing with law enforcement replaces a single grant-in-aid program created under the Omnibus Crime Control and Safe Streets Act of 1968. The first full-year budget authority would be $500 million. Fifteen percent of this amount would be awarded at the discretion of the Law Enforcement Assistance Administration. The remainder would be divided among the states on the basis of population. States would be required to pass through to localities the same proportion of their grants that the old program required. The major change is that several requirements would be removed under the new program. No longer would states and localities be expected to contribute some of their own funds. In fact, special revenue sharing money for law enforcement could be used as state matching funds for other related grant-in-aid programs. The need to secure prior federal approval of a comprehensive state law enforcement plan as a condition of receiving the grant would also be eliminated, as would several minor restrictions on the uses of the money.

The Implications of Special Revenue Sharing

Special revenue sharing is an important departure from the existing methods of helping states and localities through numerous categorical grants. On first thought, special revenue sharing would also seem to differ substantially from general revenue sharing, since in each of the six categories state and local governments would be required to spend the funds for the purpose specified (transportation, rural development, and so on). In practice, however, the difference may prove to be more apparent than real. As was pointed out in Chapter 6, a state government receiving federal money for transportation may indeed use it for transportation, but then transfer some of its own funds previously used for transportation to meet other needs— say, higher education. In this case, the federal transportation grant would really finance an increase in spending on education. The broader the grant and the fewer the restrictions, the more easily can the recipient governments treat federal grants as the equivalent of general revenues.

For this reason, the special revenue sharing grants are very close to general revenue sharing, with the difference that instead of one sum of money distributed under one formula, six sums would be distributed under a number of different formulas. In practice, each recipient would be fairly free to treat the money it received as general revenues, to spend as it saw fit. The special revenue sharing funds for education are perhaps a partial exception. As was explained earlier, part of these funds would be distributed to school districts (which in many states are separate from local governments), and the provisions governing their use seem to be more restrictive than those for the other five grants.

The total amount any state or local government would receive under combined general revenue sharing and special revenue sharing would depend on the six formulas adopted for special revenue sharing and the one for general revenue sharing, and on the total amounts available for distribution under each formula.

In these circumstances, allocating funds among the six special revenue sharing programs would be important not because it would determine how much was spent for each purpose—in practice the funds would be used for various purposes—but because each revenue sharing program would have a distribution formula favoring a particular set of governmental jurisdictions. For example, a community that was specially favored by the formula used in the urban community development grant would be interested in seeing the maximum amount of federal funds devoted to that category—not because it particularly wanted to use the grant for that purpose, but because the greater the proportion of the various federal revenue sharing appropriations allotted to the urban development category, the greater would be that community's share of the total funds to be distributed. Even if it wanted to use the added funds to increase its transportation outlays, the community would still press for an increase in the urban development fund because of its favored status under the distribution formula of that fund.

To some extent, therefore, six broad revenue sharing categories whose funds are distributed by separate formulas are equivalent to one general revenue sharing fund, with the additional characteristic that the overall distribution of that fund among various governments could change each year, depending not on a change in the formulas, but on the allocation of appropriations among the six special categories.

For this reason, enactment of the President's special revenue sharing proposals might have important side effects on the congressional process and the whole complex structure of lobbies and interest groups. Compared with the current situation, congressional appropriation decisions would be less important in determining *what* the funds were ultimately spent for, but critical in determining *who* got them.

The traditional political struggles over federal grant-in-aid appropriations reflect a combination of pressures, some based on functional interests (highways or education, for instance), and some based on regional and local interests (more money for New York or Mississippi). Over all, the President's proposals for revenue sharing, if enacted, could be expected to shift some of the attention of interest groups seeking funds for particular purposes from Washington to state capitals and major cities. In Washington, on the other hand, the struggle over the distribution of federal funds among the states, regions, and cities might well intensify.

8. Welfare and Family Assistance

ONE OF THE MOST IMPORTANT objectives of federal programs since the mid-1960s has been the reduction of poverty—improving the present well-being and future opportunities of low-income groups. The programs have been of two main types: (1) human investment programs designed to improve the future income of the poor through education, manpower training, job creation, and other means; and (2) programs to provide direct income support.

While the 1972 budget increases support for some human investment programs, its primary emphasis is on income support, continuing a trend begun several years ago. The budget makes clear that the administration has adopted an active "income strategy" in dealing with poverty. The major element in this strategy is welfare reform. The Family Assistance Plan (FAP), which failed to pass the Ninety-first Congress, is being re-introduced in the Ninety-second, with some minor modifications. FAP would put a floor under the incomes of all families with children, extending federal aid for the first time to working fathers with low earnings.

The plan itself has relatively small budgetary implications for fiscal year 1972, because even if it passes, it would not come into full operation until fiscal 1973. The budget indicates that FAP would increase outlays in fiscal year 1972 by $502 million, much of which would be for gearing up to administer the new program. The future implications of FAP, however, are extremely important. Moreover, even without FAP, welfare expenditures would rise rapidly in 1972. Federal grants to the states for public assistance are estimated to rise

172

from $5.6 billion in 1971 to $6.7 billion in 1972. Both of these esti-mates are probably too low. Supplemental appropriations will be nec-essary to meet the federal government's obligations, even under the current law.

This chapter first discusses the choices that the administration faced in designing its welfare reform proposal. Then the longer run ques-tions raised by the administration's strategy for welfare reform are considered: How far and how fast should the floor under incomes be raised? What implications would different levels have for the cost of income maintenance and the shape of the nation's distribution of income?

The Welfare Problem

Public assistance or "welfare" came under sharp criticism in the 1960s. It might fairly be said that no one was satisfied with it—neither taxpayers nor administrators nor recipients. Public assistance is a patchwork system never intended to be a major bulwark against poverty. It was set up in the 1930s, when the major strategies against poverty were job creation and social insurance. Public assistance was to provide help for certain categories of people who could not work and were not yet covered by social insurance. As social insurance grew, the need for public assistance was expected to diminish.

Public assistance is basically a state responsibility. States set stan-dards of need and administer the programs. The federal government matches what the states spend, according to a complex formula. As a result, benefit levels vary widely among states, with abysmally low levels prevailing in the South and more adequate levels generally existing in the North and West.

Public assistance is not a general program of aid to the poor. Fed-eral assistance is available only for certain categories of people—the blind, the aged, the permanently and totally disabled, and families with dependent children. Aid to families with dependent children (AFDC) was designed primarily for women with children but no husband. By amendment in 1962, the states were allowed to use federal funds to aid families with unemployed fathers, but only twenty-three states had chosen to do so by 1970. The families of em-ployed men are not eligible for assistance even though they may be poorer than the families covered by the program. Not only does this exclusion of the working poor seem unfair, but it creates incentives for men with low earnings to leave their families in order to make them eligible for welfare benefits.

Since the original emphasis in public assistance was on helping those who could not help themselves, recipients were subjected to strict means tests, and until 1967 all earnings were deducted from welfare payments. Since 1967, recipients have been allowed to retain part of their earnings without any reduction in benefits (they may keep the first $30 a month plus an allowance for work-related expenses and one-third of the rest), but they still have only a limited incentive to increase their earnings.

The expected decline in public assistance never took place. Despite prosperity and extensions of social insurance, public assistance outlays, especially for the AFDC program, climbed steadily and in the mid-1960s began shooting up rapidly. Between 1966 and 1970, total money payments for AFDC (federal, state, and local) rose from $1.8 billion to $4.8 billion, or by 27 percent a year. Most of the increases occurred in the large industrial states. A variety of factors contributed to the increase—rising numbers of broken families, more liberal standards of eligibility for welfare, increases in the proportion of eligible persons applying for benefits, migration from the South to the North and from rural to urban areas. Rising unemployment contributed to further rapid increases in 1970.

By the mid-1960s, there was wide agreement that something had to be done about welfare. Some critics focused on reducing the costs of welfare to the taxpayer, especially the state and local taxpayer. Others concentrated on improving the lot of the poor, reducing the perversities and inequities of the patchwork system, and substituting a less demeaning general system of income support for the needy.

The general dissatisfaction with welfare stimulated some recommendations for drastic change. One of the most appealing plans (the negative income tax) called for

- scrapping the present welfare categories,
- guaranteeing everyone a basic benefit that would vary only according to family size, and
- reducing the basic benefit by less than one dollar for each dollar earned (the percentage reduction is called the "marginal tax rate") in order to ensure incentives to work.

Thus, if the basic benefit were $2,400 for a certain size family and the marginal tax rate were 50 percent, then a family with $2,000 in earnings would have half of the earnings deducted from the basic benefit and would receive a welfare check for $1,400 ($2,400 less half of $2,000). Its total income would be $3,400 (earnings of $2,000 plus $1,400 from welfare). Families with higher earnings would receive lower welfare benefits. A family earning $4,800 (the "break-even point") would get no benefits.

Although a negative income tax would be simpler and more equitable than the present welfare system, it is very difficult to shift from one to the other. One of the biggest problems is the existence of large interstate differences in current public assistance benefits. If the basic benefit under the new system were set low, some of the persons presently covered would be worse off. If it were set high (that is, at the levels prevailing in states with relatively high welfare benefits), the cost of shifting to the new system would be extremely large, and many persons would be added to the welfare rolls.

The welfare reform plan proposed by President Nixon in August 1969 was a compromise between the present system and a general negative income tax. For the adult welfare categories (aged, blind, disabled) the present system would be retained, although the federal contribution would be increased. The big change would be for families with children. The existing aid to families with dependent children would be eliminated in favor of the new Family Assistance Plan, essentially a negative income tax for families with children, including for the first time the working poor.

What FAP Would Do

Under the Family Assistance Plan the federal government would put a floor under the incomes of families with children. The basic benefit would be $500 each for the first two persons in the family and $300 for each additional member. Thus, the basic benefit for a family of four would be $1,600. As an inducement to work and an allowance for work-related expenses, families could earn up to $60 a month ($720 a year) without any reduction in benefits. Their benefits would be reduced by 50 percent of earnings above that amount.

The new federal program would immediately raise benefits in the eight states where maximum payments are currently below $1,600 for a family of four. In most states, however, welfare payments are already above that amount. These states would be required to maintain supplementary programs for present recipients so that no one would be made worse off by the new law. The federal government would pay 30 percent of the cost of the supplementary programs. States making supplementary payments would be allowed to reduce these payments by two dollars for each three dollars the family earned. In addition, the food stamp program, which now provides a family of four with food price reductions worth about $864 a year, would be continued.

In its first full year of operation, the proposed reform would increase the federal cost of public assistance by about $3.8 billion (see Table 8-1). However, it would result in substantial savings to the states, probably about $400 million in the first year.

The most striking effect of FAP would be to extend income support to an entirely new group—the working poor. As may be seen in

Table 8-1. Comparison of Estimated Full-year Cost of the Family Assistance Plan and the Current Welfare System, by Level of Government and Program, Fiscal Year 1972
Billions of dollars

Level of government and program	Total cost under Family Assistance Plan[a]	Cost of current welfare system	Net cost of Family Assistance Plan
Federal government	**16.1**	**12.3**	**3.8**
Payments to families with children	5.0	3.7	1.3
State fiscal relief[b]	0.6	...	0.6
Adult categories	2.5	2.1	0.4
Day care and training	0.9	0.3	0.6
Administration	0.7	0.4	0.3
Medicaid[c]	4.0	3.8	0.2
Food stamps[d]	2.4	2.0	0.4
State and local governments	**4.1**	**4.5**	**−0.4**
Payments to families	2.8	3.1	−0.3
Adult categories	1.3	1.4	−0.1
Total	**20.2**	**16.8**	**3.4**

Source: "Welfare Reform: Costs and Caseloads," Prepared by the Department of Health, Education, and Welfare for the House Committee on Ways and Means, 92 Cong. 1 sess. (February 1971; processed), Tables II-1, II-3, II-4.

a. Assuming 100 percent participation of persons eligible for the plan.

b. State fiscal relief results from a proposed 90 percent freeze on state expenditures, which would produce state savings, increasing with increased caseload over time, but would result in a net flow of funds from states to the federal government if FAP benefits are raised high enough to eliminate most of the state supplemental payments.

c. FAP would result in some increase in Medicaid coverage, but this would not occur if Medicaid is replaced by the proposed federal health insurance plan (see Chap. 11).

d. If approved, a simplified proposal for the cost of food stamps to be automatically deducted from welfare checks, with the stamps then sent directly to the client, will result in increased cost.

Table 8-2, it would alter drastically the composition of the beneficiary population. The present AFDC caseload is dominated by nonworking female heads of families. About half are black, but only 27 percent live in the South. The FAP population, in contrast, would be more than half male-headed families, predominantly working, predominantly white, and more heavily concentrated in the South, where wages are low.

The proposed reform would not extend aid to *all* poor persons. Individuals living alone or in families without children would still not be eligible for benefits unless they were aged, blind, or disabled.

Table 8-2. Distribution of Families under the Aid to Families with Dependent Children Program in 1969, and of Families Eligible for the Family Assistance Plan in 1972, by Selected Characteristics

	Percentage distribution	
Characteristic	*Aid to families with dependent children (2,400,000 families[a])*	*Family Assistance Plan (3,617,000 families)*
Sex of family head		
Male	18.2	50.1
Female	81.8	49.9
Race of family head		
White	49.3	61.4
Non-white	50.7	38.6
Region of residence		
Northeast	30.9	21.1
North central	19.8	20.3
South	26.8	42.7
West	22.5	15.9
Work experience of family head		
Worked full-time all year	7.8	30.9
Some work experience during year	10.1	37.0
No work during year	82.1	31.3
Military	0.0	0.9

Sources: Aid to families with dependent children: U.S. Department of Health, Education, and Welfare, National Center for Social Statistics, "Preliminary Report of Findings—1969 AFDC Study," NCSS Report AFDC-1(69) (March 1970; processed), Tables 28 and 29, and "Findings of the 1969 AFDC Study: Data by Census Division and Selected States," NCSS Report AFDC-3(69) (December 1970; processed), p. 2, and Tables 1 and 14; Department of Health, Education, and Welfare, *Social Security Bulletin*, Vol. 34 (March 1971), p. 53.

Family Assistance Plan: "Welfare Reform: Costs and Caseloads," Prepared by the Department of Health, Education, and Welfare for the House Committee on Ways and Means, Table VI-1.

a. Number of families receiving aid in October 1970.

The decision to exclude non-aged childless couples and unrelated individuals was made on purely budgetary grounds. The administration estimated that providing universal coverage under FAP would raise the number of recipients by some 4.5 million persons and increase net costs by almost $1 billion.

Dilemmas in the Design of FAP

Ideally, an income maintenance system would have three characteristics: (1) it would concentrate funds on those most in need, (2) it would treat people fairly and equitably, and (3) it would encourage people to work. Unfortunately, these objectives conflict; giving primary emphasis to one involves sacrificing the others, at least to some extent.

The present public assistance system was designed with primary emphasis on the first objective, assisting those most in need and least able to help themselves. It assigns people to categories based on the likelihood of their being able to work—the aged, the blind, the disabled, mothers with dependent children—and pays highest benefits to those presumed least able to work. The system has led to inequities, like the exclusion of the working poor, and disincentives, like a sharp reduction of benefits as other incomes rose. The main objective of FAP is to redress the balance by increasing equity and incentives to work.

By putting a floor under welfare benefits, FAP would narrow the disparity between high- and low-benefit states. It would thus reduce, but by no means eliminate, geographic inequities in the welfare system.

By extending aid to the working poor, FAP would reduce the disparities in treatment between families headed by males and those headed by females, but it would not eliminate them. In most states, a needy family with a female head would be eligible for supplementary benefits, while an equally needy family with a male head would be eligible only for FAP. The difference in yearly benefits might be as much as $2,000.

While it would make some major contributions toward reducing inequities, FAP would go only a small way toward improving work incentives. Families receiving FAP only would be allowed to retain the first $720 of annual earnings and half of all earnings above that without any reduction in benefits. Families also receiving supplementary benefits would be allowed to keep only one-third of their earnings above the first $720. Moreover, as is explained below, the effect of food stamps and other programs may be to reduce incentives still further.

Even these modest increases in equity and incentives would be bought at some sacrifice of the principle of concentrating funds on the neediest. Compare, for example, families of the same size in a state with no supplements, some earning outside income, others not. Since the basic benefit is $1,600 for a family of four and the marginal tax rate is 50 percent (the rate at which benefits are reduced as earnings rise), a family with earnings up to $3,920 would be receiving benefits. Another family of the same size, but with no earnings, would be struggling to live on $1,600. For the same total cost, one could design a program with a higher basic benefit and a higher marginal tax rate. Such a program would do more for the neediest families than would FAP, but it would reduce incentives to work.

In designing FAP the administration faced difficult choices. Raising the basic benefit would have several good results. It would get more money to the neediest families and further reduce the disparities among states and between families with male and those with female heads. Unless the marginal tax rate were raised, however, raising the basic benefit would raise the break-even point, adding more families to the recipient roles, and possibly discouraging some families with low earning capacity from working. Moreover, it would cost money. As is shown below, increasing the basic benefit by $100 would raise the cost of FAP by about $500 million. Further increases would cost more because of the increasing concentrations of families in the lower middle-income ranges.

Basic benefit level [1] (in dollars)	Payments to families with children (in billions of dollars)
1,600	4.3
1,700	4.8
1,800	5.2
2,200	7.7
2,400	9.4
3,000	14.4
3,600	22.3

1. Assumes that the FAP proportion of $500 for the first two members to $300 for additional members in the $1,600 plan is maintained at the higher benefit levels.

One could, of course, offset these cost increases by raising the marginal tax rate or by reducing the amount of earnings families are allowed to keep without any benefit reduction. For example, the cost of disregarding the first $720 in earnings is estimated at $840 million, an amount sufficient to cover the cost of raising the basic benefit by about $200. Alternatively, raising the marginal tax rate for all FAP recipients from 50 percent to 67 percent would free about $700 million to support a higher basic benefit. Actually the costs of this type of program are far more sensitive to changes in the marginal tax rate than to changes in the basic benefit. The net cost of a plan with a $2,000 basic benefit and a 50 percent marginal tax rate would be about the same as for a $2,400 basic benefit with a 70 percent tax rate. Similarly, the net cost of a $2,400 plan with a 30 percent tax rate would be almost as high as that of a $3,600 plan with a 50 percent tax rate.[2]

Both equity and incentives cost money. Any change in the basic benefit or the marginal tax rate involves a balancing of the three conflicting objectives: equity, incentive, and concentration on the neediest.

If it were possible to assign people to categories, based on whether or not they could be expected to work, some of the dilemmas could be avoided. A high basic benefit and a high marginal tax rate could be provided for those in the "nonworking" categories, where work incentives would be unimportant. A low basic benefit and a low marginal tax rate could be provided for the working categories. But, of course, this is precisely where the present system breaks down. Except for the obvious cases (the aged, the disabled), people cannot be so classified. And if benefits are different in the different categories, people have incentives to create situations which place them in a particular category.

Integration with Other Welfare Programs

Families in poverty are now eligible for a variety of cash and in-kind benefits that include federally supported welfare benefits, state-supported emergency and general assistance, Medicaid and Medicare, food stamps or commodity distribution, public housing, and supple-

2. Computed by Josephine Allen of the Urban Institute from U.S. Bureau of the Census, 1967 Survey of Economic Opportunity, updated to 1971.

mentary education programs. All of these are in some way based on need. Most of them are made available only to certain categories of persons (such as female-headed families) and denied to others in equal need. In some cases, net benefits are reduced gradually as income increases, giving rise to a "marginal tax" on earnings. In other programs, benefits are cut off entirely when income reaches a certain point, so that a person may suffer a severe and abrupt decline in total disposable income because he has earned an additional dollar of income. The Medicaid program offers the best example of this sort of inequity.

The current system is thus replete with both inequities—unequal treatment of equally needy persons—and "notches," or points at which a person earning a dollar more can be worse off than someone earning a dollar less. The layering of benefits from all these programs also produces very high cumulative marginal tax rates. For example, consider the case of a welfare mother with three children in Chicago who is earning $3,000 a year. Her AFDC payments and food stamps (minus social security and other taxes) would bring her total income to $5,067. If she got a much better job and began earning $5,000, her benefits would fall, her taxes would rise, and her net disposable income would be $5,310. Her additional $2,000 of earned income would make her only $243 better off! If her earnings increased by another $1,000, she would actually experience a net loss in disposable income because she would no longer be eligible for food stamps. If she were eligible for medical assistance or were one of the relatively small number of welfare families in public housing, her incentives to work might be further impaired.

These problems do not arise out of FAP. They are features of the existing welfare system. Indeed, the administration, prompted by the Senate Finance Committee, has made a valiant effort to improve the integration of some of these programs. The efforts have served mainly to illustrate the dilemma: it is impossible to reduce marginal tax rates unless more money is spent or benefits are reduced for some recipients.

Food Stamps

The relationship between FAP and food stamps is an example of the problem. The food stamp program, begun on a small scale in the early 1960s, provides coupons to the poor that may be exchanged for food at retail stores. With successive liberalizations, the program has grown sharply in recent years; its costs are estimated at $1.5 billion in 1971 and $2.0 billion in 1972.

Under the latest food stamp authorization, enacted in 1970, a poor family of four may receive $1,272 worth of food stamps a year. Families with extremely low incomes pay nothing for the stamps; as a family's income rises, it must pay up to 30 percent of that income for the stamps. A family of four with no income except FAP benefits would pay about $400 for stamps worth $1,272, receiving a net benefit of approximately $864. In some areas a family on welfare may elect to have the payments deducted from its welfare check and automatically receive the stamps along with its welfare payments. If FAP were adopted, this option would be extended to all FAP and welfare recipients. The administration estimates that another $400 million would be added to food stamp costs, as the newly eligible working poor elected to have food stamps automatically distributed with their FAP checks.

Food stamps pose several problems for FAP. Since food stamp recipients must pay more for their stamps as income rises, the marginal tax rate on earnings would be increased—from FAP's 50 percent to 65 percent, and for those receiving state supplementation, from 67 percent to 77 percent. Work incentives would thus be dulled.

Why not integrate food stamps with FAP? Since for a family of four the net value of food stamps is $864, why not increase FAP benefits to, say, $2,400, keep the 50 percent tax rate, and eliminate food stamps? But this would pose two difficulties. First, eliminating the additional "tax" now incorporated in the food stamp program would raise the break-even point, increase the number of families eligible for assistance, and add to the cost of the program. Second, and more important, poor families in states that would supplement FAP benefits would lose part or all of their current food stamp benefits. Under the current FAP plan, for example, a family might be receiving $2,600—$1,600 from FAP and $1,000 in state supplements—plus net food stamps worth $550. Under an integrated plan, that family would still receive $2,600 in cash—$2,400 from FAP and $200 from the state—and nothing in food stamps. Such an integrated plan would, in effect, take the saving from eliminating food stamps and pay it out in two ways: by raising cash benefits for the poor living in states with little or no state supplementation, and by reducing the welfare costs of states that do have supplements.

The administration has become increasingly aware of the potential costs of FAP plus the food stamp program and may even introduce an amended proposal that would eliminate food stamps for families with children and raise the FAP guarantee for such families to $2,200. States with welfare standards currently in excess of $2,200 would be required to raise their standards by the value of the food stamp bonus for such families. Food stamps would also be abandoned for aged and disabled welfare recipients in favor of a national cash minimum of $130 per person per month. The proposal would require the retention of food programs for non-aged, needy, childless couples and unrelated individuals, an unattractive expedient made necessary by the continued exclusion of such persons from federally supported welfare programs. This exclusion is, in itself, one of the largest issues to be resolved if further steps are to be taken toward developing a rational system of cash and in-kind programs.

Unemployed Fathers

A related but somewhat different problem involves the integration of FAP with state supplementation in those states in which unemployed fathers are eligible for AFDC. The present law permits, but does not require, states to aid families with unemployed fathers at levels comparable to the regular AFDC program. Since "unemployed" is defined by the number of hours a person works, rather than by earnings, families with one or more part-time earners can receive benefits, while even needier families are ineligible because the father works full time. About 120,000 families are now aided, but the problem of what to do with the unemployed fathers program once FAP is enacted is a difficult one. If the program were abolished, families now benefiting would suffer because they would be eligible only for FAP, not for state supplementation. If the program were continued, fathers working full time at low wages and receiving only FAP would have an incentive to reduce their hours of work in order to qualify for the higher benefits available from the state supplementation.

Another alternative would be to remove the hours limitation altogether and extend full benefits (including supplementation) to all families headed by males and meeting the income criterion. This solution would eliminate the disparities between male- and female-headed families in the same state, but it might have an adverse effect on incentives to work. Moreover, it would cost over $2 billion, most of which would go to families in a few states where AFDC benefits are relatively high. If the same amount were spent to increase the FAP benefit, needier families would be helped, and geographic inequities would be reduced rather than increased.

The administration has vacillated on this issue. The initial FAP proposal authorized the unemployed fathers program in all states but retained the limitation on hours. Under pressure from the Senate Finance Committee, the administration abandoned the program entirely. Since then, pressure from liberals has mounted to return to the original position, and the fate of the program is unclear. The preferable strategy would probably be to recognize the true long-run cost of continuing the program, given the likelihood of increased applications and mounting pressure to remove the hours limitation, and to redirect at least part of the probable federal outlays to raising the basic FAP benefit.

Alternative Futures

If FAP or something like it is enacted, what will happen to future welfare expenditures? Will they eventually begin to decline (or at least become a smaller part of government outlays) as economic growth continues and wage levels rise? Or will they continue to grow as they have in the recent past, perhaps constituting an increasing proportion of public outlays as the definition of "adequate income" rises along with wage levels?

The answers to these questions depend on the answers to at least two other sets of questions. First, how much emphasis is put on other public programs to reduce poverty, and how successful are these programs? If one thinks of poverty in terms of a specific level of income that is insufficient to meet basic human needs, it seems plausible that poverty can be largely eliminated by a combination of public policies. Economic growth with high employment can provide jobs at rising wages for most people. Social insurance can be improved to provide adequately for the needs of the aged, the disabled, the sick, the survivors of covered workers, and the temporarily unemployed. There is some hope that better health care, education, and vocational training can bring disadvantaged groups into the mainstream of American society so that almost everyone will be employable and no identifiable group will be stuck in marginal jobs. If all these programs were successful—a big "if"—then the number of people below the specified poverty level would decline and welfare would eventually be necessary only for a few social misfits and emergency cases.

The second question is how fast will the poverty line rise? If poverty is regarded as a relative, not an absolute, condition, then policies other than income maintenance are unlikely to solve the problem. Even if employment is high and human investment programs are successful, income will always be distributed unevenly, because ability is so distributed and because in our society substantial income rewards are offered for innovation and risk-taking. Some people will always earn substantially less than others or have greater-than-average family responsibilities. Those with incomes much below the average will always feel that they are poor and will be so regarded by others. Therefore, it may be desirable to have a permanent system that redistributes income from those able to pay taxes to those in need, and that reduces disparities in income without impairing incentives.

This seems consistent with what has actually happened. Even under existing programs, outlays for public assistance have been rising rapidly. Benefit levels have increased, and a larger proportion of the eligible population has been receiving benefits. Public concepts of what is "adequate" are apparently rising, and the stigma attached to being on welfare is declining. Since enactment of the Family Assistance Plan would bring a whole new group into the recipient population, it would presumably reduce the stigma still further. The establishment of a federal floor would probably increase pressures to raise the benefit levels, since it would be easier for proponents of liberalized benefits to exert pressure on the Congress than it would be to try to raise fifty different state standards. Moreover, it might be more equitable (as well as more feasible) to finance increases in welfare benefits if the federal government were bearing most or all of the cost, than if state and local taxes had to be raised to finance the increases.

Who Would Benefit?

Any moves to make FAP more adequate would of course involve balancing the same three objectives: helping the neediest, increasing incentives, and improving equity. This section explores the costs and implications of moving to higher benefit levels under an FAP-type of plan, with universal coverage and a moderate tax rate.

Two important characteristics of such plans should be borne in mind. First, they entail substantial transfers to those whose incomes are already well above the basic benefit. If the basic benefit were $3,000 for a family of four and the marginal tax were 50 percent, then some benefits would go to families of this size with incomes up to the break-even point of $6,000. Moreover, at this tax rate, a $100 rise in the basic benefit would raise the break-even point by $200. Hence, any increase in the basic benefit would mean not only increased payments to those already eligible, but extension of eligibility into the middle-income range. Since a great many families are concentrated in this group, raising the basic benefit by even a small amount could add considerably to the cost of the plan and the number of beneficiaries.

The second characteristic of such plans is that they involve substantial transfers from small to large families at the same income level, because the break-even level (as well as the basic benefit) is related to family size. For example, the break-even level might be $5,000 for a family of two and $10,000 for a family of six. At a given level of earnings, say $6,000, the small families would be paying taxes, and the large families would be receiving benefits. This fact may be in accord with notions of relative need, but it may also conflict both with notions of equity and with a policy of discouraging population growth.

Both the potentialities and the dilemmas of this strategy may be illustrated by comparing two specific plans with different basic benefit levels. The first plan has a basic benefit of $3,600 for a family of four; the second, $5,500. For both plans, benefits are reduced by fifty cents for each dollar of earnings above $720. (The $720 is assumed to cover work-related expenses.) The break-even point is thus $7,920 for a family of four under the $3,600 plan and $11,720 under the $5,500 plan.

The $3,600 plan essentially guarantees that no one will fall below the poverty line as now defined by the government. Many people regard this line as far too low, especially in big cities. It would clearly be next to impossible for four people to obtain decent housing, food, and clothing on $3,600 a year in New York or Chicago. The more generous $5,500 plan is similar to one proposed by the National Welfare Rights Organization. Although the benefit level sounds high (many fully employed people do not earn as much as $5,500), it is not much above the cash value of the benefits now available to a few welfare families in big cities. For example, a few four-person welfare families in New York City are estimated to be currently eligible for total benefits in cash and in kind of some $5,665.[3]

Estimates have been made of the net cost (above present welfare outlays) of transfers under both plans, assuming that they were operative in 1971.[4] The $3,600 plan would cost about $25 billion and would transfer income to about 69 million people. It is thus a transfer program of imposing magnitude when compared with current welfare programs, even though it would provide a basic benefit slightly inferior to current poverty standards. Nonetheless, the amount of redistribution effected would still be less than that currently brought about through the social security program, which in 1970 transferred some $29 billion from wage and salary earners to aged and disabled retirees and survivors of covered workers. The cost of transfers under the $5,500 plan would be some $71 billion, over and above current welfare costs and administrative costs. The plan would distribute benefits to more than half the population of the United States. This huge cost is hardly surprising, inasmuch as the basic guarantee would exceed the earnings of a substantial part of the labor force, though it would not be much above the highest welfare benefits currently available.

Under both plans, substantial benefits would go to families generally thought of as "middle income." Even under the lower plan, 34 percent of the beneficiary families would have incomes of $6,000 or more, and those families would receive about one-fourth of the total benefits. Under the higher plan, 52 percent of the beneficiaries would have incomes of $6,000 or more, and they would receive some 46 percent of the total gross benefits; 36 percent of beneficiary families would have incomes of $8,000 or more and would receive about 30 percent of the total transfers. These transfers to middle-income

3. Includes an AFDC payment of $3,780 plus food stamps, Medicaid, and public housing net benefits. Excluding the public housing bonus, which only some 8 percent of recipients in New York City receive, the total benefit package is $5,245.

4. Both computations were made using the transfer income program evaluation model developed by the Urban Institute. The data base is the March 1969 Current Population Survey projected to 1971. For a description of the methodology used, see Nelson McClung, John Moeller, and Eduardo Siguel, *Transfer Income Program Evaluation*, Working Paper 950-3 (Washington, D.C.: Urban Institute, 1971). The costs of implementing these programs should decline over time with increases in real and dollar wages. For example, assuming an annual growth in wages of 7 percent (3 percent real growth, 4 percent inflation) and no corresponding increase in benefit levels, the costs of the programs should decline by almost 15 percent by 1975 and the caseloads by about 25 percent.

families, of course, would reflect the higher benefit levels of larger families. Indeed, a disproportionate share of the benefits under both plans would go to comparatively large families. Under the $5,500 plan, families of five or more, which account for only 30 percent of recipient families, would receive 51 percent of total benefits.

Who Would Pay?

Thus far, we have considered only who would benefit. Someone would have to pay. To illustrate the possible net effect of these plans on different income classes, assume that both would be financed by adding to the positive income tax a surtax that would increase every taxpayer's current tax burden by a fixed percentage.

Financing the $3,600 plan from the current tax base would require the imposition of a 28 percent surtax to meet the estimated new transfer cost of $25 billion plus administrative overhead. The $5,500 plan would require a surtax of 78 percent, so that, for example, a taxpayer now paying a marginal tax of 35 percent of income would instead pay some 62 percent on his last dollar of income. Financing the plans in this way would, of course, entail substantial transfers from upper- to lower-income groups and—within income groups—from smaller to larger families. Under the $5,500 plan, families with incomes below $11,000 would gain *on the average*, while families with incomes above that amount would lose. Units with only one or two persons, however, would be net losers if their incomes were above $5,000, while net benefits would accrue to families of seven or eight persons with incomes as high as $15,000.

The fairness of such transfers might well be questioned, especially by middle-income wage earners with small families.

Suppose that the positive and negative tax systems are integrated so that each pay period a worker receives a check which, depending on his income class and family size, has either been reduced by his net positive tax liability or increased by his net negative tax entitlement. Under the $5,500 plan, Worker A, with a wife and no children, could earn about $7,000 a year and receive an annual paycheck some $370 lower than he received before; his co-worker earning the same nominal wage for the same work would receive an annual net "bonus" of about $1,800 if he had two children, and $2,900 if he had three. If Worker A regarded the number of one's children as a discretionary matter (not unlike other consumption choices, such as how many cars to own) he might well feel cheated.

The political opposition and complaints of unfairness generated by this horizontal redistribution of income—not to mention the opposition to major increases in the positive income tax—would probably be great. If the establishment of a minimum guarantee at or above the poverty level were seriously considered, several methods should be explored for reducing the size of the redistribution:

• Benefits could be reduced for additional family members. For example, lower (or zero) benefits could be provided for the third and subsequent children.

• Benefits could be adjusted for the cost of living or prevailing wages in the area to reduce the amount of redistribution from higher-standard to lower-standard areas, although at present the data necessary to make these judgments do not exist.

• Benefits could be reduced dollar for dollar where the beneficiary had income from other transfer programs, such as social security.

This last suggestion would be a step toward replacing other transfer programs by a single integrated income maintenance program. The prospect of abolishing the existing hodgepodge of income maintenance programs, with their varying types of inequity and inadequacy, and replacing them with an integrated system is, of course, appealing.

But such a move could not be undertaken lightly. It would involve a basic shift in the American philosophy of income maintenance. Our primary income maintenance systems—social security, unemployment insurance, and workmen's compensation—are tied to work effort and productivity. They serve the majority of Americans who spend most of their lives in the labor force, and they enjoy the strong political support of that group. In general, those who have sought to reform the welfare system have assumed that the work-related programs would continue and have directed their efforts toward broadening public assistance-type coverage to assist that minority of Americans who, for one reason or another, cannot make it in the world of work. Shifting to a single integrated income-maintenance system unrelated to work history would be a major step, whose consequences should be carefully weighed.

There is no way of accurately measuring the economic and social effects of shifting the emphasis in income maintenance programs from the idea of self-protection to that of guaranteeing the satisfaction of minimum needs. The issue undoubtedly will be debated for many years to come. In any case, it is unlikely that the problems of providing an adequate level of living for the nation's poor can be solved through a single structural reform of the income maintenance system. As the needs of the poor are diverse, so must be the tools to meet them. Despite the realization of much needed reform in our national income maintenance programs, the United States will probably continue using a variety of categorical and in-kind programs, including social services; subsidized housing, health, and day care; cash assistance for emergency and special needs; and wage-related subsidy and manpower programs for the employable poor.

9. Job Creation

THE LAST CHAPTER dealt with some of the potentialities and limitations of income maintenance programs in reducing poverty. This chapter deals with another way of alleviating poverty—raising the incomes of the poor by using public funds to create jobs. The two approaches interact. Work incentives in an income maintenance program will not be effective if no jobs exist; and to the extent that the poor find jobs, the costs of income maintenance will be reduced.

Public job creation does not figure prominently in the 1972 budget, but continued congressional interest in the subject indicates that it will be an issue in the debate over the administration's program.

Unemployment is not the sole cause of low incomes. Increasing employment opportunities for the poor cannot be expected to help the aged, the disabled, and others who are clearly outside the labor force. But a large proportion of poor families have low incomes because the breadwinner is out of work, or works only part time, or works at extremely low wages. It is possible to alleviate the poverty of these families either by income maintenance or by increasing their earnings from employment, or by some combination of the two.

Employment can be increased in at least three ways. First, fiscal and monetary policy may be used to stimulate the economy and increase the general demand for labor. Second, the capacity of the unemployed or the underemployed to earn higher wages may be enhanced by providing job training and placement services and by facilitating their movement from areas of labor surplus to areas of labor shortage. Third, public funds can be used to create jobs, either by adding more people to the public payroll or by offering subsidies to induce private industry to hire the unemployed.

The argument for job creation as a primary weapon against unemployment is essentially this: Socially useful jobs need to be done; people need work; it is logical to put the two together. It may be quicker to use public funds to create jobs than to wait for economic policy to stimulate demand. Creating jobs is less risky than training people for jobs that may not exist or in which the newly trained person may simply replace someone else, who then becomes unemployed. Job creation offers a more dignified solution than welfare and is more acceptable to politicians and perhaps also to the unemployed. This general rationale underlay the choice of public employment as a major weapon against unemployment in the 1930s.

More recently, job creation has been defended less as a primary than as a residual strategy against unemployment. It has proved difficult to use monetary and fiscal policy to reduce unemployment much below 4 percent without accelerating inflation. But at this overall level, unemployment rates remain high for some groups (teenagers, blacks, women), and considerable underemployment persists. Unemployment rates by race, age, and sex as of April 1969, when the overall unemployment rate was 3.5 percent, are shown below.[1] Manpower

	Male		Female	
Age	*White*	*Black*	*White*	*Black*
16–17 years	11.1	18.0	12.9	22.8
18–19 years	7.0	19.0	9.1	23.3
20–24 years	3.8	8.6	4.8	13.0
25 years and over	1.6	2.7	2.7	5.5

training may help to reduce the inflationary pressure and equalize unemployment rates among groups. Nevertheless, it is difficult and expensive to train many of the unemployed and place them in existing jobs. It may be quicker and cheaper to create jobs that the unemployed could fill, and useful work would be done in the process.

Opponents argue that job creation programs, without training or career advancement opportunities, result in wasteful padding of public payrolls or subsidies for the equally wasteful padding of private payrolls. The unemployed poor, they maintain, should be provided the skill training and career experience that would enable them to be

---

1. From Robert E. Hall, "Why Is the Unemployment Rate So High at Full Employment?" *Brookings Papers on Economic Activity* (3:1970), p. 391.

absorbed by the regular job market. Those who cannot be trained for a regular job should be aided through income maintenance rather than "make-work" employment.

The remainder of this chapter examines the major issues that arise in connection with job creation programs. It reviews past efforts and summarizes the state of knowledge about the usefulness of subsidized employment. Some current proposals are discussed briefly at the end.

Six Major Questions

1. *Do we need a job creation program in the 1970s?* In the 1930s this question was clearly answered in the affirmative. An extraordinary proportion of the labor force was out of work; from 1931 to 1939 the unemployment rate never dipped below 14 percent, and job creation was seen as a major instrument for returning the economy to full employment. The unemployed were not especially disadvantaged or unskilled. Most of them had worked before and could be expected to work again, but no one knew how to stimulate private demand for such large numbers of workers. Putting them to work doing something useful seemed better than having millions on relief.

By the early 1960s, when public employment once again became a subject of active debate, the economic situation was significantly different. Unemployment was substantial (5½–7 percent) but not massive, and confidence in the efficacy of fiscal and monetary policy to stimulate the economy had greatly increased. At these levels of unemployment, is there still an essential role for job creation?

2. *For whom should jobs be created?* At low levels of unemployment (in the neighborhood of 4 percent), a public employment program necessarily concentrates on the hard-core unemployed. This is likely to be a continuing requirement. But when unemployment rises to 6 or 7 percent, people with skills and working experience lose their jobs, and a number of them eventually exhaust their unemployment compensation entitlements. Can a program meeting the needs of the latter, more average, group be mounted quickly in a recession and then turned off when full employment is regained?

3. *How should the several objectives of job creation be balanced?* If the principal objective of job creation is simply to get people to work, then it does not matter much what jobs are done. The objective of

employing two men is attained if one digs a hole and the other fills it up. But with so much socially useful work to be done, the creation of useless make-work projects is wasteful of public funds and demoralizing to those employed. It would be preferable to work toward a second objective: let the job produce something that people want. But can this be done?

The problem is that "useful" jobs, like the construction of schools or dams or the provision of most public services, require a fairly high component of skilled and experienced labor, while the hard-core unemployed are mostly unskilled and inexperienced. Efforts can be made to provide training and simplify job requirements, but these measures increase the cost of the project. In general, the more emphasis that is placed on the utility of the work, the less job creation that can be attained per dollar spent. The question is how much to buy of each.

Moreover, another kind of objective should be considered—to create jobs that will develop skills and lead to advancement into better jobs. Again there is an economic tradeoff. Upgrading the worker's skills is not costless. The more emphasis that is given to training and upward mobility, the fewer the jobs that can be created per dollar spent, and the more difficult it is to mount a large-scale program.

4. *Should jobs be created in the public or in the private sector?* Job creation is usually associated with public employment, but it is also possible to subsidize private employers to hire additional workers. The choice depends on the priority given to the need for more services in the traditionally public areas, like education and conservation, and the relative cost of the two types of job creation.

5. *How attractive should the jobs be?* If conditions of work are poor and pay is low in the created jobs, people will not want to hold them, at least not for long. They may consider themselves better off if they are on welfare or are finding sporadic employment in the regular job market. On the other hand, if jobs are created at good wage levels, people will leave other jobs to hold them, and the net increase in employment may be considerably less than the number of jobs created.

6. *How large should a job creation program be?* The answer to this question depends in part on the answers to the previous ones. It depends also on estimates of the population that might respond to an offer of subsidized work, and on the priority accorded job creation relative to other public objectives.

Job Creation Programs: A Brief History

In the 1930s creating jobs for the unemployed was a major federal activity. It was carried out by two principal agencies—the Works Progress Administration (WPA) and the Public Works Administration (PWA). The two agencies had different approaches to the problem. The WPA emphasized the creation of jobs rather than the usefulness of the project. To be sure, many useful projects—ranging from the construction of post office buildings to the writing of magnificent local histories—were accomplished by the WPA. But WPA took on the unemployed and put them to work doing whatever they could do—and not all could build post offices or write history. Some could only rake leaves, or perhaps leaf raking was the only job that could be found for them. Leaf raking, though not entirely useless, would not have been given high priority on its merits were it not for the number of jobs it created. PWA, on the other hand, designed useful public works— mostly roads, schools, and other structures—and then hired people to build them, much as people have always been hired for public or private production. WPA inevitably produced more jobs, but less tangible product per dollar expended, than did PWA.

The Second World War brought an end to unemployment and with it the interest in job creation. Indeed, thirty years have passed without a major federal job-creation program. The desirability of a large federal employment subsidy program, however, was actively debated in the mid-1960s, during the formative stage of the war on poverty, but for a variety of reasons no such public employment program was launched.

In the early and mid-1960s there was an active debate over the causes and cures of unemployment. Some economists believed that unemployment was largely the result of inadequate aggregate demand. They maintained that an increase in aggregate demand would push unemployment down to 3.5 or 4 percent. Training programs were admittedly important, partly as a means of increasing skills in short supply, thereby reducing still further the level of unemployment that could be reached without causing serious inflationary problems. But major job creation programs were not needed.

An alternative explanation was offered by the "structuralists," who contended that most of the then-current unemployment resulted from a mismatch between a rising demand for skilled labor and a redundant supply of unskilled workers. They believed that neither public job creation nor increasing aggregate demand would provide the solution. Rather, they contended that major job training programs and other structural adjustments in the labor market were necessary to bring the supply of labor into line with the demand, qualitatively as well as quantitatively, and that if this were done, the jobs would be there.

Faced with the combined opposition of the aggregate demand proponents and the structuralists, proposals for public employment did not get very far. Moreover, unemployment rates were declining rapidly. By 1966, when the Vietnam buildup had pushed unemployment below 4 percent, pressure for a public employment program declined.

Although the war on poverty had no major provision for public employment as such, several of its programs contained substantial elements of job creation. One of these was the out-of-school Neighborhood Youth Corps. Although this program was originally intended as an on-the-job training program for school drop-outs aged 16–21, the Labor Department, which administered the program, concentrated on enrolling as many young people as possible and consequently put little emphasis on training and job content. As a result, most of the jobs tended to be of the make-work variety. Critics of the program believed that it should give more attention to training and to providing young people with entry into more highly skilled jobs. Defenders of the program pointed out, however, that even leaf raking got the kids off the streets at an age when it was easy to get into trouble and provided them with a bit of pocket money, and that these were useful functions in themselves.

The program began at annual cost levels of about $100 million for 100,000 jobs, and remained at about that level through the late 1960s. By 1970, greater efforts were being made to provide education, training, and placement in other jobs or federal programs for the enrollees. The 1972 budget proposes consolidation of the Neighborhood Youth Corps into special revenue sharing for manpower.

The Work Experience Program, administered by the Department of Health, Education, and Welfare (HEW), also created a substantial number of jobs. It was designed to give on-the-job training and some experience in holding a job to welfare recipients, especially potential recipients of the new "unemployed parents" category of aid to families with dependent children. The program was administered by local welfare departments, and the recipients received welfare payments rather than wages. Funds were unevenly distributed geographically, with a heavy concentration in Appalachia, especially eastern Kentucky. Local administration varied widely. In some places, there was genuine training and an effort to move the trainees into jobs in the private sector. In others—especially in eastern Kentucky, where the program came to be known as the "Happy Pappy Program"—it provided mainly work on roads and other unskilled jobs for fathers of welfare families. In 1966 the training component was turned over to the Labor Department, and in 1968 the program was transformed into Work Incentives (WIN), a training program for welfare recipients, mostly women. WIN started slowly and has had limited success in placing trainees in jobs, partly because of a lack of day care facilities. The administration is now putting substantial emphasis on WIN as a means of reducing welfare rolls. The 1972 budget proposes an increase in WIN outlays from $146 million in fiscal 1971 to $231 million in 1972.

A much smaller program, called Green Thumb, emphasized rural beautification and provided jobs to older people in rural areas. Later transformed and broadened into Operation Mainstream, administered by the Labor Department, it now provides about 12,000 jobs.

In 1966 an amendment to the Economic Opportunity Act launched the New Careers Program. New Careers was an ambitious idea stimulated by the writings of Pearl and Riessman.[2] It undertook to provide federally financed jobs for a new corps of paraprofessional workers in public service fields like health and education. Professionals in these fields (such as teachers and doctors) were scarce and often spent much of their time on routine tasks that could easily have been performed by less well trained persons. New Careers was to provide new types of paraprofessionals (like teachers' aides and pediatric assistants) who could help the skilled professionals do their jobs more effectively. New Careers also stressed the importance of the poor working with the poor, since it was thought that services could be provided more sensitively and effectively by people who had themselves experienced the problems of the poor.

The emphasis in New Careers was on the usefulness of the job, both

2. Arthur Pearl and Frank Riessman, *New Careers for the Poor: The Nonprofessional in Human Service* (Free Press, 1965).

to the holder and to society. New Careers men and women were to receive considerable training; they were to begin on career ladders that might lead to medical or educational degrees and would at least lead to jobs of clear social utility. The program has remained minuscule, serving 3,000–4,000 enrollees a year.

What Has Been Learned?

Although no major public employment program was undertaken in the 1960s, a great deal was learned from the smaller programs. Moreover, economic events of the decade changed prevailing views about the nature and cure of unemployment and the role of job creation.

First, it is now clear—as it was not in the early 1960s—that even full employment does not solve the job problems of the poor. Pushing unemployment down to 3.5 percent in the late 1960s induced inflationary shortages in some manpower categories well before it eliminated unemployment among the least skilled. Furthermore, the spread between the unemployment rate of the most employable (prime age men) and that of the least employable (women and teenagers, especially if they are black) has been increasing. A public employment or job-creation program designed for the hardest to employ would help them without causing a shortage of prime age men in the work force. It would thus reduce unemployment with less inflationary effect than would measures to increase aggregate demand.

Manpower training programs in the 1960s also proved to be considerably less successful than had been hoped. On the one hand, when unemployment was high, subsidized training programs in private industry tended to shrink, since employers were laying off workers generally. And in publicly run training programs, those who completed training could often find no jobs available. On the other hand, when unemployment was low, trainees were mainly the hard-core unemployed. Programs that succeeded in retaining and placing a high percentage of trainees (75 percent is considered a good success rate for a manpower training program) were those whose trainees were chiefly prime age men with some recent work experience. Success rates were far lower for women, teenagers, and men who had little education and had not worked for a long time. Some optimists believe that every person is trainable and that anyone who flunks or drops out should be started again. Others believe it is both more realistic and more humane to provide low-skill job opportunities for those whose propensity to failure in a training program is high.

A corollary lesson is that it is difficult to design a public employment program for those who are still left without jobs when the economy is at full employment. This group is extremely diverse—the young and the aging, the rural poor and the urban slum dweller, women with family responsibilities, and men with spotty and unpromising job histories. It is far more difficult to find suitable jobs, especially genuinely useful jobs, for these people than for the less diverse and disadvantaged groups who are among the unemployed at higher levels of unemployment.

Of course, even at 3.5 percent unemployment, people did go into programs like New Careers and did succeed in them. But their numbers were small, and many of them might have succeeded just as well in private jobs or training. There are exceptions—the welfare mother who becomes a top-notch teacher's aide or welfare worker, and who would not have made it in an office or a factory. But the suspicion remains that many of those who succeeded in New Careers were not typical of the really hard-core residual unemployed.

Another lesson, perhaps obvious a priori but certainly confirmed by experience, is that efforts to meet objectives other than job creation (usefulness to the community, upward mobility for the enrollee) increase the cost of each job created. For example, Barth and Easterbrook of the Office of Economic Opportunity estimate that at any given budget level, a New Careers type of program will buy 20 to 25 percent fewer jobs than will a simple job-creation program. An even greater investment per job is needed if construction projects are brought into the mixture of useful jobs.[3]

How have public programs performed as compared with private ones? Again, the answer depends partly on the objectives. If the main objects are the training and upward mobility of the enrollees, the private sector can apparently perform at least as efficiently as the public sector. If the objective is pure job creation, then the considerations are somewhat different. Is additional output more needed and more socially useful in the public or in the private sector? This is a question of values and priorities. Where is it easiest to ensure that the work

3. Michael C. Barth and Frank H. Easterbrook, "Planning Public Employment: A Statement of Trade-offs" (Office of Economic Opportunity, Research Division, no date; processed), Table 2.

done is truly in addition to what would have been done anyway? Here the public sector would seem to have the edge. It is extremely difficult to design a job subsidy program in the private sector that does not either subsidize employers to hire people they would have hired anyway or serve to keep marginally efficient businesses in operation.

Some interest has been expressed in the Congress in a program of wage subsidies to private firms that hire the unemployed, instead of providing income maintenance to the working poor under the Family Assistance Plan. While the federal government already has a program that subsidizes private employers to provide on-the-job training for the hard-core unemployed, the subsidy is designed, in theory at least, to pay for training costs. A subsidy for job creation would have a different emphasis. The economic theory of subsidized job creation is as follows: The hard-core unemployed are not hired usually because they are relatively unproductive workers. The value of what they would produce is less than prevailing wages. Law and custom prevent firms from cutting wages to the level at which it would pay to hire these workers. A federal subsidy paid to a business firm for hiring an otherwise insufficiently productive worker could reduce his wage cost to the firm enough to make it profitable to hire him without reducing his income below poverty levels. Thus, more jobs would be created, and the additional jobs would be concentrated among the poor.

There are several objections to such a policy. Much of the subsidy would be paid for hiring workers who would have been hired in any event. The net addition to employment induced by such a subsidy might be quite small in relation to the total subsidy cost. In addition, it may not be the generally low productivity of the poor that keeps business from hiring them; it may be managers' fears that because of their lack of reliability, production lines will be interrupted, machinery destroyed, and so on. If this is the case, *no* feasible wage subsidy would be large enough to induce substantial hiring of those most in need of jobs.

The advantage of public employment of the otherwise unemployable is that the government can give primary consideration to creating a job and secondary consideration to turning out a useful product, as was done by the WPA. Business, on the other hand, *must* put the product first and hence is less likely to hire those for whom job creation is most needed.

Finally, what would be the appropriate size of a public employment program? The answer depends on the answers to two other questions: How many potential enrollees are there, and what proportion of them would actually enroll?

Estimates of the number of potential enrollees vary widely, depending on who is included and when the estimate is made. In July 1969, 2.9 million people were counted as unemployed; by December 1970 the number was 5.0 million. A modest estimate of 1.5 million potential enrollees was made by OEO in 1968 for a program limited to urban and rural poverty areas. Much higher estimates—up to around 10 million—are obtained if one includes poor people who have dropped out of the labor force or who are currently employed but might be attracted to better jobs under a public employment program that promised steady work at the minimum wage for all who applied.

Moreover, no good estimate exists of how many of those not currently employed are actually ablebodied and ableminded. Nor does anyone know how many of those competent to participate would be successful in a given kind of program—how many in private sector training, how many in New Careers or other public sector training, how many in a simple job-creation program. No visible characteristics distinguish the unemployed who are likely to succeed in one or another of these programs from those likely to fail. The only way to find out is to bring people through the programs and observe actual successes and failures, and this has not been done.

Two alternative courses of action might be taken to determine the "proper" size of a public employment program. One would be to guarantee a job to everyone applying, and find out how many do apply. A more practical procedure would be to start at a relatively low level and, if the jobs offered at that level were quickly snapped up, to offer more until some acceptable degree of saturation is reached. This approach may be less intellectually satisfying than to estimate the right number in advance, but it would be less risky.

Current Status of Public Employment Proposals

The recession that began in 1969 and worsened throughout 1970 revived public employment as a public issue. In August 1969, the President submitted a comprehensive manpower training message to the Congress, designed to consolidate the multitude of manpower programs and give states and localities more control over the use of the funds. The administration's bill did not provide funds for public employment, but both houses of the Congress added public employment provisions. The bill that finally passed not only authorized funds for public employment directly, but also required that one-third of the funds appropriated for "regular" manpower programs be used for public employment. In fiscal 1972 the bill would have authorized over $1 billion for public employment and created over 200,000 jobs; by fiscal 1974, $1.8 billion and an estimated 360,000 jobs. In addition to these sums, appropriations of $200 million were authorized for the manpower program whenever unemployment exceeded 4.5 percent for three consecutive months, and still another $200 million if it exceeded 5 percent for three months. One-third of these amounts would also have been available for public employment.

Although the public employment program contained in the final bill was smaller than the one initially reported to the Senate by its Labor and Public Welfare Committee, it was clearly a large-scale job-creation program. At the same time, however, the other provisions of the bill placed considerable emphasis on useful jobs, training, and mobility. For example, the bill directed that an application for a public employment grant must show, among other things, that provisions had been made to review the job prospects of participants and help them to secure appropriate placement after counseling. Such requirements would have created dilemmas for the administrators. If they had carried them out in good faith, they would have had difficulty mounting the large-scale residual job-creation program implied by the amount of money and the number of jobs authorized.

In any case, the President was opposed to such a large public employment program and vetoed the bill, sacrificing his own comprehensive manpower proposals in the process. His veto message stressed his view that the bill would have "relegated large numbers of workers to permanent, subsidized employment." In rejecting the bill, he said:

Transitional and short-term public service employment can be a useful component of the nation's manpower policies. . . . But public employment that is not linked to real jobs, or which does not try to equip the individual for changes in the labor market, is not a solution. I cannot accept a bill which so fully embraces this self-defeating concept.[4]

4. *Employment and Manpower Act of 1970—Veto Message*, Message from the President of the United States, S. Doc. 91-118, 91 Cong. 2 sess. (1970), p. 2.

At the moment, prospects for public employment legislation in 1971 are uncertain. The 1972 budget does not specifically include funds for such a program. However, the administration is again proposing the consolidation of several different manpower training programs. (See Chapter 7 on special revenue sharing.) The bills embodying the President's message on special revenue sharing for manpower permit state and local governments to use these funds for public service employment if they want to, subject to two restrictions: no person could hold such a job for more than two years, and each job would have to be certified as providing training or career advancement opportunities.

Several other bills have been introduced in the Ninety-second Congress. Representative James G. O'Hara has reintroduced a major public service employment bill. Senator Gaylord Nelson and Representative Carl D. Perkins have put in bills similar to the one vetoed last year. These would authorize $500 million (100,000 jobs) when unemployment exceeded 4.5 percent for three months, and $100 million (20,000 jobs) for each additional half percentage point, up to a maximum of $1 billion (200,000 jobs) a year. Senator Nelson's bill was passed by the Senate on April 1, 1971.

Further action on public employment in this Congress will depend partly on economic developments. If unemployment rates remain high, the case for public employment will be strong. On the other hand, if the administration's fiscal policy succeeds in turning the recession around, the pressure for public employment will undoubtedly decline.

10. Social Security

THIS CHAPTER DISCUSSES the major proposals for social security currently before the Congress and then considers some basic policy issues posed by the existing organization and philosophy of the social security system.

Current Status of Social Security Proposals

Both the Senate and the House passed social security legislation in the second session of the Ninety-first Congress. The provisions of the bills were never reconciled because of the log-jam of legislation at the end of the session. In the 1972 budget the administration again proposed liberalizing social security benefits.

However, in order to enact a cost-of-living increase in social security benefits quickly, a 10 percent across-the-board increase was attached to other legislation and passed by the new Congress in March 1971. To finance these benefits, the ceiling on wages subject to social security taxes is to be raised from $7,800 to $9,000, effective January 1, 1972. Additional liberalizations in benefits are now under consideration in the Congress, and action is expected before the end of the session. These liberalizations will probably lead to further increases in effective tax rates, either through an increase in the tax rate itself or through a further increase in the ceiling on wages subject to tax.

The major proposals still under consideration are (1) an increase in widows' benefits, (2) liberalization of the retirement test, (3) an increase in the minimum monthly benefit to $100 for a single person and $150 for a couple, and (4) provision for automatic cost-of-living increases in the future. The first full-year cost of these proposed changes, plus the cost of the 10 percent across-the-board increase, are shown in Table 10-1.

A widow's benefits would be liberalized by increasing the proportion of the husband's benefit she receives after he dies. Under current law, the wife or dependent husband of a retired worker receives a benefit equal to 50 percent of the retiree's benefit. A couple therefore receives 150 percent of the basic benefit. Also under current law, when a worker dies, his widow receives a benefit equal to 82.5 percent of his benefit. Under the proposals, this would be raised to 100 percent.

The retirement test would be liberalized through an increase in the amount a recipient can earn and still receive full benefits. Under the present law, for each dollar of earnings between $1,680 and $2,880, social security benefits are reduced by half a dollar. The $1,680 would be raised to $2,000, with a 50 percent offset on all additional earnings.

Only the Senate bill would provide for a substantial increase in the minimum social security benefit. The 10 percent across-the-board in-

Table 10-1. Total First Full-year Cost of March 1971 Social Security Benefit Increases and of Other Liberalizations Proposed in 1971 by the Administration, the House, and the Senate

Millions of dollars

	Cost		
Liberalization	Administra-tion[a]	House	Senate
Passed March 1971			
10 percent increase in regular benefits	3,572	3,572	3,572
Other changes	77	77	77
Proposed			
100 percent of primary insurance amount for widows	649	689	649
Retirement test liberalization	404	404	404
$100 minimum benefit	n.p.	n.p.	1,500
Age 62 computation for men[b]	6	1,040	6
Other changes	440	108	473
Total	5,148	5,890	6,681

Sources: *Social Security Amendments of 1970*, Report of the Senate Committee on Finance, S. Rept. 91-1431, 91 Cong. 2 sess. (1970), p. 33; *Congressional Record*, daily ed., March 16, 1971, p. H 1576.

n.p. No provision.

a. Proposed costs are partially estimated by the authors.

b. Under current law, the method for computing benefits for men must take into account the average earnings up to age 65. This provision would permit taking into account average earnings up to age 62 only. The difference in costs reflects the fact that the House version would apply to persons already on the rolls as well as future retirees. The Senate provision limits the liberalization to future enrollees.

crease raised the minimum for a single retiree from $64 a month to
$70.40 and for a couple from $96 a month to $105.60. The Senate bill
would further raise these minimum amounts to $100 and $150,
respectively.

All three proposals call for automatic increases in future benefits
that would be tied to the consumer price index. These would not begin until 1973.

It is clear that a bill with these general features will pass in this session. Substantial disagreement in the Congress seems likely on only
two points: (1) the need to raise the minimum benefit, and (2) the
desirability of automatic cost-of-living increases and the associated
automatic increases in the wage ceiling (and tax rate).

The minimum social security benefit applies to those who qualify
for social security but whose previous earnings *covered by social security* were relatively low and who would otherwise receive small
monthly benefits. Increases in the minimum have been opposed in
recent years by successive administrations because many of those who
receive it have other forms of income. Many people, for example, are
well covered under civil service retirement, but also have worked the
minimum number of years in covered employment to qualify for
social security. Raising the minimum benefit under social security
would be very expensive ($1.5 billion a year under the Senate bill) and
an inefficient way to provide funds for the truly needy, since much of
the benefit would go to those who are not in low-income brackets.

There is fairly general agreement that social security benefits should
rise as the cost of living rises. In the past, increases in benefits have
been legislated at discrete intervals, roughly every two years. Until recently, these increases have adjusted benefits for past increases in the
cost of living. The last two across-the-board increases have been somewhat larger than the rise in the consumer price index. Making the increases in benefits automatic would assure beneficiaries that their
purchasing power would not be seriously eroded. Opposition to this
proposal arises from fear that the role of the Congress in setting benefits would be undermined. There is also opposition to the automatic
increase in effective tax rates proposed to pay for the increases in
benefits.

To finance the cost-of-living increases, both the administration and
the House bill would provide for biennial automatic increases in the
ceiling on wages subject to social security taxes, thus expanding the

tax base. The Senate bill called for the increased cost to be met by equal increases in the ceiling and rate. What is meant by "equal increases in the ceiling and rate" is not clear, but presumably the tax rate and the ceiling would be increased in such a way as to produce equal increments in revenue. The increases in the wage base and the tax rate would take place whether or not the system had a surplus. The social security trust funds were expected to generate an annual surplus of $6.6 billion in calendar 1971 and $8.9 billion in calendar 1972. The recent legislation reduced these near-term surpluses to $3.4 billion and $7.1 billion, respectively. But the annual surplus is expected to increase again—to $13 billion in 1973 and $16.6 billion in 1976.

Major Long-term Issues

Despite the fact that the social security system accounts for one-fifth of the budget and that the payroll tax that finances it raises more revenue than any other tax except the personal income tax, its basic structure and financing are little understood and seldom debated. Since it does make such a large claim on national resources, and one that has been increasing rapidly, more public discussion and understanding of the nature of the system is needed. Some of the issues discussed here are also dealt with in the recently submitted reports of the 1971 Advisory Council on Social Security.[1]

Is the Social Security System Insurance?

The social security system is described to the public as an insurance system. Many people think they are contributing to a trust fund, from which, if they are in need, they will get back assistance based on their contribution. But there are several inaccuracies in this insurance analogy.

Unlike private insurance benefits, the total benefits a retiree receives during his years of retirement are not closely related to the total contributions paid during his working years. The typical retiree receives benefits that exceed the total amount paid in. If beneficiaries received only what they had previously paid in, plus accumulated interest,

1. Another fairly recent review of most of the major aspects of the system was made by Joseph A. Pechman, Henry J. Aaron, and Michael K. Taussig in *Social Security: Perspectives for Reform* (Brookings Institution, 1968).

benefits today would be considerably lower than they are. In addition, a large element of income redistribution is contained in the formula that relates retirement benefits to previous covered wages. This formula provides for higher percentages to be paid to low-wage earners than to high-wage earners. In addition, at the bottom of the scale there is a floor under benefits, so that those who qualify for minimum coverage receive the benefits regardless of their past contributions. The insurance-like feature of social security lies in the fact that by paying the tax, one becomes eligible for benefits in the future.

The social security trust funds are not bank accounts in which individual workers' contributions are held until they become eligible for benefits. Indeed, the trust funds at their present levels would support only about one year's benefit payments. What we have is much more a nearly universal system of pensions for retired and disabled workers and their survivors than an insurance system.

Financing Social Security

Because social security has been characterized as insurance, many of the concepts of private insurance have been used to evaluate the financial soundness of the system. Some are appropriate, others are not. Under private pension schemes, an individual contributes from his current earnings during his working years; those contributions are invested in earning assets; the earnings from those assets support the individual's retirement pension in later years. So far as the individual is concerned, he is indeed transferring income from now to later.

In the case of a nationwide social security system, however, there is no way of avoiding the fact that each working generation supports the currently retired generation. Accumulating a surplus in the trust funds, investing that surplus in government securities (as is currently done), and using the interest earnings to pay benefits in the future does not alter this fact. Interest payments on the public debt are themselves government expenditures, and taxes must be levied to cover them. Therefore, the size of the accumulated surplus in the social security trust funds simply determines the extent to which future working generations are taxed through a payroll tax or through general revenues to provide for the retired population. In either case, each working generation is fully taxed to support the currently retired generation.

Because it is a current tax and transfer system, the annual cost of social security benefits cannot be avoided in the year when they are paid. The annual cost depends on the level of benefits and the number of beneficiaries relative to the size of the working population. Leaving the level of benefits aside, if the number of beneficiaries is small relative to the working population, the real cost of supporting them is low. Conversely, if their number is large relative to the work force, the cost of supporting them is high. This ratio between the working population and the retired population varies over time, depending on rates of population growth in earlier years.

Because of the baby boom after the Second World War, a large rise in the retired population relative to the working population is expected soon after the turn of the century. The period of high cost of supporting beneficiaries is so far in the future that it would seem to have no relevance for current policy. Because the cost of supporting the retired population will be fairly stable or actually declining during the next forty years, there is a strong temptation to increase the real benefits during this period. Payroll tax rates would have to be increased only moderately to do so. However, those benefits would be currently provided by the working generation that will begin to retire shortly after the turn of the century. In turn they will expect at least the same per capita level of benefits that they provided to the generation ahead of them and perhaps a continuing escalation of real benefits. The burden on the working population at that time will be heavy. It becomes crucial in making current social security policy to take account of future costs, because a liberalization of benefits today is not likely to be taken away in the future.

To take account of the future costs of benefits, estimates are made of the size of the beneficiary population and of the benefits it would be entitled to under current law. Estimates are also made of the size of the working population in the future and the size of expected payrolls. Tax rates are then set to generate revenues in excess of benefit payments in order to build up a surplus in the trust fund to be invested in government securities, the interest from which is designed to pay a significant fraction of future benefits. Until recently, however, as surpluses began to appear, the Congress liberalized benefits and postponed previously scheduled increases in tax rates, so that the trust fund never actually accrued substantial annual surpluses. In the past few years, on the other hand, tax rates were set so high and wages rose so rapidly that, even after major benefit liberalizations, revenues substantially exceeded expenditures.

The tendency of scheduled rates to generate large potential surpluses in the trust fund is increased by the use of the "level wage assumption" in the actuarial calculations that determine the tax rates. In estimating the need for social security taxes to cover benefits, the current practice is to assume that wages will not increase in future years. Since wages almost invariably do rise, both revenues and expenditures are underestimated in the long-range projections. But the underestimate of revenues exceeds the underestimate of expenditures, because a rise in wage levels immediately produces more revenues but affects retirement benefits only gradually as people receiving the higher wages eventually retire. As a result there are continued unexpected actuarial surpluses in the social security system, as well as sizable current surpluses. The presence of an actuarial and a very large current surplus has usually led the Congress to raise benefits. If the increase in benefits uses up more than the actuarial surplus, a recalculation of the tax rates is needed to keep the system in balance over the next seventy-five years. The calculation is again made on the level wage assumption. Wages then rise, new surpluses appear, and the process is repeated.[2]

The magnitude of the effect is substantial. Social security expenditures (excluding Medicare) for 1980 under the law in effect in 1969 were projected at $43 billion in the 1970 report of the board of trustees of the old-age, survivors, and disability insurance trust funds. Expenditures were also projected on the assumption of moderately rising wages (about 3 percent annually) and a continued liberalization of benefits in line with growing wage levels. Under these assumptions, expenditures in 1980 would be not $43 billion, but $67 billion—an increase of more than 50 percent.

In considering how social security should be financed, the fact that the system is not like a private pension fund and cannot transfer resources over time is very important. The current practice of setting tax rates high enough to build up a current surplus in the fund to pay for future benefits, and calculating those rates on the assumption that wages will not rise, is a poor way to finance the system. It contributes to decisions about benefit levels that are based on "unexpected" surpluses rather than on judgments about national priorities. Moving

2. See "Reports of the 1971 Advisory Council on Social Security" (1971; processed), section entitled "Actuarial Assumptions and Methodology," pp. 107–11, for a more detailed description of the influence of the level wage assumption.

toward a pay-as-you-go method of financing would recognize the realities of the situation and place decisions about social security benefits in the arena of national priority choices. In the near future, moving toward a pay-as-you-go system would also imply a reduction in the payroll tax rates that are scheduled under current laws. In turn, to avoid an overall loss in federal revenues, an offsetting increase in other taxes would be required. This raises directly the question of the role of payroll taxes in the federal revenue system.

Reforming the Payroll Tax

When the social security system was started, the payroll tax was 2 percent on the first $3,000 of income. The tax is now 10.4 percent on the first $7,800; and it will be 10.4 percent of the first $9,000 beginning in January 1972, and possibly the first $9,800 if the administration's health proposals are accepted. Table 10-2 shows the rate structure

Table 10-2. **Combined Employer and Employee Social Security Tax Rates on Wages and Salaries, Existing Law and House and Senate Proposals, 1969–87 and After**
Percent

	Tax rate[a]		
Year	Existing law	House proposal	Senate proposal
1969	9.6	9.6	9.6
1970	↓	↓	↓
1971	10.4	10.4	10.4
1972	↓		↓
1973	11.3		10.6
1974			↓
1975	↓	12.0	12.0
1976	11.7		
1977			
1978			
1979			
1980	11.9	13.0	13.2
1981			
1982			
1983			
1984			
1985			↓
1986	↓		14.4
1987 and after	12.1	↓	↓

Sources: *Social Security Amendments of 1970*, Report of the Senate Committee on Finance, p. 32; *Congressional Record*, daily ed., March 16, 1971, p. H 1576.
a. Includes old-age, survivors, disability, and health insurance.

scheduled in the March 1971 legislation and the ones proposed in 1970 by the House and Senate to cover benefit liberalization. As was mentioned above, the social security tax is the second largest source of federal revenue.

One reason why the payroll tax burden receives so little attention is that it is divided into two parts. The wage earner pays one part and the employer the other. But most economists agree that the entire payroll tax really falls on wages—that wages would be higher by approximately the amount of the employer's contribution if no such contribution were on the books. A study by John A. Brittain of the Brookings Institution that has not yet been published supports this contention and produces a great deal of theoretical and empirical evidence to support it.

If one accepts the view that both parts of the tax fall on wages, then low- and middle-wage earners obviously bear the heaviest burden of the tax. Those who earn less than the taxable ceiling pay 10.4 percent, not 5.2 percent, of their earnings in payroll taxes, and these rates are scheduled to rise. A family of four with income under about $8,700 pays a larger payroll tax than income tax. By 1973, as payroll tax rates rise according to schedule and income tax rates fall due to the Tax Reform Act of 1969, the payroll tax payments for a one-earner family of four will be greater than income tax payments for earnings up to $9,850. For two-earner families, the payroll tax may exceed income tax for incomes up to about $14,000.

Several proposals have been made for reducing the dependence of social security financing on regressive payroll taxes. They fall into two general categories:

First, reforming the payroll tax to take the burden off low-wage earners. This could be done by refunding the payroll taxes paid by the poor, by introducing personal exemptions into the payroll tax, or by crediting part of payroll tax paid against income tax.

Second, shifting more of the burden of paying for social security onto general revenues. At present, low-income workers receive greater benefits relative to their past contributions than do higher-income workers, whose earnings are at the taxable wage ceiling. General revenues could be used to finance some or all of this part of the social security system.

By whatever means the income redistribution part of the social security system is financed, it is important to be aware that social security is a relatively inefficient way of providing minimum incomes to the needy aged, whose prior wages were not high enough to allow for an adequate retirement income. Setting a high minimum for social security payments benefits those who, during their working lives, earned little income that was subject to social security taxes. In some cases these are indeed the needy. But increasingly they are retirees whose past and current income is relatively high. To put dollars in the hands of the needy by this route also gives dollars to those who are not needy. Broadening the Family Assistance Plan, or some similar income-maintenance arrangement, to include needy elderly people could accomplish the same objective at a lower cost; or it could provide more funds for them at the same cost.

None of this is to say that the provision of a decent retirement income should have low priority among the nation's needs. How a society provides for its elderly is one mark of its civilization and humanity. The electorate has clearly indicated its support for a program to provide income for those who have reached retirement age and their dependents. But the particular features of the present social security system sometimes lead to decisions whose effects are inconsistent with other national objectives. More explicit recognition of the facts that social security is not solely an insurance system but is in part a redistributive mechanism, that it is necessarily a pay-as-you-go system, and that it should be planned on the realistic assumption of rising wage levels, would help the nation to arrive at more rational judgments about both the level of benefits and the means of financing them.

11. Financing Medical Care

A MAJOR DEBATE IS DEVELOPING on the financing of medical care. The administration's health insurance proposal—hinted at in the budget and developed at greater length in the President's Health Message of February 18, 1971—suggests one step toward a solution to the problem. Several alternatives are also under discussion. This chapter discusses the advantages and disadvantages of the various proposals and considers the administration's plan in the context of other possible financing options.

What Is the Problem?

The financing of medical care ranks high on the list of unresolved national problems for at least three reasons. First is the concern with the nation's health itself. Despite high expenditures for health care, the United States has a poor health record compared with other industrial nations. Second is the concern with equity in access to health care. Health care is regarded by many as a basic right; unbearable financial burdens should not be placed on low-income families or on persons who happen to have extraordinarily high health care needs. The third source of concern is the rapid rise in the cost of medical care. No matter who pays—the consumer or the taxpayer—recently skyrocketing health costs have dramatized the need to find less costly ways of delivering needed care.

High Expenditures, Poor Health

In fiscal 1970, public and private outlays for medical care (excluding research) reached $61.9 billion, or almost 7 percent of gross national product, a larger percentage than in other major nations. If recent expenditure trends continue, health expenditures could exceed $110 billion by 1975—more than 8 percent of gross national product. According to one fairly conservative estimate, in 1975 Americans will spend on hospital care alone almost twice the amount spent on all medical services in 1960. Yet, fourteen industrial countries have lower infant mortality rates than the United States, and eighteen have a longer life expectancy for males at age twenty. Moreover, in comparison with other nations, the U.S. health status seems to be declining.

The medical care system cannot be held entirely accountable for the status of health in the United States. The air people breathe, the food they eat, and their personal health habits, as well as fundamental demographic factors, such as race and age, all have a major impact on the health of the population.

Some of these social and environmental factors have been favorable to health in recent years. Rising incomes have improved nutrition; widening education has improved some health habits. Others have been unfavorable. Growing urban concentration has exposed more people to air pollution. The "sex revolution" (ironically aided by medical advances in birth control techniques) has contributed to an epidemic of venereal disease. "Better food" has increased cholesterol intake. The faster pace of life has left little time for exercise and has sanctioned such timesaving relaxants as alcohol and pills, which lead to an increase in accidents, liver ailments, and drug addiction.

Nevertheless, there is reason to believe that America's poor health record is related at least in part to inadequate medical care, especially for the poor. Low-income people get the least medical attention and have on the average poorer health than the rest of the population. For example, infant mortality in 1967 in several low-income Mississippi counties was 40 to 50 per 1,000 births, in contrast to the U.S. average of 22.4, while high-income Montgomery County, Maryland, had a rate of 17 per 1,000.

Health Care As a Basic Right

Although medical care is only one factor contributing to health, it is clear that most people are not in favor of having its distribution determined entirely by personal income. Denying health care to some because they are unable to pay for it has long been regarded—in principle, if not in practice—as inequitable.

For centuries, doctors and hospitals treated the poor in emergencies on a charity basis, but the modern world increasingly regards charity medicine as demeaning and inadequate. Many people now believe that basic medical services (preventive as well as emergency) should be available as a matter of right to all citizens. Some believe that this goal can be attained only through direct governmental provision of medical services, with facilities that are publicly owned and operated and doctors and other health providers who are publicly employed. A more common view in the United States is that health rights can be assured through public financing of privately provided medical services.

Making medical care free, however, would remove this service from the discipline of the price system. Prices perform the function of alerting producers to the relative costs of alternative treatments, and of telling consumers what they have to give up to get more medical service. Once these functions of prices are abandoned, consumers and providers might overuse medical care resources. In that case, the task of conserving medical resources would have to be shifted from the price system to regulatory bodies, which have not been notably successful in other public sectors.

Rapidly Rising Prices

Even without full national financing of medical care, the cost of medical services is rising extraordinarily rapidly. Between 1960 and 1969 the index of medical care prices rose by an average of 5.2 percent a year, or more than twice as fast as the consumer price level. Hospital daily service charges have increased by more than 14 percent a year since 1965. Price increases of this magnitude have forced widespread recognition that public action is needed not only to ensure that people who need care get it, but also to ensure that whoever pays the bill does not pay a much larger bill than is necessary.

The rise in medical care prices is apparently attributable to several interacting factors: relatively slow increases in the supply of health services, rapid increases in the demand, and an absence of incentives for either patients or suppliers to use health services efficiently.

Supply Factors

The principal factor in the supply of medical services is medical manpower. Payments to physicians and other medical professionals account for about one-third of all medical care outlays. Hospital care accounts for about another 40 percent, but more than 60 percent of the latter is for salaries.

Almost all types of health manpower are widely thought to be in short supply, but the alleged "doctor shortage" has attracted particular attention. Although physicians comprise less than 10 percent of the medical care labor force, they are clearly critical to medical service. Physicians' fees have been rising faster than prices in general, and the rate of increase in recent years has been double its long-run trend. The fee increases, along with evidence of long working hours for doctors, long waiting lines and delays in getting medical appointments, and the presence of large numbers of foreign medical graduates have led many observers to believe that the doctor shortage is critical. Moreover, a shortage of doctors cannot be relieved quickly, for medical training is long and costly. The Carnegie Commission, in its recent report, advocates large increases in medical school subsidies, large increases in enrollment, and a reduction in the length of training to increase the speed with which the supply can be expanded.[1]

The essential problem, however, may be less an overall shortage of physicians than a maldistribution and inefficient use of the supply that now exists. There are striking differences within the United States in the ratio of physicians to the general population. In the New England and Middle Atlantic regions it is almost double that in the South. And in all regions, rural areas and inner-city neighborhoods are much more poorly served than are their immediate neighbors. Thus, an expansion in the supply of medical manpower might not alleviate the most critical shortages unless the geographical distribution of medical personnel were controlled.

Furthermore, the need for physicians depends on the organization of the health care system. In some prepaid groups in California, which, it is generally agreed, provide high quality care, there are about 91 physicians per 100,000 population, while the average in the United States as a whole is 147. If medical care in the rest of the country were reorganized so that the ratio of physicians to population in these prepaid groups prevailed generally, the "doctor shortage" would disappear. Similarly, if medical care were reorganized so that paramedical

---

1. *Higher Education and the Nation's Health*, A Special Report and Recommendations by the Carnegie Commission on Higher Education (McGraw-Hill, 1970), pp. 9–11.

personnel performed some services now carried out by physicians, the shortage of doctors might be reduced.

Demand Factors

The demand for medical care has risen rapidly in the United States along with rising incomes. More and more people have been demanding not only medical care, but better quality medical care. In part, such quality has meant improved hotel and restaurant services in U.S. hospitals. In part, it has led to the installation of more advanced and more expensive medical equipment both in hospitals and in doctors' offices.

Another factor contributing to (as well as reflecting) the increase in demand for medical services has been the rapid growth of health insurance. The proportion of the population with some private medical insurance has risen dramatically in the past two decades. Now 81 percent of the non-aged population has some insurance coverage, whereas only 9 percent had insurance in 1940. The sharp rise in insurance has meant that with increasing frequency the patient's medical bills are paid not directly by the patient himself, but by a third party—the insurance company. Third-party payment reduces the patient's reluctance to seek care because of the price of individual services. He has already paid, so he might as well use the services.

In recent years, Medicare and Medicaid have significantly increased the demand for medical care on the part of the aged and low-income groups and have further extended the role of third-party payment.

The prevalence of third-party payment leads not only to greater use but also to inefficient use of medical services. Few insurance policies cover all kinds of medical service. The most frequently covered service is the most expensive—inpatient hospital care. While 157 million persons have some insurance covering hospital bills, only 86 million have policies that cover visits to physicians outside the hospital, and few have insurance covering nursing home care. A particular illness can often be treated just as effectively with the patient at home or in a nursing home as in a hospital at higher cost. However, if the patient's insurance policy covers only hospital care, the doctor tends to put the patient in a hospital or keep him there longer, even though he does not require hospital care. The result is a substantial amount of unnecessary, costly hospital care.

One might suppose that the third parties themselves would exert pressure on the suppliers to keep prices down, but in fact, little pressure is exerted. Under hospitalization coverage in the Medicare program and in many private plans, the insurer pays the "reasonable costs" of the services provided.[2] It is hard to estimate what are reasonable costs, and the practice has been to reimburse hospitals for actual costs. If actual costs are reimbursed, hospitals have little incentive to hold costs down. The higher costs are passed on to the patient in the form of higher insurance premiums or, in the case of Medicare, to the taxpayer. Serious attempts to hold down reimbursement rates have been rare—in part because it is so difficult to design a reimbursement formula that rewards efficiency, maintains quality, and adequately accounts for variations in patients and their preferences.

An additional factor in escalating hospital costs has been competition among hospitals for patients and prestigious staff. This has sometimes led to the acquisition of extremely costly and underutilized equipment by several hospitals in the same neighborhood. In principle, planning for the joint use of a rarely needed facility would have kept down costs; but there has been little planning, and, more often than not, it has been ineffectual, because the planners have not represented consumer interests and because planning authorities have had little power to enforce their decisions.

Criteria for a National Financing System

A national financing scheme for health care should meet at least three criteria: (1) it should provide incentives to keep costs down without lowering quality; (2) it should relieve the financial burden on the relatively small number of families with extremely high health expenditures; and (3) it should help the poor, for whom even average expenditures are a major financial burden.

Table 11-1 shows how expenditures for medical care varied among families in 1963, before major federal programs were introduced. Average expenditures for medical care were $370, but the variation above and below the average was considerable. More than 60 percent of all families had expenditures below the national average. At the same time, about 8 percent of families had costs in excess of $1,000, a sum that would have been burdensome to almost all U.S. families at

2. For a discussion of "reasonable costs," see *Medicare and Medicaid: Problems, Issues, and Alternatives*, Report of the Staff to the Senate Finance Committee, 91 Cong. 1 sess. (1970), pp. 45–51.

Table 11-1. Distribution of Family Personal Health Expenditures, 1963

Total expenditure for health per family. in dollars	Percentage of families	Percentage of total health expenditure by all families
0– 99	29.5	3
100–299	31.5	16
300–999	30.9	45
1,000 and over	8.1	36
Total	100.0	100

Source: Ronald Andersen and Odin W. Anderson, *A Decade of Health Services* (University of Chicago Press, 1967), pp. 57–58.

that time. This 8 percent accounted for one-third of family medical expenditures. A key problem, therefore, is how to protect the unlucky few who incur major financial burdens for medical care. The second problem is how to protect the poor and the near-poor. By fiscal year 1969, average family medical expenditures had risen to $785. While this level of spending would probably not constitute too heavy a burden for families at the median income level ($9,433 in 1969), families below the median would have considerable difficulty meeting their bills. The very poor would find it impossible to spend at the national average for medical care. They would often decide in nonemergency cases to go without care, thus possibly allowing a minor problem to develop into a major one.

It is difficult, perhaps impossible, to design a health financing scheme that will meet simultaneously all the criteria of cost control, protection against catastrophic expenses, and provision of basic services to low-income groups. A program that would meet one or two of the criteria would generally be weaker on the third.

Three features of any health financing scheme determine its character and the extent to which it meets the above criteria. These features are (1) the services that are covered, (2) the extent to which the patient shares the cost, and (3) the basis on which suppliers of services are reimbursed.

Coverage

If only expensive services, such as hospitalization, are covered, they will tend to be over-used. In general, broadening the coverage will increase the efficiency with which resources are employed. In particular, coverage of ambulatory care, nursing homes, and extended care facilities will reduce the use of hospitals, and coverage of doctors' visits and diagnostic tests will encourage preventive care. Broadening coverage to include services (such as dental care or eyeglasses) that are not substitutes for those already covered will make less of a contribution to efficiency.

On the other hand, the broader the coverage, the greater the need for cost and utilization controls. Complete coverage of all medical procedures might result in skyrocketing demands for cosmetic dentistry and orthodonture, contact lenses, and minor plastic surgery, and the price of such services would rise rapidly.

Sharing Medical Costs

Medical insurance policies seldom reimburse the patient for the full costs of all medical expenditures covered by the policy. Usually the patient shares the cost of a service received with the insurance company, either through a "deductible" or through coinsurance. A deductible means that for a given illness, or for a given time period, the patient pays an initial sum before the insurance pays any benefits. Coinsurance means that beyond the deductible, the patient pays a fixed fraction of expenses, and the insurance company pays the rest. Sometimes there is a maximum charge, either to the patient or to the insurance company. (In effect, the coinsurance rate becomes either zero or 100 percent after the maximum expense claim is reached.)

Which coinsurance and deductible features are desirable depends in part on the priorities attached to the three criteria mentioned above. At a given cost (say, an average expected benefit pay-out of $500 per family), one could design an insurance program that would completely protect families against catastrophic medical expenses. The deductible would be set high, and most families would not receive any cash reimbursements; but the coinsurance rate would be set low, so that the small number of families with extremely high expenses would still not have to pay out large fractions of their income. At a very high expense level, the coinsurance rate paid by the patient would drop to zero, and the insurer would absorb all the costs of treatment.

At the opposite extreme would be an insurance program emphasizing "first-dollar" coverage. For example, the insurance might set a very low (or even zero) deductible, so that the insurance company would pay part of even small medical bills. To keep the total cost of such a program within limits, however, substantial coinsurance payments would be required, or ceilings would have to be set on insurance payments for any particular illness or time period. Alternatively, major exclusions in service coverage (such as home visits) could be imposed. This type of plan would provide current benefits to a great many participants, eliminating concern over medical bills for the majority of the insured. However, for the minority with heavy expenses, the first-dollar approach would provide inadequate protection.

How do these two types of policies compare when measured against the three basic criteria? The catastrophic plan helps families with unusually high expenses, whatever their income level, but does not solve the problem of the poor, for whom even moderate expenses are a major burden. First-dollar coverage, by contrast, helps all families, including the poor, budget for their ordinary medical expenses, but in the absence of catastrophic coverage, first-dollar plans do not help those who face enormous bills.

Catastrophic plans would probably induce more consumer pressure to hold down costs, but only if most people did not *also* have first-dollar coverage. If most people had only catastrophic coverage, they would be spending their own money for ordinary medical expenses. Some of the wasteful practices encouraged by third-party payment might be eliminated. On the other hand, under these circumstances, patients might delay checkups and postpone preventive care, with the result that they would develop more serious and costly illnesses later. First-dollar coverage encourages early treatment of illnesses, but may increase inflationary pressure by extending third-party payments into a broader sphere of medical services.

It is probably not realistic to think of a national health insurance program, whether catastrophic or first-dollar, as replacing other forms of insurance. Most people have some insurance now. If the government provided catastrophic insurance, most middle- and upper-income families would probably buy first-dollar (or at least low-deductible) coverage on their own. Conversely, if the government provided first-dollar coverage, more people would seek catastrophic coverage at their own expense. Hence, the effect of any national health insurance plan would probably be to increase the volume of medical services paid for by third parties. Thus any type of national plan would make it even more necessary to control costs—either by fixing medical prices directly or by altering the way in which third parties reimburse suppliers so as to encourage greater efficiency.

Reimbursement to Encourage Efficiency

Under any health insurance plan, the method of reimbursement of suppliers will affect medical costs and the degree of efficient use of health resources. One general approach to cost control would involve prepayment (or at least negotiation in advance) of a fee for taking care of a certain number of patients, or providing certain services, as opposed to postpayment for actual expenses incurred.

In the case of hospitals, this idea is usually called prospective budgeting. Instead of requesting reimbursement for actual costs, or even "reasonable" costs, the hospital agrees in advance to provide certain services for a fixed fee. The hospital then has an incentive to reduce its costs and to serve the patients as efficiently as possible. This financing method has been tried out in a few states and cities, but it is too early to evaluate the results.

A more comprehensive prepayment scheme is that of the health maintenance organization (HMO). A family that belongs to an HMO pays a fixed annual fee to a medical group that promises to provide all (or nearly all) required medical services. Since the family pays a fixed amount, the HMO has an incentive to keep its costs as low as possible and create a budgetary saving. Some existing prepaid group plans make physicians' salaries depend in part on the size of the saving, thus giving the physician a stake in holding down costs. Since the HMO covers virtually all medical services, decisions on treatment are not distorted by the presence or absence of insurance coverage. In addition, the HMO tends to emphasize preventive care, since it has an economic incentive to try to arrest an incipient illness before it reaches the high-cost-of-treatment stage. Finally, the HMO is alleged to be more efficient simply because a group of doctors with different specialties can operate more efficiently together than separately. They can keep central records, simplify their billing, make bulk purchases, and make more effective use of equipment and paramedical personnel.

Prepayment provides incentives for cost control to the provider of medical services, but what does it do to the quality of care? Besides eliminating truly wasteful practices, does prepayment lead to skimping on services? No definitive answers can be given, but some steps can be taken to ensure that quality is maintained. One essential step is a review procedure in which doctors and other competent professionals inspect the hospital or group practice to make sure that proper medical procedures are being followed. To be effective, the review should be made by persons not connected with the institutions being inspected. Many medical institutions now have internal review procedures, but they are often ineffective because colleagues are reluctant to criticize each other.

Second, the discipline of competition can provide checks on both quality and cost. At present, prepaid group care is only one of several available options. A family that is not satisfied with the quality of care received can transfer out of the group and seek health services from other providers. Moreover, an HMO's charge cannot get out of line with the fees of. other providers. These checks on quality and cost through consumer choice are recognized as desirable by most advocates of group practice. But in fact competition may not be enough to regulate medical care even if groups become widespread. A lack of consumer information poses one barrier to reliance on consumer choice. In addition, large capital costs and tight licensing requirements limit the entry of new competitive medical care suppliers. Especially in smaller towns and rural areas, where there are few doctors now, consumers are unlikely to have much choice. In such cases regulation of prices and monitoring of quality by outside agencies may be necessary.

Paying for National Health Care

There are various ways of paying for a national health system. At one extreme, there might be a voluntary health insurance system in which the participant pays a premium that is set at a level sufficient to cover the actuarial costs of services to him. At the other extreme, there might be a system financed entirely out of taxes, that is, compulsory payments based on income or some other criterion unrelated to use of a health system. Various combinations of taxes and premiums are possible, and indeed the distinction between the two forms of payment is often unclear. If a "premium" is compulsory or is related to ability to pay, it is in effect a tax.

Whatever terminology is used to describe it, two questions should be asked about any payment system: Does it distribute the burden of payment equitably among various segments of the population? How does it affect incentives to work?

PREMIUMS. One option is to cover part or all of the cost of the system by charging all the participants a premium analogous to a private insurance premium. If the premium is a fixed sum for everyone, however, it will be more burdensome to the poor than to those who are more affluent. If service is available only to those who pay the premium, some needy families will be unable to pay and will go without medical care.

The burden on the poor could be lessened by relating the size of the premium to income. But this procedure may impair work incentives. For example, if premiums rose by $100 for each $1,000 of income, a family would net only $900 of the extra $1,000 in earnings. If the family were also receiving public assistance, the combined effect of increased premiums and reduced benefits of public assistance when income rose would create a high "marginal tax rate" and discourage work effort (see Chapter 8).

The disincentive effect would be mitigated if the premium rose less sharply as income rose, but this would also yield smaller total payments. The difference would presumably have to be made up through taxes.

PAYROLL TAXES. If part or all of the cost of the health system were to be paid out of taxes rather than premiums, the question becomes what kind of tax would be most appropriate? Frequently suggested for health service financing is the payroll tax, which is used to finance the social security system, including Medicare benefits. Many health financing schemes call for raising the necessary revenue by increasing the social security payroll tax.

The advantages of the payroll tax are that it is easy to collect and it provides a steady flow of revenue that grows as the economy grows. In the past, there has been little political opposition to increasing the payroll tax. It is now a major source of federal revenue, but its impact on the taxpayer is disguised by the fact that it is shared by the employer and the employee. This sharing reduces its visibility to the employee, although most economists agree that both portions of the tax probably fall largely on the wage earner.

The disadvantage of the payroll tax is that it is far more burdensome to low-wage earners than to those who are better off. Since the social security payroll tax is a flat percentage of earnings up to a maximum, with no allowances for family size, it is most burdensome to large, low-wage families, especially those with more than one earner. (See Chapter 10.) Increasing the payroll tax, or any other tax on the earnings of the poor, will tend to decrease incentives to work.

GENERAL REVENUES. An alternative source of tax financing for health care is the general revenue of the federal government. In effect, using the general revenue means financing the federal contribution to the health system out of personal and corporate income taxes, since these two taxes together yield the bulk of general federal revenues. Since these taxes are more progressive than is the payroll tax, their use would shift more of the burden of paying for medical care onto higher-income groups.

A substantial portion of low-income families have high health expenditures. A 1966 study, just before Medicare and Medicaid, showed that one-third of the families with incomes between $3,000 and $5,000 spent more than 15 percent of their incomes on health services.[3] Such families may, if they are employed, bear a substantial payroll tax burden, but they are unlikely to pay much personal income tax or to bear an appreciable indirect burden from the corporate income tax. Hence, paying for a major part of their health costs through income taxes would mean shifting resources from higher- to lower-income groups.

TAX CREDITS. An indirect way of using general revenues to finance health care would be simply to allow taxpayers to subtract the premiums they pay to private insurance plans (or a fraction thereof) from their personal income tax liability. This method of federal subsidy would not explicitly involve the expenditure side of the budget at all; health subsidies would be paid by *not* collecting some taxes that would have been collected without the medical credit.

In theory, one could establish schedules of allowable tax credits that would result in almost any degree of income redistribution. At very low incomes, where income tax liabilities are nonexistent, a tax credit plan could give rebates to families for insurance premium expenses. Some tax experts, however, doubt that the sophistication of lower-income taxpayers is sufficient to assure that they will claim the benefits due to them or that the promise of a subsequent rebate is enough of an inducement to spend now.

The tax credit device would involve a minimum of federal control. The Congress might specify the characteristics of insurance plans for which credit would be allowed, but it would not review the medical subsidy in the same way it reviews expenditures. Once the general entitlement to medical credits were established, tax losses to the U.S. Treasury would simply happen, and the Congress would have to re-

3. Murray A. Tucker, "Effect of Heavy Medical Expenditures on Low Income Families," *Public Health Reports*, Vol. 85 (May 1970), p. 423.

vise the tax laws before any changes (or control) could occur. To advocates of medical tax credits, the lack of congressional control and review is desirable; to its opponents, it is anathema.

TRUST FUNDS. Trust funds are a means of earmarking certain tax receipts to finance specific expenditures. The trust fund device could be used in financing medical care by allocating a portion of the payroll tax or any other tax for a health trust fund to be used only for paying health service benefits. The advantages claimed for the trust fund device are that (a) the trust fund most clearly embodies the idea that the particular service is a basic right for all citizens and should not be subject to the ebb and flow of political fads and fancies that affect the annual appropriations process, and (b) tying revenues to a particular service makes it clear to taxpayers how much they are paying for the service, and thus they are better able to weigh the economic value of any proposed expansion or contraction of the system.

On the other side, it is argued that the sanctity of a trust fund is only a fiction because the Congress can always change the law. To the extent that the fiction is taken seriously, it removes trust fund expenditures from the scrutiny of the budget process. Experience with trust funds indicates that expenditures for a particular activity tend to be determined not by judgments about priorities but by the intake of the trust fund, even if the latter is artificially high due to some temporary demographic or economic factor. If a surplus develops in the trust fund, there is a tendency to increase expenditures from the fund, without serious consideration of their importance relative to that of expenditures financed from sources outside the trust fund.

Current National Financing Proposals

On February 18, 1971, President Nixon proposed a National Health Insurance Partnership, designed to fulfill his State of the Union pledge "to ensure that no American family will be prevented from obtaining basic medical care by inability to pay." The President's proposal is not a single plan, but a complex set of provisions designed to cover various segments of the population in different ways.

The Administration's Plan

To ensure that the working population is covered by health insurance the plan would require all employers to purchase at least a minimum standard health insurance policy for employees and their dependents. No federal subsidy would be involved. The cost would be shared by employers and employees, with the shares presumably determined through collective bargaining in unionized industries. The law would specify an initial ceiling on the employee contribution of 35 percent of the cost of the insurance, falling to 25 percent in 1976.

The minimum standard benefits would include hospital care, surgeons' and physicians' services, laboratory and X-ray on an inpatient and outpatient basis, and maternity care. All these would be subject to a deductible of $100 a person, plus two days of hospital room charges, and a coinsurance charge of 25 percent up to $5,000 in medical bills for each person. After $5,000 in bills is reached, the insurance would pay full costs up to $50,000. Preventive medical care and eye care for children would be exempted from the deductible and coinsurance provisions in order to encourage the use of these services.

This mandatory program would cover an estimated 150 million persons (full-time workers and their families), but would exclude substantial groups in the population. Federal, state, and local employees would be excluded because they are already covered by health insurance. Part-time and seasonal workers, domestics, and the self-employed would also be excluded. Arrangements would be made to enable these people to buy health insurance at group rates, but at their own expense.

For those outside the labor force or with low earnings, a variety of other provisions would be made. Medicare would continue to cover the aged, and Medicaid would be retained for welfare recipients who are blind, disabled, or aged. Two changes would be made in these programs:

• The charge of $5.30 per month for physicians' coverage under Part B of Medicare would be eliminated in July 1971, thus saving the elderly about $1.4 billion in fiscal 1972. The coverage would be paid for by raising the social security wage base to $9,800 and shifting 0.1 percent from the cash assistance portion of the social security tax rate to Medicare.

• Coinsurance and deductible charges would be increased for many Medicaid and all Medicare beneficiaries, effective in fiscal 1972. These extra charges are estimated to cost Medicare recipients $400 million and Medicaid recipients $444 million in fiscal 1972.

For needy families with children, Medicaid would be eliminated in favor of a new Family Health Insurance Plan (FHIP), to come into effect in fiscal year 1974. FHIP would provide for thirty days of hospital care, surgeons' and physicians' services, and maternity, family planning, emergency, diagnostic laboratory, and X-ray services, as well as preventive medical and eye care for children. Families with children would be eligible if they had incomes under $5,000 (for a family of four) and they were not covered by the mandatory employer program.

The federal government would pay all costs of this program for families of four with incomes under $3,000. For families with incomes between $3,000 and $5,000, FHIP would impose a schedule of rising premiums, deductibles, and coinsurance. Specifically, in moving from incomes of $3,000 to $5,000, premiums would rise from zero to about $100 per family, and the rising schedule of deductibles and coinsurance would reduce the value of the benefits in the program from $680 to $483. As a result, a welfare mother in the income range of $3,000 to $5,000 would find that for every additional $100 she earned, she would lose not only part of her welfare benefit, but about $15 worth of medical benefits as well.

One group would apparently not be covered by any part of the President's program: low-income people without children, who are neither aged, blind, disabled, nor fully employed. This group is not covered by Medicaid now (except in states that choose to extend their benefits at their own expense) or by any federally assisted welfare program. Nor would this group benefit from the administration's proposed welfare reform (see Chapter 8).

The President's program puts considerable emphasis on reorganizing medical services under health maintenance organizations. To encourage the growth of HMOs, the administration proposes $23 million in planning grants to aid potential sponsors of the new organizations, loan guarantees to enable private sponsors to raise $300 million for capital costs of HMOs, and $22 million in direct grants to offset their special costs in rural and inner city scarcity areas. Moreover, all federally assisted or mandated health programs would have to allow participants to use their benefits to meet HMO charges.

In addition to improving the organization of health care, the administration proposes to expand the supply of health personnel by providing grants to medical and dental schools, based on numbers of graduates, and additional funds to improve the medical curriculum, increase enrollment, and provide special scholarships and loans for low-income students. The Emergency Health Personnel Act, passed by the Ninety-first Congress, is to be funded to assign Public Health Service personnel to areas of shortage, such as urban ghettos.

How would the President's program provide (1) protection against catastrophic medical costs, (2) access to medical care for the poor, and (3) cost control?

For the majority of Americans who would be covered under the mandatory employer program, the administration's plan would provide protection against high expenditures by covering all expenses over $5,000 up to $50,000. This would improve the catastrophic coverage in most families' current health insurance. The principal question is whether it would provide enough protection for working families with low earnings. Families whose breadwinner earned near the minimum wage might have to spend a whole year's wages in deductibles and coinsurance before the insurance would pick up the full costs. The principal problem here is that a "financial catastrophe" cannot be defined independently of a family's income. The administration's program appears to be adequate as catastrophic coverage for families whose income is above the median, but for low-income families, the deductibles and coinsurance would prove burdensome indeed.

Coverage for the poor, under FHIP and the vestiges of Medicaid, would probably be adequate for those with very low incomes. However, families in the $3,000–$5,000 range might find it difficult to meet deductibles and coinsurance and might therefore go without needed care. Alternatively, some of the burden of caring for the near-poor might fall on local governments, which might have to pick up the premiums, deductibles, and coinsurance required under FHIP for the near-poor. As a result, the fiscal relief promised to state and local governments through federal assumption of all the costs of FHIP might prove to be limited.

The administration's system of health insurance is designed to control costs as follows: First, the plan would eliminate the inefficiencies resulting from the fact that present insurance plans often cover only hospital expenses. Second, because of coinsurance and deductibles in the basic minimum benefit package, consumers would share in the costs of treatment, thus giving them a stake in holding down both wasteful use of facilities and the prices of services. (But higher-income consumers may buy supplemental insurance to cover the deductibles and coinsurance, thereby eliminating cost consciousness.) Third, although the use of prepaid HMOs would eliminate the cost consciousness of consumers, it would shift the incentive for cost efficiencies to producers. As long as HMOs had to compete with other providers of service, there would be a check both on the quality of the service provided by them and on their annual charges. Finally, cost controls would be strengthened through the private insurance carriers, who would administer the program under a new regulatory bill to be introduced in the spring of 1971. This bill will probably propose independent review procedures, reimbursement programs that stress advance budgeting, and controls over the rate of expansion of physicians' charges—all to be administered through the private insurance carriers.

How would the financing of the administration's proposal affect equity and maintenance of work incentives?

The administration's mandatory employer program does not appear in the budget. Its costs would be shared by the employer and the employee. It is not easy to say how the burden would be distributed or what the incentive effects would be. The mandated benefit package is estimated to cost about $300 a year per employee in 1971, of which initially not more than 35 percent would be paid by the worker. Hence, in a firm not already providing health insurance, the initial effects would be that (1) the full-time employee would have about $100 deducted from his paycheck, and (2) the employer would pay $200 extra for each full-time employee. If the firm were already providing health insurance benefits for its employees, the net costs of meeting the new requirements would be less, possibly even zero. In general, the employee's share would be a heavier burden on the low-wage earner than the high-wage earner, because the former would have a higher percentage of his earnings deducted and because he would be less likely to have health insurance coverage already. Likewise, the employer's share would be a heavier burden on low-wage industries (like retail trade), both because it would constitute a higher proportion of payroll and because these industries are in fact less likely to be providing health insurance coverage already.

As time goes on, one might expect the proposed requirements to have some effects on the demand for labor. Since the cost would be a fixed amount per full-time employee, one might expect that employers would tend at the margin to hire part-time rather than full-time labor, to use over-time rather than hiring additional workers, to substitute skilled labor for unskilled and machinery for employees. Hence in the long run, one might expect wages, especially those for full-time unskilled labor, to be less than they would otherwise have been. In other words, the costs of the health benefits, like the costs of any payroll tax (see Chapter 10), are likely to come out of wages in the long run. Hence, the mandatory employer plan in effect would be financed by a kind of payroll tax, bearing more heavily on the low-wage earner. The plan might reduce the incentive of the unemployed to take low-wage jobs. Once a worker was fully employed, however, there would be no further disincentive to work since the medical "tax" would not rise as his earnings increased.

FHIP costs, on the other hand, would be met from general revenues, and hence the burden would be distributed as equitably as that of any federal program. The major financing issue relates to the possible effect of the FHIP on the work incentives of families in the $3,000–$5,000 income range. The President pointed out in his message that the increase in premiums, deductibles, and coinsurance in this income group "would induce some cost consciousness as income rises. But unlike Medicaid—with its abrupt cutoff of benefits when family income reaches a certain point—this arrangement would provide an incentive for families to improve their economic position." It is true that families in the $3,000–$5,000 income range enrolled in FHIP who move into full-time employment would not suffer any significant loss of medical subsidies. The government subsidy of FHIP would be approximately replaced by the company's premium share under the mandatory employer program. But for FHIP families whose head is employed sporadically or is self-employed, crossing the $5,000 line would mean the loss of about $400 in medical benefits. Such workers are not eligible for the employers' plan, but would be allowed to buy into similar coverage at group rates. It should be noted, however, that under the present Medicaid program, especially in states like New York or California, where benefits are high, the loss of Medicaid when income crosses the cutoff line can be in excess of $1,000 per family. The FHIP program would thus be a move in the right direction.

National Health Insurance

A number of other programs are now before the Congress. The most prominent alternative—indeed, the one the President singled out in his health message as a contrast to his own—is full national health insurance. A national health insurance bill, "The Health Security Act," has been introduced in the Congress by Senator Edward M. Kennedy and Representative Martha Griffiths.

Unlike the President's program, the Kennedy-Griffiths bill calls for a single federally administered health insurance program for everyone. Full coverage would be provided for virtually all medical expenditures (excluded are adult dental care, purely cosmetic surgery, some psychiatric costs, and some drugs) without any deductibles or coinsurance. In other words, the bill provides both first-dollar coverage and full catastrophic benefits. Since no patient would pay any part of the cost, the first question, of course, is how would costs be controlled?

The cost control features of the Kennedy-Griffiths bill involve a complicated procedure for allocating funds and negotiating prices. First, a trust fund would be established to pay for medical services. Half of the trust fund receipts would be derived from special new payroll and income taxes and half from general revenues. The rate of growth of expenditures from the trust fund would be limited to the lesser of (a) the rate of growth of the new tax receipts, or (b) the rate of growth of a composite index of cost of living, population, and services covered under the bill. The idea is to keep total medical expenditures from growing faster than the economy as a whole.

The total health budget for the year would be set prior to the start of the year and would be divided first into ten regions and then into about a hundred "health subareas," on the basis of prior medical expenditures in those areas, adjusted for price changes, population, and so on.

Within the health subareas, physicians and hospitals would be compensated according to guidelines set in the bill. The administrative agency for a subarea would divide its budget into two parts: an account for "practitioners" (physicians, dentists, etc.) and another for hospitals. Based on the size of the practitioners' account and the number of people to be served, the agency would set a "capitation" payment for each type of practitioner—the compensation a practitioner would receive for agreeing to take care of a patient, whatever his needs, for a year. Practitioners could also elect to be compensated on a fee-for-service basis, in accordance with fee schedules set by the agency, but the intention is to encourage capitation as the mode of compensation.

Similarly, hospital budgets would be set prospectively within the limits of the funds available in each subarea. Hospitals would submit budgets for the following fiscal year. These would be reviewed, revised, and approved after consultation with hospital representatives and hearings.

In short, the Kennedy-Griffiths bill would control costs by (a) specifying an expenditure limit for medical care through establishment of a trust fund and (b) specifying a procedure for subdividing funds that would place the responsibility for cost control in the hands of those who would administer the program.

The effectiveness of this procedure would depend ultimately on the ability of the complex administrative procedure to deal with the large variety of individual situations that occur in practice, and on the relative political strength of the consumers and the providers. If the providers felt that they were being inadequately compensated, they could put pressure on the Congress to increase their compensation by raising the payroll tax in the same way that overruns on prospective budgets have been financed under other government programs.

Senator Kennedy estimated that the total cost of his program in 1970 would have been $41 billion, of which $8 billion would have replaced existing federal programs and $33 billion would have been new federal expenditures. The Kennedy-Griffiths bill would have covered about 70 percent of expenditures for personal health in 1970; if this share were maintained in fiscal 1974, the proposed first year of National Health Insurance, the aggregate cost of the program would be about $70 billion.

The financing of the Kennedy-Griffiths bill would come half from new taxes and half from general revenues. The new taxes would include both a payroll tax and a new income tax. The payroll tax would be levied on all wages and salaries at a rate of 3.5 percent, to be paid entirely by the employer (or by self-employed individuals at 2.5 percent). A 1 percent tax would be levied on all income up to $15,000 a year. The "tax base" of $15,000 would be raised periodically, by $600 increments, as average income levels increased. These taxes would be substituted for the payroll tax under the Medicare program. It is estimated that 38 percent of the financing would come from the proposed employer payroll taxes, 12 percent from the proposed tax on income, and the other 50 percent from general revenue. The general revenue portion would require annual appropriation by the Congress.

Similarities and Differences

Although the administration and the supporters of national health insurance seem in some ways to be poles apart, there are important similarities in the two approaches. First, both regard protection against catastrophic expenses as an essential element in a new national health strategy. The Kennedy-Griffiths bill provides full coverage, while the administration bill retains coinsurance up to $5,000. Under the administration bill, catastrophic expenses could still be burdensome to lower middle-income families. Second, both approaches emphasize that new forms of medical care organization are essential, and both lean toward HMOs. Third, both agree that full coverage of at least basic health services for the poor is essential. Under the President's plan, however, the non-poor would still pay a substantial share of their medical bills—an arrangement that would not greatly burden the affluent, but would not improve the current situation among the lower middle-income groups, to whom health bills often mean substantial hardship. Fourth, both approaches would seek to increase the supply of medical manpower. Under the Kennedy-Griffiths plan, funds for training programs (and improving the delivery system) would be appropriated during a "tooling up" period before National Health Insurance benefits began, and would accumulate automatically in a special fund thereafter. In the administration program, annual appropriations would be relied on for these purposes. The burden of paying for health care would be differently distributed under the two programs. The emphasis on deductibles and coinsurance in the President's plan means that those who used health services would pay a higher proportion of the cost; there would be less transfer from the well to the sick than under the Kennedy-Griffiths bill. Moreover, the President's program would probably place a far heavier share of the burden on lower middle-income families (those between the poverty and the median income levels) than would the Kennedy-Griffiths bill. This is because the burden of paying for the mandatory employer program would ultimately fall on wage earners, and the fixed amount per worker would be particularly burdensome to low earners.

Finally, both approaches recognize that a tougher form of regulation of the medical care industry is needed if costs are to be controlled. They differ on what should be done.

1. The National Health Insurance approach argues that private in-

surance has failed to regulate costs and shows no hope of change. Costs must be brought under public control, and the first steps in establishing such control are to (a) centralize the expenditures through the tax system and (b) centralize the responsibility through a government administrative structure.

2. The administration's approach is to try to reform the industry by using every control short of public expenditure control. Thus the administration has called for (a) insurance policies with broader coverage to reduce the inefficient and costly overuse of hospitals; (b) charges on consumers for a broad range of medical services so as to bring pressure on producers from users to hold costs down; (c) incentives for the establishment of HMOs, designed to encourage producer efficiency; (d) explicit introduction of medical care expenditures into collective bargaining, so that unions and management could act jointly to hold down charges; and finally (e) regulation of the health insurance industry, on which many of these controls would impinge and without whose real reform no chance of cost control is possible.

Under either approach—indeed if there were no legislative change at all—a growing share of medical payments will probably be made by third parties. The third party may be the federal government, in which case there will be both a much larger federal health budget and a much larger federal bureaucracy trying to identify legitimate hospital expenses. Or the third party may be a group of private insurers regulating hospital costs and physicians' fees and acting, for all intents and purposes, as allocators of public funds. Whether costs are under control, whether quality care is purchased for the enormous sums that will be spent, will depend very much on the details of the regulatory process and the extent to which it reflects the interest of consumers of medical care.

Under both approaches a vast administrative structure would be required, either in private insurance companies or in public bodies. These regulatory bodies, public or private, besides being faced with the extraordinary complexity of fixing fees for prevention and treatment of disease, would be hampered by the present lack of knowledge as to what delivery systems and incentive structures are most efficient.

Under the National Health Insurance approach, a much larger share of national health expenditures would appear in the federal budget, perhaps as much as $70 billion in 1974. Under the administration's program, only Medicare and Medicaid and FHIP charges would be in the budget totals, and these might aggregate $16 billion by 1974. (In addition, under the administration proposal, there would be tax losses of several billion dollars to the federal treasury stemming from the deductibility of private medical insurance premiums.) But these budget totals by no means measure the net cost of health care being provided under the different plans. National Health Insurance would reduce out-of-pocket payment of fees and reduce private health insurance and state and local government outlays for health, transferring such reductions to the federal budget and taxpayer. The administration's program would also reduce out-of-pocket expenses and state expenses (by a lesser amount) and transfer these costs mainly to the premiums paid under the mandatory employers' plan. Whether Americans receive better care at less real cost would depend not on what appears in the federal budget, but on whether the changes in delivery of service and cost controls that both approaches promise were realized.

12. Environmental Quality

ENVIRONMENTAL QUALITY problems arise because neither economic nor political institutions in the United States have been designed to cope with the fact that environmental resources are scarce and valuable goods. In an earlier day a smaller, more dispersed population and a much lower level of economic activity did not tax the capacity of air and water to assimilate wastes or threaten natural recreation sites with congestion and even obliteration. Unlike other resources, the environment was free to all comers, to use as they saw fit. As population, economic activity, and urbanization grew, however, what were once plentiful environmental resources became increasingly scarce, yet they continued to be treated as if they were still free goods. Smog in the air; unsightly, foul smelling, and unsafe streams; noise and congestion in cities; the disappearance of open spaces and recreation sites swallowed up by suburban development—these are some of the manifestations of the failure of U.S. institutions to adapt to the fact that environmental resources, having become scarce, must be rationed to their best uses.

With all their imperfections, modern industries and markets are marvelously well adapted to minimizing economic costs—to finding ever more efficient means of producing goods and services. In the search for profits, and indeed, for economic survival, business firms have no option but to seek ways to minimize their costs of labor, of raw materials, of machinery and equipment. But since individual firms and consumers do not bear the equally real costs of the environmental degradation caused by their activities, the economic sys-

238

tem offers little incentive to reduce them. Business firms pour sulfurous smoke into the air, shopping center developers gobble up once-green open spaces and create new traffic congestion problems, and consumers in their automobiles add hydrocarbons to the smog-laden air. All of them impose damages on others in the form of pollution of the environment; yet they do not have to pay for these damages. Small wonder that the environment becomes degraded when it is treated as a free resource and when the economic system provides no incentives to use it sparingly.

Recognition of the crucial role of economic incentives in an effective environmental control policy is reflected increasingly in public policy statements. In its annual report for 1971, the President's Council of Economic Advisers lays great stress on the need for developing such incentives. And the chairman of the Council on Environmental Quality recently said:

We think that significant reductions in waste discharges might be more quickly and inexpensively effected if, in addition to regulatory restrictions, changes were made in the costs facing individual polluters. For example, a system of effluent or emission charges requiring payment for the amount of specific pollutants added to the environment would, it seems to me, help harness the normal competitive forces of our economy to work with us rather than against us in achieving our pollution abatement goals.[1]

In 1970 the President proposed a special tax on leaded gasoline as a means of providing incentives for the use of unleaded gasoline, and in February 1971 he proposed a special tax on industrial emission of sulfur oxides into the atmosphere.

Not only the economic but also the political institutions of the nation have failed to cope with environmental quality problems. Water pollution is inescapably related to what goes on along an entire river basin and cannot be dealt with on a community-by-community basis. Urban sprawl and traffic congestion in major metropolitan areas will not yield to piecemeal actions taken by the scores or even hundreds of jealously independent political jurisdictions that divide the governance of metropolitan areas in the United States.

Public action to improve the quality of the environment, therefore, is only partly a question of how much money federal, state, and local

1. Russell E. Train, address delivered at the Atlantic Council, Battelle Memorial Institute Conference, Department of State, Washington, D.C., Jan. 15, 1971 (processed).

governments devote to the problem. Perhaps the most critical policy issues concern the restructuring of economic and political institutions. This chapter on environmental quality reflects that fact and devotes at least as much space to questions of economic incentives and political institutions as it does to budget issues.

The concept of environmental quality covers almost every aspect of modern life and in one way or another has some relevance for most federal programs and policies. This chapter, however, deals only with those selected federal programs that are immediately and directly addressed to the problems of water and air pollution control.

Water Pollution

Water pollution has two major characteristics that should be recognized in designing public policies to control it.

First, there is the economic problem. The assimilative capacity of the nation's rivers and streams is a precious national resource. But it is given away free. Those who use this resource are not charged for it and, as one would expect, overuse it. Few people conserve anything that is provided free of charge. Pollution is the result. On the other hand, reducing pollution also has costs: higher prices for electricity resulting from expensive antipollution devices and less favorable locations for power plants; increased federal and local property levies to pay for waste treatment plants; higher costs and lower output of all those goods and services whose production heavily pollutes the water. What is needed is some mechanism to weigh the social costs of pollution against the economic costs of eliminating it—economic costs that ultimately are reflected in a slower rise in consumption as we ordinarily measure it. Fundamentally, the nation has to balance its desire for an increased supply of the usual kind of consumer goods—automobiles, television sets, clothing, and the like—against its desire for a cleaner environment. Charging polluters a tax on every unit of pollution they discharge into rivers or streams is one way of providing such a balance. The tax would be calculated to reflect society's evaluation of the damage from pollution and could be set as high or as low as that evaluation demanded. Pollutors would have powerful incentives, in their own interest, to do what society wanted—namely, to find the most efficient and effective means for reducing their output of pollutants in order to reduce the tax. In cases where no economical means for reducing pollution could be found, the tax would cause the price of the product to rise, and thus less of it would be bought and less produced. Sales and production would shift toward less polluting activities. In cases of toxic materials like mercury, where the damage can be lethal, strict prohibition may be necessary.

Second, the control of water quality requires a regional approach. Water pollution is a problem that is amenable to a wide variety of solutions. Wastes can be *prevented* through improvements in industrial processes. They can be *treated* through waste treatment plants. They can be *impounded* during periods of low water flow, when the damage they do is great, and released gradually in periods of high water flow, when the assimilative capacity of the river is at its peak. Their harmful effects can be reduced by large-scale in-stream *aeration* of the river. The river can be *flushed out* in low flow periods by water collected behind dams during high flow periods. The optimum combination of techniques depends on, among other things, the characteristics of particular river basins, lakes, or coastal areas. The assimilative capacities of rivers can break down and decompose some kinds of pollutants up to a certain amount. Consequently the amount of waste prevention or waste treatment required is greatest where large concentrations of industry and population are located on short stretches of a river and least where concentration is sparse for long stretches of the river. Upstream pollutors ruin the quality of the water for downstream users. The costs of pollution control tend to be greatest for communities upstream, while benefits are greatest for those downstream. For both technical and political reasons, therefore, improving water quality is a regional process, not solely a matter for individual communities.

The problem of policy is to design economic, political, and budgetary support mechanisms that take these factors into account in a concerted approach to pollution control. There are three potential elements in a public policy:

• the provision of incentives to industries that would cause them to recognize the scarcity of water resources and to economize in their use;

• the prevention of pollution by setting water quality standards and enforcing them through judicial procedures against industries and local communities; and

• the provision of grant assistance to local communities to encourage the building of waste treatment plants for municipal sewage.

Current federal policy relies on the last two of these three approaches and pays little attention to the first. The federal water pollution control effort is based on the required development by each state of water quality standards for each interstate lake, stream, or coastal area within its jurisdiction; it provides for federal-state negotiations and judicial enforcement of those standards against actual or potential pollutors; it seeks secondary treatment of all municipal wastes; it provides federal grants, through the states, for up to 50 percent of the cost of constructing municipal waste treatment plants and tax subsidies to industrial treatment facilities. In 1970 a new set of legislative measures was developed in the Congress and will, in all probability, be enacted in 1971. The new measures would sharply increase federal grants for municipal waste treatment facilities and strengthen the role of the federal government in setting and enforcing standards.

Major Deficiencies in Current Federal Policy

In terms of its overall structure and detailed provisions, this current federal policy has several major defects:

1. Current pollution control policies attack the problem of industrial wastes primarily by establishing standards that are enforced by the sanction of law. The alternative of levying a stiff tax (commonly called an "effluent charge") on each unit of pollutant discharged into the rivers, thereby providing a powerful incentive for each pollutor to clean up his waste discharges, has not yet been used in the water pollution control program.

The enforcement of standards through judicial procedures entails a lengthy, tedious, and often ineffective process of negotiation with states and individual pollutors. The opportunities for delay and for the erosion of standards by pollutors are numerous. As a result, enforcement efforts are subject to long delays and are usually concentrated on only a limited number of conspicuous violators. The primary incentive under an enforcement approach is for industrial pollutors to hire lawyers to delay administrative and court action.

Under the enforcement strategy, industrial pollution has continued to grow. In one river basin after another, this growth has wiped out the gains made by constructing municipal treatment facilities, as documented in a 1969 report of the General Accounting Office.

Effluent charges could be set high enough to achieve the quality of water desired. Therefore, they are in no sense "licenses to pollute," as some have characterized them. Under an enforcement policy, no firm has an incentive to reduce its pollution discharges below the level set by the standard. Under an effluent charge system, however, firms have a continuing incentive to seek new technology that will enable them to lower pollution even below the standard, since any positive amount of pollution costs them some amount in taxes.

2. Such incentives as are currently provided to industry to reduce pollution tend to bias pollution control efforts toward inefficient choices.

Between 40 and 60 percent of the waste loads treated by municipal plants come from industrial sources. The federal grants for the construction of such plants therefore represent a heavy subsidy to industry and encourage the plant owners to treat their wastes in municipal plants. But in many cases it would be much more efficient to adopt new internal production processes that generate less waste to begin with. In effect, the federal government is heavily subsidizing one particular form—and often the most expensive form—of pollution reduction. In his 1971 message to the Congress on the environment, the President proposed to attack this problem by requiring, as a condition for receiving federal waste treatment grants, that municipalities charge industrial firms portions of the project costs that are allocable to the treatment of their wastes.

The Tax Reform Act of 1969 provided a tax incentive to firms for constructing their own waste treatment facilities. Again, this biases the incentives in favor of one particular form of pollution control.

3. The federal government provides grants for the construction of municipal waste treatment facilities in accordance with priorities determined by the individual states. These priorities in turn often have no relationship to any effective plan for cleaning up pollution along river basins.

State priority lists are based on communities that are "ready to proceed." This, in turn, depends on which ones happen to have been bludgeoned by state authorities into building new or improved facilities. The situation is well outlined in the following quotations from the 1968 State of Maryland Program Plan:

Almost without exception, every sewerage project in Maryland has been undertaken at the suggestion, urging, insistence, formal orders, and, when administrative procedures are exhausted, by court action initiated by the

Health Department and the Board of Health and Mental Hygiene. . . .
They build only what they are forced to build and only then if there are
Federal and State grants immediately available . . .[2]

As the Federal Water Pollution Control Administration points out in
its 1970 report, *The Economics of Clean Water*, most states treat applicants on a first-come-first-served basis, in a situation in which bargaining power prevails, and in which the bargaining units with the
most power are often the largest pollutors.[3] As a result of this approach, highly needed plants that would substantially improve water
quality are often not built, while marginal plants are.

As a further result, a disproportionate amount of grants have
gone to small communities, which can more easily be coerced by state
authorities into constructing treatment plants. This lopsided allocation is shown in Table 12-1.

4. Pollution control has been approached primarily on the basis
of requiring uniform treatment of wastes by each community, rather
than through a river basin approach in which treatment goals are related to the characteristics of the river. Instead of budget dollars being
allocated where they would do the most good in cleaning up a river
basin, they are allocated to secure uniform secondary treatment of
wastes, which is too much in some cases and too little in others.

Treating each community as a separate entity rather than as part of
a basin-wide approach has also added to the political problems of enforcing effective pollution control plans—which are formidable in
any event. Effective pollution control plans often call for different degrees of waste treatment in different communities. This implies different tax burdens in different communities. But the communities that
pay the higher taxes are often benefiting other communities farther
down the river that may be called upon for a lesser tax effort. State
authorities cannot enforce such differential requirements on politically
independent communities. Under a river basin authority with taxing
power, a common system of taxes for municipal wastes could be imposed throughout the basin, so that all municipalities would share
equitably in the costs of cleaning up the river. The fact that upstream
Community A had to provide more expensive waste treatment facilities than did downstream Community B would not necessarily be re-

---

2. Quoted in U.S. Federal Water Pollution Control Administration, *The Economics of Clean Water* (1970), Vol. 1, p. 116.
  3. *Ibid.*

Table 12-1. Distribution of Federal Water Pollution Control Act Grants and Population, by Size of Community, January 31, 1969

Size of community	Amount of grants (millions of dollars)	Percentage of grants	Percentage of urban population, 1960[a]
Less than 2,500	173.1	15.3	0.6
2,500– 5,000	128.1	11.3	6.5
5,000– 10,000	155.9	13.7	8.5
10,000– 25,000	215.7	19.0	15.2
25,000– 50,000	150.6	13.3	12.9
50,000–125,000	143.9	12.7	} 22.1
125,000–250,000	62.5	5.5	
250,000–500,000	36.2	3.2	9.3
Over 500,000	68.8	6.1	24.8
Total	1,134.8	100.0	100.0

Sources: Grant distribution from U.S. Department of the Interior, Federal Water Pollution Control Administration, *The Economics of Clean Water*, Vol. 1: *Detailed Analysis* (1970), p. 110. Population distribution calculated from data in U.S. Department of Commerce, *Statistical Abstract of the United States, 1968*, p. 16. Figures are rounded and may not add to totals.

a. Excludes 6.5 percent of urban residents not classified by population of city of residence.

flected fully in higher taxes for Community A.[4] As a result, political resistance to the differential waste treatment requirements imposed by an efficient control plan would be muted. All taxpayers would be interested in the least-cost method of controlling pollution.[5]

Given the lack of attention to the basic economic problems involved, the failure to emphasize a regional approach, and the maldistribution of federal grant assistance, it is not surprising that progress toward controlling water pollution has been disappointingly slow, and in many areas nonexistent.

Recent Trends in Federal Programs

In 1956 the Congress amended the longstanding Federal Water Pollution Control Act and authorized federal grants to states for the

4. Some difference in taxes might be maintained in order to influence the direction of suburban development toward areas with fewer pollution problems. But the differences would not reflect the full difference in costs of treatment.

5. This solution violates the strict economic approach suggested above for industrial pollutors—that is, let each pollutor, through an effluent charge, bear the costs that his pollution imposes. Industries can adopt internal production processes and output levels to reduce the amount of industrial wastes generated, and the effluent charge provides the incentive to do so. But in the case of municipal wastes, such a range of adaptation is impossible. As a consequence, the loss of economic incentives implicit in a common-user charge system for municipal wastes is slight and is outweighed by the gain in political incentive that would result—that is, the removal of opposition to replacing a uniform treatment standard with differential treatment in each community, depending on the characteristics of the river basin. But see note 4 above.

construction of waste treatment facilities. The 1956 amendments also initiated federal efforts to establish water quality standards and to enforce them. During the decade following passage of the act, federal involvement grew very slowly, and the level of budgetary support was small. During the period 1957–65, the average annual appropriation for waste treatment facility construction—the bulk of the federal spending effort—was less than $70 million.

In 1965 the Congress passed the Water Quality Act, which renewed and sharply expanded the federal effort in this field. This act authorized substantially increased expenditures for research and development and the construction of waste treatment facilities and set forth a program for federal supervision over the establishment of water quality standards on all interstate waters. In addition, it created the Federal Water Pollution Control Administration, subsequently renamed the Federal Water Quality Administration (FWQA), now a part of the Environmental Protection Agency. In 1966, expansion of the federal effort was consolidated and reinforced by passage of the Clean Water Restoration Act, which further strengthened the research, development, and facilities grants programs.

The recent budgetary history of the federal program is shown in Table 12-2. The grant program for waste treatment facilities has accounted for the bulk of budgetary costs for water quality improve-

Table 12-2. Appropriations and Expenditures of Environmental Protection Agency for Water Pollution Control Programs, Fiscal Years 1965, 1969, 1970, 1971, and 1972
Millions of dollars

Use and type of funds	1965 actual	1969 actual	1970 actual	1971 estimated	1972 proposed
Grant program for construction of waste treatment facilities					
Appropriations	93	214	800	1,000	2,000
Expenditures	70	135	176	422	1,000
Administration, research, development, miscellaneous grants, and enforcement					
Appropriations	35	87	87	120	143
Expenditures	31	79	86	113	131
Total					
Appropriations	128	301	887	1,120	2,143
Expenditures	101	214	262	535	1,131

Sources: *The Budget of the United States Government . . . Appendix*, for fiscal years 1967, 1971, 1972, pp. 494 and 496, 625, and 803, 805, respectively; *The Budget of the United States Government, Fiscal Year 1972*, p. 113.

ment. While this program has grown rapidly since 1965, the level of appropriations has remained substantially below the amounts authorized in the basic legislation creating the program, even though in fiscal 1970 the Congress appropriated substantially more than the administration requested in its budget. In turn, actual obligations and expenditures have been at a level well below the level of appropriations.

As this program has grown, an increasing number of problems have arisen concerning the financial relationships between the federal and state governments. Under existing arrangements, any funds appropriated for waste treatment grants remain available to the federal government until they are spent. Because the law allocates the funds on a formula basis, the initial allocation provides some states with more funding than they can use. The formula allocates the first $100 million appropriated in any year among states according to population and inversely according to income, and the remainder of the appropriation according to population. Because of the heavy emphasis on population in the formula, several states are awarded a larger appropriation than they are able to use. Heretofore, that portion of the initial allocation that could not be used by a state could not be reallocated to "needy" states until eighteen months after the initial allocation. Largely for this reason, only $425 million was obligated in fiscal 1970 although the Congress appropriated $800 million that year.

Testimony of both state and local officials and of the FWQA has emphasized the difficulty created by the gap between authorization and appropriation levels. Because of the year-to-year uncertainty as to the level of actual appropriations, states and municipalities claim that they have great difficulty in designing waste treatment facilities, plans for which must be drawn up well in advance of construction. Indeed, in many cases they appear to have refused to start construction because of this lack of assured funding.

New Programs and Their Budgetary Consequences

Fiscal 1971 is the last year for which appropriations to the water pollution control program are authorized. Three proposed successors are now before the Congress. In February 1971 the President submitted a series of proposals on environmental quality, including a number addressed to the problems of water pollution. In 1970, Senators Edmund S. Muskie and William Proxmire introduced proposals that were considered but not acted upon by the Public Works Committee. These were reintroduced in 1971.

THE ADMINISTRATION'S PROGRAM, outlined in the President's message to the Congress on the environment, expands the proposals made by the administration last year. At that time it requested a $4 billion authorization for waste treatment grants, $1 billion a year for four years. Last year the FWQA had estimated that $10 billion for the construction of municipal waste treatment facilities would be needed over the next five years to keep up with population and industrial growth, to replace obsolete facilities, and to eliminate the current backlog of unmet treatment needs. The administration's proposal would have provided 40 percent of the financing.

This year the President has revised his request upward, seeking $6 billion for waste treatment grants—$2 billion a year for three years. The increase was based on two factors: First, the FWQA revised upward estimated needs, from $10 billion in five years to $12 billion in three years, because of a faster-than-expected rate of inflation and a fiscal 1971 spending level that fell below that projected and hence raised the backlog of needs. Second, the President now proposes to have the federal government assume, on an average, 50 percent of the construction cost of the treatment plant, instead of 40 percent as was originally planned. The administration also has renewed its request of last year for the establishment of a federally sponsored Environmental Financing Authority, which would issue its own bonds to investors and use the proceeds to help local communities finance their share of waste treatment plants.

The President also proposes to revise the allocation formula among states to permit greater flexibility in using the funds and to allow a greater proportion to go to the states with the highest pollution control needs. The administration program would require that specific effluent requirements be part of state-established, federally approved water quality standards. At the present time the federal government requires states to develop water quality standards meeting federal criteria and subject to federal approval. In many cases, however, the quality standards along a river do not include specific limits (that is, effluent requirements) on the amount of waste that particular industries or municipalities may discharge. As was noted above, the administration proposals would require communities receiving waste treatment grants to recover from industrial users that portion of project costs that are allocable to the treatment of their wastes.

THE MUSKIE PROPOSAL would also continue the present strategy, increase the level of authorization, provide incentives for the development of river basin authorities, and strengthen federal power in the field of water quality standards. His bill authorizes appropriations of $12.5 billion—an average of $2.5 billion a year for five fiscal years. As an incentive to river basin planning, it authorizes federal grants of up to 60 percent of the construction costs of public waste treatment facilities where there is a basin-wide planning authority, compared to the present limit of 50 percent on federal cost sharing. Like the administration proposal, the bill would require that quality standards include effluent requirements. The Muskie bill would also extend federal authority over water quality standards to all navigable waters.

Both of the above proposals would continue the existing water pollution control strategy, which involves the carrot of federal grants and the stick of enforcement and regulation.

SENATOR PROXMIRE'S PLAN calls for quite a different strategy— one that emphasizes economic incentives. Under his proposal, an effluent charge would be imposed on each industrial waste discharger in proportion to the damage its wastes cause to water quality in the river. On the one hand, the revenues collected through this charge would be used to finance pollution abatement facilities. On the other, the charges would provide substantial incentives for industry to reduce its pollution. Senator Proxmire estimates that a minimum of $1.5 billion would be collected in effluent charges in the first year following imposition of the charge. Under his proposal, grant funds from effluent charges and appropriations would be paid not only to municipalities but also to regional water quality commissions. These could provide financing for pollution abatement facilities other than waste treatment plants—in-stream aeration, low-flow augmentation works, and the like. Of course, as time passed and industry reduced its pollution in order to minimize the effluent charges, revenues would decline. Thus, the greater the decline in revenues, the greater the success of the program.

Under either the Muskie or the administration proposal, federal outlays for waste treatment facility grants would grow rapidly over the next few years, as the higher level of grants proposed in each was translated into actual federal expenditures. Net budget outlays under the Proxmire proposal would be significantly lower since, for the first several years of the program at least, most outlays would be financed by the effluent charges.

Long-term Estimates of Treatment Costs

To gain some understanding of the magnitude of the water pollution problem, a mathematical and statistical analysis was made by the International Research and Technology Corporation for this study.[6] In its initial form the analysis takes industrial technology as given, projects population and industrial activity to the year 2000 at ten-year intervals, calculates the pollutant wasteloads that would be generated, and estimates the cost of subjecting them to varying degrees of treatment.

The projected volume of some of the major water polluting wastes is shown for selected years in Table 12-3. In every major category

Table 12-3. Wasteloads Generated (before Treatment) in the United States, by Type of Waste, 1960, and Projections for 1973, 1980, and 2000, Assuming No Change in Industrial Technology in Future Years

Type of wasteload	Wasteload (billions of pounds)				Percentage of 1960 wasteload			
	1960	1973	1980	2000	1960	1973	1980	2000
Chemical oxygen demand, total	288	565	732	2,017	100	196	254	700
Biochemical oxygen demand	62	112	178	330	100	181	287	532
Suspended solids	653	918	1,077	1,393	100	141	165	213
Dissolved solids	538	1,192	2,558	3,459	100	222	475	643

Source: Leslie Ayres and Ivars Gutmanis, "A Model for Strategic Allocation of Water Pollution Abatement Funds," IRT-R-43 (Washington, D.C.: International Research and Technology Corporation, 1970; processed).

there will be very sizable increases in wastes generated, barring major waste-reducing changes in industrial technology. The growth of population, primarily in urban areas, will also give rise to large increases in wasteloads, but the growth of industry and centralized livestock feeding will be the primary causes. Table 12-4 summarizes some of the main sources of waste generation between 1960 and 1980.

Some of the wasteloads are not, of course, directly discharged into the nation's rivers, lakes, and streams, but are processed by waste treatment plants that reduce the volume of wastes discharged. Even so, if the percentages of wasteloads treated by primary and secondary

6. Leslie Ayres and Ivars Gutmanis, "A Model for Strategic Allocation of Water Pollution Abatement Funds," IRT-R-43 (Washington, D.C.: International Research and Technology Corporation, 1970; processed).

**Table 12-4. Increases in Wasteloads Generated in the United States,
by Type of Waste and Major Source, 1960–80**

Type of wasteload and major source	Increase (billions of pounds)	Percentage of total increase
Chemical oxygen demand	444	100
Municipalities	17	4
Livestock	85	19
Manufacturing	342	77
Biochemical oxygen demand	116	100
Municipalities	16	14
Livestock	22	19
Manufacturing	77	67
Suspended solids	424	100
Municipalities	24	6
Livestock	311	73
Manufacturing	89	21
Dissolved solids	2,020	100
Municipalities	38	2
Livestock	—	—
Manufacturing	1,982	98

Source: Same as Table 12-3. Figures are rounded and may not add to totals.

treatment facilities remained the same as they were in 1970 in each industry and other major sectors, the volume of wastes entering the nation's waters would continue to grow sharply, as is shown in Table 12-5.

The aim of the Federal Water Quality Administration is to have all municipal and industrial wastes handled by secondary treatment facilities or otherwise be reduced by an equivalent amount. Realization

**Table 12-5. Wasteloads Discharged in the United States in 1973, 1980, and 2000,
Assuming Continuation of 1970 Percentages of Waste Treatment
by Each Industry and Sector**

Type of wasteload	Wasteload (billions of pounds)			Percentage of 1960 wasteload		
	1973	1980	2000	1973	1980	2000
Chemical oxygen demand	440	559	1,422	153	194	494
Biochemical oxygen demand	78	99	219	126	160	353
Suspended solids	840	962	1,157	129	147	177
Dissolved solids	1,185	2,511	3,439	220	467	639

Source: Same as Table 12-3.

of this goal would bring a very marked reduction in all major pollutants except dissolved solids. The amount of pollution that would be discharged if all wastes were given uniform secondary treatment is shown in Table 12-6. These estimates assume that wastes from livestock as well as industrial wastes receive secondary treatment. However, the treatment of livestock wastes is not encompassed in the

Table 12-6. Wasteloads Discharged in the United States, Assuming Secondary Treatment of All Waste, 1973, 1980, and 2000

Type of wasteload	Wasteload (billions of pounds)			Percentage of 1960 wasteload		
	1973	1980	2000	1973	1980	2000
Chemical oxygen demand	61	77	198	21	27	69
Biochemical oxygen demand	5	8	14	8	13	23
Suspended solids	42	48	58	6	7	9
Dissolved solids	1,126	2,471	3,267	209	459	607

Source: Same as Table 12-3.

FWQA objectives, and pollution from the runoff of cattle and poultry feeding operations is a growing problem.

Uniform secondary treatment would bring a very substantial reduction in waste discharges. But to achieve these results by applying secondary treatment to all industrial and livestock water pollutants, rather than by changes in industrial processes, would incur huge annual costs: $18 billion in 1973, $27 billion in 1980, and $55 billion in the year 2000, as shown in Table 12-7. These costs are expressed in 1971 dollars and include operating expenses and annualized investment costs (assuming depreciation over 25 years and a 5½ percent interest rate).

For the livestock industry, the costs in 1973 would equal a substantial fraction of net income from livestock operations and a much higher fraction of the income of feedlot and poultry farm operators, where the problem is concentrated. For the primary metal industries, the costs would exceed $6 billion in 1980 and $11 billion in 2000. Seeking to achieve a major reduction in water pollution solely through treating wastes already generated would be a very expensive process for the nation, and its costs would show up in significantly higher prices for the food and manufactured products we buy.

The most important conclusion to be drawn from the projections is that the volume of wastes generated by population and economic growth over the next thirty years will be very large indeed, and the cost of treating it by standard methods extremely high. Finding efficient means of reducing wasteload generation should take high priority. Emphasis on changing the internal processes used in industry probably could achieve pollution control objectives at significantly lower cost.

Table 12-7. Annual Costs of Primary and Secondary Treatment of All Wastewater in the United States, by Source, 1973, 1980, and 2000

Billions of 1971 dollars[a]

Source of wastewater	1973	1980	2000
Total	18.5	27.5	55.0
Municipalities	7.0	9.5	12.0
Livestock	1.5	2.0	3.0
Manufacturing	10.0	16.0	40.0
Paper and allied products	1.3	2.0	4.5
Chemicals and allied products	3.4	5.2	18.9
Petroleum and coal products	0.6	0.6	1.1
Primary metals	3.4	6.2	11.2
Other manufacturing	1.3	2.0	4.3

Source: Same as Table 12-3.
a. Data expressed in the source in 1967 prices were increased by 17.9 percent to reflect difference in prices between 1967 and 1971.

Air Pollution

In some ways the problems of air pollution are similar to those of water pollution. Up to a point, the air can assimilate many of the wastes generated by combustion in factories, automobile engines, utility plants, and the like. But its assimilative capacity is limited—therefore scarce, therefore valuable. This capacity is a common resource of all citizens, but society charges nothing for its use. Consequently, it is overused. Air pollution is the result. As in the case of water pollution in river basins, air pollution cannot be understood in terms of individual polluting sources. Rather it is the result of a complex interaction of atmospheric conditions and pollutants in "air sheds." Differing atmospheric conditions, like differing river flows, can produce widely varying pollution consequences from the same volume of pollutant emissions.

As in the case of water pollution, air pollution can be reduced by a variety of means—treating the wastes by devices placed in smoke-

Table 12-8. Estimated Nationwide Air Pollutant Emissions, by Source, 1968
Millions of tons per year

Source	Carbon monoxide	Partic- ulates	Sulfur oxides	Hydro- carbons	Nitrogen oxides	Total
Transportation	63.8	1.2	0.8	16.6	8.1	90.5
Fuel combustion in stationary sources	1.9	8.9	24.4	0.7	10.0	45.9
Industrial processes	9.7	7.5	7.3	4.6	0.2	29.3
Solid waste disposal	7.8	1.1	0.1	1.6	0.6	11.2
Miscellaneous[a]	16.9	9.6	0.6	8.5	1.7	37.3
Total	100.1	28.3	33.2	32.0	20.6	214.2

Source: *Environmental Quality*, The First Annual Report of the Council on Environmental Quality (1970), p. 63. Figures are rounded and may not add to totals.
a. Primarily forest fires, agricultural burning, and coal waste fires.

stacks or auto engines; redesigning industrial processes and combustion engines so that they produce fewer wastes; switching to the use of less pollutant-loaded raw materials (for example, low-sulfur coal).

Some 200 million tons of five major types of pollutants were spewed into the air during 1968 in the United States. Table 12-8 lists these emissions and their chief sources.

Perhaps more striking than the absolute level of these pollutants is their growth over time. For example, electric utilities burned fossil fuel containing about 3 million tons of sulfur in 1940; by 1968 they were releasing well over 15 million tons of sulfur oxides into the air. In 1940, some 16 billion gallons of gasoline were consumed in automobiles in the United States; by the late 1960s well over 50 billion gallons were being consumed annually. Clearly, rapid economic growth and prosperity—to say nothing of the burgeoning use of automobiles for urban commuting—have been primary causes of the air pollution problem.

Unlike the case of water pollution, there are no municipal waste treatment facilities that collect and treat air pollutants. As a consequence, there has been no equivalent of the federal grant program for water pollution waste treatment facilities. Federal programs for the control of air pollution have concentrated on research and development and on the establishment of enforceable air quality standards. As in the case of water pollution, negotiations and judicial proceedings rather than economic incentives have been the chief instruments of public policy.

Federal concern with problems of air pollution developed at about the same time as concern for the degradation of water quality. The first significant legislation was passed in 1955. That law authorized modest appropriations for research, data collection, and technical assistance to state and local governments. Because of the absence of a public works construction program, federal appropriations for air quality improvement have remained substantially below the level of appropriations for water pollution control.

The early law was supplemented in 1960, when the Public Health Service was authorized to study the effects of motor vehicle exhausts on health, and in 1963 by the passage of the Clean Air Act. The latter act expanded the research effort devoted to motor vehicle exhausts and fossil fuel combustion, authorized grants to state and local agencies in support of the development of air pollution control programs, and permitted direct federal action to abate *interstate* air pollution.

The policy direction begun by the 1963 act was reinforced and broadened in both 1965 and 1967. In 1965 the Congress laid down national standards on motor vehicle pollution, which were to be applied to 1968 model vehicles. The Air Quality Act of 1967 focused on "air sheds," rather than on individual pollution sources, and sought ways of establishing effective control programs within each air shed. The act required the Department of Health, Education, and Welfare both to delineate relevant air sheds and to develop and publish air quality criteria that indicated the problems associated with various types of pollutants. It also charged HEW with developing and disseminating descriptions of the techniques available for abating air pollution, together with their costs and effectiveness. The law further requires states to establish, in each of the designated sheds, air quality standards that prescribe maximum concentrations of the pollutants indicated in the criteria documents. After the standards are set, the states must develop plans for achieving them, setting specific emission levels on individual sources and timetables for achieving compliance with the standards.

Federal appropriations and expenditures generated by this legislation[7] are shown below for 1965 and for the years 1969–72 (in millions

7. Expenditures for air pollution control include programs now carried out by the Environmental Protection Agency for fuels and vehicle research, grants to state and local control agencies, enforcement, technical assistance, and research on air pollution effects.

of dollars). While the appropriations have been relatively small, they have grown rapidly in recent years.

	1965	1969	1970	1971 (estimated)	1972 (proposed)
Appropriations	21	88	96	107	129
Expenditures	16	57	80	104	114

The Clean Air Amendments of 1970, enacted late in the year, provided for a significant increase in federal regulatory responsibility and expenditure support for the control of air pollution. The act gives the federal government authority to require that state and local pollution control authorities specify emission standards for stationary pollutant sources. In other words, local pollution control standards must explicitly state the permissible level of emission from individual utility plants, factories, incinerators, and so on. Authorization for research and operating grants to state and local agencies was increased substantially, and federal agencies were given major new responsibilities for regional air quality control. Authorization of $1 billion in appropriations for fiscal years 1971 through 1973 is included in the bill.

Most significantly, the legislation specifies that by 1975 automobile manufacturers must produce new cars and trucks whose carbon monoxide and hydrocarbon emissions are 90 percent lower than current standards and must give customers a 50,000-mile or five-year warranty that the vehicle will continue to meet emission specifications. Under certain stringent conditions, and on the showing of a good faith effort, the federal government may extend the deadline until 1976. Similar provisions are incorporated for auto emissions of nitrous oxide, with a 1976 deadline. These requirements were vigorously opposed by the auto industry, which claimed that the targets were unreachable in the time allowed, and by the administration, which wanted to retain more flexibility on goals and deadlines.

At this stage no one can predict whether the automobile industry can meet the deadline, or what the cost will be in terms of higher auto prices. One thing is virtually certain. If the deadline approaches and the target is not fully met, neither the Congress nor the administration will close down the entire automobile industry.

Alternative suggestions have been made for placing a tax on new automobiles, gradually rising each year, with the amount of the tax depending on the level of pollutant emissions. This would pro-

vide a powerful and increasing incentive for automobile manufacturers to devise engines, fuels, and control devices that reduce
pollution, in order to reduce or eliminate the tax. Moreover, while
the tax could be made quite high, and sufficient to spur major
research and engineering efforts toward pollution control, it would
avoid the "massive retaliation" characteristics of the deadline incorporated in the current law. A remedy so drastic that it forbids the
sale of automobiles is not likely to be invoked when the chips are
down, and therefore is unlikely to be effective. Little attention has
been paid to this approach, however, in either the Congress or the
administration.

In his 1972 message on the environment, the President proposed a
major new approach to one aspect of the problem of controlling air
pollution by recommending that a tax be imposed on emissions of
sulfur oxides. These are one of the major sources of air pollution and
arise primarily from the combustion of fossil fuels in stationary
sources (electric utility plants, smelters, and the like). The tax would
create an incentive for polluting firms to reduce their emissions by a
variety of techniques—using fuels with lower sulfur content, employing currently available devices to remove the sulfur content from
their exhaust cases, and seeking to develop more effective devices.
At the same time, the proposed sulfur oxide tax would point up
sharply the basic economic problem posed by pollution control objectives. Use of fuels with a lower sulfur content might mean increased
unemployment in coal mining areas that have no low-sulfur fuel. To
the extent that industrial firms and utilities cannot reduce sulfur
emissions by other means, the tax would raise the price of those products, including electricity, that consume large amounts of fuel, and
thereby discourage to some extent further expansion in their consumption.

The Total Environment

Air and water pollution are not the only environmental problems.
Noise, congestion, the disappearance of natural scenic and recreation
areas, and ugly and garish commercial developments all contribute
to the degradation of the environment. And all of these problems
share several common characteristics.

Environmental problems of all kinds stem principally from the fact that individuals, communities, and industries, each pursuing their own apparently legitimate interests, often impose costs on the rest of society, in the form of spoiling the quality of the environment. An additional one thousand autos in the rush hour impose traffic delays on tens of thousands of other travelers and add their mite to hydrocarbons in the air that all must breathe. A new factory creates jobs and output, but contributes to the pollution of air and water. Our society has not yet found a way to confront individuals and business firms with these environmental costs, and as a consequence environmental improvement must usually be sought with the more clumsy and often easy-to-avoid tools of legal regulation.

Improving environmental quality will be costly. In choosing to limit sharply the environmental pollution that economic growth entails, the nation is also choosing to sacrifice some economic growth for the sake of a better environment. That may indeed be a wise choice—but it is a choice. A more attractive environment is not something to be provided gratis in political speeches and new laws, but in hard decisions about how the nation uses its scarce resources.

Finally, in the not too distant future, environmental pollution will become an international problem. Ocean oil spills cannot be controlled by the United States alone. Air currents and rivers cross international boundaries. Furthermore, as governments move to control pollution, they will raise the costs of doing business for some industries relative to others, thus influencing the course of international trade and the impact of tariffs and quotas.

13. Transportation

FEDERAL OUTLAYS FOR transportation, primarily investments in capital facilities, will amount to $8.8 billion in fiscal 1972, an increase of 23 percent over 1970 and 106 percent since 1960. Grants-in-aid to state governments for highway construction continue to account for about 60 percent of the federal effort and support for aviation for another 20 percent. (See Tables 13-1 and 13-2.)

Five major programs were enacted in 1970, on the initiative of, or with the active support of, the administration, that provided new or expanded federal investment in urban mass transit, federal-aid highways, airport and airways development, maritime subsidies, and a federally sponsored rail passenger corporation. In these five areas the 1972 budget proposes to obligate $7.2 billion, up $1.2 billion from two years ago. Moreover, most of these programs are scheduled for sizable future increases. Thus the federal government's commitments in support of transportation have been substantially expanded.

At the same time, the 1972 budget provides for a new special revenue sharing program for transportation, which would include funds now separately allocated to urban mass transit, highway grants (except for interstate highways), and airport development grants. The funds for these programs would be consolidated into two grant funds, one for urban mass transit investment and one for general transportation. Grants from each fund would be distributed to states under separate formulas, with a provision requiring that part of the funds be passed on to local governments. The distribution of funds under the new formula would differ significantly from the distribution under current grant arrangements, and, except for mass transit investment, the separate identity of the federal programs whose funds would be consolidated into the special revenue sharing grants would disappear.

259

Table 13-1. Federal Budget Outlays for Transportation, by Major Program, Fiscal Year 1972

Program	Amount (millions of dollars)	Percentage of total
Highway	4,923	56
Aviation	1,870	21
Water	1,611	18
Other	406	5
Offsetting receipts	−19	...
Total	8,791	100

Sources: *The Budget of the United States Government, Fiscal Year 1972*, pp. 120, 271, 397, 399, 438; *The Budget of the United States Government—Appendix, Fiscal Year 1972*, pp. 354, 356–57, 363, 365.

Table 13-2. Federal Budget Outlays for Transportation, by Agency or Program, Fiscal Years 1955, 1960, 1965, 1970, and 1972

Millions of dollars

Agency or program	1955	1960	1965	1970	1972
Department of Transportation					
Highway	636	2,978	4,069	4,507	4,923
Aviation	122	508	756	1,223	1,834
Railroad	2	3	3	17	57
Coast Guard	190	238	367	588	661
Urban mass transit	0	0	11	106	327
Other	0	0	23	−8	22
Offsetting receipts	0	0	−20	−16	−19
Subtotal	950	3,727	5,209	6,417	7,805
Other agencies					
Army Corps of Engineers (navigation projects)	118	202	396	385	490
Civil Aeronautics Board	61	67	92	48	36
Maritime Administration	163	270	330	318	460
Subtotal	342	539	818	751	986
Total	1,292	4,266	6,027	7,168	8,791

Sources: 1955–65, *Setting National Priorities: The 1971 Budget*, p. 109; 1970–72, *The Budget of the United States Government, Fiscal Year 1972*, pp. 120, 271, 397, 399, 438, and *The Budget of the United States Government—Appendix, Fiscal Year 1972*, pp. 354, 356–57, 363, 365.

The following discussion of federal transportation programs treats each major program separately. Should the Congress enact the special revenue sharing proposal, however, many of the decisions about the allocation of federal support to different kinds of transportation would pass from federal to state and local decision makers.

Highways

The federal government supports investments in highway transportation primarily through grants-in-aid to state governments for a variety of construction and related purposes. It also conducts highway safety research and control programs. (See Table 13-3.) The largest single part of the federal-aid highway program is devoted to the construction of the 42,500-mile interstate system, 90 percent of the construction costs of which are paid by the federal government. Most federal outlays for highways are financed by special taxes on gasoline, oil, tires, and trucks. The revenues from these taxes flow into the highway trust fund, out of which most federal-aid highway expenditures are made.

The Federal-Aid Highway Act of 1970 significantly broadened the scope of federal highway assistance. Among other changes, the act

• raised the share of primary and secondary highway construction costs that the federal government pays from 50 percent to 70 percent, effective July 1, 1973;

• established a new program of support for "economic development" highways as a means of promoting economic growth, with the federal government paying up to 95 percent of the cost;

Table 13-3. Federal Highway Outlays, by Program, Fiscal Year 1972

Billions of dollars

Outlay category	Amount
Interstate highway program (90 percent of construction costs)	3.1
State primary and secondary road program (50 percent of construction costs)	0.7
Special programs (forest, public land, and development highways; bridge reconstruction; and so forth)	0.8
Safety and beautification programs	0.2
Administration and research	0.1
Total	4.9
Sources of funds	
Highway trust fund	*4.7*
General revenues	*0.2*
Total	*4.9*

Sources: Based on data in *The Budget of the United States Government, Fiscal Year 1972*, and *The Budget of the United States Government—Appendix, Fiscal Year 1972*.

- established a new urban highway program with emphasis on highway-using mass transit systems;
- established a new replacement program for bridges, with the federal government paying 75 percent of the cost;
- authorized a demonstration program for the elimination of rail grade crossings, and required the secretary of transportation to develop, by July 1, 1972, recommendations for a nationwide program; and
- added miscellaneous special financing for Alaska, the Virgin Islands, Guam, and American Samoa, for federal participation in state acquisition of ferryboats, and for an enlargement of federal training programs for highway workers.

If the federal highway program were making full use of all the revenues currently accruing to it, these new programs would represent simply a diversion of funds from existing purposes to the new purposes; but while current expenditures from the highway trust fund are running at $4.7 billion annually, receipts are accruing at a rate of $5.9 billion. Moreover, since highway expenditures have been held below revenues ever since 1967—primarily as an anti-inflationary device—the trust fund has built up a surplus, which by the end of 1972 will amount to $4.8 billion. The new programs incorporated in the 1970 act, combined with language in the act indicating that it is the intent of the Congress that the administration not withhold highway expenditures, represent an effort to lay the groundwork for a large expansion in federal highway expenditures in future years.

The history of the federal highway program starkly exemplifies the problem that can easily develop when long-lived trust funds are created whose revenues are dedicated to a special purpose. If revenues begin to exceed the original requirements of the program, new "requirements" tend to be created to absorb the excess revenues. The federal government is already devoting the major portion of its transportation budget to highways. What it spends on highways, however, is not set primarily by an evaluation of the nation's overall transportation system and the proper federal role in supporting that system, but by how much revenue the highway trust fund receives.

The principal, though not the sole, reason for establishing the highway trust fund in the mid-1950s was to finance the interstate system. Although the system was originally scheduled for completion in 1972, it is now expected to be finished in 1977. The Federal-Aid Highway

Act of 1970 extended the trust fund and the taxes on which it is based until that year. But at least half of the revenues accruing to the trust fund in the years ahead will not be needed for completing the interstate system. Ten years ago expenditures on the interstate system amounted to 68 percent of trust fund revenues. By fiscal 1972 these revenues will have grown so rapidly that interstate system expenditures will require only 51 percent, and by the mid-1970s this will probably drop below the 50 percent mark. A major result of extending the trust fund until 1977, therefore, will be the provision of large new revenues for financing other highway programs. The 1970 act, as was explained above, authorized a whole new series of programs and increased federal cost sharing to absorb those revenues.

If construction of the interstate system continues as scheduled, and if other federal highway expenditures were held to their present ratio to interstate system expenditures (about 50 percent), highway trust fund revenues would exceed trust fund expenditures by $1.0 to $1.5 billion in the mid-1970s. This "excess" is substantially larger than the amounts the federal government now spends for investment and research in urban mass transit and high speed rail transportation combined. Yet by a little noticed extension of the trust fund in 1970, these sums were made available for additional highway construction.

Over the next several years it will have to be decided whether the currently accruing surplus in the trust fund, plus the large balance that has accumulated in recent years, is to be devoted to further highway expenditures. The answer to that question should take account of the relative priority of various public objectives. It should not be dictated by the coincidental fact that highway trust fund revenues—based on a special tax system designed fifteen years ago—are currently running ahead of expenditures.

If the President's special revenue sharing program is enacted, consolidating a number of current transportation grant programs (including all federal highway grants except those for the interstate system), a number of new questions will arise:

First, should the new grant program absorb all the revenues of the highway trust fund except those needed for the interstate system? Under the administration's special revenue sharing proposals, there could well remain a large surplus in the highway trust fund after allocation of trust fund revenues to the interstate system and to the new special revenue sharing grant. What is to be done with the excess funds accruing to the highway trust fund that are not needed for the interstate system?

Second, how will state and local officials allocate among various modes of transportation the funds made available in the new revenue sharing grant? Chapter 7, which discusses the special revenue sharing programs, points out that some characteristics of the new proposal will tend to reduce state spending on highways, while other forces at work may maintain or increase it.

Third, would it be desirable to split this proposed special revenue sharing grant into two parts: a rural and intercity transportation fund, from which grants would be made to state governments, and funds for urban transportation, to be distributed to city governments and metropolitan transportation authorities? This approach would recognize that intercity and intracity transportation requirements are quite different and would, for the first time, give city governments direct control over large federal transportation grants.

Aviation

The Airport and Airway Development Act of 1970 made a large, long-term commitment to the development of civil aviation. It authorized a ten-year program of expenditures of "no less than" $250 million annually for grants-in-aid for airport development and a total of $2.5 billion for air navigation and traffic control facilities. In addition it empowered the secretary of transportation to make grants of $15 million a year for airport planning.

Both the *commercial airlines*, which carry passengers and freight for hire, and *general aviation*, which consists of private planes flown for business or pleasure, will benefit substantially from the new law. The federal government will continue to build and operate air navigation facilities for the use of both, to construct and operate traffic control and landing facilities at airports, and to provide grants to state and local governments for the acquisition of land and the construction and improvement of airports—but at much higher levels of expenditure than in the past. Federal Aviation Administration (FAA) outlays for building and operating terminal and en route facilities and for airport grants, will rise from $1.2 billion in fiscal 1971 to $1.4 billion in fiscal 1972 and will continue to rise thereafter, reaching about $1.6 billion in 1976, without allowing for the effects of inflation.

The newly created fiscal framework for this program is an airport and airway trust fund, similar to the highway trust fund. Substantial new user charges, together with certain taxes already in effect and appropriations from the general revenues, are pledged to this fund. The 5 percent ticket tax on domestic air passenger fares has been increased to 8 percent, and a head tax of $3 has been levied on each air passenger departing from the United States. A new tax of 5 percent has been imposed on air freight waybills. In view of these new levies, all fuel taxes previously imposed on commercial aviation have been repealed. For the first time general aviation will make more than a nominal contribution toward federal outlays. A tax of 7 cents a gallon has been levied on all fuels used by general aviation. In addition, all civil aircraft, both commercial and general, will pay an annual license or "use" fee of $25 plus 2 cents a pound on piston engine aircraft in excess of 2,500 pounds and 3.5 cents a pound on all turbine engine aircraft.

During the early years of the program, expenditures are not expected to be supported entirely by user charges, and annual appropriations from general revenues will be transferred to the trust fund to make up deficits. The estimated annual amounts by which revenues from user charges will fall short of program expenditures during the first five years are shown in Table 13-4.

Two issues are particularly important with respect to the future of the federal government's support of aviation facilities: (1) Should gen-

Table 13-4. Estimated Revenues and Expenditures for Federal Airway System, Fiscal Years 1971–76

Millions of constant dollars

| Fiscal year | User charge revenues | Expenditures | | Surplus (+) or deficit (−) on civil share[a] |
		Total	Civil share[a]	
1971	666	1,050	840	−174
1972	726	1,212	970	−244
1973	796	1,215	972	−176
1974	872	1,206	965	−93
1975	960	1,230	984	−24
1976	1,062	1,302	1,042	+20

Sources: Revenues, Jeremy J. Warford; expenditures, *Airport and Airway Revenue Act of 1970*, S. Rept 91-706, 91 Cong. 2 sess. (1970), p. 5.

a. Revenues from user charges are transferred to the Airport and Airway Trust Fund; expenditures for the federal airway system that are attributable to civil operations are made from it. Expenditures occasioned by military use of the system are not charged to the fund.

eral aviation pay a larger share of the costs in view of its heavy use of the system? And (2) are the user charges imposed for the new trust fund appropriate? General aviation has been the fastest growing segment of the aviation industry. As against 77,000 private planes in 1961, an estimated 142,000 were flying the airways in 1971, compared to 2,500 aircraft operated by commercial airlines. General aviation's use of airways and airports, as measured by landings and takeoffs, use of instrument facilities, and the like, are expected to continue growing rapidly. In 1969, however, user charges levied on general aviation amounted to $13 million and covered only 5 percent of the costs estimated by the FAA as allocable to their operations.

The 1970 Airport and Airway Revenue Act made some improvement in this situation, but still left general aviation paying only a small fraction of the costs its activities impose on the government. The new taxes on general aviation will recover about 20 to 25 percent of costs over the next ten years,[1] leaving a substantial subsidy to be paid by the general taxpayer and passengers on commercial airlines. Congestion in the airways and around major airports stems in part from the activities of general aviation, which in turn are encouraged by the subsidized services that are provided. And it would be difficult to argue that owners of private and business aircraft are in income brackets so low that they deserve a subsidy as part of a national welfare program.

The user charges imposed in the 1970 act are closely related to the number of miles flown. The passenger ticket tax is proportional to the price of the ticket, which is based roughly on distance; the fuel tax on general aviation also varies with miles flown. But the FAA's costs are related not only to the number of miles flown, but also to the number of landings and takeoffs. User charges related to these activities—for example, landing and takeoff fees that reflected the degree of congestion at particular airports—would have several advantages: (1) they would tend to discourage the excessive use of crowded major airports and would divert some traffic, particularly private planes, to smaller suburban airports; (2) they could be varied by time of day to encourage traffic during less congested periods; and (3) they would provide the FAA with some real evidence of the demand for its facilities, thus helping to guide it toward a better allocation of investment. The fees and charges imposed by the 1970 act do not permit this kind of flexibility.

1. Estimated by Jeremy J. Warford.

In summary, the federal government has embarked on a major expansion of its airways system. The 1970 act that authorized this expansion also increased the charges levied on users of the system, with a view eventually to covering the federal investment and operating costs. Within the total, however, the charges are quite low for general aviation aircraft relative to the costs they impose, and the subsidy provided will continue to encourage a very rapid growth of this form of flying. In addition, the nature of the user charges is such that they cannot be used flexibly to reduce congestion and economically ration scarce airspace around crowded terminals.

Merchant Marine Subsidies

In 1970 the administration initiated, and the Congress enthusiastically enacted, a major expansion and redirection of the merchant marine subsidy program. The new program that President Nixon signed into law on October 21, 1970 calls for the construction of three hundred ships over a ten-year period. The vessels will be built in American shipyards, and their cost will be shared by private buyers and the federal government. The government's share will be provided as a "construction-differential subsidy," that is, it will be calculated to lower the cost of the vessel to the private shipowner to an amount no greater than he would pay for a vessel of the same type if it were built in a low-cost foreign shipyard. The act also continues the "operating-differential subsidy" for U.S. flag vessels, which pays the difference between the costs of operating ships with U.S. crews and repairing them in U.S. shipyards and the costs of using foreign crews and repair yards. Since the costs of using U.S. crews and the costs of repairs in U.S. shipyards are far above foreign levels, shipowners could not meet these costs and still compete without subsidy. While a large part of the added costs of using U.S. crews results from the higher wages paid, another very large part stems from union rules, which require U.S. ships to carry many more seamen than do foreign ships of the same type.

For several reasons, which are discussed below, it is difficult to estimate the likely costs of the government's maritime programs. Taking into account both direct budgetary outlays and the higher shipping rates imposed on both business and government, it is quite likely that the ten-year cost will exceed $10 billion. The primary justification offered for the program is the contribution it makes to national defense by maintaining U.S. shipyard capacity and by keeping in existence ships crewed by U.S. seamen. However, the actual national security benefits to be derived from such a program—particularly one of this size—have never been demonstrated.[2] The major expansion of the program now in motion will be a very expensive means of securing what are, at best, very marginal benefits.

The Construction Subsidy

The construction-differential subsidy, or CDS as it is commonly known, has been available to shipowners under a provision of the Merchant Marine Act of 1936. Between 1958 and 1968, for example, 173 new ships costing $2.2 billion were built with the aid of more than $1.1 billion of CDS. Smaller amounts were provided for reconstructing and modernizing other vessels. Although the rate of expenditure of CDS funds was highly uneven during the 1960s, owing in part to budgetary constraints caused by the war in Vietnam, contracts were let for building thirteen to eighteen vessels annually in most years of the decade.

Shipbuilding will be greatly accelerated under the new maritime program. Plans call for contracts to be let for the construction of nineteen vessels in fiscal 1971, at an estimated cost of nearly $230 million in CDS funds. These ships will be the first contingent of the three hundred called for by the new program. Construction will begin on another twenty-two vessels in fiscal 1972, rising to thirty in 1973 and remaining at that level until a total of three hundred have been built.

Costs received little attention in congressional committee hearings on the President's program. Few questions were aimed at eliciting cost figures, and witnesses volunteered little information. At least a rough estimate can be made, however, of the government's share of the cost of adding three hundred new vessels to the merchant marine. Such an estimate depends on too many variables and assumptions to be highly accurate, but it is nonetheless valuable because no authoritative cost figures were published by the Maritime Administration or offered in testimony before congressional committees.

The prospective costs will depend upon a variety of administrative, legislative, and economic developments. During most of the 1960s the federal government paid 50 to 55 percent of the cost of building new

2. For a more detailed discussion of this matter see *Setting National Priorities: The 1971 Budget*, pp. 174–77.

ships added to the merchant fleet with the aid of CDS, for it cost more than twice as much to build those vessels in American shipyards as it would have cost to build them abroad. To emphasize its determination to reduce the costs of the construction-differential subsidy, the administration proposed, and the Congress enacted, a declining schedule of upper limits on the amounts of CDS that might be granted for a particular vessel between 1971 and 1976. The limit in effect in 1970 was 50 percent.

Beginning in fiscal 1971, the administration expects the CDS to be less than 45 percent of the U.S. cost of the vessel, in fiscal 1972, less than 43 percent, and so on, decreasing by 2 percent annually until a target of 35 percent is reached in 1976. These are not legal limits on the size of the CDS, which will remain at 50 percent. They are more like productivity goals, though the act nowhere calls them that. If the lowest competitive bid received from a shipyard in any of these years requires a CDS greater than the goal for that year, the Maritime Administration is authorized to negotiate a lower price with any of the bidders; but it may still award a contract that exceeds the goal for that year.

Even if the Maritime Administration and the shipbuilding industry succeed in reducing the percentage of CDS on new construction, the absolute amount of the subsidy paid on each new ship will almost certainly fall much less than proportionately. The cost of building a ship both here and abroad has been rising rapidly. A declining percentage of a rising total can still yield an increase in the absolute cost of the subsidy.

In fiscal 1972, twenty-two new vessels are to be contracted for at a total cost of nearly $520 million. The government's share is estimated to be $227.5 million. If the mixture of ship types does not change radically in future years, the average cost of the vessels will be nearly the same as in 1972, apart from an assumed annual increase of 5 percent in line with the trend of ship construction costs that persisted throughout the 1960s. Using these assumptions, the total cost of building the three hundred new ships can be calculated:

• On the assumption that CDS rates can be lowered to 35 percent by fiscal 1976 and that they will remain at 35 percent thereafter, the government's share of the cost of the construction program will exceed $3.4 billion by the time the last ship moves down the ways.

• If CDS rates cannot be reduced below 45 percent, but the construction program is continued anyway, the government will have to contribute more than $4.1 billion to bring it to completion.

The likelihood of cost escalation is high, particularly over the next few years. U.S. shipbuilding capacity is already strained. The bulk of it is taken up by Navy shipbuilding programs, for which the 1972 budget proposes a 45 percent increase in funds over the level of the late 1960s. In February 1970 only two builders bid on a major subsidized ship contract, and the low bid was 34 percent above the cost of constructing the same type of ship four years ago.

Operating-Differential Subsidy

Until recently, only cargo liners offering regular service on established trade routes have received an operating-differential subsidy (ODS). The new maritime law extends this kind of aid to U.S. flag vessels in bulk cargo carrying service. Bulk carriers transport such cargoes as oil, ore, and wheat and operate not on a regular schedule, but as shipping opportunities dictate.

The new law contains some improvements in the method of calculating the ODS, particularly in denying subsidies for wage increases that are out of line with increases elsewhere in the economy. However, the subsidy still discourages efficiency. It pays the difference between the labor costs on a U.S. ship and those on a similar foreign ship. If a shipowner secures greater efficiency—fewer crew members to a ship, for example—he simply loses some of his subsidy, and vice versa. There is little financial incentive for management to bargain hard to reduce crew size or to take other cost reducing steps. The administration proposed to eliminate the subsidy for repair costs, but the Congress rejected the proposal.

Tax Subsidies

The 1970 legislation made its most extensive change in existing law by establishing a program that will expand the government's share of the cost of adding new ships to the U.S. merchant marine and fishing fleet. The program will operate through the federal tax system and so will not be subject to the regular review that is normally a part of the annual authorization and appropriation process.

Unlike the construction-differential subsidy, which is available to only a limited number of shipowners selected by the Maritime Administration and the total amount of which is limited in each year, the tax subsidies provided under the new program will be readily available to many shipowners in amounts over which the government will have little control. The subsidies will consist of a deferral of taxes on earnings that are attributable to the operation of a U.S. flag vessel and that the owner agrees to deposit in a special fund; he uses the fund to reinvest in new vessels built in U.S. shipyards for use "in the United States foreign, Great Lakes, or noncontiguous domestic trade or in the fisheries of the United States."[3] The law eliminates the tax on any gain the shipowner realizes on the sale of a vessel if the proceeds are reinvested in any U.S.-built ship.

The subsidy granted by these provisions is in the form of tax deferral rather than tax exemption. When the owner makes a withdrawal from his fund to purchase a new vessel, the tax basis of the vessel will be reduced by the amount of the withdrawal. The owner's depreciation deductions on the new vessel will therefore be smaller than they would be otherwise; hence, it is expected that the federal government will eventually recover its earlier tax loss. Such a tax deferral plan is nothing more than a mechanism for making interest-free loans, and the ultimate subsidy is equivalent to the interest cost saved. If the tax is deferred for ten years and the interest rate is 6 percent a year, the deferral is worth 44 percent of a full tax exemption.

Until the new law was passed, the total direct and indirect costs of subsidizing the U.S. merchant marine, paid by taxpayers and consumers of shipping services, amounted to between $650 million and $750 million a year. The new law increases the subsidies substantially. Barring a change in the law, these additional subsidies represent a long-term commitment and a claim on scarce budgetary resources for a program that has not appeared near the top of most publicly proclaimed priority lists.

Rail Passenger Service

In 1970 the Congress passed, and the President signed, a bill establishing a semipublic National Railroad Passenger Corporation, commonly called "Railpax," to take over a portion of the intercity passenger service of American railroads. The Railpax law is an effort to salvage some part of these rapidly deteriorating facilities.

3. Public Law 91-469, 91 Cong. (1970), Sec. 21(a).

In contrast to its heavy investments in highways, aviation, and water transportation, the federal government has provided no significant support to rail transportation during the past fifty years. Indeed, many would argue that its substantial promotion of competing transport modes, and its excessively rigid regulation of railroads, has hastened the demise of rail passenger service.

Under the High Speed Ground Transportation Act of 1965, the federal government did begin a modest program of research and demonstrations designed to improve intercity rail passenger service. The program concentrated on subsidizing a demonstration of high speed rail transportation in the heavily traveled corridor between Boston and Washington ($10 million in the 1972 budget), and research and development of new high speed ground transportation systems ($11 million in 1972). The demonstration program, initially plagued by delays and technical problems, has had modest success in attracting passengers. But large numbers of travelers have not yet been diverted from heavily congested airlanes and highways in the northeast corridor.

The policy underlying the new program is that travelers should have the maximum feasible choice among modes of travel—a recurring theme of public intervention in transport in the United States. Intercity rail passenger service is declared to be a necessary part of a "balanced transportation system" that will allow users to have a choice. Other expected benefits are a reduction of air pollution and an end to congestion on the highways and airways and at airports.

To achieve these results, the new law empowers the Railpax corporation to take over and operate passenger services on a "basic system" designated by the secretary of transportation. Operations of the corporation will begin on May 1, 1971 and must continue at least until July 1, 1973. All passenger trains not included in the basic system may be discontinued by the railroads immediately under simplified Interstate Commerce Commission (ICC) proceedings. Carriers entering into contracts with the corporation will be relieved of financial responsibility for continuing intercity passenger service, though they are expected to operate the trains for the corporation. Carriers refusing to contract with the corporation are obliged by law to continue operating trains on the basic system until January 1, 1975 regardless of the financial outcome. Employees are accorded liberal provisions for job protection and for collective bargaining.

The secretary of transportation is authorized to make grants of up to $40 million to assist the corporation in organizing and conducting its affairs. He is further empowered to guarantee loans to the corporation of up to $100 million for improving roadbeds, purchasing new or refurbishing old rolling stock, and for other purposes; and he can lend to the railroads, or guarantee loans to them of, up to $200 million to assist them in carrying out their contracts.

Contracting railroads become common stockholders of the corporation by paying in half of their 1969 passenger service deficit in cash, in equipment, or in commitments to perform future services at the option of the corporation; but they may pay less by using either of two other formulas as finally arbitrated by the ICC. An attempt will be made to attract new capital by selling cumulative convertible preferred stock to investors other than railroads.

Despite the talk of a basic national system and the role of intercity rail passenger service in affording modal choice, both the Congress and the administration recognize that at best there will be "a minimum of such service along specific corridors," and that "a large number of [routes] hold no promise for financial success in the foreseeable future."[4] Even so, Department of Transportation spokesmen have said that intercity rail passenger service will continue for 85 to 90 percent of the people now living in metropolitan areas who currently have such service. The network will have 184 trains a day connecting 114 cities. The more optimistic forecasters expect Railpax to show profits in two to three years and a $10 million profit in five years.

As its sponsors assert, Railpax will make possible many real economies. Service can be concentrated on the shortest routes, saving as much as five hundred miles on transcontinental runs; competing trains can be eliminated; coordinated management should facilitate through service; faster and more comfortable and convenient service should be possible with new equipment on improved roadbeds; arrivals and departures can be tailored to travelers' needs; frequencies on heavily traveled routes can be increased; experiments with ticketing, baggage, and meal service can be tried.

Nevertheless, making Railpax a success will be a difficult undertaking. By 1946 nearly half of the 20,000 passenger trains operating in 1929 had been discontinued because of dwindling patronage and seri-

---

4. *Passenger Train Service*, H. Rept. 91-1580, 91 Cong. 2 sess. (1970), pp. 1, 3.

ous financial losses. By late 1970 only 360 intercity passenger trains remained, and more than 100 of those are now in discontinuance proceedings before the ICC.

The new government venture raises a host of complicated issues, of which three are particularly important:

First, one of the major obstacles to an effective rail passenger system in the United States has been the existence of train service on many routes that, under even the most optimistic forecasts, will continue to generate far too little traffic to support the service. In the past, opposition from affected communities and tortuous proceedings before the ICC have blocked attempts to pare down the rail passenger system to a set of potentially high-traffic routes. The new law recognizes this fact by cutting through existing procedures, by giving the secretary of transportation power to designate a practicable set of routes, and by allowing the railroads joining Railpax to abandon passenger service on other routes. States or communities that wish to preserve routes outside the system may retain the service only if they agree to pay two-thirds of the required subsidy. By this device the Railpax law comes to grips with at least one important aspect of the rail transportation problem.

Second, many observers believe that if rail passenger service is to be maintained, it must concentrate on relatively short routes between large population centers and must provide—in addition to speedy transportation—comfortable, courteous, and convenient service. The comparative advantage of air travel increases in proportion to the distance between major population centers. While no one knows with certainty how much traffic an improved high-speed rail service can attract, the probability of success diminishes for long-distance routes, except perhaps for a single transcontinental route chosen primarily for its scenic attractions.

The choice of routes is critically important. In January 1971 the secretary of transportation designated the routes to be included in Railpax. The system excludes two-thirds of the existing passenger mileage and eliminates half of the trains. It includes the principal high-density, short-distance routes—for example, Boston/New York/ Washington; New York/Cleveland/Chicago; and seasonally, New York/Washington/Miami. It also includes routes of longer distance and lower density, on which reasonable volumes of traffic are less likely to be secured. Local and regional interest in the maintenance of passenger service undoubtedly required that the Railpax system incorporate more mileage and longer routes than transportation factors alone would have dictated. The critical question is whether the inclusion of potential low-volume routes will endanger the Railpax corporation.

The third issue is related to the second. At some point, two questions about Railpax will have to be answered. Is part or all of the system self-supporting? If not, should the money-losing segments be maintained? There is nothing inherently wrong about providing a subsidy to maintain rail service over a particular route. The service may confer benefits that are not fully measured by passenger revenue, such as reducing congestion on highways and airlanes and pollution in the atmosphere. But the very fact that low passenger volume causes the losses that require a subsidy should be a warning that the reductions in congestion and pollution are not likely to be large. As a consequence, the ability of a route segment to support itself is probably a good initial criterion for judging whether the route should be maintained, with exceptions to be made only after a careful scrutiny of the claimed benefits of a subsidy.

If it is decided to maintain money-losing segments, the subsidy should be explicitly recognized. The law creating Railpax provides for federal loans and loan guarantees totaling $300 million. If a number of route segments prove to be money losers and it is nevertheless decided to maintain them, the subsidy should be provided explicitly and directly, rather than indirectly by raising passenger fares on other routes to cover the losses (which might in any event be self-defeating), or by allowing default on the government loan.

14. Housing

ALTHOUGH THE FEDERAL GOVERNMENT directly and indirectly affects the nation's housing in a variety of ways, two areas have been of particular concern in recent years. In 1968 the Housing and Urban Development Act set two ambitious goals for the U.S. economy in the decade 1969–78. It called for the building of 25 million new housing units and, within that total, the public subsidization of 6 million new and rehabilitated units for low- and moderate-income families.[1]

Concern over housing arises from three sources: (1) the need to construct housing to meet the anticipated increase in new households, (2) the desire to upgrade the quality of available housing, and (3) the goal of providing decent housing for poor and moderate-income families at costs that do not absorb too high a proportion of their income.

The Nixon administration, while modifying details of the 1968 targets, essentially adopted them as an expression of national policy. Although 80 percent of the housing units to be constructed would be unsubsidized, the existence of the 25 million unit goal expresses a national objective that presumably influences a wide range of public policies—monetary and fiscal measures, public support of financial institutions providing mortgage credit, and financial regulation of various kinds. The decision to aim at the construction or major rehabilitation of 6 million subsidized units reflects the view that housing for low- and moderate-income families can best be provided through subsidizing the purchase or rental of new housing rather than the occupancy of existing housing (5 million of the 6 million units would

---

1. As subsequently interpreted, the 1968 goals provide for 25 million new units plus the publicly subsidized rehabilitation of 1 million existing units. The sum of these two figures (26 million units) is usually cited as "the" housing goals. This analysis concentrates on the 25 million new units.

be new). The annual budgetary cost of subsidizing homeowner and renter costs would be about $5 billion to $6 billion when the 6 million units were completed.

The federal government affects the first part of the national housing goals—constructing 25 million new housing units in ten years—primarily through its overall economic policy. In calendar 1970, principally because of high interest rates and scarce mortgage credit, only 1.5 million new units were started, far fewer than the number contemplated in the housing goals. By late 1970 and continuing into 1971, however, interest rates fell sharply, the flow of savings into savings and loan associations increased, and mortgage credit became more plentiful. The annual rate of housing starts in early 1971 rose to 1.8 million units.

The administration's economic forecast for 1971 foresees a high level of housing starts for the year. Although, as Chapter 1 pointed out, most private forecasters are more pessimistic than the administration about overall economic conditions, they agree unanimously that 1971 will bring substantially more housing starts than 1970. If the money supply grows rapidly and credit conditions continue to ease—which the administration is relying upon to stimulate recovery—housing construction in 1971 should meet or exceed the expectations of both official and private forecasters. Housing starts approaching 2 million units might be achieved, even with a slightly less ambitious growth in the money supply than the administration seeks. Since 4 million of the 25 million housing units included in the ten-year goals are mobile homes, the construction of roughly 2 million conventional units a year would be consistent with meeting the goals, though it would not make up for the shortfall in construction during the past two years. In addition to influencing residential construction through general economic conditions, the federal government provides extensive aid to the private market through various mortgage insurance programs. Although much of the activity does not involve budget expenditures, it is the oldest and most extensive form of federal aid to housing.

Housing Assistance in the 1972 Budget

While aggregate economic policy is the government's primary instrument for achieving the overall housing goal, specific subsidies in the federal budget are the primary means of reaching the target of 6 million new and rehabilitated units for low- and moderate-income families. Federal outlays for housing assistance for low- and moderate-income families is expected to total $1.9 billion in fiscal 1972, $300 million more than in fiscal 1971 and $1 billion above the amount spent in fiscal 1968, before the new programs started. In addition, $1.5 billion in loans will be made available to low- and moderate-income families for rural housing. Thus, federal housing assistance to such families will continue to expand in 1972, but more moderately than in recent years. After three years of rapid growth, program levels are approaching the annual rates necessary to produce the federally assisted units called for by the national housing goals.

Two major programs are designed specifically to reduce the cost of housing to levels the poor can afford—low-rent public housing under which local housing authorities build, buy, or lease housing to be rented or sold to poor families, and rent supplements under which poor tenants pay one-fourth of their income in rent and the federal government pays the difference between this amount and the market rent of apartments in approved projects.

Three major programs are designed to assist moderate-income families. Under Section 235 of the National Housing Act, which provides for homeownership assistance, the federal government pays the difference between 20 percent of family income and mortgage payments on approved housing. Under Section 236 (rental assistance), the federal government pays the difference between 25 percent of family income and fair market rents in special projects. Expenditures under these programs are expected to rise from $23 million in fiscal 1970 to $450 million in 1972. These programs tend to reach households with incomes higher than the limits set for admission to public housing but too low to afford new housing without assistance. In addition, the Farmers Home Administration makes loans at subsidized interest rates to moderate-income households in rural areas.[2]

Most of the new housing starts being assisted in fiscal 1972 will be for moderate-income families rather than for the poor, as is shown in Table 14-1. Of the 478,000 assisted starts, less than 30 percent are for the poor. This apparently reflects the belief that the poor will benefit

2. For further descriptions of these programs, see *Setting National Priorities: The 1971 Budget*, pp. 86–91.

Table 14-1. Federally Assisted Housing Starts, by Program, for Fiscal Year 1968 and Estimates for Fiscal Years 1971, 1972, and 1975

Thousands of units

		1971		1972		1975ᵃ
Subsidized program	*1968 actual*	*1970 esti- mate*	*1971 esti- mate*	*1970 esti- mate*	*1971 esti- mate*	*1970 esti- mate*
For poor families						
Low-rent public housing	51	94	100	94	95	121
Rent supplements	12	13	20	32	32	30
For moderate-income families						
Homeownership	44ᵇ	141	162	128	163	144
Rental housing	15ᶜ	73	124	151	188	144
Total, excluding rural housing	122	321	406	405	478	439
Rural housingᵈ	35	101	...	147	...	147

Sources: 1968, *The Budget of the United States Government, Fiscal Year 1970*, p. 119; 1970 estimates, *Second Annual Report on National Housing Goals*, Message from the President of the United States, H. Doc. 91-292, 91 Cong. 2 sess. (1970), pp. 45–51; 1971 estimates, *The Budget of the United States Government— Appendix, Fiscal Year 1972*, pp. 496, 497, 499.

a. 1971 estimates for 1975 are not available.
b. Loans for low- and moderate-income housing.
c. Housing for the elderly and rehabilitation loans and grants.
d. Farmers Home Administration housing program. Not reestimated in 1971.

indirectly as moderate-income families move from older standard housing to new subsidized housing. Expanding assistance to moderate-income families also tends to hold down program costs because they can pay more toward their housing than can poor families. A small decline in the number of assisted starts in low-rent public housing is expected in fiscal 1972. Low-rent public housing projects have been plagued by problems of maintenance and administration. The decision not to expand these programs probably reflects the disappointment in the way existing programs are operating.

There are now so many housing programs that the administration proposes to resubmit legislation, introduced but not acted upon in 1970, to consolidate forty current subsidy and mortgage insurance programs into seven larger programs and to eliminate eleven other programs. The purpose is to simplify federal administration and enable borrowers to learn more easily whether they are eligible for subsidies, loans, or mortgage insurance. The legislation would create a single rental assistance program that would replace rental assistance (Section 236) and five smaller programs. In addition, it would establish a uniform rent formula for low-rent public housing, applicable throughout the country, under which tenants would be required to pay in rent 20 percent of the first $3,500 of income and 25 percent of income over $3,500. Because local housing authorities now use varied rent formulas under low-rent public housing, uniform treatment would result in rent reductions for many public housing tenants and rent increases for many' others. Homeownership assistance (Section 235) and four smaller programs would be consolidated. The budget proposes no major new programs to assist housing; the rising expenditures reflect primarily the impact of commitments made in prior years, mostly for subsidies to low- and moderate-income housing.

The 25 Million Goal

Two questions need to be asked about the housing goals. First, do we need so many new housing units? Second, are they likely to be built?

The basic need for new housing arises from a number of sources, of which the increase in the number of households is the most prominent. Since 1950, housing construction in the United States has fluctuated from year to year, but it has usually exceeded the number of new households formed by a substantial margin. The excess of housing starts over new households reflects primarily the replacement of previously existing housing lost through abandonment, demolition, or other causes. Since the Second World War, some of the excess has also appeared as an increase in vacant housing, which was at an abnormally low level at the end of the war. In general, the greater the excess of housing starts over new households, the more rapidly the nation replaces its older housing units and the faster it improves the quality of its housing stock. Table 14-2 shows this excess for five-year periods since 1950 and as it will be in the 1969–78 period if the housing goals are realized. The excess is calculated under two different assumptions about the growth in new households.

Reflecting the surge in birth rates in the early postwar years, new households will increase substantially in the decade of the seventies, according to Census Bureau projections. Housing construction would have to rise significantly simply to match that increase. But as Table 14-2 shows, the housing goals assume an even larger growth in housing construction than in new households. Since the housing goals call

Table 14-2. Housing Starts, New Mobile Homes, and Net New Households, Subperiods during Calendar Years 1950–69, and National Housing Goals for Fiscal Years 1969–78

Annual averages in thousands

	New housing units				Excess of total new housing
Subperiod	Total	Conventional starts	Mobile homes	Net new households	units over net new households
Actual					
1950–54	1,763	1,690	73	864	899
1955–59	1,555	1,439	116	964	591
1960–64	1,602	1,471	131	928	674
1965–69	1,696	1,415	281	1,125	571
National housing goals					
1969–78[a]	2,500	2,100	400	$\begin{cases} 1,360 \\ 1,130 \end{cases}$	$\begin{cases} 1,140 \\ 1,370 \end{cases}$

Sources: U.S. Department of Housing and Urban Development, *1969 HUD Statistical Yearbook* (1970); U.S. Bureau of the Census, *Construction Reports: Housing Starts*, C20, relevant issues; Bureau of the Census, *Current Population Reports: Population Characteristics*, Series P-20, relevant issues; *Second Annual Report on National Housing Goals*; Brookings Econometric Model, unpublished tabulations (1970).

a. The data for new housing units are the national housing goals for fiscal years 1969–78. Of the two figures for net new households, the upper is the high projection of the Bureau of the Census; the lower is the low projection of the Bureau of the Census.

for an average annual construction of 2.5 million housing units, and since new households are expected to increase at an annual rate of between 1.1 million and 1.4 million units (depending on whether the high or low census projections are used), the excess of construction over new households would average well over 1 million units a year, compared to an average of 680,000 over the past twenty years.

Table 14-3 indicates how this excess would be used, according to a detailed outline of the housing goals provided by the President in his 1970 report on housing,[3] and compares this with the experience of the 1960s. A very large increase in removals of existing housing is incorporated in the housing goals, designed to reduce to zero the number of dilapidated houses in the United States. The housing goals also allow for a large rise in housing vacancies. One-third of the 3.5 million increase in vacancies results from the incorporation in the housing goals of a large increase in the construction of second (vacation) homes. Since these homes stand vacant part of the year, their number affects the overall vacancy statistics. The remaining vacancies

3. *Second Annual Report on National Housing Goals*, Message from the President of the United States, H. Doc. 91-292, 91 Cong. 2 sess. (1970).

Table 14-3. Number of New Housing Units and Their Use, Calendar Years 1960–69, and National Housing Goals, Fiscal Years 1969–78
Millions of units

Description	Actual 1960–69	National housing goals 1969–78
New housing units[a]	16.5	25.0
Use of new units[b]	17.1	25.5
Accommodation of new households	11.0	13.5[c]
Removal of existing units[d]	5.4	8.5
Increase in vacant units	0.7	3.5
Statistical discrepancy[b]	−0.6	−0.5

Sources: Bureau of the Census, *Construction Reports: Housing Starts*, C20, relevant issues; Bureau of the Census, *Current Housing Reports: Housing Vacancies*, Series H-111, relevant issues; *Second Annual Report on National Housing Goals*, pp. 23–25, 53, 55.
a. Includes mobile homes.
b. Estimates of production and use do not exactly coincide in the past data nor in the housing goal analysis in the *Second Annual Report*.
c. High projection of the Bureau of the Census for new household formations.
d. Includes estimated scrappage of mobile homes.

reflect both the rise in the number of housing units and an increase in the vacancy *rate*, built into the goals as a means of achieving an easier supply situation and a barrier to rapid increases in rents. Since the allowances for replacement housing and for increasing vacancies are generous, some shortfall from the 25 million goal could occur and the nation would still achieve a major upgrading in the quality of the housing stock.

How realistic are these goals? What conditions are essential to their achievement? Many factors have a bearing on these questions, but the goals are examined here in the limited context of their relation to population growth and economic conditions. We will first consider the quantity of housing that is likely to be built during the remaining eight years of the housing goals and then the implications for upgrading the quality of housing.

Factors Affecting Housing Construction

The major factors affecting the demand for new housing units are changes in the size and age structure of the population, the price of housing relative to other prices, the rate of growth in real income, and monetary conditions. Sharp fluctuations in the birth rates—from very low levels in the 1930s to very high ones between 1947 and 1957—are now being reflected in the shifting composition of the adult population. Table 14-4 shows the number of new households by three broad age categories for the past twenty years, and as projected by the Census Bureau to 1979. Changes in the rate of household formation result, after some time lag, in changes in the level of housing construction. The demand for multifamily units is particularly influenced by the number of households headed by young people under the age of 25 just starting out in marriage, and by the number of elderly people, many of whom move into apartments after their children have left. The demand for single-family houses, on the other hand, responds principally to the number of households in the middle age brackets, with their need for additional space for children living at home.

Ten years ago, the number of young households began to grow more rapidly, and as Table 14-5 shows, this was accompanied by a rise in the construction of multifamily housing during the 1960s. At the same time, construction of single-family housing declined sharply, accompanying a slowdown in the rate of growth of households headed by persons from 25 to 64 years old. Toward the end of the decade, the number of households in this age bracket began to rise again and is expected to increase even more rapidly in the next few years. The con-

Table 14-4. Number of Household Formations, by Age Groupings, Subperiods during Calendar Years 1950–69, and High and Low Projections for Fiscal Years 1970–79

Thousands of households

Period	Total	Head, 25 to 64 years	Head, under 25 or over 65		
			Total	Under 25 years	Over 65 years
Actual					
1950–54	4,320	2,843	1,477	36	1,441
1955–59	4,822	2,910	1,912	405	1,507
1960–64	4,641	2,252	2,389	852	1,537
1965–69	5,624	3,077	2,547	1,235	1,312
High projection					
1970–74	6,701	4,422	2,279	887	1,392
1975–79	7,306	4,996	2,310	729	1,581
Low projection					
1970–74	5,804	3,940	1,864	714	1,150
1975–79	6,499	4,556	1,943	599	1,344

Sources: Bureau of the Census, *Current Population Reports: Population Characteristics*, Series P-20, relevant issues, and *Population Estimates*, Series P-25, No. 394, "Projections of the Number of Households and Families, 1967 to 1985" (1968).

Table 14-5. Number of New Housing Units, by Type, Subperiods during Calendar Years 1950–69

Thousands

Period	Total	Multi-unit housing	Single-unit housing	Mobile homes
1950–54	8,814	1,572	6,876	366
1955–59	7,771	1,122	6,071	578
1960–64	8,010	2,368	4,988	654
1965–69	8,479	2,773	4,301	1,405

Sources: Bureau of the Census, *Construction Reports: Housing Starts*, C20, relevant issues; Department of Housing and Urban Development, *1969 HUD Statistical Yearbook;* Brookings Econometric Model, unpublished tabulations (1970). Single-unit and multi-unit housing, 1950–58, estimated by authors.

struction of single-family units can be expected to increase to meet this rising demand.

In addition to the shift toward multifamily units that occurred in the 1960s, there was also a sharp increase in the number of mobile homes. This increase in mobile home sales is the most striking housing development of recent years. The number of mobile homes grew slowly, and yearly shipments never exceeded 125,000 units until 1963. In every year since then, shipments increased sharply except in 1966, when all housing was adversely affected by tight monetary conditions. By 1970, mobile home sales amounted to 400,000 units.

The growth in mobile homes in part reflects the fact that the cost of constructing conventional housing in recent years has been rising more rapidly than the general price level, while the cost of mobile homes has not. For many families with modest incomes, the advantages of conventional houses have been offset by their rapidly rising costs. Construction costs, which rose at about the same rate as the general price level between 1950 and 1961, began mounting more rapidly in 1961, and this relative increase has accelerated in the past several years. Rapidly rising construction costs apparently have also increased the number of multifamily units built during the 1960s at the expense of single units.

In addition to the demographic changes and the rate of increase in relative prices, two other factors influence the demand for housing—the rate of growth in real income and the tightness of money. Given the number of new households being formed, rising real income adds to the number of single housing units and decreases the number of multi-units. The degree of monetary ease or tightness also influences new housing construction. The classic case of the impact of monetary policy occurred in late 1966 and early 1967, when some 450,000 housing units were not built because of the scarcity of mortgage funds.

Projections of Construction

The number of housing starts needed to achieve the overall housing goals of 25 million units by 1978 is set forth in Table 14-6. For purposes of comparison, the actual housing starts and mobile home shipments for the years 1965–70 are also shown.

To assess some of the major elements that will affect the likelihood of achieving the housing goals, a projection to 1978 has been made of the demand for new housing units based on economic and demographic

Table 14-6. New Housing Units, Fiscal Years 1965–70, and Comparison of National Housing Goals with Projections Based on Economic Factors, by Type, Totals for Fiscal Years 1969–78, and Annual Averages for Three-Year Periods, Fiscal Years 1970–78

Thousands

Fiscal year	Single-unit starts	Multi-unit starts	Total housing starts	New mobile homes	Total new housing units
Actual:					
1965	961	565	1,526	204	1,730
1966	925	508	1,433	217	1,650
1967	743	369	1,112	229	1,341
1968	887	587	1,474	279	1,753
1969	885	715	1,600	365	1,965
1970	750	608	1,359	401	1,760
National housing goals:					
Total, 1969–78	10,761	10,242	21,003	3,963	24,966
Annual averages					
1970–72[a]	789	767	1,556	442	1,998
1973–75	1,197	1,153	2,350	417	2,767
1976–78	1,306	1,255	2,562	341	2,902
Projection based on economic factors:					
Total, 1969–78	10,709	7,666	18,375	5,006	23,380
Annual averages					
1970–72[a]	872	906	1,778	449	2,227
1973–75	1,155	760	1,915	543	2,458
1976–78	1,248	650	1,898	522	2,453

Sources: Basic data are from *Second Annual Report on National Housing Goals;* Department of Housing and Urban Development, *1969 HUD Statistical Yearbook;* U.S. Department of Commerce, Business and Defense Services Administration, *Construction Review,* Vol. 15 (December 1969), p. 16. See text for description of the alternate projection. Figures are rounded and may not add to totals.

a. 1970 figures are the actual starts for that year.

factors. The projection is grounded on past relationships between housing starts, on the one hand, and, on the other, such major factors as the level of household formation, the price of housing relative to the general price level, changes in after-tax personal income, and monetary conditions. For purposes of the projection, the economic factors have been assumed to be the most favorable that could reasonably be expected:

• The Census Bureau's high projection of household formation will be realized.

• The economy will return to relatively full employment in the near future and stay near its potential output during the rest of the period.

• Monetary policy will not be exerting any significant downward pressure on the housing market.

• Residential construction costs will rise no faster than the overall price level (during the past five years construction costs rose more rapidly than prices in general).

Under these conditions, new housing construction, including conventional housing starts and mobile home shipments, would total about 23.4 million (1969–78). This is 1.6 million below the ten-year goals.

Of the 23.4 million housing units that would be constructed, under the economic projection, only 18.4 million would be conventional housing starts, compared to 21.0 million in the housing goals. The totals projected for single-family houses are remarkably similar, the differences between the official goals and the projection being primarily in the number of multifamily units and mobile homes. The economic projection of the demand for multifamily units is 2.5 million below the housing goals, and the economic projection for mobile homes is a million units higher. The number of mobile homes could be even larger if zoning laws were more favorable to them or the number of multifamily units could increase if it became more feasible to produce them from preconstructed modular units.[4]

The economic projection also shows an annual pattern over the next eight years that differs from the one contemplated in the national goals. Based on the assumed economic factors, the projection shows a fairly steady level of housing starts each year (including mobile

4. The projections of mobile homes are based on historical relationships through the middle of the 1970s. It was assumed that thereafter the share of the market going to mobile homes would remain constant.

homes); the total fluctuates between 2.2 and 2.5 million starts per year. The national goals, however, assume a relatively low figure in the years immediately ahead, rising to a total of 2.9 million annual starts by the mid-1970s.

Both the housing goals and the economic projection contemplate a much more ambitious performance than that of the past two decades, suggesting that without major efforts to provide cheap mortgage funds, to keep down housing costs, and to remove obstacles posed by local building codes, neither may be realized. Moreover, economic factors affecting residential construction may not turn out to be as favorable as is assumed above. The effect on housing starts and mobile home shipments of several less optimistic assumptions about these factors is shown in Table 14-7. Under less favorable economic conditions, not only would less housing be built, but its composition would also change. For example, if relative construction prices continue to rise at the same rate as in the past few years, multifamily units and mobile homes would become a larger proportion of total new housing units. The average size and quality of additions to the housing stock would consequently be lower than if a more favorable assumption about relative prices were made.

Table 14-7. Comparison of National Housing Goals with Projections Based on High and Low Rates of Household Formation and Varying Economic Conditions, Ten-year Totals by Type of Housing Unit, Fiscal Years 1969–78

Millions

Type of projection	Single unit starts	Multi- unit starts	Total housing starts	New mobile homes	Total new housing units
National housing goals	10.8	10.2	21.0	4.0	25.0
Alternative projections					
High rate of household formation					
Favorable economic conditions	10.7	7.7	18.4	5.0	23.4
Slower economic growth	10.0	7.8	17.8	5.0	22.8
Unfavorable construction prices	9.8	7.9	17.8	5.2	23.0
Tight monetary policy	10.1	6.8	16.9	5.0	21.9
Low rate of household formation					
Favorable economic conditions	10.2	6.5	16.7	4.9	21.6
Slower economic growth	9.5	6.6	16.1	4.9	21.0

Sources: National housing goals, Table 14-6. Alternative projections, derived by authors. See text for details on the factors used to derive the projections. Figures are rounded and may not add to totals.

Implications

The construction shown in all of the alternative projections would be larger than the amount necessary to take care of new family formation. Table 14-8 shows the implications of producing housing at various levels in the 1969–78 period. If the economic projection, based on a high rate of household formation and favorable economic factors, were to materialize, and even if the vacancy rate rose from the present 8.6 percent to 10 percent, housing starts would sufficiently exceed household formation to provide for virtually the same very high rate of removal of older housing as is called for in the housing goals. The only difference between the official goal and the favorable economic projection lies in the vacancy rate. The economic projection allows some increase in vacancy rates from the present relatively low levels back to the levels reached during the early 1960s. The housing goals provide for a very sharp increase in vacancy rates to new highs. There is some question whether, with vacancies so high, construction would continue at the levels projected in the goals.

While a projection of less favorable economic conditions would result in the construction of fewer housing units, the number con-

Table 14-8. Comparison of National Housing Goals for New Units and Their Use with Projections Based on a High Rate of Household Formation and Contrasting Economic Conditions, Ten-year Totals, Fiscal Years 1969–78

Millions of units, except as noted

| | | Alternative projections assuming a high rate of household formation | |
| | National housing goals | Favorable economic conditions | Slower economic growth |
Description[a]			
New housing units	25.0	23.4	22.8
Use of new units	25.5	23.8	23.1
Accommodation of new households	13.5	13.5	13.5
Removal of existing units	8.5	8.4	7.8
Increase in vacant units	3.5	1.9	1.8
Vacancy rate	*11.8%*	*10.0%*	*10.0%*
Statistical discrepancy	−0.5	−0.4	−0.3

Sources: First column, Table 14-3, except vacancy rate, which is from *Second Annual Report on National Housing Goals*, p. 55. Alternative projections, derived by authors.
a. See notes to Table 14-3.

structed would still be sufficient to take care of family formation, to increase the vacancy rate to 10 percent, and to allow a substantial removal of existing units.

Summary

The economic analysis confirms that a substantial number of new units are likely to be built in the next eight years, though the number may well fall short of the 25 million postulated in the housing goals. But this does not answer the question of how many are needed.

No precise measure of need is possible. Indeed, the concept of a single number that expresses some absolute "need" is a dubious one. The higher the nation's output and income, the more resources can be devoted to improving the housing stock. The less the relative cost of housing, compared to other things, the better "buy" is housing. What can be said is that the construction of housing units in the decade of the 1970s at the level shown in the optimistic economic projection would provide for new households and some desirable increase in vacancies, while permitting the replacement of older housing at a rate well in excess of the nation's performance in the 1960s. Achievement of the official housing goals would be even more ambitious, principally in allowing for a more substantial growth in vacancies as a means of easing the supply situation. But as noted earlier, in the private market system under which most housing will be built, the existence of such high vacancies could reduce incentives to build new houses at the rates envisaged in the housing goals.

Housing Subsidies

The national housing goals encompass not only a target for total housing construction, but also the objective of building 5 million new units and rehabilitating 1 million existing units with a subsidy that will bring their price or rental cost within the range of low- and moderate-income families. The subsidies are provided by various means. In the traditional low-rent public housing programs, the federal government makes payments to local public housing authorities that enable them to provide publicly owned housing at low rents. The major expansion, however, is in programs that make payments to, or in behalf of, private tenants and homeowners sufficient to enable them to live in newly constructed housing at a cost no greater than 25 percent of their income.

The subsidy program associated with the housing goals is based on two premises. First, it is assumed that decent housing for low- and moderate-income families should be provided by building *new* housing units and subsidizing the cost of occupancy, rather than by relying chiefly on subsidizing the occupancy of older, but still decent, dwellings. Traditionally, those low- and moderate-income families who have found decent housing have done so by moving into old but still standard dwellings. Second, the current housing problems of low- and moderate-income families are associated with the existence of substandard housing; that is, it apparently is assumed that most low- and moderate-income families eligible for subsidy now live in substandard housing, and that building new units for them will lead to the removal of substandard housing from the housing stock.

The annual budgetary costs of subsidizing the occupancy of 5 million newly built and 1 million rehabilitated units by low- and moderate-income families will eventually range between $5 billion and $6 billion a year, or an average cost of $800 to $1,000 per unit.

Recent data have become available that make it possible to examine critically the basic premises on which the subsidy program is based. In 1966 and again in 1967, a large-scale survey—the Survey of Economic Opportunity (SEO)—was conducted among about 25,000 households, with particular concentration on poor families. The SEO data include considerable information about the housing and income characteristics of the poor and near-poor.

Some of the important characteristics of households occupying substandard housing are shown in Table 14-9. Substandard housing is of two kinds: dilapidated housing, and nondilapidated housing lacking certain basic facilities (hot and cold running water and separate kitchen and toilet facilities for each household in the dwelling). Of 6.5 million substandard housing units in the United States in 1966, about 1.5 million were occupied by single, nonelderly persons, largely those living in rooming houses and similar accommodations without separate kitchens and bathrooms. Housing subsidies are not particularly helpful to this group, whatever its economic problems.

Of the 5 million remaining substandard dwelling units, more than half were in rural areas and were considered substandard primarily because they lacked sanitary facilities. More than 50 percent of the

Table 14-9. Number of Substandard Housing Units, by Location and Income Class of Occupant Households, 1966

Location	Total	Occupancy[a]	
		Poor households	Moderate income households
Distribution of substandard units (millions)			
All locations	6.5	3.5	1.5
Central cities	1.6	0.8	0.5
Other urban areas	1.9	1.0	0.6
Rural areas	3.0	1.7	0.5
Distribution of substandard units excluding those occupied by single-person households under age 65 (millions)			
All locations	5.0	2.8	1.1
Central cities	0.9	0.5	0.3
Other urban areas	1.4	0.8	0.4
Rural areas	2.7	1.5	0.4
Percentage of households occupying substandard units, excluding single-person households under age 65			
All locations	9.5	27.9	7.0
Central cities	5.5	14.8	4.6
Other urban areas	5.5	20.9	4.9
Rural areas	24.3	52.3	28.3

Source: U.S. Bureau of the Census, Survey of Economic Opportunity, Spring 1966, unpublished computer tabulations. Figures are rounded and may not add to totals.

a. For purposes of this tabulation the following annual income criteria were used to define "poor" and "moderate income" households: *Poor*, elderly, less than $2,000; nonelderly single person households, less than $2,000; nonelderly multiperson households in rural areas, less than $3,000, and in urban areas, less than $4,000. *Moderate income*, elderly, $2,000–$4,000; nonelderly multiperson households in rural areas, $3,000–$4,000, and urban areas, $4,000–$8,000.

rural poor and almost 30 percent of rural households with moderate incomes lived in such housing. Only 2.3 million substandard units were in urban areas. Moreover, only a relatively small percentage of the poor and an even smaller percentage of moderate-income households in urban areas lived in substandard units. On the other hand, about 15 percent of the substandard housing was occupied by persons with better than moderate incomes. Substandard housing, in other words, is a problem particularly in rural areas. The typical poor and moderate-income household in urban areas does not live in such housing.

The real problem of the poor and moderate-income family in urban areas is shown in Table 14-10. The overwhelming proportion of low-

Table 14-10. **Percentage of Households Paying More Than 25 Percent of Their Income for Rent and Household Utilities, by Income Class and Location, 1967**[a]

Annual income, dollars	Central city		Other urban areas		Rural areas	
	Elderly	Non-elderly	Elderly	Non-elderly	Elderly	Non-elderly
Less than 2,000	85	84	72	81	29	22
2,000–3,000	74	75	69	50	26	13
3,000–4,000	55	48	40	38	b	13
4,000–6,000	25	18	37	19	b	10
All incomes	59	22	54	18	24	9

Source: Bureau of the Census, Survey of Economic Opportunity, Spring 1967, unpublished computer tabulations.
a. Based on data for renter households. Nonelderly data include only multiperson households.
b. Less than 1 percent.

income renter families in urban areas must pay more than 25 percent of their income for rent and household utilities.[5] Even large numbers of urban families with moderate incomes pay an abnormally high fraction for rent. Conversely, in rural areas, where the bulk of the substandard housing is, only a relatively modest fraction of poor households pays more than 25 percent of income for rent, and the proportion of moderate-income families is even smaller. Substandard housing and poverty are not synonymous. Poor and moderate-income families in urban areas do have a housing problem—they are forced to pay a very large percentage of their income for housing costs. To oversimplify, the rural poor live cheaply in substandard housing, while the urban poor pay dearly for standard housing.

A Different Approach

These facts suggest an alternative to the current housing subsidy policy that would disassociate the payment of housing subsidies from the construction of new units. Monetary, fiscal, and other policies could be used to achieve whatever level of overall housing construction is desired. Poor and moderate-income families, in turn, could be given housing allowances that would enable them to live in decent housing without spending an abnormally high proportion of their limited income on housing costs. But that decent housing could well

5. These data overstate the magnitude of the problem. Many households in the lower-income groups are only temporarily in that category. Because of a period of unemployment or a bad year in a small business, their income is temporarily reduced, while their housing expenditures continue. The high percentage of a temporarily reduced income that must be paid in rent is not indicative of the longer-term status of such households.

be *existing* housing, rather than new housing. Dollar for dollar, such families can normally get a better buy in older housing units. In any event, there would be no one-for-one tie between the subsidy and new units.

This policy would cost substantially less than the present one, primarily for the reasons adduced above: decent older housing is cheaper than new housing, just as a used but serviceable car is cheaper than a new car. In calculating the need for subsidy, the Department of Housing and Urban Development estimated that the minimum cost to live in decent *new* housing for a typical family of four was $1,260 a year in 1966. In the same year the Bureau of Labor Statistics, through a survey of thirty-nine major cities and four smaller cities, found that the cost to live in decent (primarily older) housing for a low-income family of four averaged $1,013 a year, though this varied from city to city.

The SEO data were used to estimate the budgetary costs of paying low- and moderate-income households a housing allowance sufficient to cover the difference between the cost to live in decent housing and 25 percent of income. Single householders less than 65 years of age were excluded on the grounds that housing is not their basic problem. Most elderly homeowners were also excluded because earlier surveys had shown that 85 percent of them owned their homes debt free. Finally, all households whose subsidy would be less than $100 a year—that is, those families whose incomes were very close to the amount necessary to afford them decent housing—were excluded on the grounds that administering such a small subsidy would involve more costs and problems than it was worth. The estimates were projected to 1976, assuming that inflation would continue but at a moderated pace, and that full employment would have been reached. The Bureau of Labor Statistics data on housing costs for 1966 were first adjusted to allow for differences in the size of families and then projected to 1976 on the basis of the inflation in rents that has already occurred and is expected to continue.

The results of the calculation are shown in Table 14-11, which necessarily overstates the budgetary costs. Any such tabulation will include some families that are normally in higher income brackets, suffer temporary reverses, and for a short time earn very low incomes. These families would presumably not be eligible for housing allowances, even though the calculations underlying Table 14-11 include

Table 14-11. **Number of Eligible Households and Cost of a Housing Allowance Program for Low- and Moderate-income Families That Subsidizes Housing Expenses in Excess of 25 Percent of Income, 1976**

Age status of household	Households receiving subsidy		Budget cost of subsidy (billions of dollars)	Average subsidy cost per household (dollars)
	Number (millions)	Percentage of all households[a]		
Elderly	2.3	16.4	1.3	530
Nonelderly	3.3	5.7	1.7	540
Total	5.6	7.8	3.0	540

Source: Derived from data in Bureau of the Census, Survey of Economic Opportunity, Spring 1967, and authors' projections of income and population to 1976. See text for economic assumptions.
a. High projection of the Bureau of the Census for new household formations.

them. It is impossible to estimate their number, but the number of eligible families and the subsidy costs would probably be reduced by perhaps 10 to 20 percent after making this adjustment.

The housing allowance approach would provide an income supplement enabling low- and moderate-income families to live in decent, though still far from expensive, housing without an excessive burden on their incomes. *It would do so at a cost of between 50 and 60 percent of the current subsidy program, primarily because it would emphasize the use of already existing housing by low- and moderate-income families.* If, at the same time, appropriate policies were pursued to ensure an adequate amount of homebuilding in the nation, the additional demand for housing by subsidized householders should not press upon the housing supply and cause a major increase in rents.

If it is true that decent housing can be secured for low- and moderate-income families more cheaply in existing housing than in new housing, it is clearly desirable to use existing housing. It would be desirable even from the point of view of those same families if the funds saved by this approach could be used to increase other income support payments. As a result, the poor and the near-poor would end up with both the means to secure decent, if older, housing and additional income as well. The extra $2 billion to $3 billion cost of pursuing a policy of building *new* housing in the subsidized program sacrifices funds that could be used as additional income for the poor for the sake of putting them in newly constructed as opposed to older but decent homes.

The success of housing allowances would depend critically on maintaining an adequate volume of housing construction in the nation. If a plentiful supply of sound and decent existing units does not continually come on the market, as middle- and upper-income families buy new dwellings, housing allowances could be largely dissipated in higher rents.

Proponents of tying housing subsidies to the construction of new units offer a major counterargument against proposals for housing allowances. They point out that a combination of zoning laws, racial discrimination, and similar restrictions would make it impossible for many recipients of housing allowances to find decent older housing. As a consequence, the allowances would simply drive up rents in low-income areas. Only government subsidized construction of low-income housing outside the inner city could provide decent housing for poor and moderate-income families. But in fact, the federal government to date has had only limited success in using housing subsidies to accomplish these purposes. Moreover, the government possesses a variety of instruments—including a wide range of grants-in-aid—to secure acceptance of less restrictive zoning and to eliminate discrimination. Success depends on overcoming political resistance and not upon the use of a particular instrument, such as subsidized new construction.

It is true, however, that the budgetary cost of the housing allowance and the number of families eligible for subsidy would rise substantially if the provision of housing allowances drove up rents for low- and moderate-income families. To be conservative, the projection of subsidy costs described earlier took this possibility into account. In the past five years, rent levels have risen only 60 percent as much as the overall cost of living. In the projection to 1976, however, it was assumed that rents would rise as fast as the cost of living. By 1976 this yielded a level of rents 7 percent higher than would occur if the relationships of the past five years continued to prevail.

To illustrate the effect of still further rent increases, the projection was reestimated on the assumption that the provision of housing allowances would drive up rents for low- and moderate-income families by an additional 10 percent, over and above the 7 percent already provided in the earlier calculation. Should this occur, the total cost of the subsidy would rise to $4.9 billion and the number of eligible households to 7.4 million. The cost of housing allowances is very sensitive to increases in rents relative to the general price index, since this not only makes the cost of allowances greater for those already receiving them, but increases the number of eligible families. Clearly, any plan for housing allowances depends for its success on a plentiful supply of housing and therefore on maintaining a substantial volume of new construction.

Housing Allowances and the Family Assistance Plan

Chapter 8 pointed to some of the difficulties of devising a family assistance plan in the face of wide variations in existing state welfare programs and in the cost of living. A uniform federal minimum welfare payment would mean much more in rural Mississippi than in the heart of New York City. But in the absence of reliable data on differences in the cost of living from area to area, a uniform federal minimum seems inevitable.

A housing allowance might provide some modest help in this dilemma. Such data as are available suggest that a very large part of area differences in the cost of living stems from differences in housing costs. The costs of food and clothing also vary regionally, but the variations are much smaller than those that characterize housing. A federal minimum welfare payment could be devised in two parts: the first part would be uniform everywhere, and the second would be a housing allowance as described above. The minimum cost of inhabiting sound and decent housing could be estimated for each area, using surveys and other statistical techniques. The value of the housing allowance would thus automatically reflect a significant part of regional differences in the cost of living. Moreover, it would not be necessary to require that the housing allowance be spent on housing. Rather, housing costs would simply enter the calculation of family allowances as a means of taking into account differences in housing costs among regions, and each family would itself determine how its assistance check was to be spent. Such an arrangement would help to minimize the danger that the sudden introduction of a major system of allowances to be spent on housing would lead to a general increase in rents.

This approach would by no means take care of all the factors that call for regional variations in welfare payments. But it would account for an important part of them and thereby assist the longer-term development of an integrated federal welfare system.

15. Agriculture

FEDERAL EXPENDITURES FOR agricultural programs will not decline materially in the next few years, and they may rise. The sharply increased competition for federal program funds and the chronic public dissatisfaction with farm programs have not generated a new and less costly approach to agricultural price support and stabilization.

The corn blight and adverse weather in the United States reduced the 1970 grain crop below expectations, and crops were below average in some other parts of the world. These events provided a windfall of budgetary receipts in the 1971 fiscal year, reducing net federal expenditures for price support and related programs from $3.8 billion in 1970 to $3.2 billion in 1971 as stocks of grain and soybeans, accumulated through price support operations in recent years, were sold back into trade channels to stabilize prices. (Events affecting the crop of one year generally influence the budgetary costs of the following fiscal year.) Some budgetary receipts may be realized from the same source in fiscal 1972, but with Commodity Credit Corporation (CCC) stocks reduced, the effects of short crops this year would be felt principally in higher farm and food prices and not in reduced CCC expenditures. The 1972 budget estimates that price support outlays will rise to $3.6 billion.

The bulk of federal expenditures for price support operations are devoted to three major crops: wheat, feed grains, and cotton. The government makes payments to producers of these three crops, both as a direct income support and as an inducement for them to divert some of their acreage from production, so as to restrict supply and strengthen prices. Various techniques are used to support the prices of other agricultural products—milk, soybeans, peanuts, sugar, and

297

tobacco. But more than three-fourths of all price support expenditures are devoted to the three major crops, and most important policy questions concern changes in those three programs.

The basic legislation that had governed farm price and income support activities since 1965 expired in 1970. The possibility that new legislation could be developed that would significantly reduce the budgetary cost of these programs, or that the current level of federal price and income support expenditures would be redirected toward those farmers who need it most, was never strong. It was lost entirely when, in the final deliberations leading to the drafting of the Agricultural Act of 1970, both the administration and the Congress tailored their proposals largely to the structure of past farm programs. In addition, the administration opposed an annual limit on federal farm payments of $20,000 per farm for all crops combined, and joined with the agriculture committees in Congress in supporting a $55,000 per farm limitation on any one crop. The latter limit—which was ultimately adopted—is so high that its effect on the budget will be relatively small.

In the early stages of planning for new legislation, the administration had discussed with the House Committee on Agriculture a number of legislative changes that could have produced substantial budgetary savings over time. The ideas put forward were to reduce the level of farm price supports, thus stimulating consumption and exports and discouraging increases in production by farmers. These actions could have resulted in a smaller excess capacity for grain production in the United States by the mid-1970s and substantially lower expenditures for price and income support programs.

Most of these trial balloons appeared in the administration's draft bill, but never received much support. Subsequent actions by the Congress extended the 1965 commodity programs for three years, with only limited changes, and for the first time in nearly ten years fixed in legislation minimum price support and payment levels for feed grains and wheat. This effectively prevents any large planned reductions in farm program expenditures through the 1974 fiscal year.

One result of the 1970 farm bill debate stands out: the administration failed in its efforts to get greater discretion for the executive in establishing farm payment formulas and price support levels. The minimum price support level for wheat is now set at $1.25 a bushel, and for corn at $1.00 a bushel. Minimum formulas for direct government payments on the major crops are also rigorously established. Thus, the farm price and income support programs are now less subject to executive branch discretion than they were under previous legislation.

However, the administration did achieve its objective of providing greater flexibility to the farmer in planting any desired combination of crops, rather than having his acreage restrictions based on a crop by crop pattern. This new "set-aside" provision will tend to increase output, since it will encourage farmers to shift land formerly in crops of relatively low value, to crops of higher value that are covered by price supports and direct payments.

The combined effects of the set-aside provision and fixed minimum price supports for wheat and feed grains will probably force higher levels of spending for the grain stabilization programs in fiscal 1973, assuming that last year's corn blight is fully overcome by the use of resistant seeds for the 1972 crop.

Consequences of Recent Legislation

Because of the 1970 legislation, the choices open to budget makers on commodity price support expenditures for the period 1971–73 are narrower than they were a year ago. Spending could easily be increased in any or all of the price support programs if that were thought to be good public policy, but the opportunities for reductions are very limited. Except for feed grains, the major commodity program decisions announced in December 1970 (for 1971 crops, which will affect budget expenditures mainly in the 1972 fiscal year) would mean budget expenditures that are substantial but still near the minimum levels allowed by law. Barring a reconsideration of the three-year price support legislation, which would be unprecedented since it was enacted only in late 1970, or unexpected changes in the world agricultural situation, price support expenditures will remain near or slightly above present levels for several years.

Price and income supports, domestic and foreign food assistance, and the Agricultural Conservation Program presented potentially important budgetary issues for 1972. For the latter two, the food stamp program, the Food for Peace program, and the level of appropriations for conservation payments are the key areas subject to legislative discretion. Most other programs of the Department of

Agriculture, including soil conservation technical assistance, agricultural research and education, meat and poultry inspection, and various programs of agricultural credit continue to receive slightly larger appropriations each year, but the sum of these incremental increases is not great enough to make the possibility of a standstill on spending for these items for 1972 a serious budgetary issue. Small increases were provided for most of these functions in the 1972 budget. Eight programs of the Department of Agriculture, together with several economic development programs of the Department of Commerce, were included in the proposed special revenue sharing category for rural community development. (See Chapter 7.) The funds allotted to these programs are not significantly different in 1972 than in 1971.

Price and Income Supports

Legislative and program decisions referred to earlier are expected to result in direct payments to farmers as shown in Table 15-1. Statutory price support and payment formulas in the wheat and cotton programs left little discretion for considering alternative expenditure levels. The one serious possibility for reducing 1972 farm program expenditures significantly below levels now estimated was lost in December 1970, when the provisions of the feed grain program for the 1971 crop were announced. Program payments to producers, now estimated at $1 billion, could have been some $500 million smaller if the administration had chosen to divert a smaller acreage

Table 15-1. Government Payments to Farmers under Feed Grain, Wheat, and Upland Cotton Programs, Crop Years 1965, 1969, 1970, and 1971[a]

Millions of dollars

Program	1965	1969	1970	1971 estimated
Feed grain	1,391	1,643	1,510	1,000
Wheat	525	858	891	797
Upland cotton	773[b]	828	918	843
Total	2,689	3,329	3,319	2,640

Sources: U.S. Department of Agriculture, Economic Research Service, *Farm Income Situation*, FIS-216 (July 1970), p. 64; *The Budget of the United States Government, Fiscal Year 1972*, p. 108.

a. Payments to farmers and other farm program costs in any crop year fall generally into the succeeding fiscal year. Thus 1971 crop year payments principally represent 1972 fiscal year expenditures.

b. Data are for 1966, since the 1965 cotton program is not comparable to subsequent years.

from feed grain production in an effort to ensure an adequate supply of grain and livestock products.

The crop of feed grains harvested in 1970 was more than 25 million tons (or 14 percent) below expectations, and 16 million tons smaller than the 1969 crop. The corn blight was the major factor in this decline, although drought also affected the western cornbelt. Given this small 1970 harvest, carryover stocks of all feed grains, at 34 million tons, will be 6 million tons below the widely accepted safe reserve level by mid-1971. The 1971 crop of feed grains must increase to at least the 1969 level of 175 million tons if reserve stocks are not to be further reduced.

In order to achieve this substantial increase in feed grain output, two conditions will be necessary: an increase of about 10 percent in the acreage planted to feed grains and the availability of seed to plant the greater acreage. But the acreage diversion announced in December 1970, combined with the probability of a shortage of blight resistant seed, may limit the increase in acreage planted to less than 10 percent. According to a survey made in March 1971, farmers at that time planned to increase corn acreage by only 6 percent.

One alternative considered by the government before its December 1970 announcement, was to require farmers to set aside 10 percent of their crop acreage instead of 20 percent, as was finally decided. Had that been done, the subsidy payment to farmers could have been set at 16 cents per bushel of corn, instead of the 32 cents at which it was actually set. This alternative would have increased the land available for crop production in 1971 by nearly 8 million acres and would probably have reduced federal expenditures by about $500 million. Some of this land would have been planted to feed grains, and expected production would be 5 to 8 million tons greater than now appears likely.

Whether to spend $500 million, or to spend $1 billion and choose the larger feed grain acreage instead of the smaller in the 1971 program was, however, a difficult question because of the possible impact on farm prices. If feed grain acreage actually increased by 10 percent in 1971, while corn blight damage turned out to be light, production might then exceed requirements by 5 to 10 percent. Prices, which are now well above the support levels, might be reduced by 15 to 20 percent, or perhaps by 25 percent (to the price support level).

At the opposite end of the spectrum, acreage might increase by as little as the 6 percent indicated in March 1971, and blight damage might exceed that in 1970. The crop would then fall short of requirements during the period October 1971–September 1972. Speculative factors, including real uncertainty about the 1972 crop, could push prices up by 10 to 20 percent over 1970–71 levels. This would reduce livestock production, especially in 1972 and 1973, leading to large increases in meat prices and in the U.S. cost of living.

If feed grain production in 1971 should recover to about 7 percent above that in 1970, a level between the high and the low possibilities discussed above, farm receipts would be comparable to those in recent years, as is shown in Table 15-2. Prices would fall from 1970–71 levels, but would remain well above pre-blight levels, which were then considered to be quite attractive to corn producers.

Table 15-2. **Feed Grain Economic Indicators, Crop Years 1965, 1969, 1970, and 1971**

Economic indicator	1965	1969	1970	1971 indicated
Feed grain production (millions of tons)	157	175	159[a]	170[b]
Estimated farm value of feed grain production (millions of dollars)	6,380	7,015	7,215	7,400[b]
Payments to farmers under feed grain program (millions of dollars)	1,391	1,643	1,510	1,000
Average farm price of corn (dollars per bushel)	1.16	1.16	1.34	1.25

Sources: U.S. Department of Agriculture (USDA), *Agricultural Statistics, 1969*, pp. 28, 36, 42, 51; USDA, Economic Research Service, *Demand and Price Situation*, DPS-127 (February 1971), p. 11, and *Farm Income Situation* (July 1970), p. 64; USDA, Crop Reporting Board, *Crop Values, 1969–1970*, Cr Pr 2-1-1 (70) (Dec. 29, 1970), p. 3.
  a. Estimated.
  b. Estimated by John A. Schnittker, Robert R. Nathan Associates.

Food for Peace

This program provides both assistance to developing countries and substantial support for farm prices and incomes. The value of shipments of agricultural commodities under the Food for Peace program (Public Law 480) peaked at just below $2 billion a year in the late 1950s, under the pressure of huge surpluses, and again in the mid-1960s, when record food aid shipments to India were required to offset the severe drought there from 1965 to 1967.

This program has been declining since 1967, both because it has been U.S. policy to reduce the level of aid and to shift it to harder terms and because expanded food production in a number of recipient countries has reduced the need for massive commodity shipments. For 1972, total budget expenditures for the program are estimated at $962 million, slightly below 1971. The program level is not rigorously limited by appropriations, however. Public Law 480 is financed by the Commodity Credit Corporation, which has a large reserve of Treasury borrowing authority. The CCC can respond immediately either to increased pressure to export farm commodities because of growing surpluses, or to urgent pleas from countries abroad to compensate for reduced agricultural production or other emergencies.

Limiting Payment to Farmers

Substantial budgetary savings could have been realized in 1972 if Congress had limited federal payments to any one agricultural producer to $10,000 for a single crop, or to $20,000 for all crops combined. Such limits would have saved $250 million and $180 million a year, respectively, assuming that the program were administered rigorously.

Recognizing that farm price supports would probably not be continued after 1970 unless some kind of payment limitation were enacted, the agriculture committees of the Congress and the administration supported a maximum payment in any one year of $55,000 per crop per farm, a level that affects 1,100 farm producers in the United States. This limit, which was adopted, will save at best about $50 million a year in federal payments. This is a start toward a worthwhile objective, but it does not alter the fact that a relatively small number of large farmers receive a very large share of federal agricultural payments. Unfortunately, under regulations issued in late 1970, many of those affected may find it possible to split their farms into smaller units to escape the new provision.

"Small Farm" Provisions of 1970 Agricultural Act

Since the early 1960s the feed grain payment program has included "small farm" provisions, authorizing larger per acre or per bushel payments to producers with twenty-five acres or less planted to feed grain. A similar provision at the ten-acre level was added to the cotton program in 1965.

Programs whose benefits are distributed in this fashion generally place subsidies in the hands of low-income families. In the 1970 act the small acreage payment feature of the grain programs was terminated, and the conditions qualifying for a special payment under the cotton program were revised to limit such benefits to producers who have ten acres of cotton or less and who reside on the farm and derive their principal income from cotton production. No such residence test or off-farm income restriction was placed on payments to commercial or even corporate farmers.

Congress missed an opportunity in 1970 to turn more attention and more funds to problems of low-income farmers by rejecting a Senate provision authorizing adjustment payments to farmers who were retiring or turning to other employment. But a new provision of the law does require the executive branch to report annually on planning and technical assistance and on overall government services available to rural people and communities.

More fundamentally, providing income support to farmers by devices that relate the amount of support to the size of the farm or the amount of production—as do the current programs—inevitably channels the bulk of the assistance to the relatively small number of large and efficient farms that produce most of the nation's agricultural output. Payment limitations and small-farmer provisions can modify but not eliminate this characteristic of price support operations. As a consequence, the price support activities of the federal government must be viewed as a means of supporting a particular industry rather than as a device to provide income for the rural poor.

Agricultural Conservation Program (ACP)

For many years, dating back to the 1950s, administrations have recommended that payments to farmers to cover a portion of the cost of designated farm practices be reduced or terminated. Each year the House and Senate Appropriations Committees have funded the program and insisted that the money be spent. Presidential determination to end the program has usually faded in the face of bipartisan congressional resistance, although some funds have been withheld by presidential order, as is shown below by the fluctuating levels of expenditure (in millions of dollars for fiscal years).

	1965	1969	1970	1971	1972
Contract authority	220.0	195.5	195.5	195.5	140.0
Expenditures	216.1	199.4	182.6	178.8	150.0

For nearly fifteen years the executive branch has seen ACP as a politically potent program with a low yield in terms of resource conservation. For example, payments were once made to encourage the application of fertilizer and lime to soils, a practice that is generally profitable and requires no subsidy. Executive branch reviews over the years have forced the revision or termination of the most flagrant output-increasing programs and have increased the purely conservation components of the programs. This process proceeded far enough to cause the administration, in its initial budget decisions in the fall of 1970, to rename ACP the Rural Environmental Assistance Program (REAP), and to continue to fund it, but at a reduced level. Before the budget was submitted, however, this program was grouped with others to become part of the newly proposed special revenue sharing category for rural community development. If the President's proposals are enacted, continuation of these conservation payments would depend on decisions taken by each state.

16. Expenditures Outside the Budget

ACCORDING TO A LAWYER'S CLICHÉ, the Constitution is what the Supreme Court says it is. What is constitutional, in other words, depends on judgment and may change over time. Similarly, government revenues and expenditures are what the budget says they are. In many cases, whether expenditures under a federal program are shown in the budget depends on how the program is organized. A program whose expenditures are included in budget totals may be restructured so that its economic impact remains unchanged but part or all of its expenditures are dropped from the budget. A number of such changes have occurred over the past ten years. These changes have significantly affected the apparent growth in federal expenditures and have made it difficult to compare the budget totals of one year with those of preceding years. Without such changes,

- the growth in federal outlays between 1965 and 1970 would have been not $78 billion but $90 billion;
- the growth in federal outlays from 1970 to 1972 would be not $33 billion but $50 billion;
- outlays for housing and community development, shown as $4.5 billion in the 1972 budget, would be $20.1 billion.

The difference between official budget outlays and the adjusted estimates presented below has three sources. (1) The activities of certain agencies once included in the budget are now excluded. (2) The legal form of some kinds of financial assistance to the private sector has been altered, causing major changes in the impact of such assistance on the budget but few if any changes in its effect on the economy or

306

in the value of the aid to the recipient. (3) The activities of some agencies are understated because proceeds from sales of assets are subtracted from the agencies' payments in calculating budget outlays. Both Democratic and Republican administrations have modified budgetary accounting along these lines.

Changes in Budget Coverage

Whether to include the outlays of a particular organization in the budget is usually easy to decide. In some cases, however, the issue is not clear cut. Agencies once included in, but now excluded from, the budget are

• the Federal National Mortgage Association (FNMA), which buys and sells government insured and guaranteed mortgages;

• the Federal Home Loan Banks (FHLBs), which lend funds to member savings and loan associations and savings banks and perform certain other functions;

• the Federal Intermediate Credit Banks, which lend to local financing institutions in agricultural areas;

• the Banks for Cooperatives, which finance the operation of farmers' cooperatives; and

• the Federal Land Banks, which make long-term real estate loans to farmers and ranchers through 616 local federal land bank associations.

These agencies occupy a no-man's-land between the public and private sectors. They raise capital by selling their own obligations and lend to private individuals and institutions. In these respects, their activities resemble those of private investment banks or finance companies. However, they enjoy the direct or indirect backing of the U.S. government and therefore can sell their obligations more easily and cheaply than can purely private organizations. The government also has a voice in the volume of their credit operations. Therefore, whether they should be included in the budget is an open question. More important, many of these agencies were only recently excluded from the budget; consequently, the increase in budget outlays shown in published figures can be misleading, since earlier totals include these agencies while the latest ones do not.

The criteria for deciding whether the expenditures and revenues of a particular agency should be included in the budget are legal, not economic. The unified budget concept, adopted in 1968 and currently used to present federal budgetary data, includes the expenditures of an agency if the federal government owns some of the outstanding stock or controls the agency by electing a majority of its board of directors. Under this criterion, for example, net mortgage purchases by FNMA appeared as a budget outlay until late 1968, when FNMA repurchased all outstanding stock held by the Treasury Department. Both before and after its removal from the budget, FNMA financed these mortgages principally through the sale of its own bonds and through mandatory sales of stock to investors from whom it bought mortgages.

No basic changes in the nature of FNMA's operations occurred because its operations were removed from the federal budget. While its net expenditures grew spectacularly, from $38 million in 1965 to $4.8 billion in 1970, the budget showed a reduction in FNMA outlays to zero in 1970. During the period when FNMA was rapidly increasing its activities, its budget outlays vanished, for the legally compelling but economically trivial reason that the Treasury sold its FNMA stock.

Expenditures of the FHLBs were for many years included in the federal cash budget, the closest predecessor in accounting concept to the unified budget. When the unified budget was adopted in 1968, however, the expenditures of the home loan banks were excluded, since the federal government had long since ceased to own stock in these banks. But they perform functions very similar to those of FNMA. The twelve regional FHLBs make "advances" or loans to member financial institutions, mostly savings and loan associations and savings banks. They finance these operations through proceeds from the sale of bonds, notes, and stock to member institutions. The directors of each of the twelve regional FHLBs are elected by member financial institutions. But policy is set by the Federal Home Loan Bank Board, composed of three presidential appointees; and in some cases, policies must be reviewed by the secretary of the treasury. Despite practical control by the federal government, it was the legal independence of the FHLBs that led to the exclusion of their lending activities from the unified budget.

The adjusted outlays shown below include for all years the net outlays of FNMA, the FHLBs, the Federal Intermediate Credit Banks, the Banks for Cooperatives, and the Federal Land Banks.

New Forms of Federal Assistance

The federal government for many years has lent money to individuals, businesses, and various organizations—to assist in building houses, hospitals, and college dormitories, for example. These loans were made to assist borrowers who would be hindered in achieving socially desirable objectives if they were forced to borrow in regular credit markets. The federal loans are usually made under more liberal terms—such as smaller down payments, lower interest rates, longer repayment periods, or larger size—than the borrower could obtain from a commercial lender. For example, suppose that a borrower could obtain a twenty-year, $10,000 loan at 3 percent annual interest from the government and could borrow the same amount for the same period from a commercial lender at 8 percent. As is shown in Table 16-1, access to federal credit would save the borrower $346.37 annually in interest payments for twenty years.

The government has recently curtailed direct lending. Instead, it guarantees repayment on loans that borrowers obtain from commercial lenders and makes supplemental payments to reduce the cost of repaying the loan to some predetermined level. In the example shown in Table 16-1, the government could lend $10,000 at 3 percent and receive repayments of $672.15 a year for twenty years. Alternatively, the

Table 16-1. Illustration of the Value of Federal Below-market Interest Rate Loans and Annual Supplements Relative to Commercial Loans

Details of transaction	Commercial loan	Government loan	Annual supplement
Amount borrowed	$10,000	$10,000	$10,000
Interest rate	8 percent	3 percent	8 percent
Duration of loan	20 years	20 years	20 years
Annual repayment	$1,018.52	$672.15	$1,018.52
Annual supplement	0	0	$346.37
Net annual repayment (line 4 minus line 5)	$1,018.52	$672.15	$672.15
Annual subsidy to borrower compared to commercial loan	none	$346.37	$346.37
Budget cost			
First year	0	$10,000	$346.37
Second and all succeeding years	0	−$672.15	$346.37
Present value of subsidy discounted at 8 percent	0	$3,400.00	$3,400.00

Source: Calculated by authors.

government might agree to pay the borrower $346.37 a year for twenty years if the borrower obtained a loan at the commercial rate of 8 percent.

Apart from administrative differences, the two forms of assistance leave the borrower in the same position—in debt by $10,000 and obliged to pay $672.15 a year for twenty years to pay off the loan. The two forms of assistance would therefore induce similar behavior by investors and consumers, and their impact on economic activity would therefore be similar. If the budget is to show how government decisions affect private spending, both forms of credit assistance should receive the same accounting treatment.

In practice, the direct loan affects the budget quite differently than does the supplemental payment. The direct loan appears as a $10,000 outlay when it is made; in subsequent years, the repayments would be recorded as *negative* budget outlays of $672.15 a year. Under the supplemental payment approach, on the other hand, government expenditures of $346.37 would appear in the budget each year for the life of the loan. In addition, the government might be called upon to pay the lender if the borrower defaulted on his repayments. (The cost of this guarantee is not shown in Table 16-1.)

Several of the direct loan programs have been changed to supplementary payment programs in recent years:

College housing. Since 1950 the federal government has made forty-year, 3 percent loans to colleges and eligible hospitals for the construction of housing, student centers, dining facilities, and infirmaries. The Housing and Urban Development Act of 1968 authorized the government to make debt service grants to such institutions in order to make repayment costs on commercial loans the same as they would be under the direct loan programs.

Hospital construction. In fiscal 1971 the government began making interest subsidy payments to assist states, public agencies, and non-profit organizations to build and modernize hospitals and other health facilities. These subsidies partially supplant construction grants and direct loans previously made to the same organizations.

Academic facilities construction. To assist in the modernization and expansion of institutions of higher learning, the federal government has made fifty-year loans covering three-fourths of the cost of academic facilities. In 1970 this program was replaced by interest subsidies designed to accomplish the same purpose.

Student loans. A number of programs, including grants and direct loans, help students pay for higher education. The largest and fastest growing form of assistance is a loan guarantee, combined with an interest supplement, which enables students to borrow commercially at a lower net cost.

The federal government has also used supplemental payments most extensively to encourage the construction or purchase of housing by low- and moderate-income families, and in programs of rental assistance and rent supplements. In each case, the federal government makes payments to property owners sufficient to reduce the cost of housing to a specified fraction of the occupant's income—20 percent for homeowners, 25 percent for renters—subject to limits on the maximum federal payment. The payments encourage businessmen to build and finance houses for sale or rent to eligible low- and moderate-income families. Under the low-rent public housing program, the federal government goes even further, paying the full debt service cost on bonds sold by local housing authorities to finance the construction of low-rent public housing. For decision makers concerned primarily with the current year's budget, the supplemental payment approach has the overwhelming advantage of putting off until tomorrow the budgetary consequences of today's actions.

The supplemental payment technique has been used extensively only in recent years. To improve comparability among expenditure levels in different years, all supplemental payment programs were converted into direct loan programs in computing the adjusted budget outlays shown in Table 16–2.

Sales of Assets

The size of two major direct lending programs is disguised in the budget by special conventions applicable to them. One is administered by the Farmers Home Administration (FmHA), which provides a rapidly growing volume of low-interest home loans to low- and moderate-income households. FmHA sells the loans, together with a repayment guarantee, to private investors. In addition, it supplements the interest proceeds sufficiently to enable investors to buy these loans at face value. FmHA's budget outlays equal the dollar volume of loans disbursed, plus the costs of the interest supplements, minus the proceeds from loan repayments and loan sales.

Table 16-2. Official and Adjusted Budget Outlays, by Source of Differences, Fiscal Years 1965, 1970, 1971, and 1972

Billions of dollars

Budget description and source of adjustment	Amount				Change			
	1965	1970	1971	1972	1965–70	1970–71	1971–72	1965–72
Official budget outlays	118.4	196.6	212.8	229.2	78.2	16.2	16.5	110.9
Additive adjustments to official budget outlays								
Agencies excluded from the official budget	1.2	9.7	6.9	7.7	8.5	–2.8	0.8	6.5
Excess of subsidized housing construction over associated subsidy payments	0.2	2.8	6.0	7.0	2.6	3.2	1.0	6.8
Excess of subsidized loan volume over associated subsidy payments	⋯	0.7	1.3	3.2	0.7	0.6	1.9	3.2
Loan volume offset by asset sales	1.1	1.3	2.5	3.5	0.2	1.2	1.0	2.4
Total: Adjusted budget outlays	120.9	211.1	229.5	250.6	90.2	18.4	21.1	129.7
Excess of adjusted over official outlays	2.5	14.5	16.7	21.4	12.0	2.2	4.7	18.9

Sources: Official outlays, *The Budget of the United States Government, Fiscal Year 1972*, Table 18; adjustments, derived from data in *The Budget of the United States Government—Appendix, Fiscal Year 1972*. Figures are rounded and may not add to totals.

This method of accounting leads to the odd circumstance that loan activity may increase while budget expenditures are falling. From fiscal 1970 to 1971, for example, loan activity was projected to grow from $780 million to $996 million; over the same period, budget expenditures fell from $125 million to − $456 million, as sales of previously held loans increased.

The Export-Import Bank engages in similar operations. It lends funds to assist importers and exporters, then sells the loans to private investors. The proceeds from the sale of loans are offset against net loans in computing outlays by the Export-Import Bank. (A bill currently before the Congress and already passed by the Senate in April 1971 would remove *all* of the outlays of the Export-Import Bank from the federal budget. If enacted, this bill would result in an apparent reduction of $290 million in the 1972 budget.)

Adjusted Expenditures

To illustrate the impact of the budgetary conventions just described on the level and functional distribution of outlays, expenditures have been adjusted to include (1) the expenditures of major agencies formerly included in the budget but now excluded; (2) the volume of loans or housing construction undertaken in connection with supplemental payment programs (that is, the conversion of interest supplements into equivalent direct, low-interest loans); and (3) the loan activities of FmHA and the Export-Import Bank *without* offsetting sales of assets.

Table 16-2 shows the growing importance of these items since 1965. The excess of adjusted budget expenditures over official expenditures rises from $2.5 billion in 1965 to $14.5 billion in 1970, largely because of the exclusion of the Federal National Mortgage Association and the Federal Home Loan Bank Board from the federal budget. The further rise to $21.4 billion projected for 1972 is due largely to the growing importance of interest subsidy payments of various kinds, a trend that is expected to continue well past 1972.

The budget adjustments are largest in program areas—such as housing and education—where loans, housing subsidies, and other forms of credit assistance are most common. As is shown in Table 16-3, adjusted expenditures on housing and community development

Table 16-3. Adjusted Budget Outlays and Excess over Official Budget Outlays, by Program Area, Fiscal Years 1965, 1970, 1971, and 1972
Millions of dollars

Program area	1965		1970		1971		1972	
	Adjusted budget outlays	Excess over official budget outlays	Adjusted budget outlays	Excess over official budget outlays	Adjusted budget outlays	Excess over official budget outlays	Adjusted budget outlays	Excess over official budget outlays
Housing and community development	2,024	1,736	14,761	11,796	17,348	13,490	20,124	15,629
Higher education	427	13	2,111	730	2,571	1,113	4,030	2,728
Agriculture (less price supports)	1,305	165	3,418	1,806	2,739	1,552	3,355	1,778
Other	117,163	575	190,776	146	206,822	570	223,108	1,250
Total	**120,919**	**2,489**	**211,066**	**14,478**	**229,480**	**16,725**	**250,617**	**21,385**

Sources: Same as Table 16-2. Figures are rounded and may not add to totals.

are four times as large as official expenditures in fiscal 1972. The use of interest credits and other deferred or off-the-budget outlays to assist students and colleges is growing. In other fields their use is negligible.

Perhaps the most important aspect of the excluded outlays is their impact on credit markets. In 1972 the $21 billion of excluded outlays will give rise to approximately $21 billion of borrowing by government-sponsored organizations, private sponsors of subsidized housing, or individuals. The $11.6 billion official deficit therefore understates substantially the borrowing to which government action will give rise in 1972.

Although lumping together all excluded items and adding them to the budget totals helps in understanding the impact of government actions on the credit market, it sharply exaggerates their impact on national income and output. Most of the excluded items are loans, not purchases of goods and services or transfer payments. Unlike the latter two types of expenditures, loans do not increase the income of recipients dollar for dollar with the loan. Receiving a $1,000 loan that must be repaid is obviously not the same as receiving a $1,000 salary check or a $1,000 pension. In judging the impact of the federal budget on the nation's output and income, loans cannot be treated as equivalent to other expenditures. Indeed, the national income accounts measure of federal expenditures, which many economists consider most appropriate for analyzing the output and income consequences of federal spending, excludes loan outlays altogether.

To the extent that the items composing the $21 billion of budget adjustments carry a commitment for future subsidies—lower-than-market interest rates or subsidized rents for tenants—they do, in effect, raise the income of the recipient. Some of the excluded items carry no direct subsidy: FNMA's buying of mortgages, for example, is primarily a means of improving the flow of credit. Other items do carry long-term subsidy commitments. But the value of that commitment to the recipient is measured neither by the full amount of the loan involved (which is too large a measure) nor by a single year's subsidy (which is too small a measure). The next section provides an estimate of the current value of long-term subsidy commitments associated with the budget adjustment items. Such an estimate is directly comparable with other expenditures in the budget and can be added to those expenditures to arrive at an adjusted total that has economic meaning.

Measuring Long-term Subsidy Commitments

When the government agrees to pay part of the interest on a long-term loan or part of the housing costs of a low-income family, it commits itself to a stream of expenditures for many years to come. The value to a borrower of the commitment to pay part of his interest costs on a loan is less than the total size of the loan, since the borrower will pay some of the interest costs and must repay the principal. On the other hand, the commitment is obviously worth more than the single year's expenditure that appears in any federal budget, since the subsidy will continue for many years. Similarly, when the federal government promises to pay a rent supplement for forty years, the builder of the subsidized housing does not base his construction plans only on the first year's payments, but rather on the present value of the assurance that such payments will be made for forty years.

In each case the government could provide the subsidy in the form of a one-time grant, thereby reducing the size of the loan or the cost of housing so that repayments would be exactly equal to what they would be with an annual subsidy. In the example of Table 16-1, the annual interest and repayment costs of a $10,000 loan could be reduced from $1,018 dollars to $672 *either* by the government's agreeing to pay $346 a year for twenty years *or* by the government's making a one-time grant of $3,400, which would reduce the size of the loan to the point where the borrower himself could repay $672 a year at market rates of interest. In technical terms, the *present value* of a commitment to pay $346 a year for twenty years is $3,400.

The recipient of the subsidized loan (or the low-income home owner) gets the same benefit whether the government commits itself to pay a stream of annual subsidies or makes the equivalent initial capital grant; in either case his economic decisions should be the same.

By identifying each program under which the government commits itself to pay long-term interest or housing assistance subsidies and then calculating the present value of the subsidy, it is possible to translate subsidy commitments into capital grant equivalents. When capital grants are made, they become part of the budget total. Similarly, the capital grant equivalents of the subsidy commitments can be added to the budget totals to form new totals. Thus the full economic value and impact of the deferred expenditures involved in long-term subsidy

Table 16-4. Actual and Full Employment Budgets, Adjusted to Include Long-term Subsidy Commitments, Fiscal Years 1965, 1970, 1971, and 1972

Billions of dollars

Budget description and adjustment[a]	1965	1970	1971	1972
Actual GNP basis				
Budget surplus (+) or deficit (−)	−1.6	−2.8	−18.6	−11.6
Effect on budget balance of including capital grant equivalent of long-term subsidy commitments	−0.3	−3.6	−4.8	−6.0
Adjusted surplus (+) or deficit (−)	−1.9	−6.4	−23.4	−17.6
Full employment GNP basis				
Budget surplus (+) or deficit (−)	+2.2	+2.6	+1.4	+0.1
Effect on budget balance of including capital grant equivalent of long-term subsidy commitments	−0.3	−3.6	−4.8	−6.0
Adjusted surplus (+) or deficit (−)	+1.9	−1.0	−3.4	−5.9

Sources: Table 16-3; *The Budget of the United States Government, Fiscal Year 1972*, and *The Budget of the United States Government—Appendix, Fiscal Year 1972*; full employment budget surplus for 1965 estimated by authors.

a. The adjustment includes loans or supplemental payments under the following programs: low-rent public housing, homeownership assistance, rental assistance, rent supplements, Farmers Home Administration loans to individuals with low to moderate incomes, below market interest rate loans under section 221(d)(3) of the National Housing Act, hospital construction assistance, college housing, and student loan interest subsidies.

commitments are made comparable to capital grant items already included in the budget.

Table 16-4 shows the capital grant equivalents (present value) of loans at below market interest rates and of supplemental payments made under the major programs mentioned in this chapter: low-rent public housing, homeownership assistance, rental assistance, rent supplements, FmHA loans, below market interest rate housing loans, hospital construction assistance, college housing, and student loan interest subsidies. Because numerous smaller programs of a similar nature are excluded, a complete adjustment would be larger than that shown in the table. The table also shows the adjusted budget surplus or deficit after inclusion of the capital grant equivalents, using both the actual and full employment budget concepts.

If federal outlays were defined to include net capital grant equivalents, $6 billion would have to be added to fiscal 1972 expenditure totals, compared to $4.8 billion in 1971 and $300 million in 1965. The full employment budget, which shows a small and declining surplus over the three years 1970 to 1972, would show a rising deficit over the same period—from $1 billion in 1970 to $3.4 billion in 1971 and to $5.9 billion in 1972. While the level of the full employment surplus would be substantially reduced (and converted to a deficit) by the redefinition, its change from 1971 to 1972 would not be so greatly affected as to alter the conclusions reached in Chapter 1 about the economic impact of the 1972 budget.

17. The Fiscal Dividend Through 1976

THE DECISIONS TAKEN in the 1972 budget will affect not only that fiscal year but subsequent years as well. Some of the large new programs it proposes—revenue sharing, family assistance, and health insurance, for example—would have substantially larger costs in 1973 and later years than in 1972. Increased appropriations for such items as water pollution control and naval shipbuilding would also give rise to increased expenditures beyond 1972. To evaluate the broad impact of 1972 budget decisions and determine how the new commitments relate to the budgetary resources available, revenues and expenditures must be projected several years ahead.

This chapter provides such a projection through fiscal 1976. It does not forecast what expenditures and revenues will actually be, since those will depend on future decisions with respect to program expansion, new programs, or changes in tax laws. Rather, using certain reasonable assumptions about the course of economic activity in the next five years, it attempts to project expenditures for existing federal programs and the new ones proposed in the 1972 budget, and to estimate budget revenues under existing tax laws. The difference between projected revenues and expenditures is the *fiscal dividend*—the money available in future years for discretionary use by the President and the Congress to expand existing programs, to create new ones, to reduce taxes, or to hold as a surplus for economic stabilization purposes.

In brief, this projection shows that, between fiscal 1972 and 1974, there will be no fiscal dividend. Total federal expenditures under existing programs and those proposed in the 1972 budget will grow by as

319

much as full employment revenues, even after taking into account further reductions in Vietnam war costs. Since the full employment budget presented in 1972 was just in balance, and precarious balance at that, there will be no potential excess of full employment revenues over already committed expenditures by 1974, barring a decision to increase tax rates or to reduce spending on existing programs. After 1974, the projection shows that the "built-in" growth of expenditures will moderate somewhat, and revenues will grow slightly faster than in the prior period. By 1976, full employment revenues may exceed currently projected expenditures—but only by an amount roughly equal to 1 percent of gross national product.

The Projections

Three major elements go into the projection. First, some explicit assumptions must be made about economic conditions. The projection assumes that unemployment will fall to 4 percent by calendar 1973 and remain at that level. Thus, after 1973 the projected budgets are also full employment budgets, in the sense that the projected revenues are based on full employment conditions. The labor force at full employment is projected to grow by about 1.7 percent a year, average hours of work to decline slightly in line with long-term trends, and output per manhour in the private economy to grow by 3 percent a year. Given these assumptions, full employment GNP in dollars of constant purchasing power should grow by about 4.3 percent a year. Inflation is assumed to continue but at a moderated pace, with price increases tapering off from the 5.6 percent rate of late 1970 to 2.7 percent in 1974 and holding at that level thereafter. The ratio of corporate profits to GNP is assumed to return almost, but not quite, to the level of the late 1960s. The major elements of the economic projection are shown in Table 17-1.

Revenues

Next, the federal tax revenues that would be yielded under existing laws are determined on the basis of the economic projection. Over the next several years, full employment revenues will be affected not only by the rate of growth of GNP at full employment, but also by several changes already enacted in various provisions of the tax laws. For example, the current social security law calls for increases in payroll

**Table 17-1. Economic Indicators Used in Budget Projections,
Calendar Years 1970, 1974, and 1976**

Dollar amounts in billions

Economic indicator	1970 actual	1974 projected	1976 projected
GNP, current dollars	977	1,380	1,585
GNP, 1970 dollars	977	1,205	1,310
Personal income less transfers, current dollars	723	1,010	1,155
Corporate profits before taxes, current dollars	82	140	165
Unemployment rate, percent	4.9	4.0	4.0
Private GNP deflator, index	100.0	114.5	121.0

Sources: 1970, *Economic Indicators* (February 1971); projections, Brookings Budget Projection Model.

tax rates in 1973 and again in 1976. The Tax Reform Act of 1969 provides for a series of personal income tax reductions that are scheduled to take effect by stages between 1970 and 1973. The 1969 act also repealed the investment tax credit, which will lead to higher revenues over the period. Finally, the administration has recently liberalized certain rules on business depreciation accounting, thereby reducing taxes on corporations and unincorporated businesses. The results of the revenue projections, taking into account both the growth in GNP and the already scheduled changes in effective tax rates, are shown in Table 17-2.

If no tax changes were scheduled, economic growth would raise full employment revenues from $233 billion in 1972 to $270 billion in 1974 and $316 billion in 1976, an average annual increase of slightly less than $19 billion in the former period and $23 billion in the latter. (As Table 17-2 shows, the assumption of full employment conditions in 1974 and 1976 makes full employment revenues and actual revenues the same in those two years.) However, the Tax Reform Act of 1969, more liberal depreciation rules, and certain other changes in the tax code will reduce the level of, and the rate of growth in, revenues. Net losses from these changes will be about $3.3 billion in 1972, $9 billion in 1974, and $10.5 billion in 1976. Increases in the payroll tax rate will offset $5 billion of these losses in 1974 and $7 billion in 1976. Reductions in income tax rates in the 1960s and the tax reliefs provided in the 1969 reform law, coupled with past and prospective increases in payroll tax rates, are steadily increasing the relative importance of payroll taxes in the federal revenue system. In 1960, payroll taxes accounted for 11.5 percent of federal revenues. By 1972, their share will rise to 21.6 percent and by 1976 to 23.2 percent.

Table 17-2. Projected Federal Revenues, by Source, Fiscal Years 1972, 1974, and 1976
Billions of dollars

Source	1972	1974	1976
Revenues under tax laws in effect before the Tax Reform Act of 1969	**220.9**	**270.3**	**315.8**
Individual income taxes	99.5	127.6	154.7
Corporation income taxes	35.7	46.3	53.6
Social insurance taxes and contributions	57.6	64.5	72.8
Excise taxes	17.5	19.6	21.0
All other taxes	10.6	12.3	13.7
Adjustments, net	**−3.3**	**−4.3**	**−3.8**
Effect of 1969 Reform Act	−2.1	−5.6	−6.4
Depreciation liberalization	−2.7	−3.6	−4.3
Acceleration of estate and gift taxes	+1.5	…	…
Increase in payroll tax rates	…	+4.9	+6.9
Total revenues	**217.6**	**266.0**	**312.0**
Full employment revenues under tax laws in effect before the Tax Reform Act of 1969	**232.6**	**270.3**	**315.8**
Adjustments, net	**−3.3**	**−4.3**	**−3.8**
Total full employment revenues	**229.3**	**266.0**	**312.0**

Sources: *The Budget of the United States Government, Fiscal Year 1972*, and Brookings Budget Projection Model.

Expenditures

The final step in the projections is to estimate expenditures in 1974 and 1976 resulting from existing programs and from those currently proposed by the administration. Even in the absence of decisions to start additional new programs or to broaden existing ones, expenditures can be expected to increase sharply over the next four years.

Continued inflation will play a significant role. A federal government policy now incorporated in law gives federal military and civilian employees salary increases comparable to those received in the private sector. As private wages and salaries increase, in line with the assumption built into the economic forecast, so will federal pay. Price increases also will be reflected in higher federal expenditures. In some cases—such as payments to physicians and hospitals under Medicare —the increases will automatically be translated into higher federal expenditures by the laws under which these programs are conducted. In other cases, no automatic adjustment will result. Thus the Congress must take explicit action to adjust veterans pensions and social security benefits if the cost of living rises. If construction prices rise, additional appropriations must be provided to keep the real value of government construction programs from falling. The projections assume that such action will be taken. Past experience shows that, on balance, this is a reasonable assumption.

Federal expenditures will also rise because of increasing workloads and growing numbers of beneficiaries of federal programs. One important example is the increase in welfare recipients, particularly those receiving aid to families with dependent children (AFDC). Over the past three years, the AFDC caseload has grown by 74 percent. The projection assumes continued caseload growth, but at a sharply decreased rate (falling from a 12 percent rate of growth in 1973 to a 7 percent growth in 1976). Other examples of increasing workloads or numbers of program beneficiaries adding to federal expenditures are the rising numbers of older citizens receiving social security benefits, a growing number of visitors to national parks, and returning veterans from Vietnam receiving G.I. educational benefits.

Another cause of expenditure growth, noted earlier, is that only part of the costs of many new programs proposed by the administration show up in the 1972 budget. The costs of those programs will rise in succeeding years. General revenue sharing, the Family Assistance Plan, and health insurance for the poor are the major proposals in this category. As an exception to the general rule of excluding possible effects of future policy decisions, the projection assumes that the proposed $1,600 minimum benefit for a family of four under the Family Assistance Plan will rise to $2,200 by 1976, with one-third of the increase accounted for by the rise in the cost of living. (The $2,200 is exclusive of the value of food stamps.) This change was made because it would be unrealistic to expect the minimum benefit to remain fixed once the program was adopted.

Several major assumptions entered into the projection of the defense budget. First, the current defense posture, as measured by an appropriations request of $79 billion, was assumed to remain unchanged in real terms over the next four years, except for further decreases in Vietnam costs. Second, it was assumed that Vietnam expenditures would be reduced from $8.6 billion in the 1972 budget to $2 billion in 1974 and $1 billion in 1976, the residual expenditures representing the cost of military and economic assistance in the area. Third, the dollar costs of the non-Vietnam budget were allowed to reflect the pay and price increases resulting from the general economic assumptions built into the projection. Fourth, an additional $2 billion was projected as the minimum cost of moving toward an all volunteer armed force (on top of the $1.2 billion included in the 1972 budget). On the basis of these assumptions, the defense budget would rise to $88 billion in 1976.

Several other factors will give rise to larger federal expenditures over the next four years, even in the absence of new policy decisions. The 1972 budget, in a number of areas, calls for appropriations in excess of expenditures; for example, appropriations for water pollution control grants are $2 billion, while expenditures are only $1 billion. In the normal course of events, expenditures will rise to the higher level made possible by appropriations unless the appropriation levels are explicitly reduced by a policy decision in subsequent budgets. The budget proposes a number of financial transactions—principally the sale of loans held in government portfolios—that would have the effect of reducing expenditures. But past experience suggests that actual sales of loans seldom meet expectations; in any event, it is most unlikely that they could be sustained for several years at the level contemplated in the budget. The projection assumes that these transactions in subsequent budgets will bring in only half the amount proposed for 1972, in effect adding $2.5 billion to federal expenditures. Finally, the projection assumes that in subsequent budgets, the administration will continue to propose various economies and savings and, optimistically, that enough of these will be enacted to result in cumulative budget savings of $2 billion by 1976.

These assumptions are translated in Table 17-3 into projections of federal outlays. Over the four-year projection period, expenditures on existing programs would grow by $36 billion because of wage and price increases. In the first two years (1972–74), the overall price index for government expenditures (including the effect of wage increases) would rise by about 4 percent a year and in the second period by slightly more than 3 percent a year. Increases in workload and in program beneficiaries would add $20 billion to government outlays during the four-year period. Currently proposed new programs would add another $11 billion to expenditures. Savings of $7.5 billion from Vietnam troop withdrawals and modest reductions in some existing programs could offset about $9.5 billion of these increases. If all these factors are taken into account, by 1974 total outlays would rise $37 billion above the $229 billion proposed in the 1972 budget. By 1976 they would increase further to a total of $295 billion.

Table 17-3. Projected Changes in Federal Outlays, Fiscal Years 1972–74 and 1974–76, and Selected Total Outlays, Fiscal Years 1972, 1974, and 1976

Billions of dollars

Cause of change	Change in outlays	
	1972 to 1974	*1974 to 1976*
Existing programs		
Pay increases	4.5	4.5
Price increases	13.8	12.9
Increases in workloads and program beneficiaries	9.5	10.4
Excess of appropriations over outlays	6.0	...
Financial adjustments	2.5	...
New programs		
Family assistance	3.0	1.0
Health insurance	1.5	0.5
Revenue sharing	1.7	1.0
All volunteer army	2.0	...
Reductions		
Vietnam costs	−6.5	−1.0
Economies and cutbacks	−1.0	−1.0
Total change	37.0	28.3

Category of outlay	Total outlay		
	1972	*1974*	*1976*
Total federal outlays	**229.2**	**266**	**295**
Defense	76.0	82	88
Nondefense	153.2	184	207
Public assistance[a]	6.9	12	15
Social security[b]	37.6	44	51
Medicare	9.0	10½	12
Medicaid (including health insurance)	3.4	6	7½
Total grants-in-aid (including revenue sharing)	38.3	45	51

Sources: Same as Table 17-2.
a. Including Family Assistance Plan.
b. Old-age, survivors, and disability insurance (OASDI) payments.

The Fiscal Dividend

Projections of revenues and expenditures at full employment are shown below for 1972, 1974, and 1976, and of the fiscal dividend (revenues minus expenditures) for the latter two years (in billions of dollars).

	1972	*1974*	*1976*
Revenues	229.3	266	312
Expenditures	229.2	266	295
Fiscal dividend	—	0	+17

If the projections are correct, there will be no fiscal dividend between 1972 and 1974. Expenditures resulting from existing and currently proposed programs will equal the revenues yielded under the present tax laws. Broadening existing programs or adding new ones between now and 1974 (beyond those in the 1972 budget), would require either increases in tax rates, reductions in other programs, or a decision to run a sizable deficit in the full employment budget.

By 1976 the fiscal situation would ease, with the growth of revenues exceeding the "built-in" growth of expenditures by a sufficient amount to yield a $17 billion fiscal dividend. The reasons for the difference between the results for 1974 and for 1976 are shown in Table 17-4. In the first two years of the projection period, expenditures rise particularly sharply. Built-in expenditure increases will amount to $36 billion. Although troop withdrawals from Vietnam should provide some budgetary savings, these would be offset by the full-year costs of new programs proposed in the 1972 budget. In the following two years, the growth in expenditures would be reduced. Built-in increases would be $8.5 billion less than in the prior period. At the same time, the increase in full employment revenues would be larger, principally because the same percentage rate of economic growth would be applied to a higher base.

The Impact of Social Security Programs

The projection of expenditures assumes that social security benefits will rise sufficiently between 1972 and 1976 to offset increases in the

Table 17-4. Major Changes in Outlays and Full Employment Revenues Influencing the Fiscal Dividend, Fiscal Years 1974 and 1976

Billions of dollars

Major change	1972 to 1974	1974 to 1976
Outlays, net	**37.0**	**28.3**
Pay, price, workload, and so forth	36.3	27.8
New programs	8.2	2.5
Reductions (Vietnam and other)	−7.5	−2.0
Full employment revenues, net	**36.7**	**46.0**
Increases due to economic growth	37.7	45.5
Additional losses due to scheduled changes in tax laws	−5.9	−1.5
Changes in payroll taxes	4.9	2.0

Sources: Same as Table 17-2.

cost of living. In March 1971, when the Congress enacted a 10 percent social security benefit increase, it postponed any decision on the administration's proposal to make future cost-of-living adjustments an automatic feature of the law. History leaves little doubt, however, that the Congress will raise benefit levels by at least as much as cost-of-living increases. On the revenue side, the projection assumes that the increases in social security tax rates scheduled in the current law for 1973 and 1976 will take effect, and that the ceiling on taxable wages—recently increased to $9,000 effective January 1, 1972, and which the administration has proposed increasing to $9,800—will thereafter be raised in line with increases in average wage rates.

The revenues yielded by the social security payroll taxes will substantially exceed expenditures, even after allowing for cost-of-living increases. In 1974 the social security trust funds (including Medicare) could have an annual surplus of $12 billion and in 1976, $15 billion. The total accumulated surplus in these trust funds could rise from $50 billion at the end of fiscal 1972 to about $100 billion by the end of 1976.

The relationship of the social security surpluses to the fiscal dividend is shown in Table 17-5. By maintaining a large trust fund surplus, the government gains fiscal leeway to make increases in other programs. But, in past years, the appearance of large surpluses often has led the Congress to increase benefits and postpone scheduled increases in tax rates. Quite probably, the large potential surpluses in the trust funds over the next several years will also lead to benefit increases in excess of advances in the cost of living, or to reductions in scheduled tax rates. To the extent that either occurs, the fiscal dividend will be reduced.

Table 17-5. The Fiscal Dividend in Relation to Social Security Surpluses and the Balance of Other Revenues and Outlays, Fiscal Years 1972, 1974, and 1976

Billions of dollars

Description	1972	1974	1976
Fiscal dividend	**+0.1**	**0**	**+17**
Surplus in the social security trust fund	+8.1[a]	+12	+15
Balance of other revenues and outlays	−8.0	−12	+2

Sources: Tables 17-2 and 17-3; *Special Analyses, Budget of the United States Government, Fiscal Year 1972*, p. 27; Brookings Budget Projection Model.

a. Before changes made by the Congress in the Social Security amendments of 1971, enacted in March 1971.

Comparison with Official Estimates

The 1972 budget projects revenues and expenditures to 1976 and estimates a fiscal dividend of $30 billion in that year, compared to the $17 billion estimated here. The budget projections are not given in detail, but some of the sources of this difference can be inferred. On the revenue side, the budget estimate for 1976 is slightly higher than the one shown here—$315 billion as against $312 billion. This difference probably reflects incorporation in the official projection of slightly higher payroll tax rates than those that were enacted by the Congress in March 1971 and used in making the projections described in this chapter.

The major source of divergence is in expenditures, where the official estimates are $10 billion lower than those presented in this chapter. Three particular assumptions underlying the projections described in this chapter probably account for most of the difference between them and the official projections: (1) the assumption that the 1972 excess of appropriations over expenditures in certain programs will lead to higher expenditures in the future; (2) the more pessimistic estimate of future sales of financial assets; and (3) the assumption that the minimum family assistance benefit will be raised to $2,200 by 1976.

The Full Employment Surplus

Under the full employment conditions that are assumed to exist from 1973 onward, it is quite possible that a budget surplus may be necessary, in which case expenditures could not be allowed to rise sufficiently to match revenues. Whether such a surplus will be needed depends on the strength of private market demand. If private demand is strong, a full employment budget surplus would be needed to avoid inflationary pressure. Although tight money and high interest rates could be called upon to do part of this anti-inflationary job, such monetary policies would especially depress residential construction and investment by state and local governments. Hence, given a national policy of encouraging both of these sectors, excess private demand in the mid-1970s would call for a surplus in the full employment budget.

Should private demand be weak in the mid-1970s, maintaining full employment without inflation could well be consistent with a balanced budget or with a deficit, together with a relatively easy money policy. But projecting market demand four or five years ahead is a very difficult undertaking. In both its 1970 and 1971 Economic Reports, the Council of Economic Advisers argued that the state of the economy in the mid-1970s would probably require a full employment surplus. In its 1971 report, the council estimated the required surplus to be equal to 1 percent of GNP, if a level of residential construction sufficient to meet the housing goals were to be achieved. With the 1976 GNP projected in Table 17-1, this would imply a surplus of $16 billion —almost precisely the same as the gap between revenues and expenditures projected here. Otto Eckstein of Harvard University, using a detailed forecasting model, has estimated that a comparable surplus would be necessary under full employment conditions in the mid-1970s. Former Council Chairman Gardner Ackley has also projected the surplus required in fiscal 1976. He finds that if private investment is strong enough to account for the same share of GNP as it did in the late 1960s, a surplus of $11 billion to $12 billion would be required, while the assumption of a weak private investment share would call for a deficit of $9 billion.

Different observers thus offer different estimates of the likely need for a sizable full employment surplus in the middle of this decade. At this stage, perhaps the most that can be said is that proponents of new federal initiatives should not assume that most or all of the $17 billion potential surplus in 1976 will be automatically available for new spending programs.

The Impact of Inflation

Rising prices and wages lead to increased federal revenues, but they also generate increases in federal spending. Does the increase in revenues exceed the rise in spending, so that inflation increases the fiscal dividend? There is no easy answer to this question. Estimating the impact of inflation on revenues is not difficult, since the relationship of federal revenues to the changes in money incomes that accompany inflation can be approximated without large errors. But the relationship between inflation and expenditures is more complex, depending on, among other factors, how completely and how quickly the Congress and the administration increase appropriations to take into account the effects of inflation on the costs of what the government buys, grants, or transfers.

The federal expenditures projected in this chapter reflect several assumptions about the effects of inflation. In some cases, higher prices are quickly and automatically translated into larger expenditures. Where there is no automatic response to higher prices, the projection assumes that spending is increased by legislative or executive action, after a certain delay. Advances in the cost of living, for example, are assumed to be reflected in public assistance payments, veterans' pensions, and social security benefits one year later.

Since prices do not change by the same percentage for each commodity or service the government buys, the projection translates what happens to the overall price index (the private GNP deflator) into price changes in a way that reflects recent relationships among particular goods or services. For example, the prices of medical services and construction have been rising more rapidly, and the prices of industrial goods less rapidly, than the general price level.

With these assumptions (which are supported by past experience) it is possible to examine the impact on the fiscal dividend of alternative inflationary paths, as is done in Table 17-6 for fiscal 1976. The table shows that inflation increases federal revenues by more than it increases expenditures. In general, federal expenditures rise about 1 percent for each 1 percent increase in the price index; revenues, on the other hand, usually rise more than 1 percent for each 1 percent increase in prices. While some of the goods and services the government buys are subject to less-than-average price increases, a roughly equal amount is subject to above-average price increases. Government revenues, on the other hand, reflect the progressive features of the individual income tax; as money incomes rise along with higher prices,

Table 17-6. The Fiscal Dividend for Fiscal Year 1976 under Alternative Assumptions about the Path of Inflation

Billions of dollars

| | Full | | Fiscal dividend | |
| | employment | | Current | 1972 |
Assumptions	revenues	Outlays	dollars	dollars
Basic projection: Inflation continues but tapers off to a 2.7 percent rate by 1973	312	295	17	15
Zero inflation: Prices rise in 1971, but not thereafter	273	270	3	3
Continued inflation: Prices rise at 4 percent per year through 1976	330	304	26	22

Sources: Tables 17-2 and 17-3 and Brookings Budget Projection Model.

many taxpayers move into higher brackets and pay a larger fraction of their income in taxes. As a consequence, rising prices and wages generate larger increases in revenues than in expenditures, and thereby raise the fiscal dividend.

The expenditure estimates are not adjusted for the lower or higher interest payments on the public debt that would accompany different assumptions about inflation. The amount by which inflation affects government interest payments could be quite considerable, depending on the degree to which interest rates reflect inflation. Since the effect of rising prices on federal interest payments is not taken into account in the calculations underlying Table 17-6, the way in which government expenditures are affected by inflation could be significantly understated in the examples shown there. The degree to which the fiscal dividend responds to inflation is, therefore, overstated in the table, but most probably not by so much as to eliminate the finding that inflation tends to raise the dividend.

While inflation does tend to raise the fiscal dividend and thus provide more resources to the public sector, it is hardly an ideal way of doing so. If the nation decides to devote additional resources to public spending, an explicit increase in taxes is a more rational and equitable way of doing so. Inflation, in addition to transferring real resources to the government, arbitrarily redistributes real income in the population, helping some persons and penalizing others. Tax increases, on the other hand, can be designed to transfer resources to the government on the basis of legislatively designed criteria and without the additional, arbitrary redistribution of incomes that accompanies inflation.

Implications

Economic growth, combined with reduced costs in Vietnam, will make available substantial additional resources to the federal government over the next several years. But most of these additional resources have already been implicitly committed under existing or proposed expenditure programs. Indeed, between now and 1974, it is likely that all of the funds made available by economic growth and savings in Vietnam will be absorbed by expenditures to which we are already committed and new programs already proposed in the budget. Only in the years after 1974 will uncommitted resources become available, and then only in relatively small amounts. Although the federal budget accounts for roughly 20 percent of GNP, by 1976, under present tax laws, the amount available for discretionary use by the President and the Congress will amount to only $17 billion (1 percent of GNP), and even some of that may have to be held as a full employment surplus. Another way to evaluate the $17 billion is to compare it with the cost of various program proposals currently being debated. It is less than half the difference in budgetary costs between the Nixon administration's health insurance proposals and those embodied in the Kennedy-Griffiths bill (see Chapter 11). It is roughly equal to the current cost of expanding the minimum payment under the Family Assistance Plan to $3,600. Since most of the fiscal dividend would show up as a surplus in the social security trust funds, however, it may never be available for other programs if the Congress decides to use the surplus for liberalization of social security benefits or reductions in scheduled payroll tax rates.

Should the nation decide that high-priority public needs would be left unsatisfied with a fiscal dividend of this size, three major alternatives would be available. The first is to incur a deficit in the full employment budget. In the short run, while unemployment and idle plant capacity are high, such a course might transfer additional resources to the government without substantially adding to inflationary pressure. But once private demand has returned to more normal levels (as is assumed for the later years of this projection), an attempt to provide more resources for the public sector through budget deficits runs a high risk of reaccelerating inflation, or of necessitating such a tight monetary policy that housing and investment goals would be seriously jeopardized.

A second means of securing additional resources is through tax increases. A decision to raise taxes implies a judgment that, on the margin, public needs have a higher priority than private. Between 1970 and 1976, gross national product measured in constant 1970 dollars will grow by $330 billion. Of that amount, $180 billion will probably go toward increased per capita consumer spending. Each 5 percent increase in the individual income tax (for example, through a 5 percent surcharge on existing taxes) would transfer to the government about $6.5 billion of that growth in potential consumption, again measured in dollars of constant purchasing power.

The third way to increase the resources available for urgent and important government programs is to curtail some existing programs. Here the decision would depend on whether the benefits to the nation from the programs in which spending is cut are significantly less than the benefits from private spending and from programs to which the resources are transferred. For example, Chapter 3 describes several alternative defense postures and the cost of each. One of those alternatives would, by 1976, cost $12 billion less than the present defense posture. It would provide fewer conventional forces to meet contingencies arising in Asia and a slower introduction of new strategic weapons systems. A decision to increase outlays in education, for example, and to finance them with savings made possible by adopting the lower defense posture would imply that any risks involved are not large and that what we lose in defense readiness is relatively less important than the benefits gained from greater expenditures on education.

The central lesson from the projections made in this chapter is that, under existing tax laws, most of the resources flowing to the government over the next several years from economic growth and Vietnam withdrawals have already been committed. As a consequence, the pursuit of new and expanded high-priority objectives by the federal government, including substantial further increases in aid to state and local governments, will require some difficult choices. To have more of some things we must sacrifice some of others, either in private goods and services or existing public goods and services. One such choice was made in 1969, when, through the Tax Reform Act, it was judged that private spending should take priority over public spending. Those who believe that certain public needs should now take top priority must seek either to reverse that decision through tax increases, or find low-priority areas of public spending from which resources can be withdrawn.

Continuing Problems in Some Older Programs

A YEAR AGO, *Setting National Priorities: The 1971 Budget* examined five older public programs and raised a number of questions about their benefits in relation to the budgetary costs they imposed. This postscript briefly summarizes what action, if any, was taken on those programs during the last session of the Congress.

Farm Price Supports

The problem: Benefits accrue primarily to higher income farmers. Subsidies are larger than needed to achieve supply management objectives.

Congressional action in 1970: Basically, the new agricultural act continues present subsidy programs. It limits subsidy payments to $55,000 per farmer for any one crop, affecting 1,100 farmers for a budgetary saving of about $50 million, as compared to widely suggested limitations of $20,000 per farmer for all crops, which would affect 10,000 farmers for a budgetary saving of $180 million.

Impacted Aid[1]

The problem: The distribution of funds is not related to education needs; the formula by which funds are distributed contains many anomalies.

---

1. Grants for elementary and secondary education to school districts that have a significant number of children of federal employees.

Congressional action in 1970: The administration's proposals for reforming the program would have corrected many anomalies, but the Congress rejected them and increased appropriations for impacted aid above the President's request. The President cited the increase as one of the reasons for his veto of the bill. The 1972 budget proposes that the impacted aid program be included as one part of the special revenue sharing grant for education. The formula for the distribution of the new grant incorporates some aspects of the current impacted aid distributional formula.

Merchant Marine Subsidies

The problem: The direct and indirect costs of the subsidies are very high relative to the increase in national security imputed thereto. The operating subsidy actively discourages improvements in efficiency on American ships.

Congressional action in 1970: The administration proposed an expansion of the subsidy program, which the Congress enacted after enthusiastically enlarging it. Minor changes were made in the operating subsidy formula, but basic obstacles to increased efficiency remain.

Public Works Projects

The problem: Numerous projects for water resource investments of doubtful value are undertaken each year. The congressional appropriation procedure encourages substantial additions to the list of new projects the administration annually proposes.

Congressional action in 1970: Appropriation procedures remain unchanged. The Congress provided funds to start sixty-eight new projects, compared to eighteen proposed by the administration.

General Aviation

The problem: Extensive airway facilities are made available to owners of private aircraft at charges covering only 5 percent of costs, thereby encouraging excessive growth of general aviation and airway congestion. Charges are levied in ways that make it difficult to use them to reduce congestion.

Congressional action in 1970: The administration proposed a major program to expand airway facilities, which the Congress enacted. The new program increases the user charges imposed on general aviation, but not by enough to recover more than from 20 to 25 percent of the costs that general aviation imposes on the federal government. Such charges on general aviation (and on commercial airlines as well) are still levied in a manner that makes it difficult to use them to ration scarce airspace and relieve congestion.